365 days with Calvin

A unique collection of 365
readings from the writings
of **John Calvin,** selected and
edited by Joel R. Beeke

RHB DayOne

© Day One Publications 2008
First printed 2008
Second printing 2009

ISBN 978–1–84625–114–6

Unless otherwise stated, all Scripture quotations are from
the **Authorized Version (King James Version)** Crown Copyright

British Library Cataloguing in Publication Data available

Published by Day One Publications
Ryelands Road, Leominster, HR6 8NZ
☎ 01568 613 740 FAX 01568 611 473
email—sales@dayone.co.uk
web site—www.dayone.co.uk
North American—e-mail—sales@dayonebookstore.com
North American web site—www.dayonebookstore.com

Jointly published with

Reformation Heritage Books RHB
2965 Leonard St., NE
Grand Rapids, MI 49525
Phone 616-977-0599 / Fax 616-285-3246
e-mail: orders@heritagebooks.org
website: www.heritagebooks.org

Cover designed by Kathryn Chedgzoy
Printed in the United States of America

Dedication

For

Calvin Beeke

my only son,
my loyal friend,
my skilful hunting-guide,
my dedicated employee—
enjoy your 365 days with your namesake

Soli Deo Gloria!

COMMENDATION

Daily devotionals—spiritual aids to help us be accountable for a life of disciplined reading of Scripture and prayer—have been around for centuries and need a certain caliber of excellence and insight if they are to prove of lasting value through 365 days! Of those I'd like to spend a year with as my spiritual guide and mentor, John Calvin is most certainly one of them. Joel Beeke guides us through the Reformer's writings to help us discover the help and insight that every Christian needs to live a God-honoring life for Jesus Christ.

Derek W. H. Thomas
John E. Richards Professor of Theology, Reformed Theological Seminary
Minister of Teaching, First Presbyterian Church, Jackson, MS
Editorial Director, Alliance of Confessing Evangelicals

Though *365 Days with Calvin* is being published to commemorate the 500th anniversary of Calvin's birth (July 2009), I have been impressed throughout its preparation with the timelessness of Calvin's writings. Calvin is truly an experientially Reformed writer, stressing both what true Christian believers experience in their pilgrimage walk with God and what they should do to grow in the grace and knowledge of the Lord Jesus Christ. Here is practical Christianity at its finest: Calvin pointing us to Christ, directing us in our Christian walk, challenging us to examine ourselves and showing us how to grow—all the while underscoring our dependency on the Holy Spirit. We cannot help but notice when working with Calvin his stunning repertoire of diverse experiences that, by God's grace, produced a remarkably mature Christian. I trust that you, too, will find it a joy to sit at Calvin's feet.

This compilation has been organized in a simple, straightforward manner. The selections from January through May are drawn from Calvin's Old Testament commentaries; June through September, from his New Testament commentaries; October, from his sermons on Ephesians; November 1–16, from his sermons on Timothy and Titus; November 17–30, from his sermons on 2 Samuel; and December, from his sermons on Galatians. To promote readability for today's reader, the selections have been edited in a contemporary but sensitive way that still remains true to Calvin. When quoting the day's text being expounded, the style of using italics without quotation marks, as utilized by the translators of Calvin's commentaries, has been retained.

Each day's selection contains four parts: the text, a suggested further reading, Calvin's comments, and a meditation on those comments designed to stimulate further reflection, examination, and action. To gain the most from each reading, don't neglect reading both the chapter from which the daily text is taken as well as the suggested further reading.

In addition to the Day One staff, my heartfelt thanks is extended to Pauline Timmer for ably assisting me in compiling the selections, and to Derek Naves, Phyllis TenElshof, and Kate DeVries for their editorial assistance. Thanks, too, to Michael Haykin for coauthoring the short biography of Calvin included in this volume. As always, I am most grateful to my dear wife, Mary, for her unflagging love and support, and to my children, Calvin, Esther, and Lydia, for all the joy they bring to their father's heart.

May your 365 days with Calvin be a year of rich growth for you.

Joel R. Beeke

John Calvin (Jean Cauvin) was so self-effacing that he only wrote about himself three times in his works: in *Reply to Sadoleto* (1539), the preface to his *Commentary on the Psalms* (1557), and on his deathbed to fellow ministers of Geneva (April 28, 1564), which was recorded by Jean Pinant. After Calvin's death on May 27, 1564, friends discovered that Calvin had given orders to be buried without a tombstone.[1] Four days after his death, the *Geneva Register* simply wrote: "Calvin est allé à Dieu le 27 Mai de la presente année" ("Calvin went to God May 27 of the present year"). Shaping this longing for obscurity was Calvin's sincere desire that only God be glorified. In examining Calvin's life and ministry, may we remain true to this driving motif of Calvin to promote only God.

Early Years

Calvin was born July 10, 1509, in Noyon, Picardy, in north-eastern France, to Gerard (d.1531) and Jeanne Cauvin (d.1515). Theodore Beza (1519–1605), Calvin's earliest biographer, describes Calvin's parents as "widely respected and in comfortable circumstances."[2] Calvin's father expected Calvin to study for the priesthood. So, in 1520 or 1521, young Calvin was sent to Paris to prepare for the priesthood.

About five years later, Calvin's father realized more money could be made in law than in the priesthood, so he sent his son to Orleans to study law. This sudden, dramatic change is noteworthy for two reasons. First, Calvin's legal training fostered in him qualities of mind—clarity, precision, and caution—that later served him well as a Bible commentator and theologian. Second, the University of Orleans was where Calvin first came into contact with Reformation truth. One of his tutors was Melchior Wolmar (1497–1560), an evangelical, who began teaching Greek to Calvin and may well have shared his faith with Calvin. Learning Greek was an important step, for it would open greater riches of the New Testament for Calvin.

Conversion

The date of Calvin's conversion is widely disputed among Reformation scholars. Most scholars cite it as 1533 or early 1534. T.H.L. Parker, however, argues for an earlier date, 1529–1530,[3] as do several recent scholars, including James I. Packer. Though we prefer the traditional date, more important for our purposes is Calvin's account of his conversion. This is what he writes in his preface to his *Commentary on the Psalms* (1557):

To this pursuit [of the study of law] I endeavoured faithfully to apply myself, in obedience to the will of my father; but God, by the secret guidance of his providence, at length gave a different direction to my course. At first, since I was too obstinately devoted to the superstitions of Popery to be easily extricated from so profound an abyss of mire, God by a sudden conversion subdued and brought my mind to a teachable frame, which was more hardened in such matters than might have been expected from one at my early period of life. Having thus received some taste and knowledge of true godliness, I was immediately inflamed with so intense a desire to make progress therein, that although I did not altogether leave off other studies, I yet pursued them with less ardour.4

Five important aspects of this brief, yet longest, account of Calvin's own writing about his conversion should be noted: First, prior to his conversion, Calvin says he was "obstinately devoted to the superstitions of Popery." He likens himself to a man sunk in a bog, for whom rescue is possible only by an outside hand. Calvin was introduced to papal superstition at an early age. His mother took her son on pilgrimages to shrines and altars to see relics and pray to God and the saints.5 Calvin felt so stuck in this bog of superstition that only God could deliver him.

Second, Calvin ascribes his rescue to God alone. He mentions no humans used by God to bring him to saving faith. He says nothing of Wolmar; or his cousin, Pierre Olivétain (1506–1538), who translated the New Testament into French; or the early Protestant martyr Étienne de la Forge, with whom Calvin lodged in Paris.6 Nor does he mention influential works written by Reformers such as Martin Luther (1483–1546). This emphasis on the absolute sovereignty of God in salvation, however, was typical of Calvin and the Reformers.

Third, Calvin says his conversion was "sudden," taken from the Latin *subita*, which can mean "unexpected." Calvin's conversion was not the result of his own wish or intent.7 Indeed, Calvin was known to be resistant to change. But God broke into his life, causing a dramatic upheaval that changed his view of God and led him to embrace evangelical doctrine.

Fourth, God overcame Calvin's natural stubbornness. As Calvin says, God "subdued and brought my mind to a teachable frame."

Fifth, Calvin was so "inspired by a taste of true religion" that he lost interest in studying the law. In respect to his father, he did not immediately drop out of the law program, but that study became less critical than his primary goal to progress in true godliness.

Some scholars depict Calvin as cold and unemotional. But this account of his conversion reveals an unusually ardent nature. As James A. de Jong has said, all one has to do is examine Calvin's prayers to find "an experiential believer of considerable ... warmth."[8] Calvin's conversion was nothing less than an unreserved, wholehearted commitment to the living God. This ardent commitment is evident in his crest, or seal, which shows a heart upon an open hand, with the motto underneath: "My heart I give Thee, Lord, eagerly and earnestly."

Calvin Comes to Geneva

In less than a year, people began to flock to Calvin to be taught pure doctrine. Teaching the evangelical faith was dangerous in France, and Calvin was soon forced to flee because of persecution. He went to Basel in January 1535, where the elderly Erasmus (1466/1469–1536); Heinrich Bullinger (1504–1575), friend and successor of Huldreich Zwingli (1484–1531) at Zurich; Guillaume Farel (1489–1565); and Pierre Olivétain were staying. While there, Calvin began working on *Institutes of the Christian Religion,* which would later become a classic work of Reformed theology.

After a year or so at Basel, Calvin went to Italy. He settled in Ferrara, where he hoped to work as secretary to Princess Renée, sister-in-law of Francis I, King of France. Calvin wanted to live there permanently as an obscure scholar, but that did not work out, so he returned to France. He only stayed there six months because he could not agree with the conditions of the Edict of Lyons (May 31, 1536), which "allowed heretics to live in the kingdom on the condition that they were reconciled to Rome within six months."[9]

Calvin planned to go to Strasbourg to gain some support from Martin Bucer (1491–1551), the German Reformer, and carve out for himself the quiet life of a scholar in "some obscure corner," but the main road was closed. So he took a different route by way of Geneva, intending to stay one night there.

Not long before Calvin's arrival, Geneva (pop. around 15,000) had declared itself pro-Reformation, largely due to the fiery preaching of Guillaume Farel, an indefatigable evangelist, and Pierre Viret (1511–1571). Calvin describes the condition of Geneva in his preface to his *Commentary on the Psalms*: "Popery had been driven from [Geneva] by the exertions of ... [Guillaume Farel], and Peter Viret; but matters were not yet brought to a settled state, and the city was divided into unholy and dangerous factions."[10]

Farel discovered that Calvin was staying in the city and went to see him. He knew of Calvin from reading the first edition of the *Institutes* (1536).[11] He discerned that Calvin was just the sort of man to assist him in Geneva, especially since Farel was more of a pioneer and evangelist than pastor and teacher. He asked Calvin to stay in Geneva and help him. Calvin was adamant about going to Strasbourg. Farel persisted. Calvin later wrote, "Finding that he gained nothing by entreaties, [Farel] proceeded to utter an imprecation that God would curse my retirement, and the tranquility of the studies which I sought, if I should withdraw and refuse to give assistance." Calvin was stricken with terror, feeling "as if God had from heaven laid his mighty hand upon me to arrest me."[12] So Calvin stayed in Geneva.

Calvin's commentary on Matthew 8:19 captures the essence of his encounter with Farel. Matthew tells about a scribe who comes to our Lord Jesus and tells him that he would follow Him wherever He would go. Calvin writes:

We must bear in mind that he was a scribe, who had been accustomed to a quiet and easy life, had enjoyed honour, and was ill-fitted to endure reproaches, poverty, persecutions, and the cross. He wishes indeed to follow Christ, but dreams of an easy and agreeable life, and of dwellings filled with every convenience; whereas the disciples of Christ must walk among thorns, and march to the cross amidst uninterrupted afflictions. The more eager he is, the less he is prepared. He seems as if he wished to fight in the shade and at ease, neither annoyed by sweat nor by dust, and beyond the reach of the weapons of war.... Let us therefore look upon ourselves as warned, in his person, not to boast lightly and at ease, that we will be the disciples of Christ, while we are taking no thought of the cross, or of afflictions; but, on the contrary, to consider early what sort of condition awaits us. The first lesson which he [i.e., Christ] gives us, on entering his school, is *to deny ourselves, and take up his cross* (Matt. 16:24).[13]

Calvin's First Ministry in Geneva (1536–1538)

During his first ministry in Geneva, Calvin was plagued by dissensions in the city, especially by some Anabaptists. He also had rather tense relations with the city council. Early on, Calvin concluded that if Geneva was to become thoroughly Reformed, the church needed a confession to which all citizens in Geneva should subscribe. Then, too, a pattern of discipline should be introduced so that everyone would not only formally embrace the Protestant faith but would become more disciplined under the Word of God. Calvin believed the church needed the authority to excommunicate immoral people so that the purity of the church might be maintained.

The city council was prepared to have a common confession of faith but was not so willing to vest the power of excommunication in the preachers. They feared that such great power could lead to civil unrest; besides, who knows what unstable preachers might do? They might even excommunicate a city councilman! So the council insisted that the ultimate authority of excommunication should remain under its own control.

This tension between the church and the government was exacerbated when Calvin and his fellow preachers in Geneva tried to foster a more disciplined life in the city. Many Genevans resented this intrusion from foreign or "outside preachers." By 1538, some opponents of Calvin's vision of the church had been elected to the city council. When Calvin and Farel insisted that certain people needed to be excommunicated before Easter 1538, the city council reneged. When the Reformers then refused to administer the Lord's Supper at all, the city council exiled Calvin and Farel from Geneva for insubordination. That was less than two years after their arrival.

Calvin received the expulsion with mixed emotions. "Geneva is bound on my heart so fully, I would have gladly given my life for its welfare," he wrote. At the same time, he said, "My Master's will be done. If we had served men, we would have been ill rewarded, but we serve a good Master who will reward us, even in expulsion."[14]

Calvin in Strasbourg (1538–1541)

Calvin wanted to go to Basel, but he heeded Martin Bucer's pressing invitation to take leadership of the French-speaking Protestant refugee congregation of nearly five hundred people in Strasbourg. Calvin lived in Strasbourg for three years—some of the happiest years of his life. Not only could he freely follow his long-cherished desire of pursuing his scholarly career in Strasbourg, but his experience there, under the influence of Bucer, impacted him a number of ways.

First, Bucer inspired Calvin to be a biblical commentator. Though Calvin viewed Bucer as a mentor of keen insight and learning, he felt that Bucer's biblical expositions were too long-winded. Bucer influenced Calvin to begin his career as a great biblical commentator in Strasbourg, which was something in which Calvin would far excel his mentor.

Second, Calvin was impressed by the church order that Bucer established in Strasbourg. Bucer promoted four offices: doctor/teacher, pastor, elder, and deacon. Calvin later implemented this structure in Geneva as the model he regarded as most biblical.

Third, Calvin was impressed with the order of worship that Bucer introduced into the life of the Strasbourg church. While in Strasbourg, Calvin created an order for worship according to the local practice. His later order of worship in Geneva leaned heavily upon this work.

Fourth, Calvin was impressed by the school system that Bucer and his educational leader, Johann Sturm (1507–1589), established in Strasbourg. Calvin taught in Sturm's new academy, which later served as a model for

Calvin's own Geneva Academy for the training of ministers and young people.

Finally, Calvin was impressed with a young Anabaptist widow in Strasbourg, Idelette de Bure (c.1499–1549), whom he later married. Calvin was so impressed with Idelette that he once said he would rather travel to eternity in her shoes than in anyone else's in the world. Calvin's nine years of marriage with Idelette, however, were not unclouded ones. The one child given to them, Jacques, died shortly after his birth. The Roman Catholics viewed Calvin's inability to have children as an act of God's judgment against him, but Calvin's response was that he had myriads of spiritual children all over the world of whom Rome was utterly unaware. Though Calvin inherited Idelette's two children, a son and a daughter, by a previous marriage and became their only surviving parent after her death, nothing could replace his loyal partner. Idelette's death was a heavy blow. Calvin wrote to a friend, "I am forced to go on, but I hardly have courage to do so."[15]

Calvin's Second Ministry in Geneva (1541–1564)

By 1541, Roman Catholics appeared to be making headway in nudging Geneva back to Catholicism. Cardinal Jacopo Sadoleto (1477–1547), the reforming bishop of Carpentras, had written a public letter to the Genevans, pleading with them to return to the Holy Mother Church. The Genevan city council asked Calvin to respond, which he did most effectively in his *Answer to Sadoleto,* one of the best early summaries of the Reformed church's doctrinal position. Recognizing the need for strong, Protestant leadership, the city council invited Calvin to return to Geneva. After reluctantly agreeing to do so, Calvin promptly threw himself into the hard work of reforming Geneva. That task would consume the last twenty-four years of his life. Calvin's second ministry in Geneva can be divided into two parts: years of opposition and years of support.

Years of Opposition (1541–1555)

In Geneva, one of Calvin's first responsibilities was to write various laws for the new republic. He drafted a new order of worship, a new catechism, and a new church ordinance, all of which, with various amendments, were eventually approved by the city council. Calvin offered a church/society structure that would cultivate the sharing of power between the church and the state as two separate kingdoms. Calvin's structure, which was greatly influenced by Bucer, would resonate in varying degrees throughout the European continent.

Calvin's *Ecclesiastical Ordinances,* which clearly defined the order of congregational life, gave the Reformed church autonomy in matters of faith and morals. The church was to exercise its power through four orders of ministry: pastors, doctors (i.e., teachers or lecturers), elders, and deacons.[16] The pastors were to preach frequently, to fervently engage in intercessory prayer, to faithfully administer the sacraments, and to conscientiously shepherd the congregation. The doctors were to focus on the theological training of seminarians and pastors, provide regular theological lectures, instruct the young, and guard the church's doctrinal purity. The elders, who were laymen, were responsible for assisting the pastors in maintaining supervision and discipline over the lives of members. They were also to engage in consistent intercessory prayer. The deacons were divided into two orders—the first to manage the church's resources and give administrative oversight; the second, to visit the sick and needy and lead the church in the ministry of mercy and charity.

The pastors and doctors formed a group called the Venerable Company, which met weekly for Bible study. Calvin moderated the Venerable Company and presented its recommendations to the city councils. The pastors and elders met in a body called the Consistory once a week to provide pastoral counsel, censure conduct, and draw in new members. The deacons also met weekly to carry out their tasks.[17]

Alongside this church structure, the city formed a pyramid of three councils that included the smallest and most powerful council of twenty-four (usually called the city council) and the larger, less powerful city councils of sixty and one hundred. Neither the ecclesiastic nor the civic side of Geneva fully achieved its goals but managed to work together despite unresolved tension for many years. For example, all the city councils had some say in choosing the church's elders, but the pastors themselves were allowed to choose the pastors.

The rumor that Calvin was a tyrant in Geneva and ruled with an iron hand is patently false. Calvin never held a civic office in Geneva. He was not even a citizen of the city until well into the 1550s. His position was not secure in Geneva until 1555, when his enemies (the Libertines) failed to be re-elected to the city council.

Whatever influence Calvin had in Geneva during the 1540s and the first half of the 1550s was based on the moral authority of his preaching, teaching, and wisdom. Even then, the city council often operated against his judgment and recommendations. For example, Calvin wanted weekly communion, but the city council insisted that communion should be administered only four times a year. Then, too, Calvin faced major battles with various individuals, including the Reformed humanist Sebastian Castellio (1513–1563), the council-leader Ami Perrin, the free-thinker Jacques Gruet, the ex-Carmelite Jerome Bolsec (d.1584), the rambunctious Philibert Berthelier, and the anti-trinitarian Michael

Servetus (c.1511–1553). Prolonged battles with each of these men took a heavy toll on Calvin in the midst of these busy years.

Despite formidable opposition, Calvin maintained an intense preaching schedule. Until 1549, Calvin preached twice on Sunday, at one of the two morning services, then again in the afternoon. He also spoke three times during the week.[18] In October 1549, the number of sermons increased from once every other day to once a day by order of the city council.[19]

Calvin's frequent, faithful preaching bore fruit in the conversion of individual Genevans. In due time, the city councils also swung Calvin's way.

Years of Support (1555–1564)

When the Libertines were defeated in 1555, the city council finally became supportive of Calvin and conceded the long-disputed right of excommunication to the Consistory. Geneva became Calvin's city at last! For the last nine years of his life, Calvin implemented many of his long-cherished visions. In his final decade, more than any other, Calvin revealed his skill as an able teacher of theology, a biblical writer, a faithful preacher, a wise counselor, and a seasoned church leader.

In 1558, Calvin established the Geneva Academy, which was divided into a "private school" (schola privata) for elementary instruction and a "public school" (schola publica), which offered more advanced studies in biblical languages and theology. Calvin's friend and successor, Theodore Beza, served as the first rector of the school. Students came to the academy from all over the world. When Calvin died, the school had 1,200 junior and 300 senior students. Men trained for the ministry fanned out from Geneva into many other countries in Europe. Most went to France, where the Reformed movement grew to about 10 percent of the population prior to the St Bartholomew Day massacre. A significant number of pastors and lay leaders also went to Britain (e.g., John Knox, the reformer of Scotland), Germany (e.g., Caspar Olevianus, the reformer of the Palatinate), and the Netherlands (e.g., the Marnix brothers, lay leaders of the Reformed movement there). In those countries, Calvin's followers—often with his assistance—adopted various confessional statements to strengthen the Reformed cause. Eventually, the academy evolved into the University of Geneva.

In 1559, Calvin completed his final definitive edition of the Institutes, which became the most famous book of Reformed theology ever written. Following the overall structure of the Apostles' Creed, Calvin divided this work into four books. The first book is on God the Creator, and man, brought into creation by God. This book discusses the providence of God and the oversight of God over all things. The second book covers the fall of man into sin, the character of sin, and the work of Christ in redeeming man from sin. The third book explains how the Holy Spirit applies redemption to mankind. The fourth book is primarily on the church—the character of the church from a positive point of view, the negative deformation of the church in the Middle Ages, and, finally, the proper relationship of church and state.

Calvin wrote many more works in his last decade, including commentaries, sermons, and treatises on a great variety of subjects. He also wrote voluminous letters from his study and his sickbed encouraging and instructing pastors and persecuted believers throughout Europe to persevere in the doctrines of grace. He was a spiritual and practical counselor to thousands. To his fellow ministers gathered around his deathbed, Calvin said, "God has given me grace to write what I have written as faithfully as it was in my power. I have not falsified a single passage of the Scriptures, nor given it a wrong interpretation to the best of my knowledge."[20]

Counting his posthumous works, Calvin's collected writings fill fifty-nine large folio volumes in the *Corpus Reformatorum* (a 101-volume set of important Reformation works) and twelve volumes of *Supplementa Calviniana*.[21] This includes commentaries on twenty-four of the thirty-nine Old Testament books and twenty-four of the twenty-seven New Testament books (all except 2 and 3 John and Revelation). The biblical fidelity, practicality, and experiential depth of Calvin's writings are unsurpassed in Protestant history.

To the end of his life, however, Calvin viewed his most important work in Geneva as "proclaiming the Word of God" and "instructing believers in wholesome doctrine." Though he was heavily involved in pastoring pastors and people, the center of his ministry was preaching the gospel. In 1561, Beza claimed in a letter to Farel that over a thousand people heard Calvin preach on a daily basis.[22] Calvin himself repeatedly said that it is through preaching that God reveals Himself in judgment and mercy, turning hearts to obedience, confirming the faith of believers, and building up and purifying the church.

Calvin delivered his sermons from memory without prepared texts. His method of preaching was like that of Zwingli and some church fathers, such as John Chrysostom (*c.*347–407). He did not choose a single text or isolated passage. Rather, he preached steadily through book after book of the Bible, often taking the better part of the year to complete a Bible book. On Sundays, he concentrated on the New Testament, except for a few Psalms on Sunday afternoons, interrupting his method only on special feast days such as Christmas and Easter. During the week, he preached through the Old Testament, book by book.[23] T.H.L. Parker notes: "Those in Geneva who listened Sunday after Sunday, day after day, and did not shut their ears ... received a training in Christianity such as had been given to few congregations in Europe since the days of the fathers."[24] And in the words of Steve Lawson: "Calvin's preaching was biblical in its substance, sequential in its pattern, direct in its message, extemporaneous in its delivery, exegetical in its approach, accessible in its simplicity, pastoral in its tone, polemic in its defense of the truth, passionate in its outreach, and doxological in its conclusion."[25] It was also practical and experiential in its emphases.

Calvin's last years were packed with evangelistic endeavors, particularly in France, but also as far away as Brazil. Geneva-trained ministers and missionaries also planted churches in the Netherlands, Italy, Poland, Germany, Hungary, England, and Scotland. Everywhere Calvin's advice was sought and gladly given.[26]

Calvin's Death and Influence

Calvin's health could not keep pace with his incredible workload. During the last years of his life, he battled numerous diseases. Doctors, fellow Reformers, students, and friends advised him to stop working, but his answer was: "What! Would my Lord find me idle?"[27] As noted at the beginning of this biographical sketch, he died May 27, 1564, at the age of fifty-five. He was granted his wish to be buried in a plain wooden coffin in an unmarked grave, so that human glory would not rob God of the exclusive glory that He deserves.

Soli Deo Gloria (the glory of God alone) is what Calvin's life and theology are all about. This is the common theme of Calvin the theologian, Calvin the reformer, Calvin the pastor-counselor, Calvin the churchman, Calvin the evangelist, and Calvin the writer. In every area of his personal life and ministry, Calvin was wholeheartedly committed to God and his glory and yearned only to promote the pre-eminence of Christ in dependency on the Spirit.

Primarily through his writings, Calvin's influence has lived on through the centuries and permeated millions of hearts. Today that influence is commonly called Calvinism and is nearly synonymous with the Reformed faith. The threefold influence of Calvin's Calvinism has been summarized by Burk Parsons as "devotion, doctrine, and doxology—the heart's devotion to the biblical God, the mind's pursuit of the biblical doctrine of God, and the entire being's surrender to doxology."[28]

Calvinism's greatest influence was in Britain and its colonies of North America, the Netherlands, Hungary, and parts of Germany. In all of these areas, and many more around the world, including Poland, Italy, Brazil, South Africa, Malawi, Zambia, Australia, New Zealand,

Singapore, South Korea, China, the Philippines, Russia, Egypt, Pakistan, India, and Israel, Calvinism is still being propagated today. Truly, Calvinism has a bright future, for it offers much to people who seek to believe and practice the whole counsel of God. Calvinism aims to do so with both clear-headed faith and warm-hearted piety, producing vibrant living in the home, the church, and the market place to the glory of God.

Today, Calvin's legacy is extended to us in additional ways. David Hall suggests ten key areas that our culture is different because of Calvin. He includes education, care for the poor, ethics, church autonomy, collegial governing, decentralized politics, parity among professions, economics, the Psalter, and printing books.[29]

The devotional *365 Days with Calvin* aims to capture some of Calvin's authentic devotional piety and doxology that promotes God's whole counsel. Cotton Mather writes that John Cotton, on being asked why in his later days he indulged nightly studies, pleasantly replied, "Because I love to sweeten my mouth with a piece of Calvin before I go to sleep."[30] It is our prayer that this spirit of genuine piety that so enveloped Calvin and Cotton may also penetrate you as you read this book.

Joel R. Beeke and Michael A. G. Haykin

Notes

1   **G.R. Potter** and **M. Greengrass,** *John Calvin* (New York: St Martin's Press, 1983), 171.

2   *The Life of John Calvin* in *The Banner of Truth*, 227–228 (1982), 11.

3   **T.H.L. Parker,** *John Calvin: A Biography* (Philadelphia: Westminster Press, 1975), 22, 162–5.

4   *Commentary on The Book of Psalms*, trans. **James Anderson** (reprinted Grand Rapids: Baker Book House, 1979), 1:xl-xli.

5   **Ronald S. Wallace,** *Calvin, Geneva and the Reformation* (Grand Rapids: Baker Book House, 1988), 2.

6   **Wallace,** *Calvin, Geneva and the Reformation*, 7.

7   **Parker,** *John Calvin,* 163.

8   Cited **J. Nigel Westhead,** "Calvin and Experimental Knowledge of God" in *Adorning the Doctrine: Papers read at the 1995 Westminster Conference* (London: The Westminster Conference, 1995), 16.

9   **Parker,** *John Calvin*, 52.

10   *Commentary on The Book of Psalms*, 1:xlii.

11   Remarkably, Calvin wrote the *Institutes* at the age of twenty-six, only a few years after his conversion. The first edition consisted of six chapters that covered the law (the Ten Commandments), a summary of faith (Apostles' Creed), prayer (the Lord's Prayer), the sacraments, and Christian liberty and responsibility. It was immediately hailed by

Protestants as a major achievement in producing an apology for and an introduction to the Protestant faith. The first edition was only one-fifth the size of the final edition that would appear in 1559, five years before Calvin died. Calvin continued to work for most of his life expanding and refining his theological classic. Cf. **Francois Wendel,** *Calvin: Origins and Development of His Religious Thought,* trans. **Philip Mairet** (Grand Rapids: Baker, 2002), 111–49.

12 Preface to the *Commentary on the Psalms*, 1:xlii.

13 *Commentary on a Harmony of the Evangelists, Matthew, Mark, and Luke*, trans. **William Pringle** vol. 1 (reprinted Grand Rapids: Baker Book House, 1979), 388.

14 Cited **John T. McNeill,** *The History and Character of Calvinism* (Oxford: Oxford University Press, 1954), 143.

15 **McNeill,** *History and Character of Calvinism*, 156–7.

16 **David F. Wright,** "Calvin's Role in Church History," in *The Cambridge Companion to John Calvin,* ed. **Donald K. McKim** (Cambridge: Cambridge University Press, 2004), 284.

17 **Derek Thomas,** "Reforming the Church," in **Joel R. Beeke,** *Living for God's Glory: An Introduction to Calvinism* (Lake Mary, FL: Reformation Trust, 2008), 225–7.

18 **T.H.L. Parker,** *The Oracles of God: An Introduction to the Preaching of John Calvin* (London: Lutterworth Press, 1947), 33.

19 **Parker,** *Oracles,* 39.

20 Cited **Parker,** *John Calvin,* 154.

21 **Karl Gottlieb Bretschneider et al.** eds., *Corpus Reformatorum,* 101 vols. (Halle: Schwetske, 1863–1900). The Calvin works comprise Series 2 of this collection, *Ioannis Calvini, Opera Quae Supersunt Omnia,* vols. 29–87. Cf. **Robert Reymond,** *John Calvin: His Life and Influence* (Fearn, Tain, Ross-shire, UK: Christian Focus, 2004), 13n.

22 **David W. Hall,** *The Legacy of John Calvin: His Influence on the Modern World* (Phillipsburg, NJ: P & R, 2008), 60.

23 **T.H.L. Parker,** *Portrait of Calvin* (London: SCM Press, 1954), 82.

24 **Parker,** *John Calvin,* 92.

25 **Steven J. Lawson,** "The Preacher of God's Word," in *John Calvin: A Heart for Devotion, Doctrine, and Doxology,* ed. **Burk Parsons** (Lake Mary, FL: Reformation Trust, 2008), 72–79.

26 **Joel Beeke,** "Calvin's Evangelism," *Puritan Reformed Spirituality* (Darlington, UK: Evangelical Press, 2004), chapter 3.

27 *The Life of John Calvin* in *The Banner of Truth,* 227–228 (1982), 56–7.

28 *John Calvin: A Heart for Devotion, Doctrine, and Doxology,* 5.

29 **Hall,** *Legacy of John Calvin,* 13–41.

30 **Cotton Mather,** *The Great Works of Christ in America,* vol. 1 (reprinted Edinburgh: Banner of Truth Trust, 1979), 274.

Light out of Darkness

And God said, Let there be light: and there was light. And God saw the light, that it was good: and God divided the light from the darkness.
Genesis 1:3–4
SUGGESTED FURTHER READING: 2 Corinthians 4:3–6

It was proper that the light, by which the world was to be adorned with excellent beauty, should be created first. It was not by inconsideration or by accident that the light preceded the sun and the moon. We are prone to tie the power of God to those instruments which he employs. The sun and moon supply us with light. According to our notions, we so include their power to give light that if they were taken away from the world, it would seem impossible for any light to remain. But the Lord, by the very order of creation, holds the light, which he imparts to us without the sun and moon. Further, it is certain from the context that he created the light to be interchanged with darkness.

And God saw the light. Moses introduces God here as surveying his work that he might take pleasure in it. But Moses also does that to teach us that God has made nothing without reason and design. We ought not to understand these words as if God did not know that his work was good till it was finished. But the meaning of the passage is that the work, such as we now see it, was approved by God. Therefore nothing remains for us but to acquiesce in this judgment of God. This admonition is useful. For whereas man ought to apply all his senses to admiring contemplation of the works of God, we see what license he allows himself in detracting from them.

FOR MEDITATION: God's creative power should never cease to amaze us. He speaks and light immediately exists. We commonly take light for granted and attribute its presence entirely to the means by which God provides it. But we should rather see it as a blessing from our Father and, as Calvin says, apply all our senses in admiring contemplation of it.

God's Provisions in Nature

And God blessed them, and God said unto them, Be fruitful, and multiply, and replenish the earth, and subdue it: and have dominion over the fish of the sea, and over the fowl of the air, and over every living thing that moveth upon the earth. Genesis 1:28

SUGGESTED FURTHER READING: Psalm 8

God here confirms what he said before about dominion. Man was created with the condition that he should subject the earth to himself; but now he is put in possession of his right, when he hears what has been given to him by the Lord. Moses expresses this more fully in the next verse when he says that God is granting to man the herbs and the fruits. It is of great importance that we touch nothing of God's bounty but what we know he has permitted us to touch since we cannot enjoy anything with a good conscience unless we receive it as from the hand of God. Therefore Paul teaches us that in eating and drinking, we sin unless faith be present (Rom. 14:23).

We are instructed to seek from God alone whatever is necessary for us. In the very use of his gifts, we are to meditate on his goodness and paternal care. For God in effect says, "Behold, I have prepared food for you before you were formed. Acknowledge me, therefore, as your Father, who has so diligently provided for you when you were not yet created. Moreover, my care for you has proceeded still further. It was your business to nurture the things provided for you, but I have taken even this charge upon myself. Wherefore, though you are, in a sense, constituted the father of the earthly family, it is not for you to be over-anxious about the sustenance of animals."

FOR MEDITATION: God has wondrously provided for our needs and given us dominion over the earth he created. It is not, therefore, a sin to use what God has given for our use. Nevertheless, our dominion is to be benevolent and wise; we are not to abuse or recklessly consume God's good creation but to care for it as good stewards.

Holy Work

*And the L*ORD *God took the man, and put him into the garden of Eden to dress it and to keep it.* Genesis 2:15

SUGGESTED FURTHER READING: Matthew 25:14–30

Moses now says that the earth was given to man with the condition that he cultivate it. It follows, then, that man was created to employ himself in work and not to lie down in idleness. Labor, truly, was created pleasant and full of delight, entirely exempt from all trouble and weariness. Since God ordained that man should cultivate the ground, he also condemned all indolent repose. Nothing is more contrary to the order of nature than to spend life eating, drinking, and sleeping while having no work to do. Moses says Adam was given the custody of the garden. That shows us that we possess the things that God has given to us on the condition that we be content with a frugal and moderate use of them and that we also take care of what remains.

Let him who possesses a field so partake of its yearly fruits that he does not suffer the ground to be injured by his negligence. Let him labor to hand it down to posterity, either as he received it or even better cultivated. Let him so feed on its fruits that he neither dissipates it by luxury nor permits it to be marred or ruined by neglect. Moreover, so that economy and diligence with those good things which God has given us to enjoy may flourish among us, let every one regard himself as the steward of God in all things that he possesses. Then he will neither conduct himself dissolutely nor corrupt by abuse those things which God requires to be preserved.

FOR MEDITATION: Hard work is a gift from God, not a curse of sin; therefore, let us joy in work well done. Diligent and conscientious work brings glory to our Creator as we fulfill an important aspect of his will for humanity. Do you work "as unto God" or "as unto men"?

Creation Groaning

And unto Adam he said, Because thou hast hearkened unto the voice of thy wife, and hast eaten of the tree, of which I commanded thee, saying, Thou shalt not eat of it: cursed is the ground for thy sake; in sorrow shalt thou eat of it all the days of thy life. Genesis 3:17

SUGGESTED FURTHER READING: Romans 8:18–25

In response to Adam's sin, God announces that the earth will be cursed. Since Scripture tells us the *blessing* of the earth refers to the fertility which God infuses into the earth by his secret power, so the *curse* is the opposite privation, in which God withdraws his favor from the earth. Thus the condition of the world varies with respect to men, according to whether God is angry with them or shows them his favor. We may add that punishment is exacted, not from the earth itself, but from man alone. For the earth does not bear fruit for itself but to supply food to us. The Lord, however, determined that his anger should, like a deluge, overflow all parts of the earth, so that wherever man might look, the atrocity of his sin should meet his eyes.

Before the fall, the world was a fair and delightful mirror of God's favor and paternal indulgence toward man. Now, all the elements show us that we are cursed. And although (as David says) the earth is still full of the mercy of God (Ps. 33:5), yet we now see signs of his dreadful alienation from us. If we are unmoved by those signs, we betray our blindness and insensibility. Lest sadness and horror should overwhelm us, though, the Lord also sprinkles everywhere the tokens of his goodness. Moreover, though the blessing of God is never seen as pure and transparent as it first appeared to man in his innocence, yet, if what remains behind be considered in itself, David truly and properly exclaims, "The earth is full of the mercy of God."

FOR MEDITATION: The disturbing savagery of the natural world around us is the result of our sin. The suffering and pain in animals is the consequence of our transgression. Should that not move us to mourn our sin and its consequences for all of creation?

Finding Peace in Suffering

In the sweat of thy face shalt thou eat bread, till thou return unto the ground; for out of it wast thou taken: for dust thou art, and unto dust shalt thou return. Genesis 3:19
SUGGESTED FURTHER READING: Philippians 3

Those who meekly submit to their sufferings present acceptable obedience to God if this cross-bearing along with increased knowledge of sin teaches them to be humble.

Truly it is by faith alone that one can offer such a sacrifice to God. But the faithful also labor in procuring a livelihood with the advantage of being stimulated to repentance and customizing themselves to the mortification of the flesh. God often remits a portion of this curse to his own children lest they sink beneath the burden. Psalm 127:2 says, "It is vain for you to rise up early, to sit up late, to eat the bread of sorrows: for so he giveth his beloved sleep."

As those things which have been polluted in Adam are repaired by the grace of Christ, the pious feel more deeply that God is good and enjoy the sweetness of his paternal indulgence. But because even at best the flesh is to be subdued, it not infrequently happens that the pious are worn down with hard labor and with hunger. So it is best that when we are admonished of the miseries of the present life, we should weep over our sins and seek relief from the grace of Christ, which not only can assuage the bitterness of grief but mingle sweetness with it.

FOR MEDITATION: When we feel overwhelmed with work, illness, or other difficulties, it helps us to bring those matters to God in prayer. Why is this so? How does Christ our Savior graciously teach us to be humble as well as to enjoy the sweetness of his presence?

Running from Sin

If thou doest well, shalt thou not be accepted? and if thou doest not well, sin lieth at the door. And unto thee shall be his desire, and thou shalt rule over him. Genesis 4:7
SUGGESTED FURTHER READING: Ecclesiastes 8:1–14

God will pronounce a dreadful sentence against Cain if the man hardens his mind in wickedness and indulges himself in his crime. The warning is emphatic; God not only repels Cain's unjust complaint but shows that Cain could have no greater adversary than the sin that he inwardly cherishes.

God so binds the impious man in these concise words that he can find no refuge. It is as if he says, "Your obstinacy will not profit you, for, though you would have nothing to do with me, your sin will give you no rest but will sharply drive you on, pursue you, urge you, and never allow you to escape." Cain rages in vain but to no profit. He is guilty by his own inward conviction even though no one accuses him. The expression "sin lieth at the door" refers to the interior judgment of the conscience that convinces man of his sin and besieges him on every side.

The impious may imagine that God slumbers in heaven. They may strive to repel fear of his judgment. But sin will perpetually draw these reluctant fugitives back to the tribunal from which they flee.

The expression of Moses has peculiar energy. *Sin lieth at the door*, meaning the sinner is not immediately tormented with the fear of judgment. Rather, gathering around him whatever delights he can to deceive himself, he appears to walk in free space and to revel in pleasant meadows. However, when he comes to the door, he meets *sin*, which keeps constant guard. Then conscience, which before was at liberty, is arrested, and he receives double punishment for the delay.

FOR MEDITATION: When we sin and God convicts us of that sin, we run from judgment in many different ways. But why is it impossible to escape the effects of sin? What kind of punishment can we expect when we finally stop running?

Righteous Noah

And the LORD *said unto Noah, Come thou and all thy house into the ark; for thee have I seen righteous before me in this generation.* Genesis 7:1
SUGGESTED FURTHER READING: Romans 3:21–26

Our duty is to hear God speaking to us. We are not through depraved fastidiousness to reject those exercises by which he cherishes or excites or confirms our faith, even though our faith is tender, or languishing, or weak. Nor must we reject those exercises as superfluous. *For thee have I seen righteous,* God says.

When the Lord says he preserves Noah because he is a righteous man, he seems to attribute salvation to the merit of works. For if Noah is saved because he is righteous, it follows that we should also deserve life because of good works. But here we must cautiously weigh the design of God, which is to save one man, in contrast with the whole world, so that he might condemn the unrighteousness of all men. The punishment that God is about to inflict on the world is just, seeing that one man is left in whom righteousness is cultivated, and for his sake God was propitious to his entire family.

Should anyone object that this passage proves that God respects works in saving men, the response is that this is not repugnant to gratuitous acceptance, since God accepts those gifts which he himself has conferred upon his servants. We must observe, in the first place, that God loves men freely. He finds nothing in them but what is worthy of hatred, since all men are born as children of wrath and are heirs of eternal malediction. But God adopts them to himself in Christ and justifies them by his mere mercy. After he has reconciled them unto himself, he regenerates them by his Spirit to new life and righteousness. Out of this flow good works, which of necessity are pleasing to God himself.

FOR MEDITATION: Even the most holy saints have only a shred of the obedience required of them by God. No matter how long we have been growing in the Lord, we must stand under the blood of Jesus Christ the righteous and nowhere else. How can we remember this truth more often and more gratefully?

The Covenant Divide

And the LORD *said unto her, Two nations are in thy womb, and two manner of people shall be separated from thy bowels; and the one people shall be stronger than the other people; and the elder shall serve the younger.* Genesis 25:23

SUGGESTED FURTHER READING: Deuteronomy 2:1–8

God says that the contention between the twin brothers in Rebekah's womb implies something far greater than itself; it means that there will be discord between the brothers and their posterity. The expression, *two nations are in thy womb,* is emphatic. Since Jacob and Esau were twins, and therefore of one blood, their mother did not suppose that they would become so separated that they would become heads of two, distinct nations. Yet God declares that dissension will take place between these brothers who were by nature joined together.

Second, he describes what will happen to their progeny. One nation will have victory over the other because they cannot be equal. The cause of the contest between them is because one is chosen by God and the other rejected. The reprobate gives way reluctantly to the godly, so it necessarily follows that the children of God must undergo many troubles and contests because of their adoption.

Third, the Lord affirms that the order of nature will be inverted. The younger son will be victor over the elder. This victory does not simply refer to earthly riches and wealth. Rather, this oracle teaches Isaac and Rebekah that the covenant of salvation will not be made with both brothers and their people but will be reserved only for the posterity of Jacob. In the beginning, the covenant promise is general and refers to all the seed of Abraham. Now it is restricted to one part of that seed.

FOR MEDITATION: The gospel of Jesus Christ still divides brothers. Sadly, this division often perpetuates itself through the generations, creating separate nations—some of which support Christianity while others are hostile to it. What a responsibility this gives us to present the gospel to succeeding generations of both nations! How can we fulfill this responsibility more?

Jacob Have I Loved

And the LORD *said unto her, Two nations are in thy womb, and two manner of people shall be separated from thy bowels; and the one people shall be stronger than the other people; and the elder shall serve the younger.* Genesis 25:23

SUGGESTED FURTHER READING: Romans 9:1–29

There is conflict between the children in Rebekah's womb because God chooses to divide the seed of Isaac (of which the condition appears to be one and the same), adopting one part and rejecting the other. One part obtains the name and privilege of the church, while the rest are reckoned strangers. One part receives the blessing of which the other is deprived. We know that because later the descendents of Esau were cut off from the body of the church, while the covenant of grace was deposited in the family of Jacob.

If we seek the cause of this choice of God, it is not found in nature, for the origin of both nations was the same. It is not found in merit, either, because the heads of both nations were enclosed in their mother's womb when the contention began. To humble the pride of the flesh, God determined to take away from men any reason for confidence or boasting. He might have brought forth Jacob first from the womb, but he made the other the first-born, who, at length, was to become the inferior brother.

Why does God by design invert the order that he himself appointed? It is to teach us that, without regard to dignity, Jacob was to be the heir of the promised benediction. He was gratuitously elected. God gave preference to Jacob over his brother Esau by making him the father of the church. Jacob was not granted this as a reward for his merits, nor did he obtain this by his own efforts. Rather, he was elected purely by the grace of God. But when an entire people are the subject of discourse, reference is made not to secret election, which is confirmed to a few, but to common adoption, which spreads as widely as the external preaching of the Word.

FOR MEDITATION: The election of the deceitful Jacob is one of the clearest demonstrations of sovereign grace. It should be no less clear to us in the example of every man, woman, and child who comes to faith in Christ. Are you a debtor to sovereign grace?

Committing our Way to God

And Jacob sent and called Rachel and Leah to the field unto his flock.
Genesis 31:4
SUGGESTED FURTHER READING: Psalm 37:1–7

Jacob sends for his wives so he can explain his intention to leave their father. He also wishes to persuade them to accompany him in his flight. It is his duty as a good husband to take them away with him; therefore, it is necessary to inform them about his plan.

Jacob is not blind to the many dangers of the journey. It will be difficult to take women who have never left their father's house on a long journey to a remote region. Moreover, there is reason to fear that they, in seeking protection for themselves, might betray their husband to his enemies.

Jacob acts with great care in choosing to expose himself to danger rather than to fail in his duty as a good husband and master of his family. If his wives refuse to accompany him, the call of God will compel Jacob to leave on his own. But God grants what is far more desirable; the entire family agrees to come with him. In addition, his wives, who have often torn the house apart with fighting, now freely consent to go with Jacob into exile. So the Lord also allows us to succeed, when we in good faith discharge our duty and shun nothing that he commands.

In seeing how Jacob calls his wives to him into the field, we infer what an anxious life he led. Certainly it would be more convenient for him to stay home with his wives. He is already advanced in age and worn down with many toils, so he has great need of their service. Yet he is satisfied with a cottage in which he might watch over his flock and lives apart from them.

If there is a particle of equity in Laban and his sons, they will find no cause for envying Jacob in this situation.

FOR MEDITATION: How many times have we abandoned our duties because we thought that success could only come through disobedience? Perhaps you have been asked to leave comfortable circumstances to follow God's leading. How does God care for us when we follow him?

Humility

And Pharaoh said unto his brethren, What is your occupation? And they said unto Pharaoh, Thy servants are shepherds, both we, and also our fathers. Genesis 47:3
SUGGESTED FURTHER READING: Matthew 23

This passage teaches us how much better it is to possess a remote corner in the courts of the Lord than to dwell in the midst of ungodly palaces. The design of God was to keep the sons of Jacob in a degraded position until he would restore them to the land of Canaan. His purpose was to preserve them in unity till the promised deliverance should take place; therefore, they did not conceal the fact that they were shepherds.

We must beware lest the desire of empty honor should elate us when the Lord reveals no other way of salvation than of bringing us under discipline. Let us willingly be without honor for a time so that hereafter angels may receive us to participate in their eternal glory. By this example of Jacob's sons, those who are asked to do humble work are taught that they have no need to be ashamed of their lot. It ought to be enough, and more than enough, for them that the mode of living that they pursue is lawful and acceptable to God.

The remaining confession of the brethren that they were shepherds (verse 4) was not unattended with a sense of shame; they said they had come to sojourn in Egypt because of hunger. The advantage that arose because of their circumstances was not to be despised. For they came to Egypt few in number and perishing with hunger and were so branded with infamy that scarcely anyone would deign to speak with them. The glory of God that afterward shone upon them was ever so much more illustrious when, in the third century from that time, God wonderfully led them forth out of Egypt as a mighty nation.

FOR MEDITATION: It is a constant temptation to present ourselves as more important than we really are. This reveals both pride on our part and dissatisfaction with the lot God has chosen for us. We would do well to speak the truth as Joseph's brothers did.

Testing God

And all the congregation of the children of Israel journeyed from the wilderness of Sin, after their journeys, according to the commandment of the LORD, and pitched in Rephidim: and there was no water for the people to drink. Exodus 17:1

SUGGESTED FURTHER READING: Psalm 78:12–22

A double accusation is brought against the children of Israel; first, for insulting God by quarreling and chiding with him, and second, for tempting him. Both arose from unbelief caused by ingratitude. It was vile of God's people to so soon forget what he had so graciously given them. He had brought them supplies when they were suffering from hunger, so why did they not fly to him when they were oppressed by thirst? It is plain that God's former favor was ill-bestowed upon these people since it so directly vanished in their ingratitude.

Their unbelief is also apparent because they neither expected nor asked anything of God. Pride is also apparent in their daring to chide him. Indeed, what almost always happens is that we who do not depend on God's providence nor rest on his promises provoke him to contend with us. We rush impetuously against him. The brutal violence of passion hurries us to madness, unless we are persuaded that God will in due time be our helper, and we are submissive to his will.

In the beginning of the chapter, Moses indicates that the Israelites journeyed according to the commandment, or, as the Hebrew expresses it, "the mouth" of God, as if he would praise their obedience. From that we understand that when they first left Egypt, the children of Israel were sufficiently disposed to their duty. Then a temptation occurred that interrupted them from proceeding in the right way. That example warns us that when we undertake anything at God's bidding, we should beware that nothing should hinder our perseverance. None are fitted to act rightly but those who are well prepared to endure the assaults of temptation.

FOR MEDITATION: How many undeserved blessings have we disregarded when we have forgotten God's gracious provisions and made ungrateful demands of him! How can you be more submissive to his will today?

Mercy to a Thousand Generations

Thou shalt not make unto thee any graven image, or any likeness of any thing that is in heaven above, or that is in the earth beneath, or that is in the water under the earth: Thou shalt not bow down thyself to them, nor serve them: for I the LORD thy God am a jealous God, visiting the iniquity of the fathers upon the children unto the third and fourth generation of them that hate me; and shewing mercy unto thousands of them that love me, and keep my commandments. Exodus 20:4–6

SUGGESTED FURTHER READING: Micah 7:14–20

God is characterized here as a husband who will tolerate no rival. He will assert his rights as a husband, since his rivalry is nothing more than retaining what is his own. He will exclude all rivals of his honor. Considering God's sacred covenant with the Jews, Moses seems to be alluding here to the violation of this spiritual marriage. But though he begins with a threat, God, who far prefers mercy to severity, gently allures his own to himself rather than compels them to allegiance. He declares that he will be merciful to a thousand generations, as the original Hebrew says in verse 6, while he only denounces punishment on the third and fourth generations.

To encourage worshipers to earnest piety, God declares that he will be kind not only to them but to their posterity, even for a thousand generations. This is proof of his inestimable kindness, even indulgence, for he deigns to bind himself to his servants, to whom he owes nothing, and to acknowledge his favor toward them and their seed.

It is wrong to infer merit from the promised reward, however, because God does not say that he will be faithful or just toward the keepers of his law. Rather, he only promises to be merciful. Let the most perfect then come forward, for they can require nothing better of God than his favor to them on the grounds of his gratuitous liberality.

FOR MEDITATION: The implications and consequences of our present actions extend to the next generation and beyond. Seeing that our conduct has such consequences, should we not flee from sin and seek to be more like Christ? Are there specific ways to do this today?

Mental Murder

Thou shalt not kill. Exodus 20:13
SUGGESTED FURTHER READING: Genesis 4:3–10

This commandment has two parts: first, that we should not vex, or oppress, or be at enmity with others; and, second, that we should live at peace with others without exciting quarrels. We should aid, as much as possible, those who are unjustly oppressed. And we should strive to resist the wicked lest they injure others. Christ, in teaching the true sense of the law, speaks against those transgressors who have committed murder, saying they are in danger of the judgment. So is anyone who is angry with his brother without a cause. He adds, "Whosoever shall say to his brother, Raca, shall be in danger of the council: but whosoever shall say, Thou fool, shall be in danger of hell fire" (Matt. 5:22). Contrary to what some have supposed, Jesus does not offer a new law here, as if to cast blame upon his Father. But he shows the folly and perversity of those interpreters of the law who only insist on the external appearance and husk of things, since the doctrine of God must rather be estimated from a due consideration of his nature.

If a man carries a weapon for the purpose of killing a man, earthly judges will find him guilty of violence. God, who is a spiritual lawgiver, goes even further. With him, anger is counted as murder; yea, inasmuch as God pierces to the most secret feelings, he holds even concealed hatred to be murder. John writes, "Whosoever hateth his brother is a murderer" (1 John 3:15); i.e., hatred conceived in the heart is sufficient for his condemnation, although it may not openly appear.

FOR MEDITATION: How can we feel morally superior to murderers? Are not we ourselves often murderers in our thoughts and words?

Vultures under Cover

Thou shalt not steal. Exodus 20:15
SUGGESTED FURTHER READING: Nehemiah 5

Charity is the goal of the law. The rule of charity is that every one's rights should be safely preserved and that no one should do to another what he would not do to himself. In defiance of the law are thieves who secretly steal the property of others, seek to gain from the loss of others, accumulate wealth by unlawful practices, and are more devoted to their private advantage than to equity. Rape or plundering is theft, since there is no difference between robbing one's neighbor by fraud or by force.

So that God might warn his people against all fraudulent injustice, he uses the word *steal* in Exodus 20:15, which is something we naturally abhor as disgraceful. Still, we know that men bury their misdeeds under many coverings and that they convert those deeds into praise by false pretexts. By craft and low cunning their deeds appear as prudence, and those who cleverly overreach others, take in the simple, and insidiously oppress the poor are spoken of as provident and circumspect. The world boasts of vices as if they were virtues and freely excuses those in sin. But God wipes away this gloss when he pronounces all unjust means of gain to be theft.

An affirmative precept is connected with the prohibition *Thou shalt not steal,* for those who do not steal must also inculcate liberality and kindness and the other duties whereby human society is maintained. So that we may not be condemned as thieves by God, we must endeavor, as far as possible, to ensure that others should safely keep what they possess and that we promote our neighbor's advantage no less than our own.

FOR MEDITATION: Think about your first reactions when you hear of another person's misfortune, particularly someone who has harmed or hurt you. Are you most concerned with their profit or with yours? How can the prohibition on stealing apply to you?

Wanting More

Thou shalt not covet thy neighbour's house, thou shalt not covet thy neighbour's wife, nor his man-servant, nor his maid-servant, nor his ox, nor his ass, nor any thing that is thy neighbour's. Exodus 20:17
SUGGESTED FURTHER READING: Romans 7:7–25

Though it was God's design to arouse men to sincerely obey the entire law, yet their hypocrisy and indifference were so great that it was necessary to stimulate them more sharply and to press them more closely, lest they seek subterfuge under pretence of the obscurity of the doctrine. For if men had only heard, "Thou shalt not kill, nor commit adultery, nor steal," they might have supposed their duty was fully performed by mere outward observance of the law. It was necessary, then, that God should give a separate admonition to men so that they not only abstained from evil-doing but also obeyed what was previously commanded with the sincere affection of the heart.

Paul gathers from this commandment that the whole law is spiritual (Rom. 7:4, 14). He explains that God, by his condemnation of lust, sufficiently showed that he not only imposed obedience on our hands and feet but also put restraint upon our minds, lest they desire to do what is unlawful.

Paul also confesses that once he slept in easy self-deceit but then was awakened by this single word of the law; for when he was considered blameless in the eyes of men, he was persuaded that he was righteous before God. He was once puffed up with confidence in his righteousness and expected salvation by his works, but, when he perceived the true meaning of the commandment *Thou shalt not covet,* he realized that the law was raised as it were to life, and Paul himself died because he was convinced he was a transgressor and saw the sure curse hanging above him.

FOR MEDITATION: God demands conformity to his law in both our external actions and our internal thoughts. Many of us are careful to maintain an outwardly upright life, but are we just as diligent to cultivate holiness in our thoughts? Since we are unable to do that on our own, are we not in desperate need of a Savior?

The Source of All Gifts

See, I have called by name Bezaleel the son of Uri, the son of Hur, of the tribe of Judah. Exodus 31:2

SUGGESTED FURTHER READING: 1 Corinthians 12

The call of Bezaleel was special because God entrusted to him an unusual and by no means ordinary work, yet we know that no one excels even in the most despised and humble handicraft unless God's Spirit works in him. For, although "there are diversities of gifts," it is still the same Spirit from whom these gifts flow (1 Cor. 12:4). God has seen fit to distribute and measure these gifts out to every person. This is not only so with the spiritual gifts that follow regeneration but also in all the branches of knowledge that come into use in common life.

It is, therefore, wrong to ascribe the means of our support partly to nature and God's blessing, and partly to the industry of man, since man's industry itself is a blessing from God. The poets are more correct who acknowledge that everything in nature, including the arts, comes from God, and that therefore everything ought to be accounted as divine inventions.

Understanding this doctrine is useful, first, because all things that refer to the support and defense of life should excite our gratitude, and whatever seems to be derived from man's ingenuity should be regarded as proofs of God's paternal solicitude for us. Second, we should honor God as the author of so many good things, since he sanctifies them for our use. Moses applies many epithets to the Spirit, because he is speaking of a remarkable work. Yet we must conclude that whatever ability is possessed by anyone emanates from one only source, God. The one difference is Bezaleel, who was endued with consummate excellence, while God makes distribution to others according to his pleasure.

FOR MEDITATION: We seldom recognize the gifts God has given us for what they really are: *gifts!* Let us make the gifts we have received reasons for greater praise to God instead of greater reliance on ourselves. Do you feel responsible to use your gifts diligently for God's glory?

Seeing God's Hand

And it shall be, when the LORD *thy God shall have brought thee into the land which he sware unto thy fathers, to Abraham, to Isaac, and to Jacob, to give thee great and goodly cities, which thou buildest not ... then beware lest thou forget the* LORD. Deuteronomy 6:10, 12

SUGGESTED FURTHER READING: Psalm 78:52–64

Wealth and prosperity may blind men's minds so that they do not sufficiently attend to modesty and moderation but rather grow wanton in their lusts and intoxicate themselves with pleasures. So God prescribes against this error. Moses admonishes us to beware lest we forget God when we have been liberally and luxuriously treated by him because he knows that it is common for abundance to lead to arrogance.

Moses does this, first, by showing how base and unworthy our ingratitude would be if God loaded us with many excellent benefits and we then cast away the recollection of him. His goodness was inestimable in giving people cities built by the hands of others and in transferring to them whatever others had prepared by their great labor and industry. So their impiety was even more detestable in neglecting him when he daily set himself before them in this abundant store of blessing.

Let us learn from this passage that we are invited by God's liberality to honor him, and that whenever he deals kindly with us, he places his glory before our eyes. On the other hand, we should remember that what ought to be seen as vehicles to lift up our minds on high are, by our own fault, converted into obstacles, and that therefore we ought to be more on guard against them.

FOR MEDITATION: It is logical that great blessings from God's hand would motivate us to praise him all the more. Sadly, however, we often take these blessings for granted and no longer recognize our dependence on him for everything. What blessings do you often take for granted?

What God Requires

And now, Israel, what doth the LORD *thy God require of thee, but to fear the* LORD *thy God, to walk in all his ways, and to love him, and to serve the* LORD *thy God with all thy heart and with all thy soul.* Deuteronomy 10:12
SUGGESTED FURTHER READING: Micah 6:1–9

We would now consider what is the sum of the contents of the law, as well as the aim and object of its instructions. Paul elicits the true goal of the law when he declares that its end is "charity out of a pure heart, and of a good conscience, and of faith unfeigned" (1 Tim. 1:5). Even in Paul's day, the law had false interpreters, who, Paul says, "turned aside unto vain jangling," when they swerved from its true objective.

Now, as the law is contained in two tables, so also Moses reduces it to two objectives: that we should love God with all our heart, and our neighbor as ourselves. Though he does not unite the two objectives in one passage, yet Christ, by whose Spirit Paul spoke, explains that to us in Matthew 22:37. When Jesus was asked what was the greatest commandment of the law, he replied that it was the first: that God should be loved. The second greatest commandment was to love our neighbor. So, the perfection of righteousness, which is set before us in the law, consists of two parts: that we should serve God with true piety, and that we should conduct ourselves toward others according to the rule of charity. That is also what Paul says, for faith, which he calls the source of charity, includes the love of God.

The declaration of Christ stands sure, that the law requires nothing of us but that we should love God and our neighbor. From that we understand that what is required of us to live a good life is piety and justice.

FOR MEDITATION: Piety and justice are such simple concepts and yet so difficult to put into practice. The way of the law is clear: looking to Jesus as fulfiller of the law, let us pray for the grace needed to follow it.

A Land of Pure Delight

And the LORD *spake unto Moses that selfsame day, saying, Get thee up into this mountain Abarim, unto mount Nebo, which is in the land of Moab, that is over against Jericho; and behold the land of Canaan, which I give unto the children of Israel for a possession: and die in the mount whither thou goest up, and be gathered unto thy people; as Aaron thy brother died in mount Hor, and was gathered unto his people.*
Deuteronomy 32:48–50
SUGGESTED FURTHER READING: Philippians 1:20–24

We naturally fly from death; no one hastens toward it of his own accord. Thus Moses would never have voluntarily entered the tomb unless he could hope for a better life to come.

Wherefore, though our carnal sense may be averse to death, let our faith prevail to overcome all its terrors, for, as Paul teaches, God's children, who desire not to "be unclothed," still long to be "clothed upon, that mortality may be swallowed up of life" (2 Cor. 5:4). Even so, Moses' obedience was remarkable; he prepared himself no less willingly for death than as if he had been invited to some joyful banquet. He and other holy men had so consecrated themselves to God that they were ready to live or to die according to God's pleasure.

Note the consolation that is referred to here; the pain of Moses' death was alleviated by the permission he received from God to behold the land of Canaan. For this reason Moses was commanded to go to the top of the mountain. Though Moses would have been satisfied with the mere promise of God and even the deprivation of this blessing, he may not have been made more cheerful at the thought of leaving his people on the threshold of their inheritance. Faith does not altogether deprive God's children of human feelings, but our heavenly Father in his indulgence has compassion on their infirmity. Thus, though Moses was sorry to be withheld from entering the Promised Land, he was supported by a seasonable remedy, that he might not be hindered in his course by this impediment.

FOR MEDITATION: Isaac Watts writes, "Could we but climb where Moses stood / And view the landscape o'er / Not Jordan's stream nor death's cold flood / Should fright us from the shore." How do we view death? Does a glimpse of the Promised Land ease our fears as we approach our end?

When the Sun Stood Still

Then spake Joshua to the LORD in the day when the LORD delivered up the Amorites before the children of Israel, and he said in the sight of Israel, Sun, stand thou still upon Gibeon; and thou, Moon, in the valley of Ajalon. Joshua 10:12

SUGGESTED FURTHER READING: Genesis 1

Christ inspires such faith in believers (Matt. 16:20; Luke 17:6) that mountains and seas are removed at their command. Faith borrows the confidence of command from the word on which it is founded.

Caution must be used here, however, lest anyone presume to give forth rash commands in his own strength. Joshua did not attempt to check the course of the sun before God instructed him about the purpose for doing so. He is said to have spoken with God, but those words do not sufficiently express the modesty and submission that become a servant of God uttering such a prayer. Let it suffice to say that Joshua asked God to grant what he desired, and on obtaining his request, became the free and magnanimous herald of an incredible miracle. Joshua would never have ventured in the presence of all the people to so confidently command the sun if he had not been thoroughly conscious of his vocation. Without it, he might have exposed himself to a base and shameful affront. With it, he opens his mouth without hesitation and tells the sun and the moon to deviate from the perpetual law of nature, adjuring them by the boundless power of God with which he was invested.

In kindness to the human race, God divides the day from the night in the daily course of the sun, and constantly whirls the immense orb with indefatigable swiftness. The Lord displayed his singular favour toward his church in the day of Joshua, when he was pleased to halt the sun for a short time till the enemies of Israel were destroyed.

FOR MEDITATION: As the disciples, who cried out, "Who can this be?" when Jesus calmed the storm, so we should cry out, "Who can compare to our great God?" when we see his mighty hand in creation. What mighty acts have we seen him perform in response to our cries for deliverance?

Rebellious Clay

So Joshua smote all the country of the hills, and of the south, and of the vale, and of the springs, and all their kings: he left none remaining, but utterly destroyed all that breathed, as the LORD *God of Israel commanded.* Joshua 10:40
SUGGESTED FURTHER READING: Job 40:1–14

Divine authority is again interposed in the text to acquit Joshua of any charge of cruelty. Since God had destined the swords of his people for the slaughter of the Amorites, Joshua could do nothing but obey his command. By such a decree all mouths are stopped and all minds restrained from passing censure.

When reading that Joshua slew all who came his way, even though they threw down their arms and begged for mercy, we may be disturbed, but when we read further that God had commanded Joshua to do so, we have no ground for pronouncing sentence on Joshua anymore than we do against those who pronounce sentence on criminals.

We might also think the children and the women that Joshua slew were without blame. If so, let us remember that the judgment seat of heaven is not subject to our laws. Rather, when we see how green plants are burned in the judgment, let us who are dry wood fear a heavier judgment for ourselves. Certainly, any person who thoroughly examines himself will find that he deserves a hundred deaths. Why then should not the Lord find grounds for the death of an infant that has only passed from its mother's womb? In vain should we murmur or complain that God has doomed all the offspring of an accursed race to the same destruction, for the potter has absolute power over his own vessels and over his own clay.

FOR MEDITATION: Passages like this selection from Joshua often incite rebellion in our hearts. Like Job, we must learn to put our hands over our mouths and humble ourselves before Almighty God, knowing that he who created all creatures also will determine, sovereignly and justly, what is right for them.

Ungodly Society

Blessed is the man that walketh not in the counsel of the ungodly, nor standeth in the way of sinners, nor sitteth in the seat of the scornful.
Psalm 1:1
SUGGESTED FURTHER READING: Proverbs 1:8–19

The psalmist says it shall go well with God's devout servants whose constant endeavor is to progress in the study of his law. Most people derided the conduct of the saints as mere simplicity and regarded their labor as useless. So it was important that the righteous should be confirmed in the way of holiness. This is done, first, by considering the miserable condition of all men who are without the blessing of God. It is supported by the conviction that God favors no one but those who zealously devote themselves to the study of divine truth. Moreover, as corruption has always prevailed in the world to such a degree that the general direction of men's lives is nothing but a continual departure from the law of God, the psalmist admonishes believers to beware of being affected by the ungodliness of the multitude around them. Beginning with a declaration of his abhorrence of the wicked, the psalmist teaches us how impossible it is for anyone to meditate upon God's law without first withdrawing and separating himself from the society of the ungodly. This is surely a needful admonition, for we see how thoughtlessly men will throw themselves into the snares of Satan and how few there are who guard against the enticements of sin.

To be fully apprized of our danger, we must remember that the world is fraught with deadly corruption. The first step to living well is to renounce the company of the ungodly, otherwise their conduct is sure to infect us with its pollution.

FOR MEDITATION: Calvin's comment that it is impossible to meditate upon God's law when surrounded by the ungodly is very applicable today. Cell phones, iPods, e-mail, and other technology can dominate our lives and surround us with ungodly influences. In our use of these technologies, are we taking care to avoid what the psalmist warns us against in Psalm 1:1?

A Well-Planted Tree

And he shall be like a tree planted by the rivers of water, that bringeth forth his fruit in his season; his leaf also shall not wither; and whatsoever he doeth shall prosper. Psalm 1:3
SUGGESTED FURTHER READING: 1 Kings 3:5–14

The psalmist here uses a metaphor to confirm the statement he made in the preceding verse. He shows us how those who fear God are to be accounted happy, not because of an evanescent and empty gladness, but because of their desirable condition. These words imply a contrast between the vigor of a tree planted in a well-watered area, and the condition of one that flourishes beautifully for a time, yet soon withers because of the barrenness of the soil in which it is placed.

The ungodly are sometimes like the cedars of Lebanon (Ps. 37:35). They have such an overflowing abundance of wealth and honor that they seem to lack nothing. But however high they may rise, and however far and wide they may spread their branches, they are poorly rooted in the ground and lack enough moisture to derive nourishment. So eventually their beauty withers away. Only the blessing of God can preserve and prosper those whom he plants.

God also allows the godly to bring forth fruit in season, the psalmist says, meaning that the children of God will flourish by being watered with the secret influences of divine grace, so that whatever befalls them is conducive to their salvation. The ungodly, on the other hand, will be carried away by a sudden storm or consumed by scorching heat. The godly will also bring forth fruit in their season, meaning that the fruit they produce will be fully mature. The ungodly, by contrast, may appear to be producing fruit but in the end will produce nothing that comes to perfection.

FOR MEDITATION: We often read of men and women who do not fear God and yet seem to be prospering. But in time, their leaves will wither and their fruits will not ripen to perfection. Consider the bigger picture before envying those who do not believe in God.

A Ruler of Iron

Thou shalt break them with a rod of iron; thou shalt dash them in pieces like a potter's vessel. Psalm 2:9
SUGGESTED FURTHER READING: Isaiah 63:1–6

Christ has such power that he reigns over even those who are averse to his authority and refuse to obey him. Psalm 2:9 implies that everyone will not voluntarily receive Christ's yoke; many will be stiff-necked and rebellious. But even those he will subdue by force and compel them to submit to him.

The beauty and glory of the kingdom David speaks of here are obvious when people willingly run to Christ in the day of his power and show themselves as his obedient subjects. But the greater number of people will rise up against this king with a violence that spurns all restraint. So the psalmist states here that this king will prove himself superior to all such opposition. God exhibited a specimen of this unconquerable power in war primarily in the person of David, who vanquished and overthrew many enemies by force of arms. But the prediction is more fully verified in Christ, who, neither by sword nor spear, but by the breath of his mouth, smites the ungodly to their utter destruction.

While the prophets in other parts of Scripture celebrate the meekness, the mercy, and the gentleness of our Lord, the psalmist describes him here as rigorous, austere, and full of terror. But his severe and dreadful sovereignty is set before us here only to strike alarm into his enemies. Furthermore, it is not at all inconsistent with the kindness with which Christ tenderly and sweetly cherishes his people. He who is a loving shepherd to his gentle sheep must also treat wild beasts with severity, either to convert them from their cruelty or effectually to restrain it.

FOR MEDITATION: One day, every knee will bow to Christ the King. Think about that today as you interact with people and hear what they are doing. Will they and you bow in adoration or terror before the Son of the living God?

Ruling in Submission to God

Be wise now therefore, O ye kings: be instructed, ye judges of the earth. Serve the LORD *with fear, and rejoice with trembling.* Psalm 2:10–11
SUGGESTED FURTHER READING: 2 Samuel 23:1–7

The psalmist now addresses kings and rulers who are not easily brought to submission and who are often prevented from learning what is right by the foolish conceit of their own wisdom. The psalmist warns these rulers that until they learn to fear God, they will remain destitute of all right understanding. Furthermore, since they have become so secure in themselves that they no longer obey God, strong measures may be employed to bring them to fear God and recover from their rebelliousness.

These rulers must not suppose, however, that the service to which God calls them is grievous. The psalmist says they are to *rejoice* at how pleasant and desirable such service will be. But lest they persist in being wanton and intoxicated with vain pleasures, imagining themselves to be happy while remaining enemies of God, he exhorts them by the words *with fear* to be a humble and dutiful submission.

What a difference there is between the pleasant and cheerful state of a peaceful conscience, which the faithful enjoy in fearing God and having his favor, and the fear of the wicked, who with unbridled insolence are dominated by contempt and forgetfulness of God. The language of the prophet implies that if the proud continue to rejoice in the gratification of the lusts of the flesh, they will progress to their own destruction. The only true and salutary joy is that which comes from resting in the fear and reverence of God.

FOR MEDITATION: The world has changed little since David wrote this psalm; kings and rulers of the earth still refuse to bow before the Lord. If we are so easily tempted to depend on our own strength, how much more must prominent leaders be so inclined? Resolve to be constant in prayer for the powerful men and women of our world to submit their lives to the Lord.

Defending our Cause

But thou, O LORD, art a shield for me; my glory, and the lifter up of mine head. Psalm 3:3
SUGGESTED FURTHER READING: 2 Samuel 15:1–30

In dependence on God, David courageously encounters enemies who are waging an ungodly and wicked war against him to prevent him from becoming king. Having acknowledged his sin, David now considers the merits of his present cause.

Likewise it becomes the servants of God to respond like David when molested by the wicked. Having mourned over their sins and humbly come to the mercy of God, they may now fix their eyes on the obvious and immediate cause of their afflictions and call upon God to help them. When undeservedly subjected to evil treatment, especially that which opposes the truth of God, they should be greatly encouraged by the assurance that God will maintain his promises to help them against such perfidious treatment.

David might appear to have claimed these things without grounds, seeing he had deprived himself of the approbation and help of God by offending him. But David was persuaded that he was not utterly cut off from the favor of God and that God's decision to make him king remained unchanged, so he allowed himself to hope for a favorable resolution of his present trial. In comparing God to a *shield*, David means that he was defended by God's power. He also says that God is *his glory*, because God would maintain and defend the royal dignity that he was pleased to confer upon David. Because of this, David is so bold that he declares he can walk with an uplifted head.

FOR MEDITATION: The knowledge that we are sinners should not keep us from fighting for God's truth. If the accusation of sin was enough to silence God's children, no one would be left to herald his truth. Having confessed our sin, we should not be afraid of calling our cause righteous and go forward in God's strength.

Righteous Before God

Hear me when I call, O God of my righteousness: thou hast enlarged me when I was in distress; have mercy upon me, and hear my prayer. Psalm 4:1

SUGGESTED FURTHER READING: Matthew 1:18–25

David was in the uttermost distress and, indeed, was almost consumed by a long series of calamities. But he did not sink under his sorrow, nor was he so broken in heart that he could not approach God as his deliverer.

In his prayer, David testifies that, even when he is utterly deprived of all earthly succor, he can still hope in God. Moreover, he addresses his Maker as *the God of his righteousness*, which is like calling him the vindicator of his right. David appeals to God this way because people everywhere are condemning him. His innocence is besmirched by the slanderous reports of his enemies and the perverse judgments of the common people.

We should carefully note David's reaction to this cruel and unjust treatment. For while nothing is more painful to us than to be falsely condemned and to endure wrongful violence and slander for doing well, such affliction often daily befalls the saints. It becomes us to learn under such hardship to turn away from the enticements of the world and to depend wholly upon God.

Righteousness is to be understood here as a good cause. David makes God the witness of his own righteousness as he complains of the malicious and wrongful conduct of men toward him. By his example, he teaches us that if our uprightness is not acknowledged by the world, we should not despair because God in heaven will vindicate our cause. Even the heathen know there is no better stage for virtue than a man's own conscience. But our greatest consolation is to know that, when men vaunt themselves over us wrongfully, we may stand righteous in the view of God and of the angels.

FOR MEDITATION: What comfort it is to know that we are vindicated in the eyes of God! This knowledge eases the intensity of the pain resulting from false accusations and a tarnished reputation. Remember and emulate David's reaction the next time that you suffer for the right.

Sure Hope for Deliverance

For thou art not a God that hath pleasure in wickedness: neither shall evil dwell with thee. The foolish shall not stand in thy sight: thou hatest all workers of iniquity. Thou shalt destroy them that speak leasing: the LORD *will abhor the bloody and deceitful man.* Psalm 5:4–6

SUGGESTED FURTHER READING: Daniel 6

Here David makes the malice and wickedness of his enemies an argument to enforce his prayer for divine favor. The language is abrupt, but the stammering of the saints is more acceptable to God than rhetoric, be it ever so fine and glittering. David's objective here is to show that the cruelty and treachery of his enemies is so intense that it is impossible for it to continue. God must arrest them in their course.

His reasoning is grounded upon the nature of God. Since righteousness and upright dealings are pleasing to God, David concludes that God will eventually take vengeance on men who persist in wickedness. How is it possible for them to escape unpunished, seeing that God is the judge of the world?

This passage is worthy of special attention. Often we are greatly discouraged by the unbounded insolence of the wicked. If God does not immediately restrain this wickedness, we are stupefied and dismayed or cast down into despair. But David finds encouragement and confidence in such circumstances. The more his enemies proceed against him in lawlessness, the more earnestly he asks for help from God, whose official work it is to destroy the wicked because he hates all wickedness.

Let the godly, therefore, learn when they suffer violence, deceit, and injustice, to come to God so they may be encouraged by the certain hope of his deliverance.

FOR MEDITATION: God *will* judge the wicked. They will not prosper. Those truths are so simple yet so hard for us to believe. Do not let the prosperity of the wicked create doubt in your heart; rather, let it encourage you in the certain hope of deliverance.

Stirring up the Godly

But let all those that put their trust in thee rejoice: let them ever shout for joy, because thou defendest them: let them also that love thy name be joyful in thee. Psalm 5:11

SUGGESTED FURTHER READING: Philippians 4

To urge God to grant him deliverance, David now argues that the effect of this action will stir up the godly to exercise greater trust in God and encourage them to give praise and thanks to him. This passage teaches us that we are ungrateful to God if we do not take encouragement and comfort from whatever blessings he confers upon our neighbors, since by those actions he proves that he is always ready to bestow his goodness upon all the godly. Accordingly, we may rejoice because, as David says, *thou defendest them.* Whenever God bestows blessings upon some of the faithful, the rest may be assured that he also will show himself beneficent toward them.

This passage enforces the teaching that true joy proceeds from no other source but God and his protection. We may be exposed to a thousand deaths, but we may be consoled in the valleys of death, knowing that we are covered and defended by the hand of God. The vain shadows of this world cannot beguile us when we take shelter under the wings of God.

We ought also particularly to notice the statement that those who trust in the Lord *love his name.* Memories of God must be sweet to us. They must fill our hearts with joy and ravish us with love as we taste of his goodness. By contrast, unbelievers wish the name of God to be buried and shun memories of him with horror.

FOR MEDITATION: What an awesome perspective this passage gives us! Do we often begrudge the blessings others receive and accuse God of unfairness in not dispensing the same blessings to us? Here we see the great joy we should have for others and the great comfort we can derive from the blessings they receive.

Arise, our God

Arise, O LORD; let not man prevail: let the heathen be judged in thy sight.
Psalm 9:19
SUGGESTED FURTHER READING: Revelation 20:11–15

One more reason to induce God to avenge the injuries done to his people
is that *man may not prevail,* David says, for when God arises, the
ungodly must fall down and give way. When the wicked become
audaciously insolent or have great power to work mischief, is it not
because God is still and gives them loose reins? But, when God does
arise, he will put a stop to their proud tumults and break their strength
and power with his nod alone.

In praying for God to arise, we learn that no matter how insolent and
proud and boastful our enemies may be, they are still under the hand of
God and can do no more than what he permits them to do. Furthermore,
God can, whenever he pleases, render all their endeavors vain and
ineffectual. The psalmist, therefore, in speaking of the wicked, calls them
man. The word in the original is derived from a root signifying misery or
wretchedness. So it is as if the psalmist calls these enemies mortal or frail
man.

The psalmist also beseeches God to *judge the heathen in his sight.* God
does this when he compels evildoers, by one means or another, to appear
before his judgment seat. Unless such unbelievers are dragged by force
into the presence of God, they will turn their backs upon God as much as
they can to exclude from their minds all thoughts of him as their Judge.

FOR MEDITATION: Are you ever tempted to despair, thinking that wicked
people may bring you down, especially when you are walking in
dependence on God? Remind yourself of this Psalm's lesson that God is
powerful enough to undo all wickedness with one word. How might he
arise in your life, proving his almighty power against evildoers?

Testimony in Adversity

The words of the LORD are pure words: as silver tried in a furnace of earth, purified seven times. Psalm 12:6

SUGGESTED FURTHER READING: Isaiah 45:18–25

God promises nothing in vain or to disappoint people, says the psalmist. This may seem a small matter, but when we consider more closely and attentively how prone we are to distrust and doubting, we will soon perceive the importance of realizing that our faith is supported by the assurance that God is not deceitful, that he does not delude or beguile us with empty words, and that he does not magnify his power or his goodness. Whatever he promises in word he will perform in deed.

We may frankly confess as David that *the words of the LORD are pure.* But those who liberally extol the truth of God's word while lying in the shade and living in ease may think differently when they begin to struggle with adversity. They may not openly pour forth blasphemies against God, but they may privately charge him with not keeping his word. When God delays to assist us, we may question his fidelity to his promises and murmur as if he has deceived us.

No truth is more generally received among people than that God is true, but few give him credit for this when they are in the midst of adversity. It is, therefore, necessary for us to cut off distrust. Whenever any doubt respecting the faithfulness of God's promises steals in upon us, we immediately ought to lift up a shield against it and affirm that the words of the Lord are pure.

FOR MEDITATION: What adversity are you facing today? How is it affecting your attitude toward God and his promises? Remember: the words of the Lord are pure. Rest in them.

The Church Besmirched

LORD, who shall abide in thy tabernacle? who shall dwell in thy holy hill?
Psalm 15:1
SUGGESTED FURTHER READING: Matthew 13:24–30

If we wish to be reckoned as children of God, we must obey the Holy
Ghost, who teaches that we must show ourselves to be God's children by
living a holy and upright life. It is not enough to serve God by outward
ceremonies; we must also live uprightly and without doing wrong to our
neighbor.

Too often we see the church of God defaced by impurity. To prevent
us from stumbling at what appears so offensive, we must distinguish
between those who are permanent citizens of the church and strangers
who are mingled among them for a time. This is a highly necessary
warning. It is given so that when the temple of God is tainted by
impurities, we may not be filled with such disgust and chagrin that we
withdraw from it. By impurities, I mean the vices of a corrupt and
polluted life. If religion continues to be pure in doctrine and worship, we
may not stumble so much at the sins that people commit to rend the
unity of the church.

Yet the experience of all ages teaches us the danger of being tempted
to lose heart when we behold sin and corruption in the church of God.
The church should be free from all pollution and to shine in uncorrupted
purity, yet she cherishes in her bosom many ungodly hypocrites or
wicked persons. Some people separate themselves from the fellowship of
the godly because they do not believe that a church in which vices are
tolerated can be a true church. But in Matthew 25:32, Christ justly claims
as his peculiar office that he will one day separate the sheep from the
goats. He thereby admonishes us to bear the evils that we do not have the
power to correct until all things become ripe, and the proper season of
purging the church arrives.

FOR MEDITATION: Gandhi reportedly said, "I like your Christ; I do not
like your Christians. Your Christians are so unlike your Christ." We
ought to mourn for the church when those outside it can see so much evil
in it. How should we evangelize such people?

Speaking Ill of a Neighbor

LORD, *who shall abide in thy tabernacle? who shall dwell in thy holy hill?*
He that backbiteth not with his tongue, nor doeth evil to his neighbour,
nor taketh up a reproach against his neighbour. Psalm 15:1, 3
SUGGESTED FURTHER READING: James 3

After briefly naming the virtues of those who desire to have a place in the
church, David now names vices from which believers should be free.

First, they must not be slanderers or detractors; second, that they must
restrain themselves from doing anything mischievous or injurious to their
neighbors; and, third, they must not give credence to backbiting and false
reports.

David names backbiting and reproach as the first injustice by which
neighbors are injured. If a good name is a treasure more precious than all
the riches of the world (Prov. 22:1), we can inflict no greater injury than
to wound a person's reputation. Not every injurious word is condemned
here; rather, the psalmist specifically refers to the disease and lust of
detraction that stir a malicious person to spread false reports. At the
same time, we cannot doubt that the Holy Spirit's design is to condemn
all false and wicked accusations.

In the clause that follows, the psalmist says the children of God should
be far removed from the more general injustice of doing *evil to his*
neighbour. The word *neighbour* here refers not only to those whom we
often speak to and enjoy friendship with, but also to people whom we
are bound to by the ties of humanity and a common nature. The psalmist
uses these terms to clearly show the odiousness of what he condemns and
to urge the saints to greatly abhor all wrong dealings with people, since
every person who hurts his neighbor violates the fundamental law of
human society.

FOR MEDITATION: The sins David mentions are easy to commit. We can
refer to these sins in many ways, but in the end, slander against our
neighbor is a serious sin. Do we realize how wrong it is to speak ill of our
neighbor, and that, if we persist in doing so, we will be unwelcome in the
Lord's house?

Ministering to the Saints

But to the saints that are in the earth, and to the excellent, in whom is all my delight. Psalm 16:3

SUGGESTED FURTHER READING: Matthew 25:31–46

One way of rightly serving God is to endeavor to do good to his holy servants. Because our good deeds cannot extend to God, it is to the saints in his place that we are to exercise charity. When people mutually exert themselves in doing good to one another, they yield right and acceptable service to God. We doubtless ought to extend charity even to those who are unworthy of it, as our heavenly Father "maketh his sun to rise on the evil and on the good" (Matt. 5:45), but David justly favors the saints over others and places them in a higher rank.

Though I do not deny that this doctrine is comprehended in the words of David, I think he goes somewhat farther, intimating that he will unite himself with the devout worshipers of God and be their associate or companion. Likewise the children of God ought to be joined together by the bond of fraternal unity, so they may serve and call upon their Father with the same affection and zeal.

After confessing that he can find nothing in himself to bring to God and is indebted to God for everything he has, David sets his affections upon the saints. God wills that he should be magnified and exalted in the assembly of the just, whom he has adopted into his family, that they may live together with one accord under his authority and under the guidance of his Holy Spirit.

FOR MEDITATION: Exercising charity toward saints on behalf of God adds a whole new perspective to holy living. In what ways can our treatment of fellow believers be a reflection of how we esteem God himself?

Finding Peace

Therefore my heart is glad, and my glory rejoiceth: my flesh also shall rest in hope. Psalm 16:9
SUGGESTED FURTHER READING: Nehemiah 8:9–12

In this verse the psalmist commends the inestimable fruit of faith. Under the protection of God, we not only enjoy mental tranquility but also live with joy and cheer. The essential part of a happy life is tranquility of conscience and of mind, whereas there is no greater unhappiness than to be tossed with a multiplicity of cares and fears.

The ungodly, however intoxicated with the spirit of thoughtlessness or stupidity, do not experience true joy or serene mental peace; rather, terrible agitations often come upon them and trouble them to constrain them to awake from their lethargy. In short, calm rejoicing is the lot of the person who has learned to place confidence in God alone, and to commit his life and safety to God's protection.

When encompassed with innumerable troubles, let us then be persuaded that the only remedy is to direct our eyes toward God. If we do this, faith will not only ease our minds but will also replenish us with fullness of joy. That is not without cause, for true believers not only have joy in the secret affection of their heart but also manifest it with the tongue in glorifying God as the one who protects them and secures their salvation.

FOR MEDITATION: The Christian life is characterized by deep, true joy, even in the midst of affliction. Do you know this kind of faith? How does directing our eyes to God bring peace in any circumstance?

Lasting Joy

Thou wilt show me the path of life: in thy presence is fullness of joy; at thy right hand there are pleasures forevermore. Psalm 16:11
SUGGESTED FURTHER READING: Proverbs 5:1–14

When God is reconciled to us, we have all things necessary for happiness. The phrase *thy presence* (i.e., the countenance of God) may be understood both as God beholding us or our beholding God. The fatherly favor that God displays in looking upon us with a serene countenance precedes our joy and is the first cause of it. Yet this does not cheer us until, on our part, we behold it shining upon us.

David also uses this clause to distinctly express to whom those *pleasures* belong. God has in his hands such a full and overflowing abundance of pleasures that these pleasures are sufficient to replenish and satisfy the whole world. So why does a dismal and deadly darkness envelop the greater part of mankind? It can only be because God does not look upon all men equally with his friendly and fatherly countenance. And because he does not open the eyes of all men to seek joy in him and nowhere else.

Fullness of joy stands in contrast to the evanescent allurements of this transitory world. People who divert themselves with the miserable pleasures of the world will eventually find themselves unsatisfied, famished, and disappointed. People may excessively intoxicate and glut themselves with worldly pleasures, but instead of being satisfied, they will in time become wearied of them to the point of loathing.

The pleasures of this world will vanish like dreams. David says the only true and solid joy in which the minds of men may rest cannot be found anywhere else but in God. None but the faithful who are content with God's grace alone can be truly and perfectly happy.

FOR MEDITATION: The pleasures of evil evaporate quickly and leave nothing but bitterness. So why are we so often lured by earthly things? Why do we look for happiness in ungodly entertainment? Do not be fooled by the promises of the world. Seek the joy that is pure and eternal.

Lasting Satisfaction

As for me, I will behold thy face in righteousness: I shall be satisfied, when I awake, with thy likeness. Psalm 17:15
SUGGESTED FURTHER READING: Jeremiah 31:10–14

Some interpreters, with more subtlety than propriety, restrict the meaning of this verse to the resurrection at the last day. That supposes David did not expect to experience a blessed joy in his heart until the life to come. It also suspends every longing desire after it until attaining that life. I readily admit that the satisfaction David speaks of will not be perfect before the last coming of Christ, but as saints, we do find great enjoyment when God causes some rays of the knowledge of his love to enter into our hearts. David justly calls this peace or joy of the Holy Spirit *satisfaction*.

The ungodly may be at ease and have abundance, even to bursting, of good things, but their desire is insatiable. They feed upon wind or earthly things without tasting spiritual things, in which there is substance. Then they are stupefied through the pungent remorse of conscience that torments them so they cannot enjoy the good things they possess. They do not have composed and tranquil minds but are kept unhappy by inward passions that perplex and agitate them.

Only the grace of God can give us contentment and prevent us from being distracted by irregular desires.

Thus I have no doubt that David alludes in this verse to the empty joys of the world that only famish the soul while they sharpen and increase the appetite. That shows us that only those who seek felicity in the enjoyment of God alone partake of true and substantial happiness.

FOR MEDITATION: Satisfaction in God is the only true satisfaction that lasts. It is also the best antidote for worldliness. How can you cultivate such satisfaction today? This is the only way to find more joy in serving God and find worldliness less desirable.

Crying to God in Distress

In my distress I called upon the LORD, *and cried unto my God: he heard my voice out of his temple, and my cry came before him, even into his ears.* Psalm 18:6

SUGGESTED FURTHER READING: 1 Peter 3:8–12

When David nearly plunged into the gulf of death, he raised his heart to heaven in prayer. Such an example of true faith is set before our eyes so that no calamities, however great and oppressive, may hinder us from praying. Prayer brought David the wonderful effects of which he later speaks, when his deliverance was effected by the power of God.

In saying that he *cried* to the Lord, David stresses the ardor and earnestness of his affection for God in prayer. By calling God *my God*, David separates himself from gross despisers of God, or hypocrites, who call upon the Divine Majesty in a confused manner in a time of tumultuous necessity, but who do not come to God familiarly and with a pure heart since they know nothing of his fatherly favor and goodness.

So then, as we approach God in prayer, faith must go before to illumine the way and to fully persuade us that he is our Father. Then the gate opens, and we may converse freely with him, and he with us. By calling God his God and putting him on his side, David also intimates that God is opposed to David's enemies. This also shows us that the psalmist was motivated by true piety and the fear of God.

The word *temple* that David uses here does not mean the earthly sanctuary of God; it means heaven, for the description that immediately follows cannot be applied to an earthly sanctuary. In using this term, David says that when he was forsaken and abandoned in the world, and all men shut their ears to his cry for help, God stretched forth his hand from heaven to save him.

FOR MEDITATION: It is hard to trust ears we cannot see. But, as Calvin points out, faith illumines the way and persuades us that God hears our cries. David had that kind of faith; in revealing how he cried out to God when he was in grave danger, the psalmist assures us that we, too, will find God's ears open to our prayers.

Seeing God in the Storm

Then the earth shook and trembled; the foundations also of the hills moved and were shaken, because he was wroth. Psalm 18:7
SUGGESTED FURTHER READING: Mark 4:35–41

God's answers to David's prayers were so powerful that it was impossible for the psalmist to sufficiently extol his Creator. He thus sets forth images of changes in the sky and the earth to show the power of God's intervention.

If natural things always flowed in an even course, the power of God would not be so perceptible. But when God changes the face of the sky by sudden rain, or by loud thunder, or by dreadful tempests, those who were sleeping and insensible must necessarily awaken and tremble with the consciousness of a presiding God. Such sudden and unforeseen changes clearly manifest the presence of the great Author of nature.

No doubt, when the sky is unclouded and tranquil, we see sufficient evidences of the majesty of God, but many men will not stir their minds to reflect upon that majesty until it comes nearer to them in a threatening manner. David thus recounts the sudden changes by which we are usually moved and dismayed. He introduces God at one time clothed with a dark cloud; at another, throwing the air into confusion by tempests, rending it by the boisterous violence of winds, by launching the lightning, and by darting down hailstones and thunderbolts.

In short, the psalmist shows us that the God who chooses to cause all parts of the world to tremble by his power also chooses to manifest himself as the deliverer of David. In doing so, he shows he can be known openly and by signs as clearly as when he displays his power to all the creatures both above and beneath the earth.

FOR MEDITATION: God makes himself known to us in many ways. Do not let the physical and chemical causes of thunderstorms or earthquakes blind you to the majesty of the God behind them. See him when the earth shakes, when the hills move, and when we ourselves tremble at his anger.

Reflecting Him

Day unto day uttereth speech, and night unto night showeth knowledge.
Psalm 19:2
SUGGESTED FURTHER READING: Romans 1:18–32

If we were as attentive as we ought to be, even one day and one night would suffice to show us the glory of God. But in addition, we see the sun and the moon perform daily revolutions; the sun by day appearing over our heads, and the moon succeeding in its turn. The sun ascends by degrees while at the same time coming closer to us. Later, it bends its course to depart from us by little and little. Variations in the length of days and nights are regulated by a law so uniform that they recur at the same point of time in every successive year. In this we have a brighter testimony of the glory of God.

With the highest reason, David declares that, although God should not speak a single word to men, yet the orderly and useful succession of days and nights eloquently proclaims the glory of God. So there is left to men no pretext for ignorance; for, since the days and nights perform for us so well and so carefully the office of teachers, we may acquire, if we are duly attentive, a sufficient amount of knowledge under their instruction.

FOR MEDITATION: How often does the sunrise draw our thoughts toward God? What about the orderly progression of seasons? What do the sun, moon, and stars say about God? How can we remedy our common neglect of Him reflected in nature?

Fearing No Evil

Yea, though I walk through the valley of the shadow of death, I will fear no evil: for thou art with me; thy rod and thy staff they comfort me.
Psalm 23:4
SUGGESTED FURTHER READING: Daniel 3

Even in prosperity, David did not forget that he was a man but meditated on the adversities that might come upon him. Certainly, the reason why we are so terrified when God exercises us with the cross, is because every man by nature, in order that he may sleep soundly and undisturbed, has wrapped himself in carnal security.

But there is a great difference between the sleep of stupidity and the repose that faith produces. Since God tries our faith by adversity, it follows that no one truly confides in God but he who is armed with invincible constancy for resisting the fears with which he may be assailed. David did not say that he was devoid of all fears but only that he would surmount fear no matter where his shepherd would lead him.

This appears more clearly from the context. In the first place David says, *I will fear no evil*. Immediately after that he adds the reason for this. He openly acknowledges that he seeks a remedy against his fear in contemplating and having his eyes fixed on the staff of his shepherd: *For thy rod and thy staff they comfort me*. What need would he have of such consolation if he had not been disquieted and agitated with fear?

Therefore, we should keep in mind that, when David reflects on the adversities that might befall him, he becomes victorious over fear and temptations by casting himself on the protection of God.

FOR MEDITATION: It was the Lord's strength and protection that delivered David from captivity to fear, not his own. If the evils you are facing have revealed your own weaknesses, do not despair. Trust the Lord to protect you and deliver you from fear.

Confessing God's Good Pleasure

Remember not the sins of my youth, nor my transgressions: according to thy mercy remember thou me for thy goodness' sake, O LORD. Psalm 25:7

SUGGESTED FURTHER READING: Psalm 103

When David mentions the sins he committed in his youth, he does not imply that he does not remember the sins he committed in later years. Rather, he means to show that he considers himself worthy of much greater condemnation for past and present sin.

In the first place, as David considered that he has not only lately committed sin but for a long time has heaped up sin upon sin, he bows under the accumulated load. Second, he intimates that if God should deal with him according to the rigor of law, not only the sins of yesterday or of a few days will come into judgment against him. All the offenses he has committed, even from his infancy, might now with justice be laid to his charge.

Accordingly, as God terrifies us by his judgments and tokens of his wrath, let us remember not only the sins that we have lately committed, but also the transgressions of the past. That will offer us ground for renewed shame and lamentation before God as we plead for mercy.

In his supplication for pardon, David pleads upon the ground of God's mere good pleasure. He says, *According to thy mercy remember me for thy goodness' sake.* When God casts our sins into oblivion, he beholds us with fatherly regard. David can find no other cause to account for this paternal regard of God but that God is good. Hence it follows that there is nothing to induce God to receive us into his favor but his own good pleasure.

FOR MEDITATION: If we step back from our daily grind and survey the mountain of sin we have been heaping up over a lifetime, how can we possibly arrive at any conclusion but the one David suggests? God's mercy to us flows from no other source than his good pleasure. How should this change our way of thinking and our actions today?

Teaching Sinners the Way

Good and upright is the LORD: *therefore will he teach sinners in the way.*
Psalm 25:8
SUGGESTED FURTHER READING: Psalm 71

Pausing briefly from prayer, David takes time to meditate upon the goodness of God so that he may return with renewed ardor to prayer.

Likewise the faithful feel that their hearts will soon languish in prayer unless they stir themselves up with new incitements. It is difficult to steadfastly and unweariedly persevere in prayer. Indeed, as fuel must frequently be added to preserve a fire, so prayer requires helps so that it will not languish and at length be extinguished.

Desirous to encourage himself to persevere in prayer, David affirms that God is *good and upright*. Gathering new strength by meditating on this truth, he will return with more alacrity to prayer. But let us also observe this consequence; that in being good and upright, God stretches forth his hand *to sinners* to bring them back in *the way*.

To attribute to God an uprightness that he exercises only toward the worthy and the meritorious is a cold view of his character and of little advantage to sinners, yet the world commonly believes that God is good to no one but believers. How can scarcely one in a hundred apply for the mercy of God, if not because so many limit it to those who are worthy of it?

On the contrary, David says God gives proof of his uprightness when he shows transgressors *the way*, which means the same thing as calling them to repentance and teaching them to live uprightly. Indeed, if the goodness of God did not penetrate even to hell, no one would ever partake of his goodness.

FOR MEDITATION: Isn't it wonderful that God teaches *sinners* the way? If it were not for this, how many of us would be saved and be on the way of holiness? Not one. David uses truths like this to help him pray. Try reflecting on the mercy of God before you pray.

Whom Shall I Fear?

The LORD is my light and my salvation; whom shall I fear? the LORD is the strength of my life; of whom shall I be afraid? Psalm 27:1
SUGGESTED FURTHER READING: Romans 8:31–39

All our fears arise from this source: we are too anxious about our life and fail to acknowledge that God is our preserver. We can have no tranquility until we are persuaded that our life is sufficiently protected by God's omnipotent power.

Let us learn to value God's power to protect us so that all our fears are put to flight. Because of the infirmity of the flesh, the minds of the faithful cannot at all times be entirely devoid of fear. But let us immediately recover courage, and, from the high tower of our confidence, look down upon all our dangers with contempt. Those who have never tasted the grace of God tremble because they refuse to rely on him. They imagine that he is often incensed against them or at least far removed from them. But with the promises of God before our eyes and the grace that they offer, our unbelief grievously wrongs God if we do not with unshrinking courage boldly set him against all our enemies.

God kindly allures us to himself and assures us that he will take care of our safety. When we embrace his promises and believe him to be faithful, we should also highly extol his power so that our hearts are ravished with admiration of himself. We must mark well this comparison: what are all creatures to God, and how does he protect them? Moreover, we must further extend this confidence to banish all fears from our consciences. Like Paul, we can then speak of our eternal salvation by boldly exclaiming, "If God be for us, who can be against us?" (Rom. 8:31).

FOR MEDITATION: When an affliction or danger provokes anxious fear in us, what does that say about our trust in God? How can we daily trust in God as our preserver so that fears do not overwhelm us?

Releasing Fear to God

Into thine hand I commit my spirit: thou hast redeemed me, O LORD God of truth. Psalm 31:5
SUGGESTED FURTHER READING: Luke 23:44–47

Though many things may distress us all, scarcely one person of a hundred wisely commits his life into God's hand. Multitudes live from day to day as merry and careless as if they were in a quiet nest, free from all disturbances. But when they encounter something that truly terrifies them, they are ready to die in anguish. They do not betake themselves to God, either because they deceive themselves with vain delusions, flattering themselves that all will yet be well, or because they are so stricken with dread and stupefied with amazement that they have no desire for God's fatherly care.

As various tempests of grief disturb us and even sometimes throw us down or drag us from the direct path of duty, or at least remove us from our post, the only remedy for setting our fears to rest is to consider that God, who is the author of our life, is also our preserver. Trusting in him is the only way to lighten our burdens and preserve us from being swallowed up by excessive sorrow.

Seeing, therefore, that God condescends to take care of our lives and to support us, let us learn always to flee to this asylum. The more that we are exposed to danger, the more we should carefully meditate upon this.

This confidence will help us discharge our duty with alacrity as well as constantly and fearlessly struggle onward to the end of our course. How then can so many people be slothful and indifferent, and others so perfidiously forsake their duty? How can they be so overwhelmed with anxiety and terrified of dangers and inconveniences that they leave no room for the operation of the providence of God?

FOR MEDITATION: Few comforts are as great as that which comes from committing one's life to God's hand. Regardless of what storms arise, peace is to be found in God. What do you most fear? Consider what comfort you may find if you release your fear to God.

Deliverance from Fear

I sought the LORD, and he heard me, and delivered me from all my fears.
Psalm 34:4
SUGGESTED FURTHER READING: 2 Timothy 4:9–22

David did not look upon his dangers with a calm and untroubled mind, as if at a distance and from some elevated position. He was grievously tormented with innumerable cares and justly spoke of his fear and terror. By saying "fears," he reveals he was greatly terrified, not by one, but by a variety of distracting troubles.

On one hand, David saw a cruel death awaiting him, while on the other, he may have been filled with the fear that Achish would send him to Saul, since the ungodly are likely to gratify themselves by making sport of the children of God. David had already been betrayed once and might well have concluded that even if he escaped, the hired assassins of Saul might be laying in wait for him on all sides. The hatred Achish had against David for the death of Goliath and the destruction of his army might also have given David reason to fear. Achish might wreak his vengeance upon David. Furthermore, he was so cruel that he likely would not be appeased by subjecting David to an easy death.

We ought to note what David says here about seeking the Lord, who *delivered me from all my fears*, so that if at any time we are terrified because of the dangers that surround us, we might not be prevented by a lack of courage from calling upon God. Even David, who is known to have surpassed others in heroism and bravery, did not have a heart of iron to repel all fears and alarms but was sometimes greatly disquieted and smitten with fear.

FOR MEDITATION: What fears are you battling today? How can you cast them upon God and leave them with him without becoming indifferent about them?

Surrounded by Angels

The angel of the LORD *encampeth round about them that fear him, and delivereth them.* Psalm 34:7
SUGGESTED FURTHER READING: 2 Kings 6:8–19

Though the faithful are exposed to many dangers, they may be assured that God is the faithful guardian of their life. The power of God alone would be sufficient, but in mercy for our infirmity God employs angels as his ministering spirits to protect us. It helps confirm our faith to know that God has innumerable legions of angels that are ready to serve as often as he is pleased to help us. What is more, the angels that are called principalities and powers are always intent on preserving our life because they know that this duty is entrusted to them.

God indeed designates with propriety the wall of his church and every kind of fortress and place of defense to her. But in accommodation to the measure and extent of our imperfection, he shows us his power to aid us through the work of his angels. Moreover, what the psalmist says about one angel can be applied to all other angels, for they are "ministering spirits, sent forth to minister for them who shall be heirs of salvation" (Heb. 1:14). In other places Scripture teaches us that, whenever it pleases God and whenever he knows it to be for our benefit, he appoints many angels to take care of his people (2 Kings 6:15; Ps. 41:11).

So, however great is the number of our enemies and the dangers by which we are surrounded, the angels of God, who are armed with invincible power, constantly watch over us and array themselves on every side to deliver us from all evil.

FOR MEDITATION: How often we forget about God's armies of angels that surround us to protect us! How could this change the way we face each day? Ask God to open your eyes to this blessing, and thank him for it.

Seeking Peace

Depart from evil, and do good; seek peace, and pursue it. Psalm 34:14
SUGGESTED FURTHER READING: Jeremiah 29:4–7

The children of God are to abstain from all evil, the psalmist says, as well as devote themselves to doing good to their neighbors. As it often happens, the man who is liberal toward some is also prodigal toward some, or at least helps many by acts of kindness and wrongs others by defrauding and injuring them.

With much propriety, David begins by saying those who want their lives to be approved before God should abstain from doing evil. On the other hand, many think that, since they have neither defrauded, nor wronged, nor injured any man, they have discharged the duty God requires of them. But with equal propriety is the precept given to also do good to our neighbor. It is not the will of God that his servants should be idle but rather that they should aid one another, desiring each other's welfare and prosperity, and promoting it as much as they can.

David next commands us to maintain peace: *Seek peace, and pursue it.* We know that peace is maintained by gentleness and forbearance. But we have often dealt with men of a fretful, or factious, or stubborn spirit, or with those who always seem ready to stir up strife upon the slightest occasion. Some wicked people irritate us and alienate themselves from the minds of good men, while others industriously strive to find grounds of contention. So the psalmist teaches us that we ought not only to seek peace, but if at any time it seems to flee from us, we must use every effort to pursue it.

In our personal affairs we should be meek and condescending and endeavor as much as possible to maintain peace, even though maintaining it causes us much trouble and inconvenience.

FOR MEDITATION: At times we are tempted to focus so completely on our battles with sin and avoiding evil that we neglect the other part of our Christian duty: the Christian life must also be active. David reminds us of that in this verse. Ask for grace today to both avoid evil and to do good.

Fasting for Humility

But as for me, when they were sick, my clothing was sackcloth: I humbled my soul with fasting; and my prayer returned into mine own bosom. Psalm 35:13

SUGGESTED FURTHER READING: Matthew 6:16–18

The psalmist here presents putting on *sackcloth* and *fasting* as helps to prayer. The faithful pray even after their meals and do not regard daily fasting as necessary for prayer. Nor do they consider it necessary to put on sackcloth whenever they come into the presence of God. But those who lived in ancient times resorted to these exercises when an urgent necessity pressed upon them. In a time of public calamity or danger, believers put on sackcloth and fasted, believing that by so humbling themselves before God and acknowledging their guilt, they might appease his wrath. Likewise, when someone was personally afflicted, he devoted himself to greater earnestness in prayer by putting on sackcloth and engaging in fasting as tokens of grief.

When David put on sackcloth, it was to show that he had taken upon himself the sins of his enemies and begged for God's mercy for them while they were exerting all their power to destroy him. Although we may regard the wearing of sackcloth and sitting in ashes as legal ceremonies, yet the exercise of fasting as people did in the time of David should remain in force today.

When God calls us to repentance by showing us signs of his displeasure, let us bear in mind that we ought not only to pray to him in an ordinary manner but also to use such means that are fitting to promote our humility.

FOR MEDITATION: Though the outward observance of fasting has been a source of pride for some, it is intended to promote humility. We must use it likewise, neglecting neither fasting nor the humility it signifies.

Facing Severe Affliction

My heart was hot within me, while I was musing the fire burned: then spake I with my tongue. Psalm 39:3
SUGGESTED FURTHER READING: Matthew 26:69–75

The psalmist now illustrates his great grief by using a simile. He tells us that his sorrow, when internally suppressed, becomes inflamed as the ardent passion of his soul continues to increase in strength. From this we learn that the more strenuously a person sets out to obey God, using all his efforts to exercise patience, the more vigorously he is assailed by temptation. For Satan, while not so troublesome to the indifferent and careless and seldom looks near them, displays all his forces against the believer. If, therefore, at any time we feel ardent emotions struggling and raising commotion in our breasts, we should remember this conflict of David so that our courage will not fail us, or at least that our infirmity may not drive us headlong to despair.

Whenever the flesh puts forth efforts and kindles a fire in our hearts, let us know that we are afflicted with the same kind of temptation that caused so much pain and trouble for David. At the end of the verse, the psalmist acknowledges that the severity of his affliction eventually overcame him, and he allowed foolish and unadvised words to pass from his lips.

In this David personally sets before us a mirror of human infirmity so that, being warned by the danger to which we are exposed, we may learn to seek protection under the shadow of God's wings. *Then spake I with my tongue* is not a superfluous mode of expression but a true and full confession of sin, in which David says that he not only gave way to sinful murmuring but had even uttered loud complaints.

FOR MEDITATION: How do you cope with major afflictions? How could meditating on the sufferings of Christ and the sovereign, paternal providence of God help us better cope when trials arise?

Keeping Watch over Us

Awake, why sleepest thou, O LORD? arise, cast us not off forever. Psalm 44:23

SUGGESTED FURTHER READING: Isaiah 43:1–7

In this verse the saints express the desire that God, in pity for them, will at length send them help and deliver them. Although God allows the saints to plead with him in this babbling manner, asking him to rise up or awaken, they should be fully persuaded that God continually keeps watch for their safety and defense.

We must guard against the notion of Epicurus, whose god, having his abode in heaven, delighted only in idleness and pleasure. But since the insensibility of our nature is so great that we do not fully comprehend the care that God has for us, the godly here request that God will be pleased to give them some evidence that he is neither forgetful of them nor slow to help them.

Likewise we must firmly believe that God ceases not to regard us, even though he appears to be doing so. Yet such assurance is of faith and not of the flesh, that is to say, it is not natural to us. Thus the faithful often give utterance before God to this contrary sentiment, which they conceive from the state of things as they see it. In doing so, they discharge from their breasts those morbid affections that belong to the corruption of our nature, and which then allows faith to shine forth in its pure and native character.

It may be objected that though nothing is more holy than prayer, prayer may become defiled when some forward imagination of the flesh is mingled with it. I confess that is true, but in using the freedom which the Lord grants to us, let us consider that in the goodness and mercy by which he sustains us, God wipes away this fault so that our prayers are not defiled by it.

FOR MEDITATION: Just as our eyelids protect our eyes every moment of a day, so God watches over us and protects us moment by moment. Think of some ways that God protects you without your being aware of it.

The Lord of Hosts

The LORD *of hosts is with us; the God of Jacob is our refuge. Selah.*
Psalm 46:7
SUGGESTED FURTHER READING: Matthew 26:47–56

In this verse we are taught how we should apply to our own use the things which the Scriptures record about the infinite power of God. We will be able to do this when we believe we are counted among those whom God has embraced with his fatherly love and whom he cherishes. The psalmist here alludes to the adoption by which Israel was separated from the common condition of all the other nations of the earth. Apart from this, the description of the power of God would only inspire us with dread.

Confident boasting, then, arises from the fact that God has chosen us for his peculiar people to show forth his power in preserving and defending us. The prophet, after celebrating the power of God by calling him *the* LORD *of hosts* or "the God of armies," immediately adds another epithet, *the God of Jacob*, by which he confirms the covenant God made of old with Abraham, that his posterity to whom the inheritance of the promised grace belongs, should not doubt that God also favors them.

So that our faith may rest truly and firmly in God, we must take into consideration two parts of his character: his immeasurable power, by which he is able to subdue the entire world, and his fatherly love, which he has manifested in his Word. When these two attributes of God join together, nothing can hinder us from believing that we can defy all the enemies who may rise up against us.

FOR MEDITATION: If we want to draw any comfort from knowing that God is the LORD of hosts, we must make sure that we are on his side. This is the most crucial issue of all. Then all our hope can be in the one who is both all-powerful and loving.

Imparting Wisdom

My mouth shall speak of wisdom; and the meditation of my heart shall be of understanding. Psalm 49:3

SUGGESTED FURTHER READING: Proverbs 8:1–12

The prophet rightly applies commendatory terms to the doctrine which he is about to communicate. He does this by speaking as one who would apply his own mind to instruction rather than to only assume the office of exhortation. He puts himself forward as a humble scholar, who, in acting the part of teacher, also has a concern for his own improvement.

All ministers of God should have a similar spirit, disposing them to regard God as their own teacher as well as of the common people. They must first embrace that divine word which they then preach to others.

The psalmist had another goal in mind. He prefers to give deference and weight to the doctrine he teaches by announcing that he has no intention to offer fancies of his own but to advance only what he has learned in the school of God. This is the true method of instruction to be followed in the church.

The man who holds the office of teacher must apply himself to receiving truth before attempting to communicate it. In this manner he becomes the means of conveying to the hands of others what God has committed to his own. Wisdom is not the growth of human genius. It must be sought from above. It is impossible for anyone to speak with the propriety and knowledge necessary for the edification of the church who has not, in the first place, been taught at the feet of the Lord.

FOR MEDITATION: It is easy for us to think we are capable of dispensing wisdom and understanding, but we cannot do so without first receiving it from God himself. Let us remember that we have nothing to give that we have not first received—and that we are to use what we have received for the edification of all around us.

Invitation through Warning

Now consider this, ye that forget God, lest I tear you in pieces, and there be none to deliver. Psalm 50:22
SUGGESTED FURTHER READING: Isaiah 55

This verse offers the kind of severe teaching that is absolutely necessary in dealing with hardened hypocrites, who otherwise would deride all instruction. While the psalmist threatens his listeners with the intent of alarming them, he also offers them the hope of pardon if they hasten to avail themselves of it.

To prevent them from further delay, he warns them of the severity and suddenness of divine judgment. He also charges them with base ingratitude for forgetting God. What remarkable proof we have here of the grace of God in extending the type of mercy to corrupt men who have impiously profaned his worship, who audaciously and sacrilegiously mocked his forbearance, and who abandoned themselves to scandalous crimes!

In calling them to repentance, God extends to sinners the hope of reconciliation with himself so that they may venture to appear in the presence of his majesty. Can we conceive of greater clemency than this, to invite to himself and into the bosom of the church such perfidious apostates and violators of his covenant, who have departed from the doctrine of godliness in which they were brought up?

Great as it is, we would do well to reflect that it is no greater than what we ourselves have experienced. We too, have drifted away from the Lord, and only in his singular mercy have been brought back by the Lord into his fold.

FOR MEDITATION: As parents, we often warn our children about threatening dangers even as we protect them from those dangers. With that in mind, how do God's warnings to us in chapters such as Psalm 50 and Isaiah 55 and books like Hebrews and Revelation actually promote the perseverance of the saints?

Sinning against God

Against thee, thee only, have I sinned, and done this evil in thy sight: that thou mightest be justified when thou speakest, and be clear when thou judgest. Psalm 51:4
SUGGESTED FURTHER READING: Psalm 32

Some believe that the psalmist here reverts to the circumstance of his sin, though it was committed against man and was concealed from every eye but of God. No one was aware of the double wrong that David had inflicted upon Uriah nor of the wanton manner in which he had exposed his army to danger. His crime which was unknown to men might be said to have been committed exclusively against God. Others think that David here intimates that, however deeply he was conscious of having injured men, he was primarily distressed about having violated the law of God.

But I believe David is saying here that even if the world pardoned him, God was the judge before whom David had to appear. Conscience hailed him to God's bar. Thus the voice of man offered no relief to him, however much others might be disposed to forgive or to excuse or to flatter. David's eyes and soul were directed to God, regardless of what man might think or say.

To one who is overwhelmed with the dreadfulness of having offended God and thus is subject to his sentence, no other accuser is needed. God is to the sinner more than a thousand men. There is every reason here to believe that to prevent his mind from being soothed into false peace by the flatteries of his court, David fully recognized the judgment of God upon his offense. It was an intolerable burden, even if he should escape trouble from the hands of his fellow creatures. This will be the experience of every true penitent.

FOR MEDITATION: It is a blessing (though often a painful one) to realize that God is our judge. Our guilty consciences are often relieved by the forgiveness of others, but we should not rest until we are assured of God's forgiveness.

A Willing Sacrifice

I will freely sacrifice unto thee: I will praise thy name, O LORD; *for it is good.* Psalm 54:6
SUGGESTED FURTHER READING: 1 Samuel 1

If deliverance is granted to David, he promises he will offer sacrifice and praise in gratitude. There can be no doubt here that David will return thanks to God in a formal manner when he has the opportunity to do so.

Though God principally looks at the inward sentiment of the heart, he does not excuse the neglect of such rites that the law has prescribed. David promises to testify his appreciation of the favor that he received from God in the manner common to all the people of God. His sacrifice thus becomes the means of exciting others to their duty by his example.

He would also *freely sacrifice*. David does not allude here to the fact that sacrifices of thanksgiving were at the option of worshipers, but rather that he would pay his vow with alacrity and cheerfulness after he had escaped his present dangers.

In general, men make big promises to God when they are under the pressure of affliction, but after they are rescued they soon relapse into the carelessness that is natural to them and forget the goodness of the Lord. But David truly promises to sacrifice freely and in another manner than the hypocrite, whose religion is the offspring of servility and constraint.

This passage teaches us that we cannot look for acceptance in the presence of God unless we also bring to his service a willing mind.

FOR MEDITATION: It is easy to promise service and devotion when we need God's deliverance. But let us make sure that, by God's grace, we follow through with what we promised to demonstrate our thankfulness to God.

Understanding their End

Until I went into the sanctuary of God; then understood I their end.
Psalm 73:17
SUGGESTED FURTHER READING: Revelation 20:11–21:8

The *end* of the wicked that David mentions here does not refer to their exit from the world or their departure from the present life, which is true of all men. Why then did David need to enter into the sanctuary of God to understand that? No, the word *end* here refers to the judgments of God, by which he makes clear that, even when God is thought to be asleep, he is only delaying for a time the execution of the punishment that the wicked deserve.

This must be further explained. If we would learn from God what the condition of the ungodly is, we must understand that, after they have flourished for a short time, they will suddenly decay. Though they happen to enjoy a time of prosperity now and until death, yet that means nothing compared to the nothingness of their life.

God declares that all the wicked shall perish in misery. If we see him executing vengeance upon the wicked in this life, we must remember that it is the judgment of God. On the contrary, if we do not see punishment inflicted on them in this world, let us not presume that they have escaped punishment or that they are the objects of divine favor and approbation. Rather, let us suspend our judgment, since the last day has not yet arrived.

In short, if we would rightly profit by addressing ourselves to the consideration of the works of God, we must first beseech him to open our eyes, for only sheer fools would presume to be clear-sighted and of a penetrating judgment. Second, we must give all due respect to God's Word by assigning to it that authority to which it is entitled.

FOR MEDITATION: We miss so much truth around us when we fail to observe the world through the lens of the Bible. The wicked often prosper and, without God's revelation of their end, we might be tempted to envy them. Thank God for his Word, by which we can see this more clearly and remain more content with what we possess. How else can this truth promote genuine contentment and keep us from controversies?

Held by my Right Hand

Nevertheless I am continually with thee: thou hast held me by my right hand. Psalm 73:23

SUGGESTED FURTHER READING: 2 Timothy 1:6–12; 4:17–18

When the psalmist speaks of God "holding him by the right hand," he means that he was, by the wonderful power of God, drawn back from the deep gulf into which the reprobate cast themselves. He ascribes wholly to the grace of God that he was restrained from breaking into open blesphemies and from hardening himself in error. That he was brought to condemn himself of foolishness, he also ascribes wholly to the grace of God, who stretched out his hand to hold up the psalmist and prevented him from a fall that would have destroyed him.

From this we see how precious our salvation is in the sight of God, for when we wander far from him, he continues to look upon us with a watchful eye and to stretch forth his hand to bring us to himself. We must beware of perverting this doctrine by making it a pretext for slothfulness. Yet experience teaches us that when we are sunk in drowsiness and insensibility, God exercises care for us. Even when we are fugitives and wanderers from him, he is still near us.

There is no temptation, be it ever so slight, that would not easily overwhelm us if we were not upheld and sustained by the power of God. The reason why we do not succumb, even in the severest conflicts, is because we receive the help of the Holy Spirit. He does not always put power in us in an evident and striking manner (for he often perfects it in our weakness), but it is enough that he succors us. Though we may be ignorant and unconscious of it, he upholds us when we stumble and lifts us up when we have fallen.

FOR MEDITATION: God's faithfulness becomes so clear when we wander from him and he does not fail to hold us by our hand. Beginning with your childhood, meditate on God's faithfulness toward you throughout your entire life.

Our Truest Service

That they might set their hope in God, and not forget the works of God, but keep his commandments. Psalm 78:7
SUGGESTED FURTHER READING: Jeremiah 17:1–8

The psalmist here explains the way the doctrine which he has stated should be applied. First, after finding out that they are instrumental in maintaining the pure worship of God and that they are to provide leadership for the salvation of their children, the fathers should be more powerfully stirred up to instruct their children.

Second, the children, who are inflamed with greater zeal, should eagerly press forward in acquiring divine knowledge. They must not allow their minds to wander in vain speculations. Rather, they should aim at, or keep their eyes directed to, the right mark. It is an unhappy and wretched toil to be "ever learning, and never able to come to the knowledge of the truth" (2 Tim. 3:7).

When we hear the purpose for which the law was given, we may easily learn the true and most successful method of deriving benefit from it. The inspired writer places trust first, assigning it the highest rank. He then requires observance of the holy commandments of God. In the middle is remembering the works of God, which serves to confirm and strengthen faith. In short, he says the sum of heavenly wisdom consists of this: men who have their hearts fixed on God by a true and unfeigned faith, call upon him. To maintain and cherish confidence in God, the believer must meditate in earnest upon his benefits and then yield to him unfeigned and devoted obedience.

We learn from this that the true service of God begins with faith. If we transfer our trust and confidence to anyone else, we defraud God of the chief part of his honor.

FOR MEDITATION: How often we place our hope and trust in others besides our Maker! As Calvin says, "the true service of God begins with faith." Are you convinced that trusting other things before God is a great insult to him and a great sin? How can this truth impact your life today?

The Erosion of Trust

Therefore the LORD *heard this, and was wroth: so a fire was kindled against Jacob, and anger also came up against Israel; because they believed not in God, and trusted not in his salvation.* Psalm 78:21–22
SUGGESTED FURTHER READING: John 3:14–21

To remove all thought that divine wrath was unduly severe, the enormity of the guilt of the Israelites is described by the psalmist: *They believed not in God, and trusted not in his salvation.* Indisputably, promises were made to the Israelites which they should have assented to. However, extreme infatuation which carried them away from God prevented them from yielding to those promises.

Trusting in the salvation of God means leaning upon his fatherly providence and regarding him as sufficient to supply all our needs. From this we learn how hateful unbelief is in the sight of God. We learn what the true nature of faith is and what its fruits are. True faith is when men quietly submit themselves to God, being persuaded that their salvation is singularly precious in his sight. It is being fully assured that God will give them whatever they need. We are led to surrender ourselves to him to be governed according to his good pleasure.

Faith is the root of true piety. It teaches us to hope for and to desire every blessing from God. It also persuades us to be obedient to him, even while those who distrust him are murmuring and rebelling against him.

Furthermore, the prophet teaches that pretences to faith, which are made by those who do not hope for salvation from God, rest upon false grounds. When we believe in God, the hope of salvation is speedily produced in our minds. This hope renders to him the praise of every blessing.

FOR MEDITATION: Trusting God's salvation is the essence of spiritual life. Unbelief is pledging allegiance to Satan. How can we learn to exercise faith more consistently and to hate unbelief more profoundly?

Guarding against Hypocrisy

Nevertheless they did flatter him with their mouth, and they lied unto him with their tongues. Psalm 78:36
SUGGESTED FURTHER READING: Matthew 15:1–20

We are not to suppose that the psalmist is saying these people made no acknowledgment of God, but he does intimate that, because the confession of their mouth did not proceed from the heart, it was therefore constrained and not voluntary. This is well worthy of notice, for from it we learn that we are constrained by duty to guard against the gross hypocrisy of uttering with the tongue before others one thing, while thinking something different in our hearts.

We also learn that we should beware of the hidden hypocrisy of the sinner, who, being constrained by fear, flatters God in a slavish manner, while yet, if he could, shunning the judgment of God. Most people are mortally smitten with this disease, for though divine majesty elicits some kind of awe from them, yet they would be grateful if the light of divine truth would be completely extinguished. It is not enough to yield assent to the divine word unless that is accompanied with true and pure affection, so that our hearts are not double or divided.

The psalmist points out in the next verse the cause and source of dissimulation is that such people are not steadfast and faithful (Ps. 78:37). By this he intimates that whatever does not proceed from unfeigned purity of heart is considered lying and deceit in the sight of God. Since uprightness is everywhere required in the law, the psalmist accuses hypocrites with covenant-breaking because they have not kept the covenant of God with the fidelity that is required. As I have observed elsewhere, we can presuppose a mutual relation and correspondence between the covenant of God and our faith, in order that the unfeigned consent of the latter may attest to the faithfulness of the former.

FOR MEDITATION: Whether or not we are guilty of hypocrisy can be a daunting question. Do we love God, and are we thankful for him and his will? Or do we serve him because we fear him, all the while wishing that he would cease to exist? Let us pray much for living, vital reality in our Christianity.

A Doorkeeper in God's House

For a day in thy courts is better than a thousand. Psalm 84:10
SUGGESTED FURTHER READING: 3 John

Unlike many people who want to live without knowing why, wishing simply that their life may be prolonged, David says that his purpose for living is to serve God. He sets a higher value on one day that is spent in God's service than a long time that is spent among worldly people from whom true religion is banished. Because it is lawful for only priests to enter into the innermost courts of the temple, David declares that, if he were simply permitted to have a place at the porch, he would be content with the humble station of acting as a doorkeeper.

The value that David sets upon being in the sanctuary of God is striking in his comparison that *he would rather be a doorkeeper in the house of my God, than to dwell in the tents of wickedness.* David would rather be cast into a common and unhonored place, providing that is among the people of God, than to be exalted to the highest rank of honor among unbelievers. That is a rare example of godliness indeed! Many people want to occupy a place in the church, but ambition has such sway over their minds that few are content to be numbered among the common and undistinguished class.

Almost all of us are carried away with the frantic desire of rising to distinction and cannot think of being at ease until we have attained some state of eminence.

FOR MEDITATION: When personal ambition takes over in our lives, we often succeed in turning the house of God into a "tent of wickedness." If it is better for us to dwell in God's house, even as a nobody, than to achieve recognition among the ungodly of this world, how then should we live? What changes should we make in our lives?

Deep Forgiveness

If his children forsake my law, and walk not in my judgments; If they break my statutes, and keep not my commandments ... Psalm 89:30–31
SUGGESTED FURTHER READING: 2 Samuel 12:1–14

The psalmist does not speak of total apostasy here, implying the total absence of godliness in people who forsake God's law and do not walk in his judgments. But sometimes the faithful cast off the yoke of God and break forth into sin in such a way that the fear of God seems to be extinguished in them. Therefore it is necessary for God to promise the pardon even of heinous sins, so that those who commit them are not overwhelmed with despair.

David, who seems by outward appearances to be wholly deprived of the Spirit of God, thus prays to be restored to him. God provides hope of pardon even for those who commit detestable and deadly transgressions so that the enormity of their sins may not keep them back or hinder them from seeking reconciliation with him.

From this we may condemn the undue severity of the fathers whose scruples did not allow them to receive those who repented from falling for the second or third time. Due care must be taken lest by too great a forbearance we give loose reins to people to commit iniquity. But there is no less danger in exercising an extreme degree of rigor. We should note that when God declares that he will show himself merciful toward sinners who have violated his law and broken his commandments, he purposely employs those odious terms to excite our hatred and detestation of sin, not to entice us to commit it.

Although the faithful may not always act in a manner worthy of the grace of God and may therefore deserve to be rejected by him, yet he will be merciful to them because the remission of sins is an essential article promised in God's covenant with us.

FOR MEDITATION: What a comfort it is to know that God's forgiveness is deep enough to cover all sin and terrible times of backsliding! Praise God for this forgiveness and for its purpose: to make sin more repulsive and Christ more attractive. How does its depth motivate us toward holiness rather than sinfulness?

Lovingkindness in Punishment

Then will I visit their transgression with the rod, and their iniquity with stripes. Nevertheless my loving-kindness will I not utterly take from him, nor suffer my faithfulness to fail. Psalm 89:32–33
SUGGESTED FURTHER READING: Hebrews 12:3–13

God does not adopt us as his children to encourage us to commit sin with greater boldness. We read here of the chastisement that God uses to show us that he hates sin. In this, he warns us of what we deserve when we offend him. He also invites and exhorts us to repent of our sins. His fatherly chastisement then, which operates as medicine, holds the line between undue indulgence, which encourages sin, and extreme severity, which pushes people to destruction.

Whenever God punishes the sins of true believers, he does so with wholesome moderation. It is therefore our duty to take the punishment that he inflicts upon us as medicine for us. For God has nothing else in view than to correct the vices of his children so that, having thoroughly purged them of sin, he may restore them anew to his favor and friendship. According to the words of Paul in 1 Corinthians 11:32, the faithful "are chastened of the Lord, that [they] should not be condemned with the world." Lest they be overwhelmed with the weight of chastisement, God restrains his hand and makes considerate allowance for their infirmity.

Thus God's promise is fulfilled, that *my loving-kindness will I not utterly take from [them]*, even when he is angry with his children. For while God is correcting them for their profit and salvation, he does not cease to love them.

FOR MEDITATION: Believers will *never* experience the wrath of God that they deserve. Though they do feel his discipline, such discipline is the act of a loving Father, not an angry Judge. The rod and stripes may be terribly painful, but they are used with love. God's lovingkindness is not taken away from those who believe. How does this comfort you?

Keeping an Eternal Perspective

For a thousand years in thy sight are but as yesterday when it is past, and as a watch in the night. Psalm 90:4

SUGGESTED FURTHER READING: Luke 12:16–21

We know that people who have completed the circle of life are forthwith taken out of the world, yet the knowledge of this frailty fails to make a deep impression on our hearts because we do not lift our eyes above the world. Moses awakens us by showing us the eternal perspective of God, without which we do not perceive how speedily our life vanishes away.

The imagination that we shall have a long life is like a profound sleep in which we are all benumbed. Only meditating upon the heavenly life can swallow up this foolish fancy respecting the length of our continuance upon earth. To those who are blind to eternity, Moses presents the view of God as Judge. "O Lord!" he seems to say, "If men would only reflect upon that eternity from which Thou beholdest the inconstant circling of the world, they would not make so great an account of the present life."

The reason that unbelievers indulge in pleasures is that they have their hearts too much set upon the world and do not taste the pleasures of a celestial eternity.

Hence we learn the application of this teaching. Why do we have such great anxiety about our life that nothing satisfies us? Do we continually molest ourselves because we foolishly imagine that we shall nestle in this world forever?

Moses does not only contrast a thousand years with one day; he also contrasts them with *yesterday*, which is already gone. For whatever is still before our eyes captivates our minds. But we are less affected with the recollection of what is past. So, let us elevate our minds by faith to God's heavenly throne, from which he declares that this earthly life is nothing compared with what is yet to come.

FOR MEDITATION: Maintaining an eternal perspective is difficult. But isn't our failure to do so the reason why we find ourselves falling into worldliness so often? Yesterday is past. We must keep the next thousand years in perspective.

Directing the Work of our Hands

And let the beauty of the Lord *our God be upon us: and establish thou the work of our hands upon us; yea, the work of our hands establish thou it.* Psalm 90:17
SUGGESTED FURTHER READING: Nehemiah 6:10–19

God has promised that the church will be perpetuated to the end of the world. In a special manner that should lead us to pray for the welfare of the church as well as for our posterity, who are yet unborn. We should also note the word *beauty*, for in it we learn that the love that God bears toward us is unparalleled. In enriching us with his gifts, God gains nothing for himself, yet he would have the splendor and beauty of his character manifested in bountifully dealing with us, as if his beauty would be obscured when he ceases to do us good.

In the clause *establish thou the work of our hands upon us*, Moses intimates that we cannot undertake or attempt anything with the prospect of success unless God becomes our guide and counselor and governs us by his Spirit. It then follows that the reason why the enterprises and efforts of worldly men have a disastrous end is that, in not following God, they pervert order and throw everything into confusion.

Though God converts to good in the end whatever Satan and the reprobate plot and practice against him or his people, yet the church, which God rules with undisturbed sway, has in this respect a special privilege. By his providence, which is incomprehensible to us, he directs his work with the reprobate externally but governs his believing people internally by his Holy Spirit. Therefore we can properly say that he orders or directs the work of their hands.

FOR MEDITATION: How often haven't we found that, despite our native abilities and best efforts, we are unable to make progress in some task? At other times, with the Lord's blessing, we can accomplish things far beyond our normal abilities. It is humbling and also refreshing to recognize that we are so dependent on the Lord's blessing. In what areas in your life has this recently been manifested?

The Purpose of the Sabbath

It is a good thing to give thanks unto the LORD, *and to sing praises unto thy name, O most High.* Psalm 92:1
SUGGESTED FURTHER READING: Isaiah 1:12–18

As the psalm's inscription says, the Jews were in the habit of singing Psalm 92 on the Sabbath day. It is apparent in other passages that other psalms were also applied to this use. As the words may be literally read in the Hebrew, *it is good for giving thanks unto the* LORD. The psalmist says it is good to have a certain day set apart for singing the praises of God; it is a useful arrangement that one day is chosen on which the Lord's people can celebrate God's works.

The reason the psalmist dedicates this psalm to the Sabbath is obvious. The day is not to be holy in the sense of our being devoted to idleness, as if idleness could be acceptable worship to God, but in the sense of separating ourselves from all other occupations so that we can meditate upon divine works. Because our minds are inconstant, we are apt to wander from God when exposed to various distractions. We need to be disentangled from all cares if we would seriously apply ourselves to the praises of God.

The psalmist teaches us that rightly observing the Sabbath does not consist of idleness, as some absurdly imagine, but in the celebration of the divine name. The argument that he makes is drawn from the profitableness of service, for nothing is more encouraging than to know that our labor is not in vain and that what we engage in meets with divine approbation.

FOR MEDITATION: The Lord did not give us the Sabbath so that we might fritter it away doing nothing profitable. It is given so that we might focus on him and on his Word, and keeping it is a matter of the heart. Take a moment to re-examine how you spend your Sabbaths. Is there room for improvement?

When his Ways are Incomprehensible

O LORD, how great are thy works! and thy thoughts are very deep. Psalm 92:5
SUGGESTED FURTHER READING: Psalm 139

Having spoken in general of the works of God, the psalmist proceeds to speak more particularly of God's justice in governing the world. Though God may postpone the punishment of the wicked, in due time he shows that he does not overlook or fail to perceive their sins. Furthermore, though God exercises his own children with the cross, he proves in the end that he is not indifferent to their welfare.

The Psalmist makes this particular point because much darkness is thrown upon the scheme of divine providence because of the inequality and disorder that prevail in human affairs. We see the wicked triumphing and applauding their own good fortune, as if there were no judge above. They also take advantage of divine forbearance for additional excesses because they are under the impression that they have escaped God's hand. The temptation is aggravated by the stupidity and blindness of heart that lead them to imagine that God exerts no control over the world and sits idle in heaven.

We know how quickly we can sink under the troubles of the flesh. The psalmist, therefore, intentionally selects this occasion to show the watchful care exerted by God over the human family. He begins by using the language of exclamation, for such is the dreadful distemper and disorder by which our understandings are confounded that we cannot comprehend the method of God's works, even when it is most apparent. We are to notice that the inspired writer is not speaking here of the work of God in the creation of the heavens and earth, nor of his providential government of the world in general, but only of the judgments that he executes amongst men.

FOR MEDITATION: At times, life seems cruel and unfair. We see wickedness and injustice flourish all around us while goodness and justice suffer. We can only maintain a proper perspective by trusting that God is in control, says the psalmist. When has such trust been rewarded in your own life?

Curbing Rebellion against God's Deep Ways

O LORD, how great are thy works! and thy thoughts are very deep. Psalm
92:5
SUGGESTED FURTHER READING: Romans 11:33–36

God governs the world in a manner that we are often unable to
comprehend. Were things under our own management, we would invert
the order that God observes. Since that is not the case, we may perversely
argue with God for not hastening sooner to help the righteous and to
punish the wicked.

It strikes us in the highest degree inconsistent with the perfections of
God that he should bear with the wicked when they rage against him,
when they rush without restraint into the most daring acts of iniquity,
and when they persecute at will the good and the innocent. It seems
intolerable to us that God should subject his own people to the injustice
and violence of the wicked while failing to check abounding falsehood,
deceit, plunder, bloodshed, and every species of enormity. Why does he
suffer his truth to be obscured and his holy name to be trampled under
foot? Such is the greatness of the divine operation and the depth of divine
counsel that cause the psalmist to break forth in admiration.

It is no doubt true that God has displayed incomprehensible depth of
power and wisdom in the fabric of the universe; but what the psalmist
especially has in view here is to check our tendency to murmur against
God when he does not pursue our plan in his providential management.
When his ways do not agree with the general ideas of men, we ought to
contemplate them with reverence, remembering that God, to better try
our obedience, has lifted his deep and mysterious judgments far above
our conceptions.

FOR MEDITATION: How easily our hearts rise up in rebellion and unbelief
when God does not act as we think he should! This psalm is a wonderful
corrective to that spirit. What steps can we take to remind ourselves who
is Creator and who is creature when we contemplate God's ways in the
world?

Strengthening Covenant Promises

He hath remembered his covenant for ever, the word which he commanded to a thousand generations. Psalm 105:8

SUGGESTED FURTHER READING: Genesis 15

God made a covenant with Abraham and by solemn oath also promised to be the God of Abraham's seed. To give greater assurance of the truth of his promise, God graciously renewed his covenant with Isaac and Jacob. The effect of extending the vow to posterity is that God's faithfulness might take deeper hold of the hearts of his people. Also, when God's grace is renewed on recurring occasions, it becomes better known and more illustrious among men. Accordingly, this covenant is proved more steadfast and immovable, for what is affirmed concerning each of the patriarchs belongs equally to them all.

It is said that God "swore to Isaac." Had God not before sworn that to Abraham? Undoubtedly he had. It is also said that it was established to Jacob for a law, and for an everlasting covenant. Does this mean the covenant was previously only temporal and transitory and that it then changed its nature? Such an idea is altogether at variance with the meaning of the sacred writer. By these different forms of expression the psalmist asserts that the covenant was fully and perfectly confirmed, so that, if the calling was perhaps obscure for one man, it might become more evident by God's transmitting it to posterity. By this means the truth of the covenant was better manifested.

Here we are once more reminded that God with great kindness considers our weakness when, both by his oath and by frequently repeating his word, he ratifies what he formerly promised to us. Our ingratitude then appears fouler in disbelieving him when he not only speaks but also swears.

FOR MEDITATION: The promises that God makes to his people also extend to their posterity, which includes sinners like us. How does each manifestation of God's covenant promises help strengthen believers' responses to their covenant commitments?

Qualified for Service

He sent Moses his servant; and Aaron whom he had chosen. Psalm
105:26
SUGGESTED FURTHER READING: Psalm 77:11–20

Here the prophet briefly refers to the deliverance of God's people. If the
Egyptians of their own accord had allowed the people of Israel to leave
Egypt, neither the service of Moses nor miracles of God would have been
required.

But God determined that his people should be delivered in such a way
that denial of its author would be impossible. Moses is called his *servant*
to teach us that he was not self-appointed to his office and that he
attempted nothing by his own authority. Rather, as the minister of God,
Moses executed the office with which he was entrusted. The same is true
of Aaron, who is said to have been *chosen*. What is attributed in
particular to each of these eminent men applies equally to both.
Therefore Psalm 105:26 is basically saying: God sent Moses and Aaron,
his servants, not because of their intrinsic fitness or because they
spontaneously offered their service to God, but because God chose them.

This passage teaches us that those who are engaged in active and
useful service for the church are not exclusively qualified for it by their
own exertions or by their own talents, but are stirred by God to serve.
Moses was a man of heroic virtue, but in himself, he was nothing.
Accordingly, the psalmist would say all that is accounted worthy of
remembering in Moses as well as Aaron is to be ascribed to God alone.
Whatever men do for the welfare of the church, they owe the power of
doing so to God, who, of his free goodness, has been pleased thus to
honor them.

FOR MEDITATION: This teaching goes against every natural inclination of
our hearts. How easily we take pride in ourselves when God blesses our
work, as if we were somehow ultimately responsible! The honor, Calvin
says, belongs to God alone. How does this both humble us and fill us
with gratitude?

Conquered by Frogs

He turned their waters into blood, and slew their fish. Their land brought forth frogs in abundance, in the chambers of their kings. Psalm 105:29–30

SUGGESTED FURTHER READING: Exodus 8:1–15

The plague of water being turned into blood was especially grievous to the Egyptians because water was one of the two great means of supporting life. The power of God shone forth brighter considering that the land of Egypt was well irrigated, yet the Egyptians were parched with drought. It is said that *their land brought forth frogs* and entered even *the chambers of their kings.* God thus manifestly showed that he was the author of the miracle, for though all Egypt swarmed with frogs, the courts of the kings should have been exempt from this nuisance. The term *kings* denotes either the nobles of the realm or the king's sons, who were brought up in expectation of royal power, for at that time, as is well known, only one king reigned over all Egypt.

From this we learn how, by a kind of mockery, God easily humbles those who pride themselves in the flesh. He did not gather an army to fight against the Egyptians, nor did he forthwith arm his angels or thunder out of heaven. But God brought forth frogs in Egypt, which contemptuously trampled upon the pride of that haughty nation and held in contempt the whole world besides. It would have been no disgrace for Egypt to have been conquered by powerful enemies, but consider how dishonorable it was to be vanquished by frogs!

By this God showed that he has no need of powerful hosts to destroy the wicked, for he can do this, even seemingly in sport, whenever he pleases.

FOR MEDITATION: Calvin provides us with a unique reminder of how deluded we are when we think we are in control. Whether by great natural disasters or by an army of frogs, God will remind us that *he* is the one in control. How does the Holy Spirit teach us experientially to relinquish control of our lives to God?

Remembered with Favor

Remember me, O LORD, *with the favour that thou bearest unto thy people: O visit me with thy salvation.* Psalm 106:4

SUGGESTED FURTHER READING: Psalm 30

The prophet here declares his chief desire is that God would extend to him the love that he bears toward the church. He might thus participate in all the blessings which, from the very first, God bestowed upon his chosen and which he day by day continues to bestow on them. The prophet desires this not only for himself but also, in the name of the universal church, offers up a prayer for all, that by his example he might stimulate the faithful to present similar petitions.

Remember me, says he, *with the favour that thou bearest unto thy people*; that is to say, grant to me the same unmerited kindness that thou art pleased to confer upon thy people, so that I may never be cut off from thy church but will always be included among the number of thy children. The phrase *favour toward thy people* refers passively to the love that God graciously bears to his elect. The prophet uses it to indicate the marks of God's love. From this gracious source flows the proof that God actually and experimentally gives grace to his people.

The prophet considers being numbered among the people of God as the summit of true happiness because by this means he feels that God is reconciled to him. Nothing is more desirable than this. Also, he experiences that God is bountiful. The term *remember* refers to the circumstance of time. As we shall see toward the end of the psalm, it was written when the people were in such a sad and calamitous state that the faithful might have entertained some secret apprehension that God had forgotten them.

FOR MEDITATION: Are you, by grace, one of God's chosen people? If you are numbered among the elect, you will never be forgotten but will be remembered with favor. That should comfort you in the darkest hours.

Provoking God

Many times did he deliver them; but they provoked him with their counsel, and were brought low for their iniquity. Psalm 106:43
SUGGESTED FURTHER READING: Numbers 14

The wickedness and perversity of people becomes more evident when even God's severe chastisements fail to produce reformation. The prophet deduces that the detestable hardness of people's hearts continues. They are not bent to obedience despite all the benefits they have received from God. Indeed, in the time of their afflictions, they groan under the burden of those afflictions, but when God mitigates their punishment and grants them wonderful deliverance, how can their subsequent backsliding then be excused?

Bear in mind that we have a picture here as in a mirror of the nature of all mankind. If God uses the same means that he used for the Israelites to reclaim the majority of the sons of men, how is it that comparatively few do not continue in the very same state as they were? He may humble us with the severity of his rod or melt us with his kindness, but the effect is only temporary, because, though he visits us with correction upon correction or heaps kindness upon kindness upon us, we very soon relapse into our wonted vicious practices.

The Jews did not cease from backsliding, but, as the psalmist says, *provoked him with their counsel.* They then received a just recompense of reward in being oppressed by their iniquity. Moreover, though these backsliders deserved their afflictions, yet God still heard their groanings. In his unwearied kindness, God did not cease to strive with them even in their perverseness of spirit.

FOR MEDITATION: This passage is a clear demonstration of our need for the miracle of regeneration. Unless a person is changed from the inside out, all the chastisements or all the blessings in the world will not turn him to God. What impact do God's chastisements have on you?

Triumphing in Praise

*Save us, O L*ORD *our God, and gather us from among the heathen, to give thanks unto thy holy name, and to triumph in thy praise.* Psalm 106:47

SUGGESTED FURTHER READING: Acts 2:40–47

This psalm was composed during the sad and calamitous dispersion of the people of Israel. It was necessary for the people to be completely humbled to prevent them from further murmuring against God's dispensations. Seeing that God had extended pardon to their fathers, who were undeserving of it, he aimed to inspire their children with the hope of forgiveness, provided they carefully and cordially sought to be reconciled to him. This was especially the case because of God solemnly remembering his covenant with them. Through faith they might draw near to God, even though his anger had not yet turned away.

Moreover, God had chosen them to be his peculiar people, so they could call upon him to collect into one body their dissevered and bleeding members. For, according to the prediction of Moses, "If any of thine be driven out unto the outmost parts of heaven, from thence will the LORD thy God gather thee, and from thence will he fetch thee" (Deut. 30:4). This prediction eventually came true when the widely separated multitude was gathered together and grew in the unity of the faith. For though the people of Israel never regained their earthly kingdom and polity, yet they were grafted with the Gentiles into the body of Christ, which was a more preferable gathering.

Wherever they were, the children of God were united with each other and to the Gentile converts by the holy and spiritual bond of faith. Together they constituted one church that extended over the whole earth. They came together to fulfill the purpose of their redemption from captivity, namely, that they might celebrate the name of God and employ themselves continually in praising him.

FOR MEDITATION: The psalmist asks for deliverance for the people of Israel so that they might give thanks and triumph in praising God. This is a great lesson for us to remember when we ask the Lord for blessings: our ultimate motive should be his glory, not simply our comfort. What means can we use to learn this transforming lesson more profoundly and consistently?

Grateful in Danger

Such as sit in darkness and in the shadow of death, being bound in affliction and iron. Psalm 107:10

SUGGESTED FURTHER READING: Matthew 14:22–33

The Spirit of God mentions many dangers in which God shows his power and grace in protecting and delivering people. The world calls these vicissitudes the sport of fortune; hardly one in a hundred people ascribe them to the superintending providence of God.

But God expects a very different kind of practical wisdom from us, namely, that we should meditate on his judgments in a time of adversity and on his goodness in delivering us from danger. For surely it is not by mere chance that a person falls into the hands of enemies or robbers; neither is it by chance that a person is rescued from them. But what we must constantly keep in mind is that all afflictions are God's rod, and therefore there is no remedy for them other than God's grace.

If a person falls into the hands of robbers or thieves and is not instantly murdered, but, giving up all hope of life, expects death at any moment, surely his deliverance is striking proof of the grace of God. This grace is even more illustrious considering the few who escape from such danger. Such circumstances, then, ought not to diminish our praises of God.

The prophet charges people with ingratitude who, after they have been wonderfully saved, very soon lose sight of the deliverance granted to them. To strengthen the charge, he brings forward their sighs and cries as a testimony against them. For when they are in dangerous straits, they confess in good earnest that God is their deliverer. Why then do these confessions disappear when they enjoy peace and quietness?

FOR MEDITATION: Cries to God for deliverance come so easily and so naturally to our lips when we are unable to help ourselves. Why then does praise feel so difficult when things are going well? Are we so foolish to think that we can take care of ourselves in the good times, as if we are any less dependent on God?

Waiting for God

Let this be the reward of mine adversaries from the LORD, *and of them that speak evil against my soul.* Psalm 109:20

SUGGESTED FURTHER READING: Isaiah 30:18–26

David did not rashly or unadvisedly utter curses against his enemies but strictly adhered to what the Spirit dictated. I acknowledge that many people pretend to have similar confidence and hope, but who nevertheless recklessly rush beyond the bounds of temperance and moderation. But what David beheld by the unclouded eye of faith, he also uttered with the zeal of a sound mind; for, having devoted himself to the cultivation of piety under the protection of God's hand, he was aware that the day was approaching when his enemies would experience the punishment they had earned.

We learn that David's trust was placed in God alone. He did not look to people to direct his course according to whether the world smiled or frowned upon him. We can be sure that whoever places his dependence on people will find that the most trifling incident will annoy him.

Therefore, even if the whole world abandons us, we, like this holy man, should lift up our heads to heaven and look there for our defender and deliverer. If God intends to use human instruments for our deliverance, he will soon raise up people to accomplish that purpose. But if he chooses to try our faith by depriving us of all earthly assistance, we should not regard that as any negative reflection upon the glory of his name. Rather, we should wait until the proper time when God fully makes known his decision in which we can calmly acquiesce.

FOR MEDITATION: Patience in waiting for an answer to prayer, especially a prayer for deliverance, must be consciously cultivated if we are to avoid losing confidence in God and his ways. But while waiting is a challenge, the Spirit often uses it to teach us to look to heaven, not people, for deliverance. What lessons have you learned about the Lord or about yourself while waiting on him in prayer?

Assurance of his Protection

The LORD shall send the rod of thy strength out of Zion: rule thou in the midst of thine enemies. Psalm 110:2
SUGGESTED FURTHER READING: Psalm 2

It is astonishing that though the whole world has united to oppose Christ's kingdom, the church has continued to spread and prosper. David here encourages the godly not to be dispirited by the foolhardy attempts of those who presume to introduce discord and disorder into the kingdom of Christ, for God will use his invincible power to maintain the glory of his sacred throne.

When our minds are agitated by various commotions, let us confidently rest, knowing that no matter how much the world rages against Christ, they will never be able to hurl him from the right hand of the Father. Moreover, because he does not reign on his own account but for our salvation, we may rest assured that we will be protected and preserved from all ills under the guardianship of this invincible King.

Doubtless our condition in this world will include many hardships, but God's will is that Christ's kingdom should be encompassed with many enemies, his design being to keep us in a state of constant warfare. Therefore it becomes us to exercise patience and meekness, and, assured of God's aid, boldly to consider the rage of the whole world as nothing.

This passage also tells us about the calling of the Gentiles. If God had not told us about the extension of Christ's kingdom to the Gentiles, we could not today be regarded as his people. But since the wall is broken between Jew and Gentile (Eph. 2:14), and the gospel promulgated, we too have been gathered into the body of the church, and know that Christ puts forth his power to uphold and defend us.

FOR MEDITATION: Although believers are troubled by worldly enemies or by internal discord and disorder, we can be assured that the church of Christ will be restored to peace. We can look to heaven, confident that God will not allow evil to triumph but will uphold and defend his bride. How does this comfort us here and now?

Delighting in his Commands

Praise ye the LORD. *Blessed is the man that feareth the* LORD, *that delighteth greatly in his commandments.* Psalm 112:1
SUGGESTED FURTHER READING: James 2:14–26

In the second clause of the verse, the prophet specifies that the fear of God includes *delighting greatly in his commandments*. The addition of this explanatory clause is quite apparent, for while people boldly condemn the law of God, yet it is also common for them to pretend that they fear God. The prophet refutes such impiety when he acknowledges that no one is a true worshiper of God who does not also endeavor to keep God's law. The prophet makes a significant distinction between a willing and prompt effort to keep the law, and one that merely consists of servile and constrained obedience.

We must, therefore, cheerfully embrace the law of God in such a manner that our love of it, with all its sweetness, may overcome all allurements of the flesh. Mere attention to the law is fruitless. A person cannot be regarded as a genuine observer of the law unless he truly delights in the law of God and renders obedience that is agreeable to God.

In considering the passage at large, the prophet affirms that the worshipers of God who delight in his Commandments are *blessed*, thus guarding us against the very dangerous deception that the ungodly practice upon themselves in imagining that they can reap a sort of happiness from doing evil.

FOR MEDITATION: Calvin offers a sobering test of our fear of God here: do we truly delight in obeying God's commands or do we only submit out of mere obligation or duty? Do you esteem his smiles and frowns to be of greater value than the smiles and frowns of people? Do you welcome any means he may employ to urge us on to obedience?

Praiseworthy Liberality

He hath dispersed, he hath given to the poor; his righteousness endureth forever; his horn shall be exalted with honour. Psalm 112:9
SUGGESTED FURTHER READING: Mark 12:38–44

The righteous will never lose the fruit and the reward of their liberality, the psalmist says. First, they will be honored for their *dispersing*. They do not give sparingly and grudgingly, unlike some who imagine that they fulfill their duty to the poor by doling out a small pittance to them. The righteous give as liberally as necessity requires and their means allow; for a liberal heart does not necessarily mean that the person possesses a large portion of the wealth of this world. The prophet's point is that the righteous are never parsimonious but rather are always ready to give to others as they are able.

Next he says *they give to the poor*, meaning they do not offer charity at random but with prudence and discretion to meet the needs of the poor. We are aware that unnecessary and superfluous expenditures for the sake of ostentation are frequently lauded by the world; consequently, a larger quantity of the good things of life is squandered away in luxury and ambition than is dispensed in prudent charity. The prophet instructs us that truly praiseworthy liberality does not consist of distributing our goods without any regard to the objects upon whom they are conferred and the purposes to which they are applied, but in relieving the needs of the truly needy and expending money on proper and lawful things.

This passage is quoted by Paul (2 Cor. 9:9), in which he says it is easy for God to bless us with plenty so that we may exercise our bounty freely, deliberately, and impartially. This accords best with the design of the prophet.

FOR MEDITATION: We can easily fall into a sort of a mechanical habit of giving, lacking the spirit the psalmist talks about here. But we should always have our eyes open for opportunities to give liberally, spontaneously, and quietly to people who are truly in need. Can you think of any such opportunities today?

Resting in God's Favor

Return unto thy rest, O my soul; for the LORD *hath dealt bountifully with thee.* Psalm 116:7
SUGGESTED FURTHER READING: Psalm 145

David now tells himself to rest because God has shown favor to him.

Is the experience of the grace of God enough to allay the fear and trepidation of our minds? That is what David seems to indicate here in saying that, since he has experienced the relief of divine aid, he can now return to rest. But if the faithful regain their peace of mind only after God manifests himself as their deliverer, what room is there for the exercise of faith, and what power will the promises have to quiet our souls?

Surely, waiting calmly and silently for indications of God's favor which is concealed from us is the undoubted evidence of faith. As strong faith quiets the conscience and composes the spirit, so, according to Paul, "the peace of God, which passeth all understanding," reigns supremely there (Phil. 4:7). Hence the godly remain unmoved, though the world around them seems to be falling into ruin.

What does it mean to *return unto thy rest*? However much the children of God may be driven hither and thither, yet they constantly derive support from the Word of God so that they cannot totally and finally fall away. In confiding in his promises, they throw themselves upon God's providence even while they are sorely distressed by disquieting fears and sadly buffeted by the storms of temptation. No sooner does God come to their assistance, than inward peace takes possession of their minds. Also, in the manifestation of God's grace, they are given grounds for joy and gladness.

This latter kind of quietness is what David asks for, declaring that, even though he has experienced much to cause agitation of mind, it is now time for him to delight himself calmly in God.

FOR MEDITATION: The storms of life can so agitate our minds and spirits that our only option is to run in desperation to the Rock of our salvation. There we not only find relief from the temptations and attacks of life, but, by grace, we also are inwardly restored to rest, assured that God will care for us. Have you experienced this peace that passes understanding?

The Wonder of his Benefits

What shall I render unto the LORD for all his benefits toward me? Psalm 116:12

SUGGESTED FURTHER READING: Psalm 136

The psalmist now exclaims that the multitude of God's benefits to him is so great that he cannot find adequate language to express his gratitude. His question is emphatic, *What shall I render unto the LORD?*, indicating that it was not his desire but the means that were inadequate to render thanks to God. Acknowledging this inability, the psalmist uses the only means in his power to extol the grace of God. He seems to say, "I am exceedingly wishful to discharge my duty, but when I look around me, I find nothing that will prove an adequate recompense."

He cannot offer to God sufficient compensation for his benefits, the psalmist says, adding that he felt obligated to do so not just for one series of benefits but for a variety of innumerable benefits. "There is no benefit on account of which God has not made me a debtor to him; how should I have the means of repaying him for them?" he seems to ask. Since the means of recompense fails him, the expression of thanksgiving is the only thing he can offer that will be acceptable to God.

David's example teaches us not to treat God's benefits lightly or carelessly, for if we estimate them according to their value, that very thought ought to fill us with admiration. Each one of us has had God's benefits heaped upon us. But our pride, which carries us away into extravagant theories, causes us to forget this very doctrine of God's generosity toward us. Nonetheless, that ought to engage our unremitting attention. Furthermore, God's bounty toward us merits more praise because he expects no recompense from us, nor can receive any, for he stands in need of nothing, and we are poor and destitute in all things.

FOR MEDITATION: It is so easy to think that certain blessings are owed to us, but this is not a proper way to cultivate thankfulness to God. David's perspective is much healthier; his praise flows out of recognizing the wonder of these blessings and their source in God. What impact could this perspective have on your day today?

Vows to the Lord

I will pay my vows unto the LORD *now in the presence of all his people.*
Psalm 116:14
SUGGESTED FURTHER READING: Deuteronomy 23:15–25

David's steadfast piety now shines forth in his willingness to fulfill the vows he made to God when he was in the midst of danger. He did not forget those promises, as most people do. When the hand of God lies heavy upon them, many people ask for God's help, but shortly after receiving that help they soon bury in oblivion the deliverance that they have received.

In speaking of the true worship of God, the Holy Spirit properly connects by an indissoluble bond these two parts of worship: "Call upon me in the day of trouble" and, after your deliverance, glorify me (Ps. 50:15). If any regard it absurd for the faithful to enter into a covenant with God by making vows to him in hopes of procuring his approbation, I must explain that they do not promise the sacrifice of praise to soothe him by their flatteries, as if he were a mortal like themselves. Also, they do not attempt to bind God to themselves by proposing some reward, for David previously protested that he would not offer any recompense.

The intent of vows, first, is that the children of God may have their hearts strengthened with the confidence of obtaining whatever they ask. Second, it is that they may be stimulated to offer up more gratitude to God for his mercies. The privilege of vowing may surely be conceded to the children of God in their infirmity, for by this means their most merciful Father allows them to enter into familiar conversation with him, provided they make their vows for the right purpose. Whatever happens, nothing may be attempted without God's permission.

FOR MEDITATION: Many of us might be uncomfortable making vows to God, thinking of that as bargaining with the Almighty. But if we are able to leave behind the notion of repaying God (as David did), such vows can be a great stimulus for praise, worship, and service. How have you "paid" your vows "unto the LORD"?

God's Wondrous Law

Open thou mine eyes, that I may behold wondrous things out of thy law.
Psalm 119:18
SUGGESTED FURTHER READING: Psalm 19

God gives light to us to see the wonder of his Word, the prophet says. We are blind to the gospel even in the midst of the clearest light until God removes the veil of blindness from our eyes.

The psalmist confesses that his eyes were shut, making him unable to discern the light of the heavenly doctrine until God, by the invisible grace of his Spirit, opened them. The psalmist seems to be deploring his own blindness as well as that of the whole human race. But he tells us that the remedy is at hand, provided we do not, by trusting our own wisdom, reject the gracious illumination that God offers to us.

Let us realize that we do not receive the illumination of the Spirit of God to make us condemn God's law and take pleasure in secret revelations, like many fanatics who do not regard themselves spiritual unless they reject the Word of God and put in its place their own wild speculations.

The prophet's goal is very different. He wishes to inform us that God illumines us so we are able to discern the light of life that God manifests in his Word. He mentions the *wondrous things* of the law to humble us, to help us contemplate that law with admiration; and to convince us of our great need of God's grace to comprehend the mysteries of his Word which surpass our limited capacity. The law includes not only the Ten Commandments but also the covenant of eternal salvation with all its provisions, which God has made with us. Knowing that Christ, "in whom are hid all the treasures of wisdom and knowledge," "is the end of the law," we need not be surprised that the prophet commends it and the sublime mysteries which it contains (Col. 2:3; Rom. 10:4).

FOR MEDITATION: When we focus on the wonders of the revelations of God's Word, we are much safer from the temptation to desire new and special revelations from God. The Bible contains so many wondrous things that a lifetime of study would not reveal them all to us; study them further to find new strength for each new day.

Disciplined to Obedience

Before I was afflicted I went astray: but now have I kept thy word. Psalm 119:67

SUGGESTED FURTHER READING: Hebrews 12:5–11

Experience demonstrates that when God deals gently with us, we often break into rebellion. Since even a prophet of God who strays needs to be corrected by forcible means, discipline is assuredly needful for us when we rebel.

The first step in obedience is the mortification of the flesh, which does not come naturally to people. So, not surprisingly, God brings us to a sense of duty by manifold afflictions. As the flesh is from time to time resistant, even when it seems to be tamed, it is no wonder to find God repeatedly subjecting us anew to the rod.

This is done in different ways. He humbles some by poverty, some by shame, some by disease, some by domestic distress, and some by hard and painful labors. He applies the appropriate remedy to the diversity of vices to which we are prone. It is now obvious how profitable is the truth of David's confession. The prophet speaks of himself even as Jeremiah (31:18) says of himself that he was "as a bullock unaccustomed to the yoke," setting before us an image of the rebellion that is natural to us all.

We are very ungrateful indeed if the fruit that we reap from chastisements does not assuage or mitigate their bitterness. So long as we are rebellious against God, we are in a state of the deepest wretchedness. The means he chooses to bend and tame us to obedience is his chastisements.

The prophet teaches us by his own example that God gives evidence of his willingness that we should become his disciples by the pains he takes to subdue our hardness. We should then at least strive to become gentle, and, laying aside all stubbornness, willingly bear the yoke that he imposes upon us.

FOR MEDITATION: If the afflictions we experience have a blessed end—our sanctification (Heb. 12:11)—shouldn't we learn to become thankful for them? Rather than simply enduring them with a stiff upper lip, we should be praising God that he did not leave us to ourselves. Are you facing afflictions today? If so, how can you shift your perception of them to offer thanks to the Lord for them?

Distancing Ourselves from Evil

Depart from me, ye evildoers: for I will keep the commandments of my God. Psalm 119:115
SUGGESTED FURTHER READING: Ephesians 5:1–21

To follow the way of the Lord without stumbling, we must endeavor to keep the greatest possible distance from worldly and wicked people, not in terms of physical separation but in terms of interacting and conversing with them.

The dangerous influence of wicked people is well evident from observing that few people keep their integrity to the end of life. The world is fraught with corruption. In addition, the extreme infirmity of our nature makes it easy for us to be infected and polluted by evil, even from the slightest contact with evildoers.

With good reason, the prophet bids the wicked to depart from him, so he may progress in the fear of God without obstruction. This statement agrees with the admonition of Paul in 2 Corinthians 6:14, "Be ye not unequally yoked together with unbelievers." It is beyond the prophet's power to chase the wicked away from him, but by these words he intimates that, from now on, he will have no more interaction with them. He emphatically designates God as *his God*, to testify that he counts him to be more worthy than all of mankind. Finding extreme wickedness universally prevalent on the earth, he chooses to separate himself from evildoers so that he might join himself wholly to God.

So that bad examples may not tempt us to evil, we are well advised to put God on our side and to abide constantly in him, for he is ours.

FOR MEDITATION: To engage with a wicked world while remaining separate from evildoers can be difficult; yet it must be done. We cannot abandon sinners in their plight, but we must ensure that their evil does not rub off on us. This requires constant prayer for wisdom and a heart and mind full of Christ and his Word.

The Only Way to Live

The righteousness of thy testimonies is everlasting: give me understanding, and I shall live. Psalm 119:144

SUGGESTED FURTHER READING: Proverbs 2

People cannot truly live destitute of the light of heavenly wisdom, the psalmist says. Unlike swine or asses, people were not created to stuff their bellies but to exercise themselves in the knowledge and service of God. When they turn away from such endeavors, life becomes worse than a thousand deaths. David stresses that the purpose of life for him was not merely to be fed with meat and drink and to enjoy earthly comforts, but to aspire after a better life, which could only be done under the guidance of faith.

That is a very necessary warning; for though it is universally acknowledged that people exceed the lower animals in intelligence, yet most people, as if deliberately, stifle whatever light God pours into their understanding. I admit that all people want to be sharp-witted. Nonetheless, few aspire to heaven and consider that the fear of God is the beginning of wisdom. As meditation upon the celestial life is buried by earthly cares, people do nothing else than plunge into the grave. While living to the world, they die to God.

In using the term *live*, the prophet names his utmost wish. He seems to say, though I am already dead, yet if thou art pleased to illumine my mind with the knowledge of heavenly truth, this grace will be sufficient to revive me.

FOR MEDITATION: If our great passion in life is to live well, we must not look for fulfillment in earthly pleasures and luxuries, for none of these will truly satisfy. Rather, we must be like David—passionate in seeking righteousness and understanding from God on how to live. That is the only way that leads to heaven.

Success at Work

It is vain for you to rise up early, to sit up late, to eat the bread of sorrows: for so he giveth his beloved sleep. Psalm 127:2
SUGGESTED FURTHER READING: Matthew 6:25–34

Solomon, the writer of this psalm, identifies two means that people believe contribute in an eminent degree to the amassing of riches. It is not surprising to find that those who become rich in a short time spare no exertion but work night and day in their occupations, allowing themselves only scanty payment from the product of their labor.

Solomon, however, says that neither living on a small salary nor diligence in work will by itself profit us. He does not forbid us to practice temperance in our diet or to rise early to engage in worldly business, but rather stirs us up to prayer and to calling upon God. He also recommends that we express gratitude for divine blessings and bring to naught whatever would obscure the grace of God.

Consequently, we shall rightly enter our worldly vocations when our hope depends exclusively upon God. Our success then will correspond to our wishes. But if a person takes no account of God as he eagerly makes haste, he will bring ruin upon himself by his precipitous course.

The design of the prophet is not to encourage men to give way to sloth, so that they think about nothing all their life long and abandon themselves to idleness. Rather, his meaning is that they execute what God has asked them to do. They should begin each day with prayer and call upon God's name, offering him their labors so that he may bless them.

FOR MEDITATION: No matter how diligent we are, if our work is not blessed by God, it will fail miserably. Sadly, this principle is far from our minds during most workdays when we so easily slip into the mentality that our success depends solely on us. Make a conscious effort today to remember that any success in work is a blessing from God.

Comfort in the Midst of Death

Though I walk in the midst of trouble, thou wilt revive me: thou shalt stretch forth thine hand against the wrath of mine enemies, and thy right hand shall save me. Psalm 138:7
SUGGESTED FURTHER READING: Psalm 23

Here David declares that God chooses to be his preserver, even if that means bringing him back to life in the midst of his troubles.

The passage well deserves our attention, for by nature we are so averse to suffering that we wish we might live safely beyond the shot of its arrows. We shrink from close contact with even the fear of death as something altogether intolerable. At the slightest approach to danger, we are immoderately afraid, as if our emergencies preclude the hope of divine deliverance.

Faith's true office is to see life in the midst of death. It is to trust the mercy of God, not to procure us universal exemption from evil, but to quicken us in the midst of death every moment of our lives. For God humbles his children under various trials so that his defense of them may be more remarkable and that he may show himself to be their deliverer as well as their preserver. In the world, believers are constantly exposed to danger. David offers the assurance that he will be safe under God's protection from all of his enemies and their efforts. He declares his hope is in the hand of God, which is stretched out for his help and will be invincible and victorious over every foe.

From this we are taught that God chooses to exercise his children with continual conflict, so that, having one foot as it were in the grave, they may flee with alarm to hide themselves under his wings, where they may abide in peace.

FOR MEDITATION: Rather than shrinking from enemies or danger, let us place our confidence in the Lord; he alone is willing and able to save us. This ought to give us a sense of peace, even in a world of trouble where enemies abound. What do you think David meant when he said, "Thou preparest a table before me in the presence of mine enemies" (Ps. 23:5a)?

Happy are the Blessed

Happy is that people, that is in such a case: yea, happy is that people, whose God is the LORD. Psalm 144:15
SUGGESTED FURTHER READING: Matthew 5:1–12

David says that those people are happy to whom divine favor has been shown and manifested.

Should anyone object that only a gross and worldly spirit would estimate man's happiness in terms of transitory gifts, I would reply that we must read the two things in connection: that those people are happy who recognize the favor of God in the abundance they enjoy. They have a sense of happiness from these transitory blessings that persuades them of their Father's care and leads them to aspire after the true inheritance of eternal blessings. There is no impropriety in calling those happy whom God blesses in this world, provided they do not show themselves blind to the improvements and uses that they make of God's mercies or foolishly and lazily overlook the author of them.

The kind providence of God in not suffering us to lack the basic needs of life is surely a striking illustration of his wonderful love. What is more desirable than to be the objects of God's care, especially if we have sufficient understanding to conclude from the liberality with which he supports us that he is our Father? For everything is to be viewed in reference to this point. It would be better for us to perish for want than to have mere brute satisfaction that forgets the main thing, that only those are happy whom God has chosen as his people.

In giving us meat and drink, God allows us to enjoy a certain measure of happiness, but it does not follow that believers who struggle through life in want and poverty are miserable, for this want, whatever it be, God can counterbalance by better consolations.

FOR MEDITATION: When God blesses us by meeting our material needs such as food, clothing, housing, and work, we may feel happy. But that happiness is incomplete if we do not look beyond the gifts to the Giver, as well as to the ultimate Gift of all, Jesus Christ our Savior.

Cleansing from the Heart

Wash you, make you clean; put away the evil of your doings from before mine eyes; cease to do evil. Isaiah 1:16

SUGGESTED FURTHER READING: 1 Samuel 15:1–11

Isaiah exhorts the Jews to repentance and shows the true way of it if they wish to have God approve their obedience. We know that nothing can please God unless it proceeds from a pure conscience; for God does not, like men, judge our works according to their outward appearance. Frequently a particular action, though performed by a very wicked man, obtains applause from men; but in the sight of God, who beholds the heart, a depraved conscience pollutes every virtue.

Haggai also teaches this, using an illustration from ancient ceremonies. He says everything that an unclean person touches is polluted, from which he concludes that nothing clean proceeds from the wicked. Isaiah declares that if integrity of heart does not sanctify people's outward worship, in vain do they offer sacrifices to God, in vain do they pray, in vain do they call on God's name. So that the Jews no longer labor to no purpose, Isaiah demands inward cleanness. He begins by saying that they need a comprehensive reformation, lest, after having discharged one part of their duty, they should imagine that this would veil other actions from the eyes of God.

Such is the manner in which we ought to deal with men who are estranged from God. We must not confine our attention to one or a few sores of a diseased body. Rather, because our aim is a true and thorough cure, we must call on them to begin anew. They must thoroughly remove the contagion so that they who were formerly hateful and abominable in the sight of God may begin to please God.

FOR MEDITATION: Have we dealt with the root of our own wickedness? If not, our good deeds will not recommend our polluted heart to God; rather, our polluted heart will taint even our best deeds. Until our hearts are thoroughly washed, we cannot cease to do evil.

Tasting the Good of the Land

If ye be willing and obedient, ye shall eat the good of the land. Isaiah 1:19
SUGGESTED FURTHER READING: Deuteronomy 28:1–14

In saying *Ye shall eat the good of the land,* Isaiah refers to the fruits that the earth yields to supply the necessities of life. In some sense, the earth may be said to be unkind when it does not produce its fruits and keeps them, as it were, in its bosom. Yet I have no doubt that Isaiah here alludes to the promises of the law, in which God declares that, for those who fear him, he will bless the earth and cause it to produce a great abundance of all good things. "The LORD shall make thee plenteous in ... the fruit of thy ground, in the land which the LORD sware unto thy fathers to give thee" (Deut. 28:11).

Yet when God offers us the conveniences of earthly life, it is not because he wishes that our attention should be confined to our present happiness. That is what hypocrites value and what entirely occupies their minds. No, he offers us *the good of the land* so that by the contemplation of it we may rise to the heavenly life, and that, by tasting so much goodness, he may prepare us for the enjoyment of eternal happiness. God was especially accustomed to act in this manner toward the ancient people, so that by tasting present benefits, as by a shadow, they might be called to heavenly inheritance.

This distinction ought to be carefully observed, so that we might apply this instruction to ourselves according to the degree of prosperity with which God has exalted us. The prophet intends to show us that true happiness, with its accompaniments, consists of obedience to God; and that the wicked, by their obstinacy, bring upon themselves every kind of calamity. Therefore all our distresses ought to be ascribed to the sins and crimes that we have committed.

FOR MEDITATION: It is proper that we welcome earthly blessings for what they are—blessings. Still, we should not forget that they point to greater things beyond this earth. Regardless of how many earthly blessings we may possess, we should strive to obtain heavenly ones. What steps can you take in your life to take neither earthly nor heavenly blessings for granted?

Teaching by Example

And many people shall go and say, Come ye, and let us go up to the mountain of the LORD, to the house of the God of Jacob; and he will teach us of his ways, and we will walk in his paths: for out of Zion shall go forth the law, and the word of the LORD from Jerusalem. Isaiah 2:3
SUGGESTED FURTHER READING: 1 John 2:1–6

People who take upon themselves the office of teaching and exhorting should not only sit down and command others but should also join and walk along with people as companions, Isaiah teaches us. Some men are very severe instructors and eager to urge others forward, yet they themselves do not move a step. But here, believers, we learn that instead of commanding people what to do, teachers should lead the way by their own example. The true method, therefore, of profitable teaching is actually performing what we demand, thereby making it evident that we speak with sincerity and earnestness.

And he will teach us of his ways. He shows, first, that God cannot be worshiped aright until we have been enlightened by doctrine; and, second, that God is the only teacher of the church on whose words we ought to hang. Nothing is less acceptable to God than foolish and erring services that men call devotion. Likewise, though God uses the agency of men in teaching, still he reserves as his own right that they must utter nothing but his word.

Had this rule been followed by those who called themselves teachers of the early church, religion would not have been so shamefully corrupted by a wide and confused diversity of superstitions. Nor is it possible that we today shall not be carried away by various errors when we are tossed about by the opinions of men. So Isaiah justly claims for God alone the power and authority to teach the church and to shut the mouths of all mortals, so that the office of teaching is committed to pastors for no other purpose than that God alone might be heard. Let those who wish to be ministers of Christ allow themselves to be regulated by Isaiah's teaching, that they may take nothing away from God's authority.

FOR MEDITATION: The same principles apply for all Christians. If we are going to bring others to Christ, we must walk alongside them, our example declaring that we are committed to what we say. All our verbal evangelism will be ineffective if we are not living as authentic Christians.

Separating Wheat from Chaff

When the Lord shall have washed away the filth of the daughters of Zion, and shall have purged the blood of Jerusalem from the midst thereof by the spirit of judgment, and by the spirit of burning. Isaiah 4:4
SUGGESTED FURTHER READING: Zechariah 13

When the church's filth has been washed away, she will be clean, and all who belong to her will truly be the elect of God. Now, it is certain that what Isaiah says here does not apply universally to the external church, into which many have been admitted under the designation of believers and who have nothing that corresponds to their profession.

The number of unbelievers in the church may even exceed the small number of true believers, as chaff often exceeds wheat in a barn. And though the captivity in Babylon was used by God as a sieve to remove a large portion of chaff, yet we know that the church was still very far from being as pure as she ought to have been. Still at that time there was, in some measure, a resemblance of that purity which will be truly and perfectly manifested after the lambs are separated from the kids (Matt. 25:32). When Isaiah speaks of those beginnings, he includes (as his custom is) a period that extends to the end, when God will bring to perfection that which he has begun.

We see the same thing today, for though chastisements and punishments do not entirely remove all spots from the church, yet when spots have been washed out, she recovers a part of her purity. She suffers no great loss by the strokes inflicted in her because, while she is diminished, she is at the same time comforted by casting out many hypocrites. For it is only by casting out offensive or corrupt matter that a diseased body can be restored to health.

In this we obtain a most useful consolation, for we tend to want a multitude of believers and to estimate by it the prosperity of the church. On the contrary, we should rather desire to be few in number in which the glory of God shines brightly. But because our own glory leads us in another direction, the consequence is that we more greatly regard a great number of men than the excellence of a few.

FOR MEDITATION: What is the use of a great number of nominal Christians if few behave like Christians in any sense of the word? The greater concern is building a holy church, not building a mega-church. How can you help your church become more holy?

The Foolishness of Building Bigger Barns

Woe unto them that join house to house, that lay field to field, till there be no place, that they may be placed alone in the midst of the earth!
Isaiah 5:8
SUGGESTED FURTHER READING: Zephaniah 1

The prophet now reproves the insatiable avarice and covetousness from which often arise acts of cheating, injustice, and violence. It is not entirely wrong for a person to add field to field and house to house, but so often the person who does so has the disposition of mind that is not satisfied once it is inflamed by the desire of gain.

Accordingly, Isaiah describes the feelings of those who never have enough, and whom wealth can never satisfy. So great is the keenness of covetous men that they want to possess everything. They want everything that is obtained by others, regarding it as something that has been taken from them. All the while they do not realize they need the assistance of others or that a man left alone can do nothing. Their only care is to scrape together as much as they can. They swallow up everything by their covetousness.

Isaiah accuses covetous and ambitious men of such folly that they wish to have other men removed from the earth so they might possess it alone. They do not realize that if they were left alone, they could not plow, or reap, or perform other offices indispensable to their subsistence, or supply themselves with the necessaries of life. For God has linked men so closely together that they need the assistance and labor of each other. No one but a madman would disdain other men as hurtful or useless to him. Ambitious men cannot enjoy their renown alone but amid a multitude. How blind, therefore, are those who wish to drive and chase away others so that they might reign alone!

FOR MEDITATION: Calvin makes clear the foolishness of insatiable covetousness. Why, then, do we find ourselves constantly moving in this direction? Let us look to the example of Christ and pray for strength to resist this temptation today.

Touched by the Sign

And he laid it upon my mouth, and said, Lo, this hath touched thy lips; and thine iniquity is taken away, and thy sin purged. Isaiah 6:7
SUGGESTED FURTHER READING: 1 Corinthians 11:23–26

In these verses, we learn that truth must never be separated from the signs of it, though it should be distinguished from them. We perceive and feel a sign, such as the bread which is put into our hands by the minister in the Lord's Supper. Because we ought to seek Christ in heaven, our thoughts should be carried thither. But also, by the hand of the minister Christ's body is presented to be actually enjoyed by the godly, who rise by faith to fellowship with Christ. The sign of Christ is bestowed upon the godly, who raise their thoughts to him by faith; for he cannot deceive them.

We also learn from this passage that the sacraments are never separate from the Word of God. The angel does not act like a dumb person here, but, having given the sign, the angel immediately adds doctrine to show what was intended by the sign. The sign would have been no sacrament if doctrine had not been added, for by doctrine Isaiah learned the purpose for which the coal was applied to his mouth.

Let us therefore learn that the chief part of the sacraments is the Word, and that without the Word, they become absolute corruptions.

In sum, this text teaches that there is nothing to prevent Isaiah, who has been perfectly cleansed and is free from all pollution, from appearing as God's representative here on earth.

FOR MEDITATION: The next time you partake of a sacrament, meditate on the importance of both the sign and the doctrine that it presents. How do Word and sacrament work together in a practical way to strengthen your faith?

Our Wonderful Counselor

For unto us a child is born, unto us a son is given: and the government shall be upon his shoulder: and his name shall be called Wonderful, Counsellor, The mighty God, The everlasting Father, The Prince of Peace. Isaiah 9:6
SUGGESTED FURTHER READING: Luke 24:13–35

The titles Isaiah uses for Christ are not foreign to its subject but are adapted to the case in hand, for the prophet describes what Christ will become to believers. Rather than speaking of Christ's mysterious essence, Isaiah applauds his excellent attributes, which we perceive and experience by faith. This ought to be most carefully considered, because so many people are satisfied with the mere name of Christ and do not see his power and energy, which ought to be chiefly regarded.

By the title *Wonderful*, Isaiah rouses the minds of the godly to earnest attention that they may expect from Christ something more excellent than what is seen in the ordinary course of God's works. It is as if the prophet says that in Christ are hidden the invaluable treasures of wonderful things (Col. 2:3). Indeed, the redemption that Christ brings surpasses even the creation of the world. The grace of God that will be exhibited in Christ exceeds all miracles.

Next, Isaiah uses the term *Counsellor* to show that the Redeemer will come endowed with absolute wisdom. The prophet does not reason here about the hidden essence of Christ but about the power that Christ displays toward us. It is not because Christ Jesus knows all his Father's secrets that the prophet calls him Counselor, but rather that he proceeds from the bosom of the Father (John 1:18) and is therefore in every respect the highest and most perfect teacher.

Likewise, we are not permitted to get wisdom from any source but from the gospel. Regarding Christ as Counselor contributes to the praise of the gospel, for our Counselor contains the perfect wisdom of God, as Paul frequently shows (1 Cor. 1:24, 30; Eph. 1:17; Col. 1:9).

FOR MEDITATION: In what way is Christ Wonderful and Counselor to us in our limited, sin-filled understanding? How can he lift us above our sinful condition to behold him in his glory?

Calling on Christ for his Gifts

And the spirit of the LORD *shall rest upon him, the spirit of wisdom and understanding, the spirit of counsel and might, the spirit of knowledge and of the fear of the* LORD. Isaiah 11:2
SUGGESTED FURTHER READING: Proverbs 4:1–13

Christ did not come empty-handed but was well supplied with every gift so that he might enrich us with them, the prophet tells us. He shows that the gifts of the Spirit are laid up in Christ, first, generally; and second, particularly, that we may go to him to obtain whatever we want.

The Messiah will enlighten us with the light of wisdom and understanding, impart counsel to us in difficulties, make us strong and courageous in battle, and bestow on us the true fear of God, which is godliness. In short, he will communicate to us all that is necessary for our life and salvation. The prophet includes all gifts here; it would be excessively foolish to attempt to conceal those that do not belong to this enumeration.

He shows that these gifts dwell in Christ so they may be communicated to us. We are called his fellows (Ps. 45:7) because strength proceeds from him as the head to the individual members. In like manner Christ causes his heavenly anointing to flow over the entire body of his church.

Hence it follows that those who are altogether barren and dry have no interest in Christ and falsely glory in his name. So whenever we feel we lack any of these gifts, let us blame our unbelief; for true faith makes us partakers of all Christ's benefits. We ought, therefore, to pray to the Lord to prevent the lusts of the flesh from ruling in us, that Christ may wholly unite us to himself. We should also observe that we ought to ask all blessings from Christ alone, for we are mistaken if we imagine that anything can be obtained from the Father any other way.

FOR MEDITATION: How amazing to think that believers may take part in all of the benefits provided in Christ! And yet our expectations often fall far below what God is willing to give us. Let us storm the throne of grace to obtain these gifts through Christ and to better appreciate the fullness of his promises.

Threatened by Enemies from Afar

They come from a far country, from the end of heaven, even the LORD, *and the weapons of his indignation, to destroy the whole land.* Isaiah 13:5

SUGGESTED FURTHER READING: Joel 1

Trouble from nearby nations does not appear to threaten Babylon, but the prophet warns that calamity will come to them from a distance. Likewise, though everything appears calm and peaceful right now and we are not at variance with our neighbors, God can bring enemies *from the end of heaven*. Therefore we cannot promise ourselves a lasting and prosperous condition when we are not threatened with an immediate danger.

If Isaiah's prediction had reached the inhabitants of Babylon, they would undoubtedly have laughed at it as a fable. Even if they had paid some respect to the prophet, they had such a strong conviction of their safety that they would have despised Isaiah's threats as idle and groundless.

Consider this example. When we preach about the present threat of the Turk, everyone thinks it is a fable because the Turk is still at a great distance from us. But we see how quickly he overtook those who were at a greater distance and were more powerful. So great is the insensibility of men that they cannot be aroused unless they are chastised and made to feel the blows.

Let this warning to the inhabitants of Babylon be a warning to us. Before it is too late, let us dread the threats that the prophets utter, so that the same thing may not happen to us as happened to those wicked men who, relying on their prosperous condition, were so terrified when the hand of God attacked and struck them that they could no longer stand but sank down bewildered.

FOR MEDITATION: The incredible shifts in alliance during the twentieth century demonstrate the truth of Isaiah's warning. The Lord can raise up enemies where we least expect them. His threats of judgment are not idle.

Guided to Safety

The way of the just is uprightness: thou, most upright, dost weigh the path of the just. Isaiah 26:7

SUGGESTED FURTHER READING: Psalm 119:1–16

Let us commit ourselves to God and follow him as our leader, and we shall be guided in safety. Though snares and artifices, strategies of the devil and wicked men, and innumerable dangers may surround us, God will enable us to escape. We will feel what the prophet says here, that our ways, even amid deep chasms, are made plain, so that there is no obstacle to hinder our progress.

Indeed, experience shows that if we are not led by God's guidance, we will not be able to push our way along rugged roads, for so great is our weakness that we shall scarcely advance a single step without stumbling at the smallest stone that comes in our way. Satan and wicked men not only entangle and delay us by many perplexities and small difficulties, but also cause us sometimes to encounter high mounds and deep pits, which even the whole world would be unable to avoid.

It is therefore proper for us to acknowledge how much we need heavenly direction. We should confess with Jeremiah, "O LORD, I know that the way of man is not in himself: it is not in man that walketh to direct his steps" (Jer. 10:23).

In vain, therefore, do men form plans and deliberate and decide about their ways, if God does not stretch out his hand. But he holds it out to the righteous and takes peculiar care of them. While the providence of God extends to all, and while God supplies the needs of young ravens and sparrows and of the smallest animals, yet he has a special fatherly kindness toward the godly and delivers them out of dangers and difficulties.

FOR MEDITATION: Consider how powerless we are in so many trials—sickness, economic woes, death, war—and in temptations such as the lust of the flesh, the lust of the eyes, and the pride of life. We should have very little trouble in acknowledging our need for the Lord to guide us in his paths! How has God guided you in his ways and kept you in safety recently? Ask for his aid again today.

Shaken out of Carelessness

Many days and years shall ye be troubled, ye careless women: for the vintage shall fail, the gathering shall not come. Isaiah 32:10

SUGGESTED FURTHER READING: Job 5:1–11

The prophet warns against the slothfulness of the Jews by declaring that those who fail to listen to his calm instruction shall be dragged forth with trembling and alarm.

The Jews are excessively anxious about earthly blessings and perishing food, so Isaiah addresses this fear by threatening a scarcity of wine and wheat. If the people were more thoroughly purified from groveling desires, the prophet might have threatened what Jeremiah deplores in Lamentations: that the sacrifices and festivals have ceased and that the holy assemblies are discontinued (Lam. 1:7).

But, because the Jews of Isaiah's time are sunk in their pleasures and have not labored to know the value of spiritual blessings, the prophet accommodates himself to their ignorance and addresses their bellies rather than their understanding. He speaks of the desolation of the fields, which would be the necessary consequence of their carelessness, for abundance and plenty commonly give rise to ease and indifference. "The Lord will therefore deprive you of all food and shake off your slothfulness, and take away all ground of confidence," he says.

We are here reminded that we ought not to sleep in the midst of prosperity nor imagine that we might expect uninterrupted prosperity in the world. Rather, we ought to use the gifts of God with moderation, if we do not wish to be suddenly aroused and be overwhelmed when we are off our guard. We will then feel heavier distress because we did not look for a change of our affairs.

FOR MEDITATION: When life is good and our material wants are supplied, even to excess, we easily become careless and wasteful. What's worse, we can become indifferent to the Creator and Provider of all things, who can turn plenty into want, Isaiah says. When have you experienced a time of want after a time of prosperity? How did that affect your relationship with the Lord?

Finding Blessing in Trouble

And am I now come up without the LORD against this land to destroy it? the LORD said unto me, Go up against this land, and destroy it. Isaiah 36:10

SUGGESTED FURTHER READING: Amos 9

Rabshakeh warns Hezekiah, King of Judah, that it is useless to assemble his forces and to make other warlike preparations against the attack of Assyria. For Hezekiah is not contending with a mortal man, but with God himself, at whose suggestion (not his own) the King of Assyria is attacking Judah. Therefore those who oppose the King of Assyria will fight against God, and all their efforts will be useless.

From this we ought to learn that, however earnestly we may be devoted to godliness, and however faithfully we may labor to advance the kingdom of Christ, we cannot expect to be free from every annoyance. Rather, we ought to be prepared to endure very heavy afflictions.

The Lord does not always recompense our piety with earthly rewards. Indeed, it would be exceedingly unsuitable for us to possess abundant wealth and enjoy outward peace and see that everything proceeds according to our wishes. For the world reckons even wicked men to be happy on the ground that they do not endure bad health or adversity, are free from the pressure of poverty, and have nothing to disturb them. In this respect, our condition would not differ at all from that of the reprobate.

Consider the example of Hezekiah, who labored with all his might to restore religion and the true worship of God, yet endured calamities so heavy and violent that he was not far from despair. We ought to constantly place this example before our eyes so that, even when we think we have discharged our duty, we may nevertheless be prepared to endure conflicts and troubles of every kind. We should then not be disturbed if enemies gain an advantage at the onset, as if all at once they would swallow us up.

FOR MEDITATION: The example of Hezekiah is a powerful corrective to the "health and wealth" gospel that is common today. Such a gospel can only bring disillusionment when troubles and trials come, as they almost always do. Our assurance of God's favor must rest in something other than external blessings—it must rest in Christ.

Standing Firm against Slander

And am I now come up without the LORD *against this land to destroy it? the* LORD *said unto me, Go up against this land, and destroy it.* Isaiah 36:10

SUGGESTED FURTHER READING: 2 Samuel 16:5–14

Rabshakeh, the field commander of the Assyrians, boasts of the greatness and power of his king in order to terrify Hezekiah. Such is the manner in which wicked men act toward us. They attack us with threatening words and try our patience with various terrors. Satan is at work in such labors, for we plainly see him speaking through the mouth of a person like Rabshakeh.

We ought, therefore, to distinguish between God's words and the words of those who falsely assume his name, for Satan resorts to various artifices to make himself appear to be like God. Rabshakeh unjustly brings many reproaches against Hezekiah, but the good king does not place his hope in his own strength and does not vaunt himself through reliance on the Egyptians. Godly men, even when they do well, must be exposed to evil reports. By these strategies Satan attacks our faith and unjustly slanders us among men.

The temptation to be terrified by such reports is highly dangerous, for we want our integrity to be well known. When we are well disposed, we take it ill if other men put a different interpretation on our conduct. Satan tries by slander to overturn all that we have done out of a good conscience. Or he accuses us of something that we are not at all guilty of. Or he loads us with unfounded slanders or contrives what never came into our minds. An upright conscience ought to be like a brazen wall to us so that we might follow the example of Hezekiah to stand unshaken against the accusations and slanders of wicked men.

FOR MEDITATION: When have you been unjustly accused of doing wrong? Did you stand unshaken in your integrity before God, or did you cower and fall before slanderous reports? How can we be more like Hezekiah when others question our character, reputation, or actions when we are sincerely following God's will?

Smitten to Repentance

And it came to pass, when King Hezekiah heard it, that he rent his clothes, and covered himself with sackcloth, and went into the house of the LORD. Isaiah 37:1

SUGGESTED FURTHER READING: 1 Chronicles 21:1–17

The modesty of holy King Hezekiah is wonderful. For after performing so many illustrious works and being adorned by the excellence of so many virtues, the king does not hesitate to prostrate himself before God. On the other hand, the courage and steadfastness of Hezekiah's faith is wonderful, for it shows the king is not hindered by the weight of the temptation of failing to freely seek God, by whom he is so severely smitten.

Scarcely one man in a hundred does not murmur if God treats him with any degree of severity or who does not bring forward his good deeds as a ground of complaint, reasoning that he has been unjustly rewarded. Other men, whose wishes are not answered by God, complain that their worship of God serves no good purpose.

We perceive nothing of this kind in Hezekiah. Though he is conscious of possessing uncommon piety, he does not shrink from confessing his guilt. Likewise, if we desire to turn away God's anger and to experience his favor in adversity, we must repent and sincerely acknowledge our guilt, for adversity does not come to us by chance but is the method by which God rouses us to repentance.

Indeed, sackcloth and ashes will be of little avail if they are not preceded by the inward feelings of the heart, for we know that hypocrites are abundantly liberal in the use of ceremonies. Yet the Holy Spirit justly commends the exercises of repentance when they are directed to their proper object.

FOR MEDITATION: When we are afflicted with sickness or sorrow, do we murmur and complain, thinking God means to destroy us? Or do we come to him in sorrow and repentance, asking for the grace to bear any affliction and for forgiveness for any sin? Let us, like Hezekiah, seek our heavenly Father in all our troubles, trusting that he will use them to make us more like our Savior, Christ Jesus, whose sufferings were for us and our salvation.

Lifting up Prayers

It may be the LORD *thy God will hear the words of Rabshakeh, whom the king of Assyria his master hath sent to reproach the living God, and will reprove the words which the* LORD *thy God hath heard: wherefore lift up thy prayer for the remnant that is left.* Isaiah 37:4
SUGGESTED FURTHER READING: Matthew 6:9–13

Hezekiah sends messengers to Isaiah, asking him to lift up prayer for the remnant of Judah. In this we learn that the duty of a prophet is not only to comfort the afflicted with the Word of the Lord but also to offer prayers for their salvation.

Pastors and ministers of the Word, therefore, should not think they have fully discharged their duty when they have exhorted and taught, if they do not also pray. This also is what all of us ought to do. Yet Hezekiah asks Isaiah to pray in a particular manner so that he might lead the way to others by his example. "To lift up prayer" is nothing more than "to pray," yet the mode of expression deserves attention, for it shows how our feelings should be regulated when we pray.

Much of Scripture tells us to lift up our hearts to heaven (Lam. 3:41), for if we do not, we will have no fear of God. Moreover, we are so dull that we may be immediately seized by gross imaginations of God. If he did not bid us look to heaven, we would choose rather to seek him at our feet. "To lift up prayer," therefore, is to pray in such a manner that our hearts do not grovel on the earth or think anything earthly or gross about God but rather ascribe to him what is suitable to his majesty. Then our warm and earnest affections may take lofty flight. It is thus said in Psalm 141:2: "Let my prayer be set forth before thee as incense; ... as the evening sacrifice."

FOR MEDITATION: How often do we lift up prayers to heaven? When do they seem to stay on the ground? What does that do to our spirit, and how is our impression of God affected?

The Overthrow of Tyrants

And it came to pass, as he was worshipping in the house of Nisroch his god, that Adrammelech and Sharezer his sons smote him with the sword; and they escaped into the land of Armenia: and Esarhaddon his son reigned in his stead. Isaiah 37:38

SUGGESTED FURTHER READING: Malachi 3

It is highly important to behold, as in a picture, the unhappy death of tyrants whom the Lord destroys without the agency of men. For when everything appears to be overthrown by a tyrant's violence, God exposes the tyrant with all his power to universal scorn. Sennacherib, who comes into Judea with a vast army, returns home with few soldiers. He is led in triumph, as it were, by God as the conqueror. But the matter does not end here, for Sennacherib is slain in the very heart of his own empire, in the metropolis, in the temple itself, where reverence defends the lowest person from the mob. He is slain, not by a foreign enemy, not by a people in a state of sedition, not by traitors, and not by servants, but by his own sons, that the murder might be even more disgraceful.

Observe that insatiable gluttons who freely wallow in the blood of others are often slain by their own followers. They are punished by those from whom they, above all others, ought to be safe. This is more shocking than if they are put to death by strangers. So God punishes the cruelty of those who, in their eagerness to enjoy power, did not spare even the innocent. Even from profane historians we find similar examples in which we may easily behold the judgments of the Lord.

In addition, the insatiable ambition of Sennacherib receives its just reward because, while he is intent on extending his territories, he cannot secure peace in his own family by leading his children to live at peace. Out of this father's neglect and undue attachment to others, conspiracy arises. Not only is this tyrant slain, but his kingdom also is soon afterwards overthrown. In the meantime, so that his successor might not dare to make any attempt against the Jews, God keeps him busy within the country with internal problems.

FOR MEDITATION: When have we despaired of tyrannical control over us, thinking we are powerless to combat it? How has God miraculously intervened, toppling evil rulers and opponents by methods we could never have imagined?

Asking for a Sign

And this shall be a sign unto thee from the LORD*, that the* LORD *will do this thing that he hath spoken.* Isaiah 38:7
SUGGESTED FURTHER READING: Judges 6:36–40

God gives us some signs of his own accord without our asking for them. He grants other signs to us when we ask for them. Signs are generally intended to help us in our weakness, but God does not for the most part wait till we have prayed for them to grant them.

Hezekiah seems to be insulting God by refusing to credit his word when he asks for a sign. We must not accuse Hezekiah of unbelief, however, because his faith is weak, for no person has faith that is perfect and complete in every respect. Nor can we blame Hezekiah for seeking assistance to support him in his weakness, for, having embraced the promise made to him by the prophet, he shows his confidence in God by seeking a remedy for distrust. If there was no weakness in man, he would not need any signs. Consequently, we need not wonder that the king asks for a sign, since on other occasions the Lord freely offers them.

Yet it is also proper to observe that Old Testament believers never rushed forward at random to ask for signs but did so only after being guided by a secret and peculiar influence of the Spirit.

The same thing might be said about miracles. If Elijah prays to God for rain and for drought (James 5:17, 18), it does not follow that others are at liberty to do the same. We must see what God permits us to do, lest by disregarding his Word we bargain with him according to the foolish desires of our flesh.

FOR MEDITATION: As Calvin says, it may not be appropriate for us to ask God for a sign. Nevertheless, we can learn from Hezekiah's example. Recognizing the imperfection and weakness of his faith, he did not despair, but rather asked God for help in overcoming his weakness. Do we do this as well?

Our Caring Shepherd

He shall feed his flock like a shepherd: he shall gather the lambs with his arm, and carry them in his bosom, and shall gently lead those that are with young. Isaiah 40:11
SUGGESTED FURTHER READING: Psalm 23

God has determined to protect and guard his church. On this account the prophet compares the Lord to a *shepherd* who expresses his infinite love toward us. Our Lord does not refuse to stoop so low as to perform toward us the office of a shepherd.

In other passages, such as Isaiah 34:2, the prophet describes the Lord as one armed with terrible power for the defense of his people. But here he ascribes a more amiable character to the Lord, so that believers may sweetly repose under his protection.

By the word *flock*, Isaiah describes the elect people whom God has undertaken to govern. We are thus reminded that God will be a shepherd to none but those who, in modesty and gentleness, will be like sheep and lambs. We ought to observe the character of this flock, for God does not choose to feed savage beasts, but lambs. We must therefore lay aside our fierceness and permit ourselves to be tamed if we wish to be gathered into the fold of which God promises that he will be guardian.

The words *he shall ... carry them in his bosom* describe God's wonderful condescension, for he not only is moved by a general feeling of regard for his whole flock, but, in proportion to the weakness of any one sheep, he also shows his care in watching, his gentleness in handling, and his patience in leading his sheep.

Isaiah leaves out nothing that belongs to the office of a good shepherd; for the shepherd ought to observe every sheep so he can treat it according to its capacity, even supporting those who are exceedingly weak. In a word, God will be mild, kind, gentle, and compassionate so that he will not drive the weak harder than what they are able to bear.

FOR MEDITATION: Without such a kindly Shepherd, who would feed us, carry us, and lead us? What a great comfort it is to know that we have a strong yet gentle Shepherd who is willing and able to care for his lambs, even the very weakest.

Weapons of the Wicked

No weapon that is formed against thee shall prosper; and every tongue that shall rise against thee in judgment thou shalt condemn. This is the heritage of the servants of the LORD, *and their righteousness is of me, saith the* LORD. Isaiah 54:17

SUGGESTED FURTHER READING: Psalm 31

Even though wicked men exert themselves to the utmost, they will gain nothing, for their attacks are guided and restrained by the secret purpose of God. The prophet makes use of the word *every* here, meaning that wicked men have *every* means of attempting many and diversified methods for destroying the church, but their efforts shall be vain and fruitless, for the Lord will restrain them. Heaven permits them, indeed, to a great extent, to try the patience of believers, but, when God so wills, he strips them of their strength and armor.

Having spoken in general of the weapons that wicked men use to attack the church, Isaiah specifically mentions the tongue, because no other *weapon* is so deadly and destructive. Not only do the wicked revile, slander, and defame the servants of God, but, as far as lies in their power, they extinguish the truth of God and alienate the hearts of men from it. That can distress us more than if life were taken from us a hundred times. Good and upright men find slander more distressing and more painful than any stroke to the body. Therefore Isaiah has good reason for mentioning this deadly weapon of the tongue.

The wicked may assail us by arms, and by the *tongue,* and by *weapons* of every kind, yet we can rely on this prediction of the prophet and hope that we shall be victorious, for victory is here promised to us. Since we are certain of victory, we ought to fight valiantly and with unshaken courage.

FOR MEDITATION: If the attacks of the enemy are in God's hands and guided by his will, why do we fear them? Their destruction and the ultimate victory of God's people is assured. Let us seek more grace to dispense with our anxieties and trust his wisdom.

Exercising True Repentance

Let the wicked forsake his way, and the unrighteous man his thoughts: and let him return unto the LORD, and he will have mercy upon him; and to our God, for he will abundantly pardon. Isaiah 55:7
SUGGESTED FURTHER READING: 2 Chronicles 7:11–22

The prophet describes the nature of repentance in three steps: first, *Let the wicked forsake his way*; second, *the unrighteous man his thoughts*; and third, *let him return unto the LORD*. Under the word *way* he includes the whole course of life. Accordingly, he demands that believers bring forth fruits of righteousness as witnesses of their new life. By adding the word *thoughts*, he intimates that we must not only correct outward actions but that those must begin with the heart; for though in the opinion of men we appear to change our life for the better, yet we will make little progress if our heart is not changed.

Thus repentance embraces a change in the whole man, including his inclinations, purposes, and works. The works of men are visible, but the root of them is concealed. So the root must first be changed so that afterward it may yield fruitful works. We must first wash from the mind all uncleanness and conquer wicked inclinations so that outward testimonies may be added afterward. If any man boasts that he has changed and yet lives as he did before, it will be vain boasting, for both conversion of the heart and change of life are necessary.

In addition, God does not command us to return to him before he applies a remedy to revolt from our former way of life, for hypocrites willingly praise what is good and right, provided they are free to crouch amid their filth. We may have nothing to do with God if we do not first withdraw from ourselves, especially when we have been alienated by wickedness. Therefore, self-denial comes first so that it may lead us to God.

FOR MEDITATION: Isaiah's description of repentance is an excellent mirror by which to examine our own hearts, minds, and lives to see if we have truly repented of our sin and turned to God. If we have truly repented, we may know with assurance that he has pardoned us.

Comparing Christ to Kings

Behold, the days come, saith the LORD, *that I will raise unto David a righteous Branch, and a King shall reign and prosper, and shall execute judgment and justice in the earth.* Jeremiah 23:5
SUGGESTED FURTHER READING: Revelation 5

Jeremiah's comparison of Christ to earthly kings should be deemed proper, for God speaks to us according to the measure of our capacities. He cannot fully express what Christ is in a few words. Still, we must bear in mind that we must rise above our consideration of earthly kings to Christ; for though he is compared to them, he is not limited by that comparison. After contemplating what our minds can comprehend of Christ, we must ascend farther and much higher than this comparison.

The difference between the righteousness of Christ and the righteousness of kings must be noted. Those who rule well can administer righteousness and judgment in no other way than being careful to render to each person his due by checking the audacity of the wicked and by defending the good and the innocent. We can expect no more than this from earthly kings.

Christ is far different, for he is not only wise in knowing what is right and best, but he also endues his own people with wisdom and knowledge. He executes both judgment and righteousness because he defends the innocent, aids those who are oppressed, gives help to the miserable, and restrains the wicked. But he also executes righteousness, because he regenerates us by his Spirit. And he executes judgment because he bridles, as it were, the devil.

We can now understand how we must mark the transcendence of Christ over earthly kings. We see the analogy, for there is some likeness and some difference. The difference between Christ and other kings is very great, yet they are alike in some things, so earthly kings are cited to us as figures and types of Christ.

FOR MEDITATION: Consider the greatest rulers who ever existed. Regardless of their wisdom, their glory, their fame, or their power, Christ far exceeds them all. He has no equal, for he is the King of kings. In what ways does he execute righteousness and judgment in your life?

Finding Peace and Happiness

In his days Judah shall be saved, and Israel shall dwell safely [i.e., find tranquility]: *and this is his name whereby he shall be called,* THE LORD OUR RIGHTEOUSNESS. Jeremiah 23:6
SUGGESTED FURTHER READING: Isaiah 26:1–13

The first requirement for a happy life is a tranquil and quiet mind. When all the things that people covet and what they think are necessary for happiness are heaped together, people cannot be other than miserable if their minds are not at ease.

It is then with good cause that tranquility is added when mention is made of salvation. Experience teaches us that we have no salvation unless we, in reliance on Christ the Mediator, have peace with God. Paul also mentions peace with God as the fruit of faith (Rom. 5:1). We can only be miserable without peace with God. Paul also says that miseries aid our salvation, for afflictions produce patience, patience exercises hope, and hope never makes us ashamed. Peace with God is the proof of salvation, because with it God truly shows that he is present with us.

We thus see how appropriate it is for the prophet to connect tranquility of mind with happiness. It is certain that we do not yet enjoy either full salvation or peace such as are promised here. But let us learn by faith what salvation and rest are, even in the midst of the agitations to which we are continually exposed, for we find rest in God only when we cast our anchor in heaven.

The prophet says Judah will be saved and that Israel will find tranquility. By this we know that he is referring to the kingdom of Christ from the beginning to the end. Therefore it is no wonder that he speaks of perfect happiness, the first-fruits of which are now beginning to appear.

FOR MEDITATION: Restlessness and agitation are normal in the midst of challenges and difficulties. Looking to Christ anchors us in hope and quiets our anxieties. Have you found rest in the Eternal Hope? How is this simply a foretaste of what is yet to come?

Called to Prophesy

I have not sent these prophets, yet they ran: I have not spoken to them, yet they prophesied. Jeremiah 23:21
SUGGESTED FURTHER READING: 2 Timothy 4:1–8

"If God is the author of my ministry, then I, though alone, am superior to the whole world. If prophets are not called by God, they may increase a hundredfold in number, but what they speak means nothing, for we must believe in God alone." That is what Jeremiah seems to be saying here. We now see the reason for his saying that the prophets *ran* but were not *sent*; that they *prophesied* but have received no commands from God.

This passage specifically teaches us that no one is worthy of being heard unless he is a true minister of God. Two things are necessary to prove that: a divine call as well as faithfulness and integrity. So we may safely reject anyone who pushes himself forward, pretending to be a prophet, for God alone may claim the right of being heard.

A simple, naked call is not sufficient for a prophet; he who is called must also faithfully labor in prophesying the words of God. Both are mentioned here, for Jeremiah says the prophets ran, though they were not sent; and they prophesied, though they were without a command from God. The same idea is repeated here in two different Hebrew clauses, but the stronger expression is found in the second clause, for sending properly refers to a call, and commanding refers to the execution of the office.

God, in the first place, chooses his prophets and commits to them the office of teaching. Then he commands them what to say, dictating to them, as it were, *his* message. Thus a prophet may not declare anything he devises but only be a herald of God's message.

FOR MEDITATION: When we hear men speak on behalf of God, how can we know that they are true prophets? Jeremiah says we can tell a prophet is true if he is called by God and speaks with faithfulness and integrity only the words of God. Think of that the next time you listen to someone whose reputation appears to be more important than the message of God's Word. Most importantly, pray for your church leaders daily, that they might simply be heralds of God's message.

Bringing Believers Together

And I will be found of you, saith the LORD: *and I will turn away your captivity, and I will gather you from all the nations, and from all the places whither I have driven you, saith the* LORD; *and I will bring you again into the place whence I caused you to be carried away captive.*
Jeremiah 29:14
SUGGESTED FURTHER READING: Revelation 7

God's people, who have been dispersed into all nations and all places, will one day be brought together, the prophet says. The same message is declared in the Psalms: "he gathereth together the outcasts [or, the dispersions] of Israel" (Psalm 147:2). Jeremiah declares this truth to Jews who are considering their dreadful dispersion and can entertain no hope.

We see how the prophet offers them hope and encourages them to struggle against this trial. The words seem to have been taken from Moses, who says that, though they will be scattered through the extreme parts of the world, yet God will gather them (Deut. 30:1–3). In Deuteronomy 30, Moses expressly reproves the unbelief of God's people if they despair of God's mercy and salvation when they are torn and scattered. He says that God's power is abundantly sufficient to gather them together, even if they are scattered to the four quarters of the world.

We now perceive the intent of the prophet. We also gain a useful teaching that God in a wonderful manner will gather his church when believers are scattered to form them into one body. For a time he may obliterate the name of the church and even its appearance. He has given us some proof of that in our time. For who could have thought that the church we now see with our eyes in some parts of our world would ever take place? How could we know that in a time of dreadful desolation everywhere, when no corner in the world could be found where two or three faithful men could dwell together, that God in a secret manner would gather his elect?

We hence see that this prophecy has not only been fulfilled at one time, but that by the grace of God it has often been manifested and is still being made manifest in the gathering together of God's church.

FOR MEDITATION: How can we believe the church is triumphant when it is constantly torn apart by schisms or frequently driven underground, such as in China or Russia? How can we grasp this promise that all believers will one day be gathered into one body to praise and worship God?

Relying on Everlasting Love

The LORD hath appeared of old unto me, saying, Yea, I have loved thee with an everlasting love: therefore with loving-kindness have I drawn thee. Jeremiah 31:3

SUGGESTED FURTHER READING: Romans 5:1–11

False imaginations may come to mind when we hear how God has in various ways and degrees been miraculously merciful toward his people. "Well, that happened before, but we do not know whether God's purpose remains the same today," we say. "Indeed, he conferred this favor on ancient people, but we do not know whether he will extend the same grace to us today."

The devil, in his craftiness, suggests these false ideas, which impede the flow of God's favor by suggesting that his goodness may not come to us. The grace of God is stopped in its course when we distinguish ourselves from the fathers and all the servants toward whom God has been so merciful.

It is, therefore, useful for us to heed the prophet who shows us that whatever blessings God has at any time conferred on his ancient people should be ascribed to his gratuitous covenant. That covenant is eternal; hence there is no doubt that God is prepared today to secure the salvation of all the godly, for he remains ever the same and never changes. His desire is to have his fidelity and constancy ever shine forth in the covenant that he has made with his church.

Since the covenant of God is inviolable and cannot fail, even if heaven and earth are brought into confusion, we ought to be assured that God will deliver us. How so? We know that because God's covenant remains the same, therefore his power to deliver us remains the same. This is how we ought to make use of this verse.

FOR MEDITATION: Because God often works differently today from how he worked during the time of Scripture, we can have difficulty believing that he cares for us and protects us with the same divine power. Such thoughts are from the evil one and dishonor God and his eternal covenant. We must quell such thoughts and trust our omnipotent, caring God; he is the same then and now.

Rejoicing on the Eve of Exile

For thus saith the LORD; Sing with gladness for Jacob, and shout among the chief of the nations: publish ye, praise ye, and say, O LORD, save thy people, the remnant of Israel. Jeremiah 31:7
SUGGESTED FURTHER READING: Acts 16:16–34

Jeremiah now asks God's people to sing and shout for joy. This prophecy is given not long before the utter destruction of the people, the city, and the temple. But the prophet's intent here is to comfort everyone, even the dead in their graves, so that all might patiently wait for the promised deliverance. The people could be assured of deliverance because it is no more difficult for God to raise the dead than to heal the sick. This prophecy becomes especially helpful when the Jews are driven into exile and become so miserably scattered that they have no hope of deliverance.

So that his teaching might more effectively enter their hearts, the prophet exhorts people to rejoice, to shout for joy, and to sing. Not only the people of God, but also strangers, are told to do so. For though the joy of believers is not like that of unbelievers, the prophet seems purposely to address his words to aliens so that the Jews might be ashamed for not believing the promises offered to them.

The prophet says, "Ye alien nations, shout for joy, for Jacob." What should Jacob do in the meantime? We now see the purpose for the prophet's vehemence in bidding all to rejoice for the redemption of the people. His intent is that this prophecy might not only bring some comfort to the miserable exiles, but also assure them that even in the midst of death they can live before God, provided they do not despair.

In short, the prophet's intent is not only to mitigate the sorrow of God's people, but also to fill them with spiritual joy so they might not cease to entertain hope and to take courage. They must not only patiently but cheerfully bear their calamities because God promises to be propitious to them.

FOR MEDITATION: Singing and shouting for joy when we face profound setbacks in life seems incredibly idealistic. Yet, if we are believers, that is what God asks us to do, for even on the eve of calamity we know that we will eventually come through safely because of the gracious hand of our Savior, Christ Jesus.

Trusting his Incredible Promises

Behold, I will bring them from the north country, and gather them from the coasts of the earth, and with them the blind and the lame, the woman with child and her that travaileth with child together: a great company shall return thither. Jeremiah 31:8

SUGGESTED FURTHER READING: Isaiah 49:1–17

Though the prophet addresses this teaching to ancient people, it contains truth that is perpetually useful. People act preposterously when they measure God's favor according to present appearances. This mistake that we almost inherit by nature involves all our thoughts and feelings. It also produces a lack of confidence in God. All of God's promises then grow cold to us, or at least lose their true value.

For when God promises anything, we look around us and ask how that can possibly be fulfilled. If our minds cannot comprehend the way and manner that a promise can come true, we then reject what has proceeded from the mouth of God. Let us carefully consider this prophetic doctrine so that when God promises what surpasses our faith and seems impossible to fulfill, this doctrine will come to our minds. Let it serve as a corrective to check our false thoughts, lest we, being preoccupied by a false and preposterous opinion, should do wrong to the power of God.

If the deliverance that God promises seems incredible to us, let us remember that God has the power to make the blind to see, the lame to walk, the pregnant and those lying in bed to undertake a journey; for he can by his power overcome all obstacles. We shall find our faith victorious, provided we learn to rely on God's promises and firmly rest on them.

FOR MEDITATION: Imagine how hard it would have been for the Jews to receive these promises in so dark a time, and yet, they were fulfilled. We often doubt God's amazing promises because our present circumstances seem so bleak. Until we learn to fully lean on God and his promises, understanding that darkness and light are both alike to him (Ps. 139:12), our faith will not be victorious. What circumstances are you facing today that require this faith?

Moving Forward

Then the king commanded Ebedmelech the Ethiopian, saying, Take from hence thirty men with thee, and take up Jeremiah the prophet out of the dungeon, before he die. Jeremiah 38:10
SUGGESTED FURTHER READING: Psalm 4

Let us be courageous when it is necessary, though we have little hope of a favorable outcome. Ebedmelech might have thought that his attempt to help Jeremiah would be in vain, however strenuously he pleaded for the prophet. He might then have relinquished the task instead of boldly undertaking it.

Likewise, those who think too much about a difficult task often talk themselves into inactivity. They think, "What effect can you possibly have? You are only one person, and your enemies are many. If the king himself has been forced to yield to the anger of wicked men, how can you as an individual have the confidence to resist them? Furthermore, such tumult will be raised that you will perish in it. Meantime, these wicked men will perhaps stone the unhappy man whom you are trying to help."

All these thoughts might have occurred to Ebedmelech, and he thus might have desisted from helping. But we see that he rested not in his own confidence but in God's favor.

Let us remember his example and hope beyond hope when God requires us to do something. When faith and duty demand anything from us, we must close our eyes to all obstacles and go forward in our work, for all events are in God's hands alone, and they will happen as he pleases. Our duty is to proceed, even if we think our labors may be in vain and will not bear fruit. Ebedmelech happily succeeds in rescuing the prophet because he acts as a pious and upright man in obeying God.

God will also extend his hand to us, whatever difficulties we encounter, for we shall overcome them by his power and help.

FOR MEDITATION: We often overanalyze situations and attempt to justify our neglect of duty. Ebedmelech did not do this, but rather stepped out in faith, trusting that he was doing the Lord's will. He left the results in God's hands. Are we doing that today?

Offering a Cup of Cold Water

For I will surely deliver thee, and thou shalt not fall by the sword, but thy life shall be for a prey unto thee: because thou hast put thy trust in me, saith the LORD. Jeremiah 39:18
SUGGESTED FURTHER READING: Philemon

God was not unmindful of the Ethiopian who helped save Jeremiah's life. Though Ebedmelech was an alien and from a barbarous nation, he alone undertook the cause of the prophet when others were either so terrified that they did not exert themselves, or else were sworn enemies of God's servant.

Ebedmelech alone dared to proceed in this hopeless situation to defend the holy man. Jeremiah says this service was so incredible that it would not go without a reward. Ebedmelech showed his concern for Jeremiah's life, but not without danger, for he knew that princes were united against him, and these ungodly men had on their side the greatest part of the court and of the common people. Ebedmelech roused himself against enemies both high and low, but God aided him so that he was not overpowered by his adversaries. In this very great danger, Ebedmelech experiences the favor of God and is protected and delivered from danger. As Jesus later says, "He who gives a cup of cold water to one of the least of my disciples shall not lose his reward" (Matt. 10:42).

No doubt the Spirit of God uses the example of Ebedmelech to rouse us to the duties of humanity to teach us to relieve the suffering of the miserable, to give them as much help as we can, and not to shun the hatred of men or any dangers that we may thereby encounter. Because we so often neglect doing good, we are told about the reward given to the Ethiopian so that we may know that, even though we should expect nothing from men when we are kind and generous, yet our work will not be in vain, for God in his wealth can render to us more than we can expect from the whole world.

FOR MEDITATION: The Lord will honor those who give a cup of cold water to the needy, and he will reject those who give nothing, regardless of how religious they are. Are we, like Ebedmelech, among the first group? In what ways can you reach out to the downtrodden and the rejected?

Obeying at All Cost

Then they said to Jeremiah, The LORD *be a true and faithful witness between us, if we do not even according to all things for the which the* LORD *thy God shall send thee to us. Whether it be good, or whether it be evil, we will obey the voice of the* LORD *our God, to whom we send thee; that it may be well with us, when we obey the voice of the* LORD *our God.* Jeremiah 42:5–6
SUGGESTED FURTHER READING: Hebrews 11:1–10

Jeremiah acts as a kind of mediator here, addressing the people in God's name as though he has been sent from heaven. The people respond by saying they will do whatever God commands. They say even more emphatically: *Whether it be good, or whether it be evil, we will obey the voice of the* LORD *our God.*

In saying this, the people do not suggest that God's word is wrong or in any way unjust; rather, they use the word *good* in the sense of being joyful, and *evil* as being sad or grievous. They ask for nothing more than that God will declare to them what pleases him, to which they will be so submissive that they will refuse him nothing, even if it is contrary to the flesh.

If this declaration proceeds from the heart, it is a testimony of true piety; for the minds of the godly ought so to be framed as to obey God without making any exception, whether he commands what is contrary to their purpose or leads them where they do not wish to go. By contrast, those who wish to make an agreement with God, saying he should require nothing but what is agreeable to them, show that they do not know what it means to serve God.

True obedience of faith requires that we renounce our desires and do not set up our own arguments and wishes against the Word of God. We do not object to what God requires of us, saying it is too hard or not quite agreeable to us. So whether it is *good* or *evil*, meaning agreeable to or contrary to the feelings of the flesh, we ought to embrace what God requires and commands. This is the foundational measure of true religion.

FOR MEDITATION: When God commands us to do something unpleasant, we often try to excuse ourselves from that particular duty, demonstrating the insincerity of our promise. Let us instead strive for the obedience of faith that Calvin talks about and renounce our selfish thoughts.

Rejecting Gospel Light

But when I speak with thee, I will open thy mouth, and thou shalt say unto them, Thus saith the Lord GOD; He that heareth, let him hear; and he that forbeareth, let him forbear: for they are a rebellious house.
Ezekiel 3:27
SUGGESTED FURTHER READING: Isaiah 6:8–13

Ambassadors are usually sent to conciliate, by courteous and friendly discourse, those with whom they have to deal. But God here follows a method completely contrary to that. Ezekiel tells us the Lord says, "He who hears, let him hear: he who forbears, let him forbear." By this the Israelites may understand that the prophet was sent to them, not because there was any hope of their becoming wise again, since they had proved by sufficiently numerous examples that they were altogether desperate, but to tell them that that the Lord will strike and wound them further, and at length inflict a deadly blow on them.

Now we see confirmation of what the prophet previously warned, that the office of teaching was given to him, not because his labor would be useful and fruitful among the common people, but that he might enflame the Israelites to madness if they still prove unwilling to grow wise.

God deals with the reprobate in various ways. Sometimes he appears doubtful that they can be cured. He sends prophets to them to exhort them to repentance. But when he sees their ingratitude in burying the light that is sent to them, God then deprives them of all doctrine. The light shines forth again but at length is succeeded by other, deeper darkness.

Therefore, as long as the doctrine of salvation shines upon us, let us hasten to repent lest God darken all our minds and senses, and deprive us of the singular benefit of having the image of his paternal favor engraved on us.

FOR MEDITATION: It is sobering to think that continued rejection or disregard of the gospel may result in its removal. With the great blessing of gospel light comes great responsibility to steward that light. What a curse it would be if we were driven into darkness as the Israelites were in Ezekiel's day!

Hastening to the Breach

Ye have not gone up into the gaps, neither made up the hedge for the house of Israel to stand in the battle in the day of the LORD. Ezekiel 13:5
SUGGESTED FURTHER READING: Nehemiah 2:11–18

The prophet identifies false prophets by saying to the approved and faithful servants of God that false prophets have not gone up into the breaches, nor built up a hedge to protect the house of Israel so they might stand in the battle in the day of Jehovah. Their teaching must be altogether rejected because they do not have the right goal in mind, Ezekiel says.

The true goal of God's servants is to consider public safety, and, when they see signs of God's wrath, to meet that wrath head-on in an attempt to prevent urgent calamity. Impostor prophets viewed the people not only as impious, but rebellious, so they saw no hope of their repentance. On the other hand, though they were blind, they could see signs of God's approaching and threatening vengeance. Hence it was their duty to go forward to the breaches.

What the prophet means by "breaches" here is any opening in a wall that allows an enemy to storm into a city. So when the iniquity of the people overflows like a deluge, it opens up a rupture through which God's wrath may pour immediately, laying waste to everything until it is reduced to nothing.

Those who desire to faithfully discharge the office of teaching ought to hasten to this breach to recall people from their impiety and to exhort them to repentance.

FOR MEDITATION: What a powerful image: abundant sin making a breach through which God's wrath can pour. Have you made any such breaches in your life? Repent and pray today for repairs before God's punishment pours.

Finding Safety in the Church

And mine hand shall be upon the prophets that see vanity, and that divine lies: they shall not be in the assembly of my people, neither shall they be written in the writing of the house of Israel, neither shall they enter into the land of Israel; and ye shall know that I am the Lord GOD. Ezekiel 13:9
SUGGESTED FURTHER READING: Hebrews 10:19–25

The Holy Spirit admonishes us not to conclude that people are true members of the church because most of them seem to excel other people. For just as the chaff lies above the wheat and suffocates it, thus hypocrites bury the sons of God, whose number is small. Hypocrites also shine forth in their own splendor, and great numbers of them seem to make them exclusively worthy of the title of the church.

Hence let us examine ourselves, searching whether we have the living root of piety and faith, which are those interior marks by which God distinguishes his children from strangers, or hypocrites.

This passage also teaches that nothing is more formidable than to be separated from God's flock. We cannot hope for safety unless God collects us into one body under one head. When we safely reside in Christ alone, we cannot be separated from Christ without falling away from all hope of safety. Christ will not and cannot be torn from his church that he is joined to by an indissoluble knot, as the head is to the body. Hence, unless we cultivate unity with the faithful, we are also cut off from Christ. Nothing, then, is more fearful than to be separated from God's people, and therefore from Christ.

Psalm 106:4 says, "Remember me, O God, in thy good will towards thy people: visit me with thy salvation." When the author of the psalm prays this way, he acknowledges that we will have true and solid happiness when the Lord embraces us along with the rest of the faithful. For God's good will toward his people is that fatherly kindness by which he embraces his elect.

If God thinks us worthy of his fatherly favor, then we may be truly confident of safety.

FOR MEDITATION: In a day when many Christians are focused only on their own individual relationship with God, this passage reminds us of the importance of the church. The church is not just a means to advance our own walk with God, but a divinely appointed institution. Connecting with the church is therefore not an option, but a requirement for true believers.

Why God Deceives the Prophets

And if the prophet be deceived when he hath spoken a thing, I the LORD have deceived that prophet, and I will stretch out my hand upon him, and will destroy him from the midst of my people Israel. Ezekiel 14:9

SUGGESTED FURTHER READING: 1 Kings 22:19–23

God does not rage like a tyrant but exercises just judgment. Also, no deceptions of doctrine are allowed without God's permission. This seems at first absurd, for God seems to battle himself when he gives freedom to Satan to pervert sound doctrine. If this perversion happens by God's authority, it seems completely contradictory. But let us always remember that God's judgments are not without reason called a profound abyss (Ps. 36:6). When we see rebellious men acting as they do, we should not expect to understand what far surpasses even the understanding of angels.

Therefore we must soberly and reverently regard God's works, especially his secret counsels. With the aid of reverence and modesty, it will be easy to reconcile these two things: that God gives birth to and cherishes and defends his church and confirms the teaching of his prophets, while at the same time he permits it to be torn and distracted by dissension.

God acts this way to punish the wickedness of men as often as he pleases when he sees them abuse his goodness and indulgence. When God lights up the flame of his doctrine, it is the sign of his inestimable pity; when he allows the church to be disturbed and men to be in some degree dissipated, that should be imputed to the wickedness of men.

Whatever the explanation may be, God says he himself deceived the false prophets, for Satan could not utter a single word unless God permitted him to do so. God not only permitted, but ordered Satan to do so to exercise his wrath against the wicked.

FOR MEDITATION: It is difficult to understand why God allows Satan freedom to rage within the church by perversions of doctrine. Nevertheless, we can take comfort in knowing that all the storms that rage are under God's control. Satan will never completely overwhelm the church or defeat God's purposes.

Boasting in the Lord

Therefore thus saith the Lord GOD; As the vine tree among the trees of the forest, which I have given to the fire for fuel, so will I give the inhabitants of Jerusalem. Ezekiel 15:6

SUGGESTED FURTHER READING: 1 Corinthians 1:26–31

That this discourse might profit us today, we must perceive that we are superior to the whole world through God's gratuitous pity, even though by nature we have nothing to boast of in ourselves. We cannot carry ourselves with pride in our reliance on God's gifts, for this would be sacrilege. We would in arrogance be snatching away from God his own praise and clothing ourselves, as it were, in his spoils.

Paul, in speaking of the Jews, shortly but clearly defines both sides of our condition: "Do we excel?" he asks (thereby making himself one with the Jews). "Are we better than the Gentiles?" (Rom. 3:1). He answers, "By no means, for Scripture denounces all of us as sinners who are cursed. Since we are all children of wrath, we can claim no superiority over the profane Gentiles."

After prostrating the pride of his own nation, the Jews, Paul asks again: "What? Are we not superior to others?" He then answers, "Yes, in every way, for the adoption, worship, law of God, and covenant confer such remarkable superiority on us that cannot be found anywhere else in the whole world."

How can the Jews excel and be preferred to others, yet excel in nothing? The answer is that they have nothing in themselves to allow them to despise the Gentiles or boast of themselves as superior because their excellence is not in themselves but in God.

FOR MEDITATION: God chooses men and women who are not worthy of his favor and pours his grace and mercy on them, making them new creatures. They may be preferred above all other people, but they can boast only in the Lord. If you have been chosen by God, do not boast in yourself; boast in the Lord for what he has done in you.

Inciting God's Wrath

Therefore thus saith the Lord GOD; *As the vine tree among the trees of the forest, which I have given to the fire for fuel, so will I give the inhabitants of Jerusalem.* Ezekiel 15:6
SUGGESTED FURTHER READING: Matthew 3:7–12

As often as we are favored with God's gifts, by which we approach him and overcome the world, we ought also to remember what we were before God took us up. Acknowledging our original condition will erode all arrogance and prevent us from being ungrateful to God.

But that is not sufficient; we must also recognize that not only has God's free grace raised us to such a height, but it also sustains us. Thus our continued state of grace is not because of our efforts but depends only on his will. Remembering our origin ought to humble us but also impress on us the sense of our infirmity. From this we learn that we cannot persevere unless God daily, yes, even momentarily, strengthens us and follows us with his favor.

Finally, if God afflicts or chastises us with his rod, we should know that he chooses this means to beat out of us the foolish confidence by which we deceive ourselves. We thus ought to diligently weigh the meaning of the phrase "the wood of the vine is useless when it is torn up," especially when dry. For although profane nations perish, yet it is not surprising that God's judgments will be even more severe toward the reprobate who are members of the church and have been enriched with spiritual gifts, yet who persist in unbelief.

The punishment of such ingratitude will make us an example to others, so that the whole world may be astonished at such dreadful signs of God's anger. The Jews will become such objects of God's wrath that they will cause hissing and abhorrence in the nations around them. They will be an astonishment and curse to the profane nations.

FOR MEDITATION: The judgments that God will exact on those who belong to his church but are not true members are a terrifying prospect! The discipline that he uses to humble our pride is to be welcomed. It may be painful, but it reminds us that we owe everything to God's grace.

The Beginning of Conversion

But if the wicked will turn from all his sins that he hath committed, and keep all my statutes, and do that which is lawful and right, he shall surely live, he shall not die. All his transgressions that he hath committed, they shall not be mentioned unto him: in his righteousness that he hath done he shall live. Ezekiel 18:21–22

SUGGESTED FURTHER READING: Ephesians 2

If this humane invitation of God does not stir us, we have no excuse. For he bears witness that he is gracious to us when we heartily desire to be reconciled to him. Still, he requires serious repentance.

A kind of half-conversion can be discerned in many who think they are safe before God if they can only bring forward something worthy of praise. But that is like a servant offering his master muddy wine, which is mixed not only with dregs but also with filth. So are the works of those who do not put away all depraved desires and strive to free themselves from corruptions of the flesh.

Note what is taught here, that the beginning of conversion is to renounce oneself and one's lusts. To that must be added another part of duty, for when anyone bids farewell to his vices, he must also devote himself in obedience to God. The prophet here joins the two together, since one cannot be separated from the other. Hence the Spirit here shortly defines what true and legitimate conversion is. He says that when someone is converted, his life is prepared for God, since God will forget all his sins. This confirms the doctrine, for God cannot be entreated as long as he imputes our sins to us. Hence, we may deem him gracious to us, for he promises that as soon as we truly repent, all our sins will be buried and no longer remembered.

The incomparable goodness of God is that he deigns to forget all our sins as soon as he sees us earnestly desirous of returning to him.

FOR MEDITATION: This text is excellent material for self-examination. If true conversion involves fleeing from our evil desires and corruptions and devoting ourselves obediently to God, it should be our regular practice to examine ourselves to make sure that, by God's grace, we have indeed done these very things. Have you?

Rescuing the Perishing

Have I any pleasure at all that the wicked should die? saith the Lord GOD: and not that he should return from his ways, and live? Ezekiel 18:23

SUGGESTED FURTHER READING: Revelation 22:16–21

God earnestly desires that those who are perishing and rushing to destruction should return to the way of safety. For this reason the gospel is spread abroad in the world. In this, God bears witness through all the ages how inclined he is to pity the lost.

The heathen may be destitute of the law and the prophets, yet they are always endued with some taste of this doctrine. True, they are suffocated by many errors, but they are also induced by a secret impulse to seek pardon from God. Also, the sense in some way is born in all people that God will be appeased by all who seek him. God bears witness to this clearly in the law and the prophets.

In the gospel, we hear how familiarly God addresses us when he promises us pardon (Luke 1:78). We can know salvation by embracing the mercy that he offers us in Christ.

It follows, then, that what the prophet now says is true, that God does not will the death of a sinner. God meets the sinner of his own accord. He is not only prepared to receive all who fly to his pity, but also calls them toward him with a loud voice when he sees how they are alienated from all hope of safety. Note also the manner in which God wishes all to be saved, namely, that they turn away from their wicked ways. God does not wish all men to be saved to renounce the difference between good and evil. Rather, he stresses that repentance, or turning aside from wicked ways, must precede pardon.

FOR MEDITATION: God cannot compromise his just character for men and women to be saved. He desires their salvation, but he still demands satisfaction for their sins. They must repent and trust in Jesus Christ and the salvation provided through him. Have you truly repented, or are you simply banking on God's loving character? His love will not compromise his justice. We must flee to Christ in true repentance.

Not Willing the Death of Sinners

Have I any pleasure at all that the wicked should die? saith the Lord GOD: and not that he should return from his ways, and live? Ezekiel 18:23

SUGGESTED FURTHER READING: Joshua 24:19–27

How does God wish all men to be saved? He does this today by the Spirit's convicting the world of sin, righteousness, and judgment by the gospel, just as he did this in days past through the law and the prophets (John 16:8). God makes clear to people their great misery so that they may come to him. He wounds that he may cure, and slays that he may give life.

We maintain that God does not will the death of sinners, since he equally calls all people to repentance and promises he is prepared to receive them if they only seriously repent. Some may object, saying that this would deny God's election, for he has predestinated a fixed number to salvation. The prophet does not speak here of God's secret counsel, but only of God calling those in misery from despair that they may apprehend the hope of pardon, and repent and embrace the offer of salvation.

If anyone again objects, saying this proves that God acts with duplicity, the answer is ready: God always wishes the same thing, though by different ways, and in a manner we cannot understand. Although God's will is simple, yet it involves great variety, as far as our senses are concerned. It is not surprising that our eyes should be so blinded by intense light that we cannot judge with certainty how God wishes all to be saved and yet has devoted the reprobate to eternal destruction and wishes them to perish. While we now look through a glass darkly, we should be content with the measure of our own intelligence (1 Cor. 13:12). When we one day are like God and see him face to face, then what is now obscure to us will become plain.

FOR MEDITATION: In dealing with texts like these, we should not try to exalt our reason over God's revelation, depriving the text of its power. Rather, we should glory in the great and free salvation offered to all who hear the gospel. This is the good news we must bring to everyone around us: God is willing to save sinners who turn to him.

Finding Sabbath Blessing

And hallow my sabbaths; and they shall be a sign between me and you, that ye may know that I am the LORD your God. Ezekiel 20:20
SUGGESTED FURTHER READING: Isaiah 58

God established the Sabbath, the day of rest, not simply to exact from people what is due to him. Nor did he establish it merely that people might rest. Therefore the prophet Ezekiel explains how God's Sabbaths should be sanctified or kept holy.

God is not satisfied by the people's merely resting from their weekly labors; rather, inward sanctification is the primary purpose of the Sabbath. In this passage God says that, if the Jews rightly observe the Sabbath, they will feel the effects of God's favor represented in the Sabbath. We have said that the Sabbath is a sacrament of regeneration; now God promises the efficacy of his Spirit if his people do not shut the door to that Spirit by their own impiety and contempt of the Sabbath. Hence we see that sacraments will not lose the blessing of the Spirit unless people render themselves unworthy of the grace offered to them in observing the sacraments.

We maintain, therefore, that there is a direct relationship between faith and the sacraments; the sacraments become effective through faith. Man's unworthiness does not detract anything from the sacraments, however, for they always retain their nature. Baptism is the laver of regeneration, even if the whole world doubts it (Titus 3:5); the Supper of Christ represents his body and blood (1 Cor. 10:16), even if there is not a spark of faith left in the world.

But we do not fully perceive the grace that is offered to us, for though spiritual things always remain the same, yet we do not experience their effect or perceive their value unless we are careful that our lack of faith does not profane what God has consecrated to our salvation.

FOR MEDITATION: How are we hallowing God's Sabbath today? Merely taking time off from work and going to church perfunctorily may be missing the most crucial benefit of all: the blessing of the Spirit in our inward sanctification. By faith we must observe the wondrous grace of the sacraments, including this sacrament of regeneration. Are there changes you need to make to your Sabbath observance?

Bowing under God's Persevering Rod

Nebuchadnezzar the king, unto all people, nations, and languages, that dwell in all the earth; Peace be multiplied unto you. I thought it good to show the signs and wonders that the high God hath wrought toward me. How great are his signs! and how mighty are his wonders! his kingdom is an everlasting kingdom, and his dominion is from generation to generation. Daniel 4:1–3
SUGGESTED FURTHER READING: Luke 15:3–7

Nebuchadnezzar here predicts the magnificence and might of his own monarchy, sending his announcement to all peoples and nations and languages that dwell on the earth. No doubt the king believes he has sufficiently paid the penalty of his former ingratitude and now ascribes glory to the one true God. Yet we also know how often he relapsed into his own superstitions and never really said farewell to them. We also see how often King Nebuchadnezzar had to be chastised before he profited by the rod of the Almighty.

Likewise, we need not be surprised if God often strikes us with his hand, since experience usually proves us to be dull, and even utterly slothful. When God, therefore, wishes to lead us to repentance, he may be compelled to continually repeat his blows, either because we are not moved when he chastises us with his hand, or we seem roused for a time, then return again to our former dullness. He is therefore compelled to redouble his blows.

We see ourselves in this story of Nebuchadnezzar as in a mirror. But the singular benefit is that, after God repeatedly chastised the king, he finally yielded. We do not know whether this confession proceeded from true and genuine repentance. I must leave that undecided. Yet without the slightest doubt, Daniel cited this edict of the king to show that the king was eventually so subdued that he confessed the God of Israel as the only God and bore witness to this among all people under his rule.

FOR MEDITATION: We are slow learners and should not be angry with God when he perseveres in chastening us to repentance. If he were not so patient and insistent, we all would have wandered far from him long ago. Is he chastising you today? What lesson can you learn from it?

Living with Unanswered Prayer

At the beginning of thy supplications the commandment came forth, and I am come to show thee; for thou art greatly beloved: therefore understand the matter, and consider the vision. Daniel 9:23
SUGGESTED FURTHER READING: Matthew 6:5–15

Our vows and prayers cannot possibly gain us favor with God unless we are already embraced by him; for in no other way do we find God's favor unless we first flee by faith to his loving kindness. Then, in reliance upon Christ as our Mediator and Advocate, we may dare to approach him as a child to a parent. For these reasons our prayers are of no avail before God unless they are in some degree founded in faith, which alone reconciles us to God. We cannot be pleasing to him without the pardon and remission of sins.

We observe also how the saints pleased God by enduring the failure to obtain their requests. Daniel endured trials for many years and was afflicted by much grief, yet he did not consider himself worthy of receiving anything by that labor. He might have concluded that all his work was in vain, for he prayed often and perseveringly without effect. But the angel now meets Daniel and frankly testifies that Daniel has found acceptance with God. He is to understand that he has not suffered any repulse, even though he has failed to obtain the object of his earnest desires.

Likewise, we may become anxious in our thoughts and inclined to despair when there appears to be no profit or fruit of our prayers, and we receive no open and immediate answer. We must then consider this instruction from the angel that even Daniel, who was most acceptable to God, was heard at length, even though he was not permitted to see with his eyes the object of his wishes. Daniel died in exile and did not see the fulfillment of the prophet's prophecies concerning the happy state of the church.

FOR MEDITATION: "Unanswered prayer" can be a tremendous burden. But it is not an indication that we are not accepted by God. Rather, we should persevere in prayer, knowing that if we are accepted with God, our prayers are heard even though we have not seen an answer yet.

Ministering as Stars

And they that be wise shall shine as the brightness of the firmament; and they that turn many to righteousness as the stars for ever and ever.
Daniel 12:3
SUGGESTED FURTHER READING: Revelation 1:9–20

Our justification is ascribed to faith because our faith directs us to Christ in whom is the complete perfection of justification. Thus our justification may be ascribed equally to the faith taught and the doctrine which teaches it.

Those who bring us this teaching are the ministers of our justification. So the assertion of the angel in this verse is that the sons of God, who are devoted entirely to God and ruled by the spirit of prudence, point out the way of life to others. In this they not only will be saved themselves, but they shall possess a glory that surpasses anything that exists in this world.

Hence, we gather that it is prudent to submit ourselves to God to be teachable as well as to carefully promote the salvation of other people. The effect of this labor will be to increase our courage and alacrity. For how great is the honor conferred upon us by our heavenly Father in willing us to be ministers of his righteousness?

As James 5:19 says, we preserve those about to perish if we bring them back into the right way. James calls us preservers, just as the angel calls us justifiers. In this neither the angel nor the apostle wish to detract from the glory of God, but by these forms of speech the Spirit represents us as ministers of justification and salvation when we unite with those who have need of our assistance and exertions.

FOR MEDITATION: The hope of reward and greater glory should spur us on to seek the salvation of those around us, regardless of the pain, suffering, and rejection that may come. What are those trials compared with the glory of the stars?

Listening to the Warning

And it shall come to pass at that day, that I will break the bow of Israel, in the valley of Jezreel. Hosea 1:5
SUGGESTED FURTHER READING: Psalm 44

The Israelites are so inflated with their present good fortune that they laugh at predictions of the judgment to come. They know that they are well furnished with arms and men and money, so think they are in every way unassailable. The prophet now warns them, declaring that all their preparations cannot prevent God from punishing them.

We see the prophet's intention here is to break down the false confidence of the people; for the Israelites believe they will not be exposed to the destruction that Hosea has predicted. They are dazzled with their own power and think themselves beyond the reach of any danger while they are well fortified on every side. But the prophet says all their fortresses will be nothing against God; for *at that day*, when the ripe time for vengeance shall come, the Lord will break all their bows, tear in pieces all their arms, and reduce their power to nothing.

We are here warned to take heed, lest anything should lead us to be deaf to God's threats. Though we have strength, though fortune smiles on us, though the whole world seemingly combines to secure our safety, yet there is no reason why we should feel safe when God declares himself opposed to and angry with us.

He can punish us whenever he pleases, depriving us of all our arms and reducing our power to nothing. Let this verse come to mind whenever God terrifies us with his warnings, for he can take away all the defenses in which we vainly trust.

FOR MEDITATION: There is no defense sufficient to resist the onslaught of God's anger. We must be sure that we enjoy his favor; nothing and no one can save us once he has decreed our destruction. Search your heart today. If you are one of his, rejoice in his wonderful grace shown to you.

Walking in the Lord's Ways

Who is wise, and he shall understand these things? prudent, and he shall know them? for the ways of the LORD *are right, and the just shall walk in them: but the transgressors shall fall therein.* Hosea 14:9
SUGGESTED FURTHER READING: Numbers 13:25–33

The just find a plain and even way in the Word of the Lord; nothing stands in their path to obstruct their course. By daily advances they attain that to which the Lords calls them, even their celestial inheritance.

The just walk in the Lord's ways because the Lord leads them by his hand. Faith will be a hundred eyes and wings to them. Hope will sustain them, for they are armed with promises and encouragements. They have stimulants whenever the Lord earnestly exhorts them, and they have his warnings that are so terrible that they keep them awake. The faithful find the best ways in the Word of the Lord, and they follow them.

By contrast, the ungodly imagine all doubts, even the least, to be mountains. When they encounter anything intricate or obscure, they are confounded and say, "I would gladly seek to know the Holy Scripture, but I meet with so many difficulties." Hence, they regard a doubt as a mountain; nay, they purposely pretend doubts so they may have some excuse when they wish to evade the truth and turn aside from following the Lord.

The ungodly stumble in the ways of Jehovah. So we might read Hosea 14:9 in terms of the ungodly as: "Though the ungodly stumble, yet the just shall always walk in those ways of the Lord," meaning there is no reason why the ungodly should hold us back by their continual stumbling and by exclaiming that the Word of God is full of offense, for we shall find in it an even way. Let us then ascribe glory to God that he is just and that his ways are right.

FOR MEDITATION: The Word of God, which clearly lays out the ways of God, has a remarkable power to divide and distinguish men from one another. One finds grace in its pages and loves to follow the Lord's paths. Another, reading the same pages, finds nothing but stumbling blocks and difficulties. Let us pray that God blesses us with his Spirit so that we find wonderful paths rather than stumbling blocks.

When Despair Leads us to God

And it shall come to pass, that whosoever shall call on the name of the LORD *shall be delivered: for in mount Zion and in Jerusalem shall be deliverance, as the* LORD *hath said, and in the remnant whom the* LORD *shall call.* Joel 2:32
SUGGESTED FURTHER READING: Matthew 11:25–30

God wants us to call on him, not only in prosperity but also in an extreme state of despair. It is as if God calls the dead to himself, declaring that he has the power to restore life to them and bring them out of the grave.

Since God invites the lost and the dead to come to him, there is no reason why even the heaviest distresses should prevent access to him for us or for our prayers, for by faith we ought to break through all these obstacles. The more grievous our troubles, the more confidence we ought to have, for God offers grace not only to the miserable but also to those in utter despair. The prophet did not threaten general evil to the Jews but declared that, before the coming of Christ, all things would be full of horror (verse 31). After this denunciation the prophet adds: *Whosoever shall call on the name of the* LORD *shall be delivered.*

Paul cites Joel's prophecy in Romans 10 and extends it to the Gentiles, so let us examine how he interprets the testimony of Joel. Paul uses these words of the prophet to prove that, since adoption is extended to the Gentiles, it is lawful for them to flee to God and to familiarly invoke him as Father. He hence proves that the gospel should be preached to the Gentiles, since invocation arises from faith; for unless God shines on us by his Word, we cannot come to him. Faith, then, is always the mother of prayer.

FOR MEDITATION: There is no situation so grave, no sin so black, that negates our invitation to repent and call on the name of the Lord and be saved. God delights in saving those who cannot save themselves. Do not doubt his power and willingness to save you when you find yourself condemning the horrendousness of your sin. Take it to him and humbly ask for his forgiveness.

Discouraged by Satan's Intrigues

Then Amaziah the priest of Bethel sent to Jeroboam king of Israel, saying, Amos hath conspired against thee in the midst of the house of Israel: the land is not able to bear all his words. For thus Amos saith, Jeroboam shall die by the sword, and Israel shall surely be led away captive out of their own land. Amos 7:10–11

SUGGESTED FURTHER READING: Luke 7:31–35

We must be watchful, not only against the open violence and cruelty of enemies, but also against their intrigues, for as Satan is a murderer, and has been so from the beginning, so he is also the father of lies. Whosoever then strenuously and constantly wishes to work for the church and for God must prepare for a contest with evil. He must resist all fears and all intrigues.

I have not said without reason that God's servants ought to be prepared against the fear of death. They must remain intrepid, though they die, and lay down their necks, if need be, while performing their office, to seal their doctrine with their own blood. On the other hand, they should be prudent, for the enemies of the truth will often assail them by flatteries. Our experiences today sufficiently prove this.

More danger, I know, has risen when enemies attempt to terrify us by such objections as: "What is your purpose for doing this? The whole world must necessarily at length be consumed by calamities. Why do you seek that religion should flourish everywhere, sound learning should be valued, and peace should prevail? The fiercest war is at hand. Once it arises, all places will be full of calamities. Savage barbarity and cruelty will follow, and religion will perish. You will cause all of this by your persistence."

These things have often been said to us. When we read this passage, we ought to notice the methods by which Satan tries to undermine the efforts of the godly and the constancy of God's servants.

FOR MEDITATION: Amos's example teaches us that we should not be surprised when we are misrepresented. With the mass media surrounding us, the possibility of intrigue and calamity is greater today than ever before. Satan easily can, and does, use these means to cast continual doubt upon the gospel and those who profess it.

Restraining Anger

And God said to Jonah, Doest thou well to be angry for the gourd? And he said, I do well to be angry, even unto death. Jonah 4:9
SUGGESTED FURTHER READING: Proverbs 16:27–33

God did not merely reprove his servant Jonah because he did not patiently bear the withering of the gourd but because he became angry, and his anger was excessive. Jonah was grieved beyond measure and without restraint, so his anger was justly condemned by God as a fault.

The answer of Jonah confirms this, for we see how obstinately the holy prophet repels the admonition of God by which he should have been restored to a right mind. Jonah was not ignorant of God's words. Why, then, was he not smitten with shame? Why was he not moved by the authority of the speaker to immediately repress the fierceness of his mind?

It often happens that, once the minds of men are blinded by a wrong feeling, they will not listen to God, even if he thunders and explodes from heaven. Since we find such an example of perverseness in this holy man, Jonah, how much more should not every one of us fear? Let us learn to repress our feelings of anger and to bridle them at the beginning, lest they burst forth to such a greater extent that we eventually become altogether obstinate.

Who would know that the holy prophet could have been brought to such obstinacy? Let us be reminded by this remarkable example how furious and unreasonable are the passions of our flesh. Therefore we ought to restrain these passions before they gather more strength than they ought.

FOR MEDITATION: Do you ever let passions rise to the level where you are totally incapable of accepting and digesting rebuke, even if it comes from God? Jonah's shocking impudence demonstrates that he had this problem. Remember his account when you next feel your passions rise, and heed its warning.

Strengthened by the Spirit

But truly I am full of power by the spirit of the LORD, *and of judgment, and of might, to declare unto Jacob his transgression, and to Israel his sin.* Micah 3:8
SUGGESTED FURTHER READING: Zechariah 4

Micah with incredible courage stands alone against the false teachers of his time. This confidence is something all God's servants should possess so they might not succumb to the empty and vain boastings of those who subvert the order of the church.

At times, God permits his pure truth to be corrupted by false teachers, who become popular among those high in honor as well as the multitude. Let us then remember the striking example of Micah lest we be discouraged and lest the firmness and invincible power of the Holy Spirit be weakened in our hearts. We may then proceed in the course of our calling to defend the name of God against all the deceptions of men, if indeed we are convinced that our service is approved by God.

Micah shows here that he was not supplied with ordinary or usual power. As God employs the labors of his servants, so he is present with them and furnishes them with suitable protection. When someone does not encounter great difficulties in discharging the office of teaching, only a common measure of the Spirit is necessary for the performance of his duties. But when someone is drawn into arduous and difficult struggles in serving the Lord, he is especially strengthened by the Lord.

We see daily examples of this, for many simple men who have never been trained up in learning have been so endued by the celestial Spirit that when they experienced great trials, they closed the mouths of great doctors who seemed to understand all oracles. By such evidences God proves that he is the same today as when he formerly endowed his servant Micah with a power that was so rare and so extraordinary.

FOR MEDITATION: The Lord grants sufficient grace to his children. We should not fear those dreaded possibilities that loom in front of us. If, like Micah, we face extraordinary trials and duties, we will be granted an extraordinary measure of the Spirit's power. The Lord will always give his children what they need to do his will.

Distinguishing the Truth

Hear this, I pray you, ye heads of the house of Jacob, and princes of the house of Israel, that abhor judgment, and pervert all equity. Micah 3:9

SUGGESTED FURTHER READING: John 16:12–16

God's servants ought to courageously break through those obstacles that Satan uses either to delay or to force them backward. In addition, the godly ought to wisely distinguish between the faithful servants of God and impostors who falsely pretend his name. Then no one who wants truly and from the heart to obey God will be deceived, for the Lord will give him the spirit of judgment and discrimination.

The reason why many miserable souls today are led to endless ruin is because they either shut their eyes or willfully involve themselves in such subterfuges as the following: "I cannot form any judgment, for I see on both sides learned and celebrated men, who are in some repute and esteemed. Some call me to the right hand and others to the left. So where am I to go? I therefore prefer to close my mouth and my ears." Seeking a cloak for their sloth, many thus manifest their ignorance, for we see that the eyes of the godly will be opened when the Lord exercises and tries their faith.

God allows discords and contentions to arise in the church so that some may choose one way and others another way. Though God relaxes the reins of Satan so that contests and turmoil of all kinds may arise in the church, it is no excuse for us not to follow what the Lord prescribes, for God will always guide us by his Spirit, provided we do not foster our own sloth.

FOR MEDITATION: In our day, indecision has become endemic. What is more, we have developed philosophies to justify our indecision. If some think one way and others another, we justify taking no position by saying the truth is too hard to discern. But God has not left us to stumble around in such uncertainty; he has given us his sure Word and his Holy Spirit. We *can* know the truth, and we must daily strive to find it.

Offering Hope in the Midst of Fear

But in the last days it shall come to pass, that the mountain of the house of the LORD shall be established in the top of the mountains, and it shall be exalted above the hills; and people shall flow unto it. Micah 4:1
SUGGESTED FURTHER READING: Psalm 46

Though the prophet publicly proclaims a promise of hope, he undoubtedly offers it only to the children of God, for others are not capable of receiving this consolation. We see the same thing in the writings of other prophets whose practice is to add consolations to threats, not for the sake of all people, but to sustain hope in the faithful, who might have despaired had not a helping hand been stretched forth to them.

We know the faithful tremble when God manifests any token of wrath, for the more one is touched with the fear of God, the more one dreads God's judgment and fears his threats. We thus see how necessary it is for prophets and teachers to moderate threats and terrors against the children of God, for they have enough fears without heaping more on them.

Formerly Micah spoke to the wicked who despised God while putting on the cloak of religion. But now the prophet turns to address the true and pious worshipers of God. In addressing the faithful of his age, his doctrine especially belongs to us now, for otherwise how could the kingdom of God have been propagated through all parts of the earth? How could the truth of the gospel have come to us and we be made partakers with the ancient people of the same adoption, unless this prophecy was fulfilled?

So the calling of the Gentiles, and consequently our salvation, is included in this prophecy of Micah.

FOR MEDITATION: The thought of God's disfavor was very distressing to godly people in Micah's day. Is it to you? They needed no more than a hint of judgment to upset them. How loud must God thunder before you listen?

Seeking Peace with Others

And he shall judge among many people, and rebuke strong nations afar off; and they shall beat their swords into plowshares, and their spears into pruning-hooks: nation shall not lift up a sword against nation, neither shall they learn war any more. Micah 4:3
SUGGESTED FURTHER READING: Isaiah 52

Micah now more fully explains how the gospel of Christ will be to the nations a standard of peace, like a banner that is raised up when soldiers engage in battle.

We learn that the real fruit of the gospel will not grow in us unless we exercise love and benevolence among one another and exert ourselves in doing good. The gospel may be purely preached among us at the present time, but when we consider how little progress we have made in brotherly love, we ought to be ashamed of our indolence. God daily proclaims that Christ is our peace with God. He graciously makes Christ propitious to us so that we may live in harmony with others. We indeed wish to be regarded as children of God and to enjoy the reconciliation obtained for us by the blood of Christ. But in the meantime, we tear one another apart and sharpen our teeth against each other. Our dispositions are cruel.

If we truly desire to be disciples of Christ, we must pay attention to the divine truth that each of us must strive to do good to his neighbor. This cannot be done without opposing our flesh, for we have a strong inclination to love self and to seek our own advantage. We must therefore put off these inordinate and sinful affections so that brotherly kindness may succeed in their place.

FOR MEDITATION: The gospel brings peace and reconciliation. When these things are absent, we can be sure the gospel is absent, no matter how much religion is present. Are we agents of peace, or do we cause strife and division wherever we go?

Understanding the Counsel of God

But they know not the thoughts of the LORD, *neither understand they his counsel: for he shall gather them as the sheaves into the floor.* Micah 4:12
SUGGESTED FURTHER READING: Isaiah 46:9–13

The prophet now speaks of the failure to understand the design and thoughts of God. If only that is brought before us, we will have little solid comfort and have nothing of much force or power.

But there is another principle that should be understood here: the thoughts of God *are* known to us who are taught in his school. The counsel of God is not hidden from us, for it is revealed to us in his Word. Our consolation, therefore, depends on a higher and more profound doctrine, which is that the faithful in their miseries ought to contemplate the counsel of God as in a mirror.

What does this mean? When God afflicts the godly, he holds a remedy in his hand; and when he throws the godly into the grave, he can restore them to life and safety. We therefore can understand the design of God to chasten his church with temporal evils. If we know this, there is no reason why the slanders of the ungodly should deject our minds. When the ungodly vomit forth all their reproaches, we ought to more firmly adhere to the counsel of God.

The pride of the ungodly should not surprise us, for if they raise their horns against God, why should they also not despise us, who are so few in number and of hardly any influence, at least compared to what they possess? The church is indeed contemptible in the eyes of the world. It is no wonder, then, if our enemies deride us and load us with ridicule and contempt when they dare to act so forwardly toward God.

It is enough for us to know that they do not understand the counsel of God.

FOR MEDITATION: When we who are believers think we cannot understand God and his ways, particularly in times of evil and even death, we can take comfort in reading his Word. It tells us what is true and what is not. It assures us that God loves us, even when evil people ridicule us for our faith.

Finding Christ as our Peace

And this man shall be the peace, when the Assyrian shall come into our land: and when he shall tread in our palaces, then shall we raise against him seven shepherds, and eight principal men. Micah 5:5
SUGGESTED FURTHER READING: Isaiah 9:1–7

How can we venture to believe the promise that in times of trouble, eventually all will be quiet and secure? Micah assures us, "this man" shall be our peace. We should thus be satisfied with the protection of the king whom God the Father gives us. Let the shadow of that king suffice us, for we shall be safe enough from all trouble.

We now see in what sense the prophet calls Christ the peace of his people, or of his church. God calls Christ his peace because he will drive far away all hurtful things. He will be armed with strength and invincible power to check all the ungodly, that they may not make war on the children of God or prevent them in their course, if they would cause any disturbances.

Christ is our peace in another way; for he reconciles us to the Father. What would it serve us to be safe from earthly annoyances if we were not certain of being reconciled with God? Unless our minds are sure of the paternal benevolence of God, we must necessarily tremble at all times, even if no one causes us any trouble. Even if all men were our friends and applauded us, our condition would still be miserable. We would surely struggle with restlessness unless our consciences were pacified with the sure confidence that God is our Father.

Christ can be our peace in no other way than by reconciling God to us. At the same time, the prophet promises that we shall lie safely under the shadow of Christ, so that we fear no evil. For though Satan furiously assails us, and the whole world becomes angry with us, we shall fear nothing if Christ keeps and protects us under his wings.

FOR MEDITATION: The only real hope for peace in our world is for men and women to find peace with God. If the human race were to turn to Christ, we would soon find our world full of peace. Let us pray, then, for the Prince of Peace to reign in our world.

What the Lord Requires

Wherewith shall I come before the LORD, *and bow myself before the high God? shall I come before him with burnt offerings, with calves of a year old? Will the* LORD *be pleased with thousands of rams, or with ten thousands of rivers of oil? shall I give my firstborn for my transgression, the fruit of my body for the sin of my soul? He hath shown thee, O man, what is good; and what doth the* LORD *require of thee, but to do justly, and to love mercy, and to walk humbly with thy God?* Micah 6:6–8
SUGGESTED FURTHER READING: 1 Samuel 15:13–35

When men litigate one with another, there is no cause so good but what an opposing party can undo. But, as the prophet suggests here, men lose all their efforts at evasions when God summons them to trial. The prophet also shows what deep roots hypocrisy has in the hearts of all people, for they will forever deceive themselves and try to deceive God.

Why do people who are proved guilty fail to immediately and in the right way come to God in repentance, but instead seek elaborate, winding excuses? It is not because they have any doubt about what is right, unless they willfully deceive themselves, but because they willfully seek the subterfuges of error. It hence appears that men perversely go astray whenever they fail to repent as they ought and fail to bring to God true integrity of heart.

It is also true that the whole world, which continues in its superstitions, is without excuse. For if we scrutinize the intentions of men, we eventually understand that people carefully and anxiously seek various superstitions because they are unwilling to come before God and to devote themselves to him without deceit and hypocrisy. Since it is so, all who desire to pacify God with their own ceremonies and other trifles cannot by any pretext escape judgment.

God has clearly and distinctly prescribed what he requires of us, but the ungodly wish to be ignorant of this. Hence their error is at all times willful. We ought to note this in the words of the prophet.

FOR MEDITATION: It is much easier to render to God anything other than a broken heart and an upright life. Sacrifices are easily obtained, but they can serve as no substitute for what the Lord really requires of us. Are we striving, by grace, to live justly, to love mercy, and to walk humbly with God?

Looking to the Lord

Therefore will I look unto the LORD; *I will wait for the God of my salvation: my God will hear me.* Micah 7:7
SUGGESTED FURTHER READING: Psalm 73

The only way the faithful may be preserved from being led away by bad examples is to fix their eyes on God and to believe that he will be their deliverer.

Nothing is more difficult for us than to refrain from doing wrong when the ungodly provoke us, for they seem to offer us good reason for retaliation. Even when no one injures us, the custom of retaliation seems just. We think that what is sanctioned by the manners and customs of our time is lawful, so that when the wicked are successful, this becomes a very strong incentive for us to follow their example.

Thus it happens that the faithful can hardly, and with no small difficulty, keep themselves within proper bounds, for they see that wickedness reigns everywhere and with impunity. Even more, when they see those who encourage wickedness increase in esteem and wealth, immediately the corrupt lust of emulation creeps in.

But when the faithful themselves are provoked by injuries, there seems to be a particularly just reason for following the example of the wicked. They say that they willfully do harm to no one, but they are only resisting an injury done to them. Or they are merely retaliating from fraud with fraud, which only seems just.

To prevent this temptation, the prophet bids the faithful to look to God. It is the same thought that is often expressed in Psalm 119; the faithful must not allow themselves to be led away by bad examples, but must continue to walk in obedience to God's Word, however great and violent the provocations they receive.

FOR MEDITATION: If we find ourselves defrauded, our minds quickly justify fraudulent dealings in return. But that is not how we are called to live, nor does it bring glory to God. Instead, we should look to God for our salvation and for his justice to prevail in whatever way he sees fit. Vengeance is his.

Receiving Comfort in Judgment

I will bear the indignation of the LORD, *because I have sinned against him, until he plead my cause, and execute judgment for me: he will bring me forth to the light, and I shall behold his righteousness.* Micah 7:9
SUGGESTED FURTHER READING: Psalm 103:1–12

After the church confesses her sin against God, she turns her eyes elsewhere. She says she was unjustly oppressed by her enemies, and they were led to do wrong by cruelty alone. She thus entertains the hope and expectation that God will defend her innocence and punish the wicked. Yet she humbly acknowledges that she too has sinned against God.

Whenever our enemies do us harm, let us lay hold of the truth that God will be our defender, for he is the patron of justice and equity. He will not abandon us to the violence of the wicked. He will at length heed our pleading, undertake our cause, and be our advocate.

In the meantime, let us be mindful of our sins so that in true humiliation before God we may not hope for the salvation that he promises to us except through his gracious pardon.

Why, then, are the faithful bidden to be of good comfort in their afflictions? Because God promises to be their Father. He receives them under his protection and testifies that his help to them shall never be wanting. But how can they be confident of this? Is it because they are worthy? Is it because they deserve something like this?

By no means, for they acknowledge themselves to be guilty when they humbly prostrate themselves before God and willingly condemn themselves before his tribunal, so that they may anticipate his judgment.

We now see how the prophet connects these two things, comfort and judgment, which might otherwise seem contradictory.

FOR MEDITATION: The wonder of grace is clearly demonstrated in God's willingness to protect and preserve those who have grievously sinned against him. Though we are sinners, we may confidently plead for the justice of God—the very justice that we have offended—against our enemies for Christ's sake.

Judging Self before Others

Shall not all these take up a parable against him, and a taunting proverb against him, and say, Woe to him that increaseth that which is not his! how long? and to him that ladeth himself with thick clay! Habakkuk 2:6
<small>SUGGESTED FURTHER READING: Psalm 119:161–176</small>

Not one of us wants to say the same thing about himself that he brings forward against others. For when a greedy man gathers things, whether right or wrong, or an ambitious man by unfair means advances himself, we instantly cry, "How long?" Though everyone is quick to say this about others, yet no one wants to say that about himself.

Let us therefore take heed that when we reprove injustice in others, we come without delay to ourselves and are impartial judges to our own actions and intent. Let us not be so blinded by self-love that we seek to absolve ourselves from the very faults that we freely condemn in others.

In general, people are more correct in their judgment of matters in which they are not involved, but when they consider matters in which they take part, they become blind. Honesty vanishes and all judgment is gone.

The prophet offers us this teaching based on the common feeling of nature, so that every one of us may restrain ourselves when we presume the office of a judge in condemning others. We are also given this proverb that we might condemn ourselves and restrain our desires when we find them advancing beyond just bounds.

FOR MEDITATION: It is so easy to see the faults of others while remaining completely ignorant of our own. But ignorance is no excuse. We must diligently examine ourselves and our lives to dispel our ignorance and find any sin that has not been dealt with.

Why Animals Suffer

I will utterly consume all things from off the land, saith the LORD. *I will consume man and beast; I will consume the fowls of the heaven, and the fishes of the sea, and the stumbling blocks with the wicked; and I will cut off man from off the land, saith the* LORD. Zephaniah 1:2–3
SUGGESTED FURTHER READING: Genesis 7

Why does God pronounce vengeance on the beasts of the field, the birds of the heaven, and the fish of the sea? For no matter how much the Jews have provoked God by their sins, innocent animals ought to be spared. If a son is not to be punished for the fault of his father (Ezek. 18:4), but only the soul that has sinned must die, why does God turn his wrath against fish and birds and animals? This seems to be a hasty and unreasonable infliction.

To answer that, let us first bear in mind that it is preposterous for us to estimate God's doings according to our judgment. Proud and perverse people do that today, for they are disposed to judge God's works with such presumption that whatever they do not approve of they think it right to fully condemn. It behooves us to judge God's ways with modesty and sobriety, confessing that his judgments are a deep abyss. When a reason for God's ways does not appear obvious, we ought to reverently and with deep humility look for the day in which that revelation comes.

Second, it is wise for us to remember that because animals were created for man's use, they must undergo much along with him. God made the birds of heaven and the fishes of the sea and all other animals subservient to man. Why, then, should we wonder that the condemnation of the one who has sovereignty over the whole earth should also extend to the animals?

The world was not willingly or naturally made subject to corruption, but because the corruption from Adam's fall diffused itself through heaven and earth.

FOR MEDITATION: The horrifying cruelty sometimes found in the animal kingdom is not natural, but is the product of our sin. Though the animals did not sin against their Creator, they too were destroyed in the flood. The next time that we are tempted to think lightly of sin, let us reflect on the incredible suffering that we have brought upon this earth and tremble at the seriousness of our sin.

Trusting in the Sun of Righteousness

But unto you that fear my name shall the Sun of righteousness arise with healing in his wings; and ye shall go forth, and grow up as calves of the stall. Malachi 4:2
SUGGESTED FURTHER READING: John 1:1–18

"Sun" is an appropriate name for Christ, for God the Father has given a much clearer light in the person of Christ than he did formerly by the law and all its appendages.

Christ is called the light of the world, not because the fathers wandered as the blind in darkness and were content with the law as with the dawn or with the moon and stars. We know how the doctrine of the law was so obscure that it may truly be said to be shadowy. When the heavens at length were opened and the gospel was made clear, it was through the rising of the Sun, which brought the full day. Hence it is the peculiar purpose of Christ to illuminate us.

On this account, the first chapter of John says that the true light which illuminates every man that comes into the world existed from the beginning. Yet this light shone in the darkness, for some sparks of reason exist in men, however blinded they became through the fall of Adam and the corruption of nature. Christ is specifically called the light with regard to the faithful, whom he delivers from the blindness by which all by nature have been afflicted, and whom he undertakes to guide by his Spirit.

The meaning, then, of the word "Sun," when applied to Christ, is that without the Light of the World we can only wander and go astray. But by his guidance we shall keep in the right way. Hence he says, "He who follows me walks not in darkness" (John 8:12).

FOR MEDITATION: Without Christ and his light, we would be doomed to wander in darkness. If you are a Christian, thank him particularly for dispelling the darkness in which you were determined to remain. You could not see the light until the Spirit opened your eyes.

Remembering the Living Word

Remember ye the law of Moses my servant, which I commanded unto him in Horeb for all Israel, with the statutes and judgments. Malachi 4:4
SUGGESTED FURTHER READING: Nahum 3

Prior to the coming of Christ, there was a kind of silence on the part of God. By ceasing to send prophets for a time, God's desire was to stimulate the Jews so they might with greater ardor seek Christ. The prophet Malachi was one of the last prophets.

Since the Jews are to be without prophets, they should more diligently obey the law and take careful heed to the doctrine of religion that it contains, the prophet says. So Malachi now bids the people to remember the law of Moses, as if to say, "Hereafter shall come the time when you will be without prophets, but your remedy will be the law. Pay careful attention to it, and beware lest you should forget it."

When God ceases to speak to people, even for the shortest time, some are carried away by their own inventions and ever inclined to vanity. We know that abundantly by experience. So, to keep the Jews from wandering and departing from the pure doctrine of the law, the prophet reminds them that they are to faithfully and constantly remember it until the Redeemer comes.

Observe that the prophetic message is not separate from the law, for all the prophecies that followed the law were like appendages; they included nothing new but were given so the people might more fully retain them in their obedience to the law.

FOR MEDITATION: Some people reason that God has not spoken for so long that it matters little what he had to say two thousand years ago. A great comfort and protection against this unbelief comes with knowing that the Word we now have is a living Word, and the Savior we have is, indeed, a risen Savior.

The Gift of Offspring

Thus hath the Lord dealt with me in the days wherein he looked on me, to take away my reproach among men. Luke 1:25

SUGGESTED FURTHER READING: Psalm 113

Elizabeth extols the goodness of God in private until the time is right for making known God's promises about her expected child. There is reason to believe that her husband has informed her in writing of the promised offspring; consequently, she affirms with great certainty and freedom that God is the author of this favor of impending life. This is confirmed by the words *wherein he looked on me, to take away my reproach*, for she believed the cause of her barrenness was that the favor of God had been withdrawn from her.

Among earthly blessings, Scripture speaks in the highest terms of the gift of offspring. Rightly so, for if the productivity of animals is God's blessing, then the increase and fruitfulness of the human race ought to be regarded as a much higher favor. It is no small honor that God, who alone is entitled to be regarded as Father, allows children of the dust to share this title with him. Let us, therefore, regard this teaching that "children are an heritage of the Lord, and the fruit of the womb is his reward" (Ps. 127:3). But Elizabeth looks further, for though barren and old, and contrary to the ordinary course of nature, she confesses that she has conceived by a remarkable miracle.

Let parents learn to be thankful to God for the children that he gives them, and let those who have no offspring acknowledge that God humbles them in this matter. Elizabeth speaks of her barrenness as a reproach *among men*, for childlessness is a temporal chastisement from which we will suffer no loss in the kingdom of heaven.

FOR MEDITATION: What have you been asking from the Lord that he has not given? How does waiting increase your focus on him rather than on what you want? How can we use the lessons we learn from waiting on God to assist childless couples and those who struggle with unanswered prayers?

Opening Up to God's Promises

And blessed is she that believed: for there shall be a performance of those things which were told her from the Lord. Luke 1:45

SUGGESTED FURTHER READING: 1 Kings 8:14–21

The truth of God does not depend on the will of men. God always remains true to his promises even if the whole world of unbelievers and liars attempts to ruin his veracity. Yet, as unbelievers are unworthy to obtain the fruit of the promises, so Scripture teaches us that by faith alone these promises are powerful for our salvation.

God offers his benefits indiscriminately to all, and faith opens its bosom to receive them, while unbelief allows them to pass out of reach. If there was any unbelief in Mary, that could not have prevented God from accomplishing his work in another way that he chose. But Mary is called "blessed" because she received by faith the blessing offered to her. That opened up the way to God for its accomplishment. Unbelief, on the other hand, shuts the gate and restrains God's hand from working so those who refuse the praise due to its power may not feel its saving effect.

We must observe also the relationship between the Word and faith. For we learn that, in the act of believing, we give assent to God, who speaks to us and holds for certain what he has promised that he will do for us. *From the Lord* has the same meaning as the common expression "on the part of God," for the promise brought by the angel proceeded from God alone. Hence we see that whether God uses the efforts of angels or of men, he wishes equal honor to be paid to his Word as if he were visibly descending from above.

FOR MEDITATION: How daunting the promises of God are sometimes, especially when they are so far beyond our expectations. Yet faith does not question how those blessings come but opens itself to the one who promised them, receiving what God gives with an open hand. How are we, by grace, opening ourselves to what God might accomplish in us? How can we forfeit great blessings through unbelief?

Filling the Hungry

He hath put down the mighty from their seats, and exalted them of low degree. He hath filled the hungry with good things; and the rich he hath sent empty away. Luke 1:52–53

SUGGESTED FURTHER READING: Isaiah 2:11–22

The dazzling luster of kings and princes may so overpower the masses that few consider there is a God above. If princes brought a scepter with them from the womb, and if the stability of their thrones was perpetual, all acknowledgment of God and of his providence might immediately disappear. When the Lord raises simple people to an exalted rank, however, he triumphs over the pride of the world and encourages simplicity and modesty in his own people.

Thus, when Mary says God *hath put down the mighty from their seats, and exalted them of low degree*, she teaches us that the world does not move and revolve by a blind impulse of fortune. Rather, all change is brought about by the providence of God. Furthermore, judgments that appear to disturb us and overthrow the entire framework of society are regulated by God with unerring justice.

This is confirmed by the following verse: *He hath filled the hungry with good things; and the rich he hath sent empty away.* For in it we realize that it is not because of people themselves but for his own good reasons that God takes pleasure in these changes. It is because the great and the rich and powerful who are lifted up by their abundance ascribe all praise to themselves and leave nothing to God.

We ought therefore to be scrupulously on our guard against being carried away by prosperity and vain satisfaction of the flesh, lest God suddenly deprive us of what we enjoy. To godly persons who experience poverty, and almost famine, and lift up their cries to God, no small consolation is afforded by the teaching that he *hath filled the hungry with good things*.

FOR MEDITATION: We can be so dazzled by rich and famous people that we praise them for their efforts at building empires. In so doing, we fail to recognize that everything belongs to God, who can reverse the fortunes of men in a single stroke. When have we seen the mighty put down and those of low degree exalted? How did that bring our focus back to our almighty God?

Possessing God

Behold, a virgin shall be with child, and shall bring forth a son, and they shall call his name Emmanuel, which being interpreted is, God with us.
Matthew 1:23
SUGGESTED FURTHER READING: John 1

The name *Emmanuel* implies a contrast between the presence of God exhibited in Christ and every other kind of presence that appeared to the ancient people before the coming of Christ. If the reason for this name began to be actually true when Christ appeared in the flesh, it follows that it was not completely, but only in part, that God was formerly united with the patriarchs of faith.

Hence arises another proof that Christ is "God manifest in the flesh" (1 Tim. 3:16). From the very beginning of the world, Christ held the office of Mediator, but as his true identity with God wholly depended on the latest revelation, he is justly called Emmanuel when he is finally clothed, as it were, with a new character. He appears in public as a priest to atone for the sins of men by the sacrifice of his body and to reconcile them to the Father by the price of his blood. In a word, he fulfills every part in the salvation of men.

The first thing we ought to consider in this name is the divine majesty of Christ. We may thus yield to him the reverence that is due to the only and eternal God. At the same time, we must not forget the fruit that God intended us to collect and receive from this name. For whenever we contemplate the person of Christ as God-man, we ought to be certain that if we are united to Christ by faith, we possess God.

FOR MEDITATION: The miracle of the Incarnation contains great mystery. How is Christ Emmanuel to you? How are we to reverence him as God manifest in the flesh in our prayers and worship? How are we to reverence him in everyday work? In short, how does it transform our everyday lives when we see and possess God?

Finding Great Joy

And the angel said unto them, Fear not: for, behold, I bring you good
tidings of great joy, which shall be to all people. Luke 2:10
SUGGESTED FURTHER READING: Philippians 4:1–9

To relieve the fear of the shepherds, the angel declares that he was sent
to them to announce the mercy of God. When people hear that God is
reconciled to them, those who have fallen down are raised, and those
who have been ruined are restored. They are, as it were, recalled from
death to life.

The angel begins his message by saying that he announces *great joy*.
Next he explains the reason for that joy: "a Savior is born." Until we
have peace with God and are reconciled to him through the grace of
Christ, all the joy that we experience is deceitful and of short duration.

Ungodly men frequently indulge in frantic and intoxicating mirth, but
if there is no one to make peace between them and God, the hidden
stings of conscience can only produce fearful torment. Besides, to
whatever extent they may flatter themselves in luxurious indulgence,
their own lusts will provide more tormentors.

The beginning of solid joy is to perceive the fatherly love of God
toward us, for that alone gives tranquility to our minds. As Paul says,
"the kingdom of God" does not consist of eating and drinking but of joy
in the Holy Spirit (Rom. 14:17).

By promising "great joy," the angel shows us that we ought, above all
things, to rejoice in the salvation brought to us by Christ. This blessing is
so great and boundless that it fully compensates for all the pains,
distresses, and anxieties of the present life.

Let us learn to be so delighted with Christ alone that the perception of
his grace may overcome us and at length remove from us all distresses of
the flesh.

FOR MEDITATION: When have you experienced the mercy of God? How
did it raise you up and restore you? By contrast, when have you pursued
worldly entertainment and possessions, thinking they will bring you joy,
only to find that you are too soon anxious and dissatisfied? Look to
Christ for the only joy that lasts.

Set up for Destruction

And Simeon blessed them, and said unto Mary his mother, Behold, this child is set for the fall and rising again of many in Israel; and for a sign which shall be spoken against. Luke 2:34
SUGGESTED FURTHER READING: John 3:22–36

Simeon predicts here that Christ was divinely appointed to cast down and destroy many in Israel. But we must observe that the ruin of unbelievers results from their own strikes against our Savior. Simeon makes that point when he says that Christ is *a sign which shall be spoken against*. When unbelievers rebel against Christ, they dash themselves against him, thus setting themselves up for ruin.

The world would not display harmony in opposing the gospel if there were no natural enmity between the Son of God and evildoers. The ambition or fury of the enemies of the gospel carries them in various directions. Dissension splits them into various sects, and a wide variety of superstitions separates idolaters from one another. But while they differ among themselves, these worldly people all agree in opposing the Son of God.

Some have said that opposition made to Christ is too plain an evidence of human depravity. That the world should thus rise against its Creator is a monstrous sight. But Scripture predicted this would happen, and the reason is very apparent. Once people have been alienated from God by sin, they always fly from him. Instances of this kind, therefore, should not take us by surprise. On the contrary, the armor of our faith ought to prepare us to fight all the contradictions of the world.

FOR MEDITATION: Why do evil people so vehemently oppose the only one in whom no guilt can be found? Why do they seemingly gain strength each day in tempting believers and bringing down the church? Simeon's words assure us that such enmity against Christ and his followers is to be expected. Rather than being surprised at it, let us take comfort in it, as it indicates that we are suffering like our Master (1 John 3:1).

Obeying Unexpected Orders

And when they were departed, behold, the angel of the Lord appeareth to Joseph in a dream, saying, Arise, and take the young child and his mother, and flee into Egypt, and be thou there until I bring thee word: for Herod will seek the young child to destroy him. Matthew 2:13
SUGGESTED FURTHER READING: 1 Corinthians 1:18–31

God has more than one way of preserving his people. This wonderful method of preserving the Son of God in the flight to Egypt teaches us it is improper to prescribe to God a fixed plan of action. Let us permit him to advance our salvation by a diversity of methods and not refuse to be humbled, so that he may more abundantly display his glory. Above all, let us not avoid the cross of suffering, by which the Son of God himself was trained from his earliest infancy.

The flight to Egypt, like the cross, may be foolishness to the world, yet it surpasses all the wisdom of the world. So that he might appear in his own time as the Savior of Judea, Christ Jesus is compelled to flee from Judea. He is then nourished in Egypt, from which nothing but what was destructive to the church of God has ever come. Who would not have regarded with amazement such an unexpected work of God?

Joseph immediately complies with the order of the angel. This is another proof of the certainty of the dream; for such promptness of obedience plainly shows that Joseph has no doubt whatsoever that it is God who tells him to take flight. Joseph's eager haste in fleeing Bethlehem may seem to have some aspect of distrust, for fleeing by night has some appearance of alarm. But it is not difficult to explain this. Joseph sees that God has appointed a method of safety, and he concludes that he should take flight because of extreme danger.

Likewise, our fear ought always to be regulated by divine instruction. If the instruction agrees with God's Word, it is not opposed to faith.

FOR MEDITATION: God's ways are not our ways—both in his plan of redemption and in his daily providences throughout our lives. What seems foolish to us may be the wisest course of all. What does God ask us to suffer today? What assurance do we have that his ways are wiser than we know in this? How can we submit more humbly and cheerfully to his will?

The Gifts of Forgiveness and Repentance

In those days came John the Baptist, preaching in the wilderness of Judea, and saying, Repent ye: for the kingdom of heaven is at hand.
Matthew 3:1–2
SUGGESTED FURTHER READING: John 8:1–11

The gospel message consists of two parts: forgiveness of sins and repentance. Matthew relates the first of these to *the kingdom of heaven.* We may thus conclude that people are in a state of deadly enmity with God. They are altogether shut out from the heavenly kingdom until God receives them into favor.

Though John, when he introduces the grace of God, urges men to repentance, yet we should remember that repentance is just as much the gift of God as inheriting the heavenly kingdom. As God freely pardons our sins and delivers us by his mercy from the condemnation of eternal death, so he also conforms us to his image so that we may live unto righteousness.

As God freely adopts us as his children, so he regenerates us by his Spirit in order that our life may testify that we do not falsely address him as our Father. In like manner, Christ washes away our sins by his blood and reconciles our heavenly Father to us by the sacrifice of his death. As a consequence of "our old man being crucified with him and the body of sin destroyed" (Rom. 6:6), he makes us "alive" unto righteousness.

The sum of the gospel here is that God through his Son takes away our sins and admits us to fellowship with him, so that we, in denying ourselves and our own nature, may "live soberly, righteously, and godly." We may thus conduct ourselves rightly on earth while meditating on the heavenly life.

FOR MEDITATION: Inheriting the kingdom of God is a great gift that involves both forgiveness and repentance, as Calvin says. These two are to be distinguished but never separated. Examine yourself today: are you both forgiven and penitent? If so, thank God today for these priceless gifts that lead to eternal life. If not, flee to Christ immediately.

Condemning Hypocrisy

But when he saw many of the Pharisees and Sadducees come to his baptism, he said unto them, O generation of vipers, who hath warned you to flee from the wrath to come? Matthew 3:7
SUGGESTED FURTHER READING: Ezekiel 33:1–20

Though the people whom John reproves are few in number, his purpose is to strike terror on all. He thus directly addresses the Pharisees and Sadducees, while at the same time issuing a warning to all people not to maintain a hypocritical appearance of repentance instead of a true affection of heart.

If John, as the messenger of the Holy Spirit, uses such severe language in addressing those who voluntarily come to be baptized and to make a public profession of faith, how should we act toward the avowed enemies of Christ, who not only obstinately reject all that belongs to sound doctrine, but whose efforts to extinguish the name of Christ are violently maintained by fire and sword?

Most certainly, if you compare the pope, his priests, and all false clergy, with the Pharisees and Sadducees, the mildest possible way of dealing with them would be to consider them as hypocrites. Those whose ears are so delicate that they cannot tolerate anything negative said against believers or unbelievers must argue not with us but with the Spirit of God.

Yet let godly teachers beware, lest while they are influenced by holy zeal against the tyrants of the church, they mingle with it the affections of the flesh. Since no vehemence that is not regulated by the wisdom of the Spirit can obtain divine approbation, let teachers restrain their feelings and surrender themselves to the Holy Spirit, asking him for guidance so that nothing may unintentionally escape them.

FOR MEDITATION: How would you respond if you knew John was addressing you as "a generation of vipers"? Would you react in anger or accept the warning against hypocrisy? Many may appear to be believers while failing to have a true change in heart. How can we best flee from all hypocrisy?

Entitled by the Spirit

The Spirit of the Lord is upon me, because he hath anointed me to preach the gospel to the poor; he hath sent me to heal the brokenhearted, to preach deliverance to the captive, and recovering of sight to the blind, to set at liberty them that are bruised. Luke 4:18

SUGGESTED FURTHER READING: Isaiah 61

In his own person and in his ministers, Christ does not act by human authority or in a personal sense, but as one who has been sent by God to restore salvation to the church. He does nothing by the suggestion or advice of men but everything by the guidance of the Spirit of God. He declares this so that the faith of the godly may be wholly founded on the authority and power of God.

The words *because he hath anointed me* are added by way of explanation. Many falsely boast that they have the Spirit of God while they are destitute of his gifts, but Christ proves that he has been endowed by the anointing of the Spirit of God.

He then states the purpose for which the graces of the Spirit are bestowed upon him. These graces are given that he might *preach the gospel to the poor.* Hence we conclude that those who are sent by God to preach the gospel are given the necessary gifts to qualify them for so important an office.

It is, therefore, ridiculous that, under the pretense of a divine calling, men totally unfit for discharging the office should take upon themselves the name of pastor. We are expressly told that the Lord anoints his servants, because the true and efficacious preaching of the gospel, as Paul says, does not lie "in the enticing words of man's wisdom," but in the heavenly power of the Spirit.

FOR MEDITATION: When God calls us to work for him, he promises to equip us for that work. What does it say, then, if we miserably fail at the duties that we undertake for him? Are we relying too much on our own strength and too little on the Spirit? Is this pursuit outside of his will? Let us use such failure to examine our dependence on the Spirit in all we do.

Becoming Poor in Spirit

Blessed are the poor in spirit: for theirs is the kingdom of heaven.
Matthew 5:3
SUGGESTED FURTHER READING: Luke 21:1–4

Luke says those who are "poor" are blessed, for they will possess the kingdom of God. Poverty for many people is a cursed and unhappy experience. Many are pressed down by distress, yet they continue to swell inwardly with pride and cruelty. So Matthew more clearly expresses the intention of Christ by saying that *the poor in spirit* are blessed. Christ thereby pronounces that only those will truly be happy who, though chastened and subdued by afflictions, submit wholly to God and with inward humility come to him for protection.

Others say those who are *poor in spirit* claim nothing for themselves. They are so completely emptied of confidence in the flesh that they acknowledge their poverty. But as the words of Luke and of Matthew must have the same meaning, there can be no doubt that *poor* here also applies to those who are oppressed and afflicted by adversity. The only difference is that Matthew, by adding *in spirit*, confines happiness only to those who, under the discipline of the cross, have learned to be humble.

In stating *for theirs is the kingdom of heaven*, Christ does not swell the minds of his own people by any unfounded belief, or harden them by unfeeling obstinacy, as the Stoics do. Rather, he leads them to the hope of eternal life and encourages them to be patient by assuring them that, by being *poor in spirit*, they will pass into the heavenly kingdom of God.

Only those who are reduced to nothing in themselves and who rely upon the mercy of God are truly *poor in spirit*, for those who are broken or overwhelmed by despair and murmur against God prove thereby to be of a proud and haughty spirit.

FOR MEDITATION: What would it take for you to become genuinely poor in spirit—loss of a job, health, child, spouse, money, or reputation? Pray that God will not have to use such losses to break your pride and self-sufficiency, but, if such losses do occur, come in true humility to him, asking for forgiveness for any haughtiness of heart. Ask him to deliver you from bitterness and pride.

Striving for Purity and Peace

Blessed are the pure in heart: for they shall see God. Blessed are the peacemakers: for they shall be called the children of God. Matthew 5:8–9
SUGGESTED FURTHER READING: Genesis 26:12–33

Purity of heart is universally acknowledged to be the mother of all virtues. Yet hardly one person in a hundred does not put craftiness in the place of the greatest virtue. Hence people are commonly considered to be happy whose cleverness is exercised in the successful practice of deceit and who gain dexterous advantages by indirect means over those with whom they deal.

Christ does not agree with this carnal reasoning. He pronounces those happy who take no delight in cunning but sincerely converse with people and express nothing by word or look that they do not feel in their hearts. Simple people are ridiculed for lack of caution and for not looking sharp enough to themselves. But Christ directs us to higher views. He bids us to consider that, if we do not have the cleverness to deceive others in this world, we will enjoy the sight of God in heaven.

Blessed are the peacemakers, he says. By "peacemakers," he means those who not only seek peace and avoid quarrels as much as possible but who also labor to settle differences among others, advise people to live at peace, and remove every reason for hatred and strife.

There are good grounds for this statement. It is tedious and irksome work to reconcile those who are at odds. People of a mild disposition who study to promote peace are compelled to endure the indignity of reproaches, complaints, and arguments from others on all sides. The reason is that everyone wants advocates to defend their cause. So that we may not depend on the favor of men, Christ directs us to look to the judgment of his Father, who is the God of peace (Rom. 15:33), and accounts us as his children when we cultivate peace, even if our efforts are not acceptable to others. *They shall be called* means to be accounted as *children of God.*

FOR MEDITATION: Are you at odds with anyone today? Are you so stung with pain from a quarrel or injury done to you that you cannot bear to think of speaking to that person? Are friends or family members likewise alienated from each other? How could you look to the judgment of God the Father to effect peace in your relationships?

Rejoicing in Persecution

Blessed are they which are persecuted for righteousness' sake: for theirs is the kingdom of heaven. Matthew 5:10

SUGGESTED FURTHER READING: Matthew 10:15–26

True disciples of Christ greatly need this instruction of Matthew, for the harder and more disagreeable it is for us to admit it, the more earnestly we ought to make being *persecuted for righteousness' sake* the subject of our meditation.

We cannot be Christ's soldiers under any other condition, for the greater part of the world will rise in hostility against us and pursue us even to death. The state of the matter is this: Satan, the prince of the world, will never cease to fill his followers with rage to carry on hostilities against believers in Christ. It is, no doubt, monstrous and unnatural that men who try to live a righteous life should be attacked and tormented in a way that they do not deserve. As Peter says, "Who is he that will harm you, if ye be followers of that which is good?' (1 Peter 3:13).

Yet, as a consequence of the unbridled wickedness of the world, too frequently good men in their righteous zeal arouse the resentments of the ungodly against them. Above all, it is normal for Christians to be hated by the majority of men, for the flesh cannot endure the doctrine of the gospel and have its vices reproved.

It is typical for the godly to inflame the hatred and provoke the rage of wicked men against them, because in their earnest desire to do what is good and right, they oppose bad causes and defend good ones as much as lies in their power. In this respect, the truth of God justly holds first rank. By the mark of persecution, Christ distinguishes his own martyrs from criminals and evildoers.

FOR MEDITATION: When have we come to the Lord objecting to the evil that others do against us for righteousness' sake? If we are never persecuted, we must ask ourselves whether or not we even stand for righteousness. How do Christ's words here transform the painful experience of persecution into blessing and reward? Consider that the next time you suffer on account of your stand for Christ and his righteousness.

Finding Grace to Obey

Think not that I am come to destroy the law, or the prophets: I am not come to destroy, but to fulfil. Matthew 5:17

SUGGESTED FURTHER READING: Galatians 3:19–29

God promised a new covenant when Christ came to earth. At the same time, he said the new covenant would not be different from the old. Rather, its purpose would be to give perpetual sanction to the covenant that he had made with his own people from the beginning. God says, "I will write my law ... in their hearts, and I will remember their iniquities no more" (Jer. 31:33–34). By these words, the Lord is far from departing from the former covenant. On the contrary, he declares that the old covenant will be confirmed and ratified when it is succeeded by the new.

With respect to this teaching, we must not imagine that the coming of Christ frees us from the authority of the law, for the law is the eternal rule of a devout and holy life. It must, therefore, be as unchangeable as the justice of God, which it embraces as constant and uniform. There is some appearance of change in some ceremonies related to the law. But it is only the use of these rituals that is abolished, not their meaning, for that meaning is more fully confirmed in the new covenant. The coming of Christ takes nothing away even from ceremonies; rather, it confirms them as shadows of the truth. When we see their full effect, we acknowledge that they are not vain or useless.

Let us therefore learn to maintain as unbreakable the sacred tie between the law and gospel, which many improperly attempt to break. It is easier to confirm the authority of the gospel when we learn that it is nothing less than a fulfillment of the law. Both unite in declaring God as their author.

FOR MEDITATION: There is no disharmony between the law and the gospel: both aim for the glory of God in saving sinners. This implies many things about how we understand the Christian life. For example, how does grace free us to obey God and walk more willingly in his ways? Do you regard obedience to God's law as a tedious trial?

Loving our Neighbor

Ye have heard that it hath been said, Thou shalt love thy neighbour, and hate thine enemy. Matthew 5:43
SUGGESTED FURTHER READING: Leviticus 19:9–18

It is astonishing that the scribes in Jesus' day came to such a point of absurdity that they limited the meaning of the word *neighbour* to benevolent persons. Nothing is more obvious or certain than that God, in speaking of loving our neighbor, is referring to the entire human race.

Every man by nature is devoted to himself. When we interrupt personal convenience to show acts of kindness, we depart from the kind of action that nature itself dictates. So, to encourage the exercise of loving others, God assures us that all people are our neighbors because they are related to us by nature. Whenever I see another person, I must of necessity behold myself as in a mirror, for that person is "my bone and my flesh" (Gen. 29:14). Though most people tend to break away from this kind of unity, their depravity does not violate the order of nature, for God is the author of brotherly love.

Hence we conclude that the precept of the law, by which we are commanded to love our neighbor, refers to all people. The love that God requires in his law does not look at what a man deserves but extends to the unworthy, the wicked, and the ungrateful. Now we see the true intent of this verse: to show that Christ restores and vindicates us from malicious falsehoods concerning God's law. He does not introduce a new law but corrects the wicked excesses of the scribes, by which the purity of the divine law had been corrupted.

FOR MEDITATION: When have you resisted helping people in trouble, saying they brought it on themselves? Have you shunned those who are ungodly or cut off those who are ungrateful? Rather than limiting the law, as the scribes did, let us be challenged by Christ's teaching to extend love to anyone in need.

Praying in Secret

But thou, when thou prayest, enter into thy closet, and when thou hast shut thy door, pray to thy Father which is in secret; and thy Father which seeth in secret shall reward thee openly. Matthew 6:6
SUGGESTED FURTHER READING: Luke 18:1–14

We are commanded in many passages to pray to God or to praise him in the public assembly, amid a crowd and before all the people. We are to do that not only to testify of our faith or gratitude before others, but also to excite them by our example to do likewise. Christ does not discourage us from such an exercise, but he does warn us to always have God before our eyes when we engage in prayer.

We must not literally interpret the words *enter into thy closet*, as if Christ asks us to avoid the presence of other people, or declares that we do not pray rightly unless there are no witnesses. He speaks in a comparative sense, saying that we should seek privacy in praying rather than before a crowd of witnesses.

It is advantageous, indeed, to believers and contributes to their pouring out prayers and groans with greater freedom before God for them to withdraw from the gaze of others. Retiring from the public is also useful for another reason: that our minds may be more free and disengaged from all distracting thoughts. Accordingly, Christ frequently chooses to hide himself from others by going to an isolated spot to pray.

But the main purpose of this verse is to correct the desire of self-glorification. Whether a person prays alone or in the presence of others, he ought to have the same feelings as if he were shut up in his closet and had no other witness but God. Furthermore, when Christ says, *thy Father shall reward thee*, he plainly declares that the reward that is promised to us in any part of Scripture is not paid as a debt, but is a free gift.

FOR MEDITATION: To spend adequate time in private prayer with God is not easy. In a world driven by productivity and bound by the clock, it can even seem like an unproductive use of time. Nothing is further from the truth, however. Then, too, praying before others can earn us praise and puff us up. That distracts us from the true aim of prayer, which is to focus on God. In light of our many failures in prayer, the reward Jesus speaks of is paid not as a debt, but as a free gift. Let us emulate our Savior in how he prayed, whether before others or in private; in both, he sought only the will and honor of his Father in heaven.

The Right Way to Pray

After this manner therefore pray ye. Matthew 6:9
SUGGESTED FURTHER READING: I Samuel 2:1–11

Jesus tells us we are free to offer six petitions to God. Nothing is more advantageous to us than such instruction. Though prayer is the most important exercise of piety, yet in forming our prayers and regulating our wishes, all our senses too often fail us. No person will pray aright unless his lips and heart are directed by the heavenly Master.

For this reason Christ tells us how to form our prayers so that they can be accounted lawful and approved by God. It is not the intent of the Son of God to prescribe the exact words we must use to limit our freedom from departing from the words he has dictated. Rather, his intent is to guide and restrain our wishes that they might not go beyond certain limits. Hence we infer that the guide for prayer that he gives us relates not to the words themselves but to the petitions they represent.

The first three petitions refer to the glory of God, without any regard to ourselves. The remaining petitions refer to those things that are necessary for our salvation. Likewise, the law of God is divided into tables, of which the former contains the duties of piety and the latter the duties of charity. So in prayer, Christ invites us to consider and seek the glory of God first and then to ask him to consider our own interests.

We know that we have the right approach to prayer if we give first place to the honor and glory of God, then earnestly give expression to ourselves and our own concerns. It would be altogether preposterous to mind only what belongs to ourselves while disregarding the kingdom of God, which is of far greater importance.

FOR MEDITATION: If our prayers seem to stumble, perhaps we are failing to honor what Christ himself taught us about formulating our prayers. Consider framing your prayers according to the guidelines offered here and in the Lord's Prayer. This may be a challenge for us, since we are not prone to be as earnest about God's kingdom and glory as we are about our own daily needs. But the Holy Spirit can help us not to rush through the God-centered part of prayer and immediately move on to the things we want. What grace we need to truly pray!

Forgiven to Forgive

And forgive us our debts, as we forgive our debtors. Matthew 6:12
SUGGESTED FURTHER READING: Matthew 18:21–35

The forgiveness from debts that we ask for in prayer is inconsistent with the way unbelievers try to purchase freedom from what they owe to others. For the creditor who receives payment for what is owed to him does not truly forgive those debts. Rather, a person forgives when he willingly and generously departs from his just claim and frees the debtor of all obligations.

If debts are freely forgiven us, all compensations disappear. There is no other meaning possible in this verse, for God grants the pardon of those who owe him debts by removing the condemnation that they deserve.

Christ adds the condition *as we forgive our debtors* so that we may not presume to approach God for forgiveness unless we are pure and free from all resentment against others. Yet the forgiveness that we ask of God does not depend on the forgiveness that we grant to others. Rather, the purpose of Christ here is to teach us how to forgive the offenses that have been committed against us. When we forgive, we give evidence of the impression of God's seal on us and ratify confidence in our own forgiveness.

Christ's intent is not to point out the reason for our forgiveness but to remind us of how we should cherish others when we want to be reconciled to God. Certainly, if the Spirit of God reigns in our hearts, every kind of ill will and revenge ought to be banished in us. The Spirit is the witness of our adoption (Rom. 8:16), so forgiving others is a mark of grace that distinguishes us as children of God rather than strangers. The name *debtors* is given, not to those who owe us money or any other service, but to those who are in debt to us because of offenses that they have committed against us.

FOR MEDITATION: When people wrong us, how easy—even satisfying—it is to hold the offense against them. Our anger rises if they do not come to us, begging for forgiveness. But if we hold on to that debt, how can we ask God to forgive the offenses we continually commit against him? When we consider the amazing, forgiving grace we find in God through his Son's satisfaction for our innumerable sins, how can we not readily and cheerfully forgive others when their offenses amount to the smallest fraction of our offenses toward God?

Guarding against Worry

Therefore I say unto you, Take no thought for your life, what ye shall eat, or what ye shall drink; nor yet for your body, what ye shall put on. Is not the life more than meat, and the body than raiment? Matthew 6:25
SUGGESTED FURTHER READING: Philippians 4:6–20

Christ reproves the excessive anxiety that people have about having enough food and clothing, but he also offers a remedy for curing this disease. When he forbids people to be anxious, he does not intend that they give up all concerns, for we know that people by nature have such concerns.

But excessive care is condemned for two reasons: either because people can annoy and vex themselves to no good purpose by being more anxious than is proper or their calling demands, or because they take more burdens on themselves than they have a right to do. They rely so heavily on their own efforts that they fail to call upon God to provide.

To guard against such excessive care, we should remember the promise that while unbelievers "rise up early, and sit up late, and eat the bread of sorrows," believers will obtain rest and sleep through the kindness of God (Ps. 127:2). Though the children of God are not free from work and anxiety, yet we can properly say they do not have to be anxious about life. They may enjoy calm repose because of their reliance on the providence of God.

It is thus clear how far we should go in caring about food. Each of us ought to work as far as his calling requires and the Lord commands; and each of us ought to be led by our own wants to call upon God. We must find the intermediate place between indolent carelessness and unnecessary torments by which unbelievers kill themselves. If we give proper attention to the words of Christ, we will find that he does not forbid every kind of care but only that which arises from distrust. *Take no thought for what ye shall eat or what ye shall drink*, he says. Distrust belongs to those who tremble for fear of poverty or hunger as if they may be short of provisions at any moment.

FOR MEDITATION: What if I lose my job, if my house payment rises beyond my ability to pay, if I have a heart attack, if I can't afford to send my children to college—do such "what ifs" keep you awake at night, fretting about life's possibilities? How can you find rest in Jesus' assurance that God will provide for you, no matter what?

Finding Fault

Judge not, that ye be not judged. Matthew 7:1
SUGGESTED FURTHER READING: James 4:1–12

"Judge not" is not an absolute prohibition against criticism. Rather, Jesus' words here are intended to cure a disease that is natural to us all.

We all have the tendency to flatter ourselves while passing severe censure on others. This vice provides us with a kind of strange enjoyment, for hardly anyone exists who is not tickled with the desire of asking about other people's faults. Yet we also acknowledge that it is an intolerable evil to overlook one's own vices while being critical of others.

The heathen in ancient times cited proverbs to condemn such inconsistencies, for the tendency to excuse ourselves while faulting others has existed in all ages as well as today. What is more, judging often includes another, worse sin, for most people who condemn others then think they have more freedom themselves to sin.

Jesus warns against the depraved eagerness for backbiting, censuring, and slandering others when he says, *Judge not.* He is not saying that believers should be blind to the faults of others, perceiving nothing, but only that they should refrain from the undue eagerness to judge. If they indulge themselves, everyone who wants to pass sentence on others will exceed the boundaries set by Christ.

Judging may also be influenced by wrongful curiosity about the actions of others. This disease includes the injustice of magnifying any trivial fault of others, as if it were a very heinous crime. In addition, it includes the insolent presumption of looking disdainfully at every action of others, passing unfavorable judgment on it even when it might be viewed in a good light.

FOR MEDITATION: This frequently quoted verse is often cited to excuse sin, contrary to Christ's original intent. Those of us who are fond of quoting it forget that we, too, will be judged by Christ himself. Does the coming Judgment Day ever humble you and rein in your quickness to judge others? The next time you are about to criticize someone, stop yourself and ask whether you could and should express that disapproval in a loving manner directly to that person (see Matt. 18:15–17).

How is Jesus' admonition not to judge a cure for the common kind of fault-finding that alienates people from others? What steps can you take to eradicate criticizing others from your thoughts and speech?

Praying for Pardon in Disease

And, behold, they brought to him a man sick of the palsy, lying on a bed: and Jesus seeing their faith said unto the sick of the palsy; Son, be of good cheer; thy sins be forgiven thee. Matthew 9:2
SUGGESTED FURTHER READING: Isaiah 2:1–5

Christ seems to offer the paralytic something different from what the sick man has requested. Since Christ intends to bestow health of body, he begins by removing the man's sin, the cause of the disease, reminding the paralytic of the origin of his disease and of the way in which he ought to pray.

People usually do not consider that the afflictions they endure are God's chastisements. They want relief from disease in the flesh, but at the same time they feel no concern about their sins. It is like a sick man who ignores his disease and only seeks relief from the present pain it causes.

The only way to obtain deliverance from all evils is to have God reconciled to us. It does sometimes happen that wicked men are freed from their distresses even when God is still their enemy. But if they think they have completely escaped punishment, the same evils may immediately return or more numerous and heavy calamities will overwhelm them. That will make it clear that their sorrows cannot be eased or ended until the wrath of God is appeased, as God declares through the prophet Amos: "As if a man did flee from a lion, and a bear met him; or went into the house, and leaned his hand on the wall, and a serpent bit him" (Amos 5:19).

Scripture frequently speaks about the promise of pardoning sin when people seek relief from punishment. So when afflictions remind us of our sins, let us first be careful to pray for pardon, so that when God is reconciled to us, he may withdraw his hand from punishing us.

FOR MEDITATION: The world abounds today with geo-political, medical, and natural crises that are crying out for justice and healing. All are merely symptomatic of the deeper problem of unforgiven sin. As we reach out to the suffering who are caught in one crisis or another, we must never make the forgiveness of sins secondary; real justice and real healing are inseparable from forgiveness. But what about you? When you suffer from cancer or heart disease or Type 1 diabetes, do you ask the Lord for forgiveness of sin? If you are not reconciled to God through Christ, forgiveness is precisely what you need. Without forgiveness of sin, healing of the body is meaningless.

Revealing Truth to Babes

At that time Jesus answered and said, I thank thee, O Father, Lord of heaven and earth, because thou hast hid these things from the wise and prudent, and hast revealed them unto babes. Matthew 11:25

SUGGESTED FURTHER READING: 1 Corinthians 2

It is no small matter that Christ here addresses the Father as *Lord of heaven and earth,* for in this manner he declares that God's will is that the wise remain blind while the ignorant and unlearned people receive the mysteries of the gospel. There are many other passages that similarly point out to us that those who arrive at salvation are freely chosen by God because he is the Creator and Governor of the world, and all nations are his.

This teaching implies two things. First, those who do not obey the gospel do so not because they lack the power of God, who could easily bring all creatures into subjection to his government. Second, some arrive at faith while others remain hardened and obstinate to it because of God's free election. For in drawing some and passing by others, God alone makes a distinction among men whose condition is by nature alike.

In choosing to reveal things to little children rather than the wise, God regards his own glory rather than the flesh, which is too apt to rise. If able and learned men lead the way, the general conviction of people would be to find faith by their own skill or work or learning. In no other way can the mercy of God be so fully known than by making a choice that clearly shows that whatever people offer in themselves is nothing.

Therefore human wisdom is justly thrown down so it may not obscure the praise of divine grace.

FOR MEDITATION: Our eyes are blind by nature, and we are unwilling and unable to open them. We do not want to see the truth. If our eyes have been opened, that should humble us; it is not on account of our wisdom or prudence but only because of God's grace. He brings us to himself when we are nothing so that we might know that he is the author and finisher of our faith.

Longing for Relief

Come unto me, all ye that labour and are heavy laden, and I will give you rest. Matthew 11:28

SUGGESTED FURTHER READING: Psalm 62

Christ now kindly invites those whom he sees are fit to become his disciples. Though he is ready to reveal the Father to all people, yet most are careless about coming to him because they are not convinced of their need to do so.

Hypocrites are not concerned about following Christ because they are too intoxicated with their own righteousness. They neither "hunger nor thirst" (Matt. 5:6) for his grace. In addition, those who are devoted to the world set no value on heavenly life. It would be useless, therefore, for Christ to invite these kinds of people to come to him. So he turns to the wretched and afflicted who labor or groan under a burden. That does not generally refer to those who are oppressed with grief and trials but specifically to those who are overwhelmed by their sins, are filled with alarm at the wrath of God, and are ready to sink under that weighty burden.

God uses various methods to humble his elect, but since most people who are loaded with afflictions still remain obstinate and rebellious, Christ specifically calls those whose consciences are distressed by the fear of eternal death. They are so inwardly pressed down by their miseries that they faint, and this very fainting prepares them for receiving God's grace. Jesus tells us that most people despise his grace because they are not sensible of their poverty, but their pride or folly is no reason to keep back those afflicted souls that long for relief.

FOR MEDITATION: Are you pressed out of measure because of the weight of your sin? Are you burdened by the thought of appearing before your eternal Maker and Judge? Do you long for relief from his impending wrath? If so, Christ kindly and gently invites you to come to him. He will give you rest.

Praising Christ Inadequately

And it came to pass, as he spake these things, a certain woman of the company lifted up her voice, and said unto him, Blessed is the womb that bare thee, and the paps which thou hast sucked. Luke 11:27
SUGGESTED FURTHER READING: Luke 18:18–34

Christ corrects what the woman says here. He does this because people are inclined to neglect even those gifts of God that they regard with astonishment and on which they bestow the highest praise.

In applauding Christ, the woman fails to mention what is most important: that in Christ salvation is exhibited to all. Her words are a feeble tribute because they fail to mention his grace and power that are extended to all. Christ justly claims for himself another kind of praise, not that his mother alone is blessed for bearing him, but that he brings to us perfect and eternal happiness.

We fail to do justice to the excellence of Christ until we consider the reason why the Father gave Christ to us. We must perceive the benefits that he brings to us so that we who are wretched in ourselves may become happy in him.

Why does Christ say nothing about himself and mention only the Word of God? He does this to open up all his treasures to us, for without the Word of God Jesus would have no conversation with us, or we with him. In communicating himself to us by the Word, he rightly and properly calls us to hear and keep that Word, so that by faith he may become ours.

We now see the difference between Christ's reply and the woman's commendation, for the blessedness that she limits to his mother is a favor that he offers freely to all. He shows us that we ought to have no ordinary esteem for him because all the treasures of life, blessedness, and glory are hidden in him (Col. 2:3). He dispenses those to us by the Word so they may be communicated to those who embrace the Word by faith; for God's free adoption of us, which we obtain by faith, is the key to the kingdom of heaven.

FOR MEDITATION: Many people praise Jesus inadequately. They esteem Jesus as a good teacher, an excellent example, and a good man, but they miss the major point of who he is and of his mission. Have you fallen prey to the temptation to focus on aspects of Jesus' ministry that are peripheral to the atonement, which was his main purpose?

Experiencing Only Temporary Faith

Yet hath he not root in himself, but dureth for a while: for when tribulation or persecution ariseth because of the word, by and by he is offended. Matthew 13:21

SUGGESTED FURTHER READING: 2 Chronicles 25

Christ says people with temporary faith eventually feel uneasy when they begin to experience the offense of the cross. Certainly, as the heat of the sun uncovers the barrenness of the soil, so persecution and the cross lay open the pride of those who are slightly influenced by but are not actually moved by earnest feelings of piety.

According to Matthew and Mark, such people are temporary. They may profess for a time that they are disciples of Christ, but they soon fall away through temptation. So they only imagine that they have true faith. According to Luke, their faith is temporary because the honor that they render to the gospel merely resembles faith.

They are not truly regenerated by the incorruptible seed that never fades, as Peter tells us (1 Peter 1:4). The words of Isaiah, "The word of our God shall stand for ever" (Isa. 40:8; 1 Peter 1:25), are only fulfilled in the hearts of believers in whom the truth of God, once fixed, never passes away but retains its vigor to the end.

Still, people who take delight in the Word of God and cherish some reverence for it do in some manner believe, for they are vastly different from unbelievers who give no credit to God when he speaks or who reject his Word.

But let us be sure from this teaching that no one partakes of true faith except those who are sealed with the Spirit of adoption and who sincerely call on God as their Father. Because that Spirit is never extinguished, it is impossible that the true faith that the Spirit engraves on the hearts of the godly will ever pass away or be destroyed.

FOR MEDITATION: We may repent of our sins outwardly and even respect God's Word, absorbing its teaching week after week at church and in Bible study, and getting a certain amount of joy from it. But if we repeatedly succumb to temptation without heart-sorrow and fail to change our ways, even when we are reprimanded by other godly people, we should beware lest our faith be only temporary.

Uprooting the Thorns

He also that received seed among the thorns is he that heareth the word; and the care of this world, and the deceitfulness of riches, choke the word, and he becometh unfruitful. Matthew 13:22

SUGGESTED FURTHER READING: Matthew 6:19–24

Jesus teaches us here about another kind of believer: those people who seem open to receiving the word of life but eventually permit other things to corrupt it and make it ineffective in their lives.

The thorns that destroy the Word's effect are the pleasures of this life, wicked desires, covetousness, and other anxieties of the flesh. Matthew mentions only the cares of this life along with covetousness, but the meaning is the same as in Luke, for in that term he includes the allurements of pleasures (which Luke mentions) and every kind of desire. Just as corn, which might be productive, no sooner rises as a stalk than it is choked by thorns and other matters injurious to its growth, so the sinful desires of the flesh prevail over the hearts of men and overcome temporary faith, thus destroying the power of the heavenly doctrine before it reaches maturity.

Though sinful desires exert their power on the hearts of people before the Word of the Lord springs up into blades of corn, initially their influence is not evident. Only when the corn matures and promises fruit do these worldly desires gradually make their appearance.

Each of us, therefore, ought to tear out the thorns in our hearts to prevent the Word of God from being choked in us, for there is no one whose heart is not filled with a vast quantity of, indeed, a thick forest of thorns. What is more, the number of thorns is so prodigious that it ought to shake off our laziness, which is the reason why most people do not trouble themselves about the thorns.

FOR MEDITATION: Has studying the Word of God become dull and tedious to you? Have you become so busy that reading the Bible has only become perfunctory? Are the sorrows and cares of life intruding on your prayers as so many thorns? If so, beware lest the thorns of life gain such root that they choke off your faith. Take the hardness of your heart to the Lord and ask him to soften it and pour new life into it.

Commending Fruit-Bearers

But he that received seed into the good ground is he that heareth the word, and understandeth it; which also beareth fruit, and bringeth forth, some an hundredfold, some sixty, some thirty. Matthew 13:23

SUGGESTED FURTHER READING: Ephesians 1

Those whom Christ refers to as good and fertile soil for the Word of God are people in whom the Word not only deeply and solidly roots itself but who also overcome every obstacle that prevents the Word from bearing fruit.

Is it possible for anyone to be pure and free from thorns? To answer that, we must realize that Christ does not refer here to those who are perfect in faith but only to those in whom the Word of God bears fruit. Though the fruit may not be profuse, yet those who do not fall away from the sincere worship of God are reckoned as good and fertile soil.

No doubt we ought to work hard to pull out thorns of worldliness in our lives, but even our hardest efforts will never succeed in removing all of them. Some thorns will always be left behind. But let us at least try to deaden those thorns so they may not choke off the fruit of the Word. This is confirmed by Christ's teaching that follows, informing us that everyone does not yield fruit in an equal degree.

The fertility of the soil that has a 30 percent yield is small compared with soil that yields 100 percent, yet our Lord classes together all soil that does not disappoint the work and expectations of the seed-sower. Hence we have no right to despise those who produce a lesser degree of excellence, for the master of the house, who gives preference to one above another because of more abundant produce, yet bestows the general designation of "good" even on inferior soils.

FOR MEDITATION: Some people seem to be naturally gifted leaders in the church, raise children in the faith with seemingly little effort, and succeed in evangelizing others at every opportunity without any hesitation. They communicate well spiritually, live close to the Lord, and are filled with Christ and genuine joy in believing. These 100 percent yielders intimidate us who struggle at producing even 30 percent. But according to our Lord, all believers are reckoned as "good soil" if the Word of God flourishes in them. Take heart in our Savior's encouragement to stand firm in the faith, and ask for grace to bear more fruit in days to come, to his praise.

Entertaining to Excess

Now it came to pass, as they went, that he entered into a certain village: and a certain woman named Martha received him into her house. Luke 10:38

SUGGESTED FURTHER READING: Ecclesiastes 3:1–8

The hospitality of Martha deserves praise. Jesus does commend it, yet he also points out two faults in it. The first is that Martha is excessive in her hospitality and carries it beyond proper bounds. Christ would prefer to be entertained in a simple manner and at moderate expense rather than to subject this holy woman to such hard work.

The second problem is that, by distracting her attention and undertaking more work than is necessary, Martha deprives herself of the blessing of Christ's visit. This excess is noted by Luke when he speaks of Martha's "much serving," for Christ is satisfied with little. It is like offering a magnificent reception to a prophet while not caring enough to listen to him. It is making such great and unnecessary preparations that all the teaching is buried. The true way of receiving prophets is to accept the advantage that God offers to us through their ministry.

We now see that the kind attention of Martha, though deserving of praise, is not unblemished. Furthermore, Martha is so delighted with her own bustling that she even despises her sister Mary's pious eagerness to receive instruction from Christ. This account warns us that in doing what is right we must take care not to think more highly of ourselves than of others.

FOR MEDITATION: Have you ever been so preoccupied with entertaining guests that you had no time to interact with them? Were you so busy in the kitchen that you never sat long enough to listen to what your guests had to say? If so, you may be doing what Martha does—opening her home to Jesus without giving him her heart. We all need to pray for grace to set our priorities rightly and to learn lifelong moderation.

Tasting Heaven and Hell

And in hell he lift up his eyes, being in torments, and seeth Abraham afar off, and Lazarus in his bosom. Luke 16:23
SUGGESTED FURTHER READING: James 2

Christ is telling a story here to describe spiritual matters in terms of people who will pull at our senses. Souls have neither fingers nor eyes and are not liable to thirst, nor do they hold such conversations among themselves as are described here between Abraham and the rich man. But our Lord draws a picture here that represents the life to come in a way that we can relate to it.

The general truth conveyed here is that believing souls that have left their bodies will have a joyful and blessed life beyond this world. The reprobate, by contrast, will endure such dreadful torments that our minds can hardly conceive of those anymore than we can conceive of the boundless glory of heaven. Only in a small measure—enlightened by the Spirit of God—can we taste by hope the glory promised to us, which far exceeds all our senses. Let it be enough to know that the vengeance of God that awaits the ungodly is so inconceivably horrible that Christ describes it in an obscure manner, only so far as is necessary to strike terror in us.

On the subjects of heaven and hell, Christ gives us slender information and in a manner fitting to restrain curiosity. The wicked are described as fearfully tormented by the misery that they feel. They beg for relief but are cut off from hope, thus experiencing double torment.

In this story we hear a conversation between people who ordinarily would have had no communication with each other. When the rich man says, "Father Abraham," he expresses the additional torment of realizing, too late, that he is cut off from the number of the children of Abraham.

FOR MEDITATION: In what way can we relate to the extreme suffering of the rich man? To the incomprehensible glory of Lazarus? Jesus offers us enough fodder to make us question how we are living today. Are we kneeling in faith before Christ, who alone can save us? Or are we relying on our conduct or the faith of our fathers to get us into heaven?

The Enticing Snare of Wealth

Then said Jesus unto his disciples, Verily I say unto you, That a rich man shall hardly enter into the kingdom of heaven. Matthew 19:23
SUGGESTED FURTHER READING: Deuteronomy 8:11–20

Lusting for wealth is such a deadly disease that it may prevent us from going to heaven, Christ tells us here.

In Mark, Christ softens the harshness of this warning by restricting it to those who place "confidence in riches." But these words are, I think, intended to confirm rather than correct the former statement. It is as if Jesus once more asserts that people ought not to think it strange that entering the kingdom of heaven is difficult for the rich because they tend to trust in their riches. Yet this teaching is highly useful to all: to the rich, that being warned of their danger, they may be on their guard; to the poor, that being satisfied with their lot, they may not so eagerly desire what would bring them more damage than gain.

It is true that riches do not by themselves hinder us from following God. Rather, one result of the depravity of the human mind is that it is scarcely possible for those who have much to avoid being intoxicated by such riches. Those who are excessively rich are held by Satan, bound, as it were, by such chains that they cannot raise their thoughts to heaven. They are so busy and entangled with possessions that they become utter slaves to this world.

The illustration of threading a camel through the eye of a needle, which follows, amplifies the difficulty of rich people entering the kingdom of heaven. It tells us the rich tend to be so swelled with pride and presumption that they cannot tolerate being reduced to the narrow places through which God makes his people pass. I think that the word "camel" here refers to a rope used by sailors rather than to the animal so named.

FOR MEDITATION: If we are wealthy, let us heed Jesus' warning here and examine ourselves closely. But let us also remember that it is not necessary to have much in order to become infatuated by wealth. How many of us do not want a bigger house, a newer car, a better rate of interest for our savings, greater advancement at work? The warning comes to all of us, regardless of poverty or riches: beware of becoming so entangled with earthly things that you lose sight of heaven.

Finding Refuge under his Wings

O Jerusalem, Jerusalem, thou that killest the prophets, and stonest them which are sent unto thee, how often would I have gathered thy children together, even as a hen gathereth her chickens under her wings, and ye would not! Matthew 23:37
SUGGESTED FURTHER READING: Romans 3:10–18

We now perceive the reason why Christ, speaking in the person of God, compares himself to "a hen." It is to inflict deeper disgrace on the wicked nation that had treated with disdain his gentle invitation. This invitation proceeds from more than maternal kindness. It is an amazing and unparalleled example of love that God does not disdain to stoop to those persuasions by which he might tame rebels into subjection.

Prophets were sent to "gather together" wandering and dispersed people into the bosom of God. By this he means that whenever the Word of God is exhibited to us, God opens his bosom to us with maternal kindness. Not satisfied with this, he condescends to the humble affection of a hen watching over her chickens. When he compares himself to a mother, he descends very far below his glory; how much more, then, when he takes the form of a hen and deigns to treat us as his chickens?

Besides, if this charge was justly brought against the ancient people who lived under the law, it is far more applicable to us. For though the complaints that we find in Isaiah are just in saying that in vain God spread out his hands every day to embrace a hard-hearted and rebellious people (Isa. 65:27), that though he rose up early (Jer. 7:13), he gained nothing by his incessant care of them; yet now, with far greater familiarity and kindness, he invites us to himself by his Son. Therefore, whenever he exhibits to us the doctrine of the gospel, dreadful vengeance awaits us if we do not quietly hide ourselves under his wings, by which he is ready to receive and shelter us. At the same time, Christ teaches us that all enjoy safety and rest who by the obedience of faith are "gathered together" to God; because *under his wings* they have an impregnable refuge.

FOR MEDITATION: If neither God's awesome majesty and power nor his gracious condescending love can draw us to him, what other proofs do we need that our hearts are deceitful and desperately wicked? Go to him with all your heart today, asking for forgiveness and mercy.

Persevering in Doing Good

And because iniquity shall abound, the love of many shall wax cold.
Matthew 24:12
SUGGESTED FURTHER READING: 2 Timothy 3

Every person ought to know how far and wide evil extends, but very few observe it. For as a consequence of the superior clearness with which the light of the gospel discovers the malice of men, even good and properly regulated minds grow cool and almost lose the desire to exercise benevolence. All reason with themselves that the duties they perform to one person or to another are thrown away, since experience and daily practice show that almost all are ungrateful, treacherous, or wicked. This is unquestionably a weighty and dangerous temptation, for what could be more unreasonable than to approve of a doctrine by which the desire of doing good and the demands of charity appear to be diminished?

When the gospel makes its appearance, charity, which ought to kindle the hearts of all men with its warmth, rather grows cool. But we must observe the source of this evil, which Christ points out, namely, that many lose courage because through their weakness they are unable to stem the flood of iniquity which flows on every hand. On the other hand, Christ requires courage from his followers to persist in striving against iniquity. Paul also enjoins us not to be weary of performing deeds of kindness and beneficence (2 Thes. 3:13).

Although the charity of many, when overwhelmed by the mass of iniquities, should give way, Christ warns believers that they must surmount this obstacle lest, overcome by bad examples, they apostatize. Therefore he repeats the statement in Matthew 24:13 that no man can be saved unless "he strive lawfully" (2 Tim. 2:5) so as to persevere to the end.

FOR MEDITATION: How often do we rationalize our way out of duties? Having observed its apparent futility, we abandon what God has commanded us to perform, as if we were excused from these duties. But this is foolish disobedience; we can neither see the ultimate end of things, nor are we called to judge which commands of God seem most useful and profitable to obey. Is there a Christian duty you have been shirking?

Ye Have Done it unto Me

And the King shall answer and say unto them, Verily I say unto you, Inasmuch as ye have done it unto one of the least of these my brethren, ye have done it unto me. Matthew 25:40
SUGGESTED FURTHER READING: Acts 9:1–18

Christ has just told us that our senses do not yet comprehend how highly he values deeds of charity. Now he openly declares that he will reckon as done to himself whatever we have bestowed on his people. We must be extremely sluggish if our compassion is not aroused by this statement that Christ is either neglected or honored in the persons of those who need our assistance. So whenever we are reluctant to assist the poor, let us place before our eyes the Son of God, to whom it would be base sacrilege to refuse anything.

By these words Christ likewise shows that he acknowledges those acts of kindness that have been performed gratuitously and without any expectation of a reward. Certainly, when he enjoins us to do good to the hungry and naked, to strangers and prisoners, from whom nothing can be expected in return, we must look to him who freely lays himself under obligation to us and allows us to place to his account what might otherwise appear to have been lost.

Inasmuch as ye have done it unto one of the least of these my brethren expressly recommends believers to our notice. In this Christ does not bid us to altogether despise unbelievers. Though a common tie binds together all the children of Adam, a still more sacred union exists among the children of God. So because those who belong to the household of faith ought to be preferred to strangers, Christ makes special mention of them.

Though Christ's design was to encourage those whose wealth and resources were abundant to relieve the poverty of brethren, yet it affords no ordinary consolation to the poor and distressed that, though shame and contempt follow them in the eyes of the world, yet the Son of God holds them as dear as his own members. Certainly, by calling them *brethren,* he confers on them inestimable honor.

FOR MEDITATION: Calvin points out the striking impact of Christ's words here. We are to treat our needy brothers and sisters as though we were relieving the needs of Christ himself. How much more gladly and sacrificially we would minister to those around us who are in need if we daily felt the weight of these words!

Advancing toward Death

Ye know that after two days is the feast of the passover, and the Son of man is betrayed to be crucified. Matthew 26:2
SUGGESTED FURTHER READING: John 10:1–18

Christ now again confirms what he formerly predicted to his disciples, but this latest prediction clearly shows how willingly he offers himself to die. It is necessary that he does so, because God could be appeased only by a sacrifice of obedience. At the same time, Christ says this to prevent the disciples from taking offense, lest they might be altogether discouraged by the thought that he will be dragged to death by necessity.

Two purposes are thus served by this statement: first, it testifies that the Son of God willingly surrenders himself to die to reconcile the world to the Father (for in no other way could the guilt of sins have been expiated or righteousness obtained for us), and, second, he did not die like one oppressed by violence from which he could not escape, but as one who voluntarily offered himself to die. He therefore declares that he comes to Jerusalem with the express intention of suffering death there, for while he was at liberty to withdraw and dwell in a safe retreat until that time came, he knowingly and willfully now comes forward at the exact time.

Though it was of no advantage to the disciples to be informed at that time of the obedience that Christ was rendering to the Father, yet afterward this doctrine contributed in no small degree to the edification of their faith. In like manner, this statement of Christ is especially helpful for us today because we behold, as in a bright mirror, the voluntary sacrifice by which all the transgressions of the world were blotted out. As we contemplate the Son of God advancing with cheerfulness and courage to death, we already behold him victorious over death.

FOR MEDITATION: The passion and crucifixion of Jesus Christ was not the tragic end of a life well lived. Rather, together with his resurrection, it was the climax of redemptive history. Jesus came to earth to give his life a ransom, and he did precisely that. What impact should the fact that the cross was his victory, not his defeat, have on our daily lives?

Possessed by Possessing

This he said, not that he cared for the poor; but because he was a thief, and had the bag, and bare what was put therein. John 12:6
SUGGESTED FURTHER READING: Ephesians 4:20–32

Judas resorts to a plausible pretext for his wickedness when he mentions *the poor,* whom he cares nothing about. We are taught by this instance what a frightful beast the desire of possessing is. The loss that Judas thinks that he has sustained by missing an opportunity for stealing excites him to such rage that he does not hesitate to betray Christ. In addition, it is probable that because what he said about the poor was defrauded, Judas not only spoke falsely to others, but likewise flattered himself inwardly, as hypocrites are prone to do. It was as if the act of betraying Christ was a trivial fault by which Judas endeavored to obtain compensation for the loss that he had sustained. He had but one reason for betraying Christ, which was to regain in some way the prey that had been snatched from his hands. For it was the indignation excited in him by the gain which he had lost that drove him to the design of betraying Christ.

It is amazing that Christ should have chosen as steward a person like Judas, whom he knew was a thief. For what other purpose might he have had than to put into this man's hands a rope for strangling himself? Mortal man can give no other reply than that the judgments of God are a deep gulf.

Yet the action of Christ ought not to be viewed as an ordinary rule that we should commit the care of the poor or anything sacred to a wicked and ungodly man. God has given us a law concerning those who are to be called to the government of the church and to other offices, and we are not at liberty to violate this law. The case was different with Christ, who, being the eternal Wisdom of God, furnished an opportunity for his secret predestination in the person of Judas.

FOR MEDITATION: How often we are prone to misjudge people—not only in thinking negatively of them when we have no right to do so, but also in thinking positively, when we are blind to their genuine faults. For those in positions of leadership, it can be an encouragement that even Christ had a traitor among his ranks. How can this provide us with emotional support in times when we are grieving that our familiar friend has lifted up his heel against us (Ps. 41:9)?

Finding Divine Vindication

When Jesus understood it, he said unto them, Why trouble ye the woman? for she hath wrought a good work upon me. Matthew 26:10
SUGGESTED FURTHER READING: Psalm 43

In his reply Christ does not merely defend the cause of one woman but likewise maintains the holy boasting of all who rest satisfied with having themselves and their works approved by God. It often happens that not only censure, but open condemnation, is pronounced on godly men who are convinced in their own consciences that what they do is agreeable to the command of God. Furthermore, they are accused of pride if they ignore the false judgments of the world and rest satisfied with being approved by God alone. Since this is a difficult temptation and it is scarcely possible not to be shaken by the agreement of many people against us, even when they are wrong, we ought to maintain this truth that none will ever be courageous and steady in acting properly unless they depend solely on the will of God.

Christ settles here the distinction between what is good and evil by his own solitary decision. By affirming what the woman has done as "a good work," when that action has already been condemned by the disciples, he represses the rashness of men who freely allow themselves to pronounce judgment.

Relying on this testimony, let us learn to set little value on any reports concerning us that are spread abroad in the world, provided we know that what men condemn, God approves. Let us learn to pay no deference to the opinions of men farther than that they may be edified by our example in obedience to God. When the world rises against us with a loud noise, let us satisfy ourselves with the consolation that what is reckoned bad on earth is pronounced good in heaven.

FOR MEDITATION: It is very often difficult to ignore the approbation or condemnation of men, especially considering the pride that lives in our hearts. Yet, as this passage makes clear, God judges actions by a different standard. We must strive to keep this in mind and to value God's evaluation to be infinitely more important than that of other men.

Submitting in Obedience

Now is my soul troubled; and what shall I say? Father, save me from this hour: but for this cause came I unto this hour. John 12:27
SUGGESTED FURTHER READING: Matthew 26:36–46

We may think it unbecoming for the Son of God to rashly utter a wish that he then immediately retracts to obey his Father. I readily admit that such is the folly of the cross that it gives offense to proud men. Yet the more the Lord of glory humbles himself, so much more illustrious is the manifestation of his vast love to us.

Besides, we ought to recollect that the human feelings, from which Christ was not exempt, were pure and free from sin in him, yet they were guided and regulated in obedience to God. There was nothing to prevent Christ from having a natural dread of death and yet be desirous of obeying God. This holds true in various respects. Hence he corrects himself by saying, *For this cause came I unto this hour.*

Christ may lawfully entertain a dread of death, yet, considering why he was sent and what his office as redeemer demands from him, he presents to his Father the dread which arises out of his natural disposition so that it may be subdued, or rather, having subdued it, he freely and willingly prepares to execute the command of God. Now, if the feelings of Christ, which were free from all sin, needed to be restrained in this manner, how earnestly ought we to apply his example to ourselves, since the numerous affections which spring from our flesh are such enemies to God. Let the godly therefore persevere in subduing themselves until they have denied themselves.

FOR MEDITATION: The unbelief that lives within us and the devious suggestions of the devil often conspire to pit our emotions against obedience to God. With these powerful emotions raging against our wills, obedience can seem utterly impossible. Yet, here we see Christ overcoming emotion and pushing forward toward the cross to purchase redemption for his people. How can we use his righteousness to resist the sway of our own emotions when they would deter us from obedience?

Rooted in the True Vine

I am the true vine, and my Father is the husbandman. John 15:1
SUGGESTED FURTHER READING: Hosea 14

Let us here remember the rule that ought to be observed in all parables, that we should not minutely examine every property of "the vine," but only take a general view of the object which Christ uses to apply his teaching.

There are three principal parts of this illustration of the vine: first, that we have no power of doing good except that which comes from Christ; second, that we, having been rooted in him, are dressed and pruned by the Father; third, that Christ removes the unfruitful branches in us so they may be thrown into the fire and burned.

Scarcely any are ashamed to acknowledge that every good thing that they possess comes from God, but after making this acknowledgment, they imagine that universal grace has been given to them as if it were implanted in them by nature. But Christ principally dwells on this, that the vital sap—all life and strength— proceeds from him alone. It follows that the nature of man is unfruitful and destitute of everything good; no man has the nature of *the true vine* till Christ is implanted in him. This is given to the elect alone by special grace.

The Father is the author of all blessings, who plants us with his hand, but the commencement of life is in Christ, in whom we take root. When he calls himself "the true vine," Christ means he is *truly* the vine. Therefore men toil to no purpose in seeking strength anywhere else, for useful fruit will proceed from nowhere but "the branches" that are rooted in Christ.

FOR MEDITATION: If we are branches of the vine, Jesus Christ, and all our life-sap flows from him, why do we so often, so quickly, and so easily turn to other sources for our spiritual strength and energy? How can we cultivate a more intimate relationship with Christ that recognizes our total and radical dependency on him?

Asking While Abiding

If ye abide in me, and my words abide in you, ye shall ask what ye will, and it shall be done unto you. John 15:7
SUGGESTED FURTHER READING: James 4

Believers often feel that they are starved and very far from that rich fatness which is necessary for yielding abundant fruit. For this reason, Scripture tells us that, whatever those who are in Christ may need, there is a remedy provided for their poverty as soon as they ask it from God. This is a very useful admonition, for the Lord often suffers us to hunger to train us to be earnest in prayer. But if we fly to him, we shall never lack what we ask for; rather, out of his inexhaustible abundance, he will supply us with everything that we need (1 Cor. 1:5).

In saying "If my words abide in you," Christ means that we must take root in him by faith; for as soon as we depart from the doctrine of the gospel, we seek Christ separately from himself. When he promises that he will grant whatever we wish, he does not give us permission to form wishes according to our own fancy. God would do what was ill fitted to promote our welfare if he were so indulgent and so ready to yield to us, for we know well that men often indulge in foolish and extravagant desires. But here he limits the wishes of his people to the rule of praying in a right manner, and that rule is subject to the good pleasure of God in all our affections. This is confirmed by the context in which the words stand; for he means that his people *will* or *desire* not riches, or honor, or anything of that nature, which the flesh foolishly desires, but the vital sap of the Holy Spirit, which enables them to bear fruit.

FOR MEDITATION: A Christian's prayer should ultimately be that God's will be done. Any petition that deviates from God's will is not appropriate. But what is God's will? The answer is found in these words: "if my words abide in you." With God's Word as our guide, we may pray in confidence, knowing that "it shall be done unto us."

Finding Hope in Prayer

Watch and pray, that ye enter not into temptation: the spirit indeed is willing, but the flesh is weak. Matthew 26:41
SUGGESTED FURTHER READING: Matthew 4:1–11

So that he may not terrify and discourage his disciples, Christ gently reproves their slothfulness, then adds consolation and good grounds for hope.

First, he reminds them that though they earnestly desire to do what is right, they must contend with the weakness of the flesh. Therefore, prayer is always necessary. We see that Christ praises their willingness so their weakness may not throw them into despair. Yet he urges them to pray because they are not sufficiently endued with the power of the Spirit.

This admonition properly relates to believers who, being regenerated by the Spirit of God, desire to do what is right but still labor under the weakness of the flesh. Though the grace of the Spirit is vigorous in them, they are "weak" according to the "flesh." And though the disciples alone have their weakness pointed out to them, yet what Christ says of them applies equally to all. So we ought to draw from this a general rule that it is our duty to keep diligent watch by praying. We do not yet possess the power of the Spirit in such a measure as not to frequently fall through the weakness of the flesh unless the Lord grants his assistance to raise us up and uphold us.

We have no reason to tremble with excessive anxiety, for an undoubted remedy is held out to us. We neither have far to seek nor seek in vain for this remedy, for Christ promises that all who are earnest in prayer shall perseveringly oppose the slothfulness of the flesh and will be victorious.

FOR MEDITATION: Watching and praying is always necessary, for we carry with us the remnants of the corruption in which we were born. While we ought to be growing daily in holiness and in the Spirit of God, we can never be confident that we can overcome our old nature on our own. The spirit may be willing, but the flesh is weak; therefore, we must watch and pray.

Restraining Reckless Zeal

Then Simon Peter having a sword drew it, and smote the high priest's servant, and cut off his right ear. The servant's name was Malchus. John 18:10
SUGGESTED FURTHER READING: Luke 9:51–55

If we see nothing faulty in the zeal of Peter, we still ought to be dissatisfied with it on the single ground that Christ declares that he is displeased with it. But we see that it is not because of Peter that Christ does not turn aside from death, and that his name is not exposed to perpetual disgrace.

In offering violence to the captain and the soldiers, Peter acts the part of a ruffian because he resists the power that God has appointed. Christ already is hated by the world more than enough, so this single deed of Peter might give further plausibility to all the accusations that Christ's enemies falsely bring against him. Besides, it is exceedingly thoughtless of Peter to attempt to prove his faith by the sword, while he cannot do so by his tongue. When called to confess Christ, Peter denies his Master, yet now, without his Master's authority, Peter raises a tumult with his sword.

Warned by so striking an example, let us learn to keep our zeal within proper bounds. As the wantonness of our flesh is always eager to attempt more than God commands, let us learn that our zeal will fail to succeed whenever we venture to undertake anything contrary to the Word of God. Sometimes the commencement of our venture gives us flattering promises, but we shall at length be punished for our rashness.

Let obedience, therefore, be the foundation of all that we undertake. We are also reminded here that those who have resolved to plead the cause of Christ do not always conduct themselves so skillfully that they do not commit some fault. Therefore, we ought to more earnestly entreat the Lord to guide us in every action by the spirit of prudence.

FOR MEDITATION: Peter's folly—first in his overzealous attack on Malchus, then in his cowardly denial of Jesus—is a humbling illustration of our own foolishness. If God does not give us grace, we will all be constantly swinging from one extreme to another, doing irreparable damage to Christ's kingdom. If God has kept you from such extremes in your public conduct, thank your Father in heaven for his mercy shown to you and pray for daily discipline and restraint.

Staying Away from Temptation

Now Peter sat without in the palace: and a damsel came unto him, saying, Thou also wast with Jesus of Galilee. But he denied before them all, saying, I know not what thou sayest. Matthew 26:69–70
SUGGESTED FURTHER READING: Judges 16

Peter's fall, which is related here, is a bright mirror of our weakness. His repentance is also a striking example of the goodness and mercy of God that is held out to us.

Therefore, this narrative which relates to a single individual contains a doctrine that may be applied to the whole church. Indeed, it is highly useful both to instruct those who cherish anxiety and fear and to comfort those who have fallen, by holding out to them the hope of pardon.

First, observe that Peter acted inconsiderately when he entered the hall of the high priest. It was his duty, no doubt, to follow his Master, but having been warned that he would revolt, he ought rather to have concealed himself in some corner so as not to have exposed himself to an occasion of sinning. Likewise, it frequently happens that believers, under an appearance of virtue, throw themselves within the reach of temptation. It is therefore our duty to pray to the Lord to restrain and keep us by his Spirit, lest, going beyond our measure, we are immediately punished.

We ought also to pray whenever we commence any undertaking that God may not permit us to fail in the midst of our efforts or at the beginning of the work but may supply us with strength till the end. Conviction of our weakness ought not to be a reason for indolence to prevent us from going wherever God calls us. Rather, it ought to restrain our rashness so we may not attempt anything beyond our calling. It also ought to stimulate us to pray that God, who has given us grace to begin well, may continue to give us grace to persevere.

FOR MEDITATION: What shame it brings to Christ when we proudly march into the jaws of temptation, thinking much of our own strength! We thus draw attention to ourselves and give unbelievers an occasion to mock God when we fail to stand for Christ. We should not willingly enter situations of great temptation, or, if we are forced to do so, we should rely on the grace of God rather than our own strength. Is there a specific area of your life for which this is applicable today?

Tears of Repentance

And Peter remembered the word of Jesus, which said unto him, Before the cock crow, thou shalt deny me thrice. And he went out, and wept bitterly. Matthew 26:75

SUGGESTED FURTHER READING: Daniel 9

Peter probably left the palace in fear, for he did not venture to weep in the presence of witnesses. In this he gives another proof of his weakness. Hence we infer that he did not deserve pardon by satisfying God but obtained it by the fatherly kindness of God.

Peter's example teaches us that we ought to entertain confident hope, even though our repentance is weak, for God does not despise weak repentance, provided it is sincere. Peter's tears, which he sheds in secret, testify before God and the angels that his repentance is true, for, having withdrawn from the eyes of men, he places himself before God and the angels. Therefore his tears flow from the deep feelings of his heart.

This deserves our attention, for we see many who purposely shed tears so long as they are seen by others but who have no sooner gone into private than they have dry eyes. There is no room to doubt that tears that do not flow on account of the judgment of God are often drawn forth by ambition and hypocrisy.

But we may ask, is weeping required in true repentance? I reply, believers often with dry eyes groan before the Lord without hypocrisy and confess their fault to obtain pardon. But those who have committed more aggravated offenses must be in no ordinary degree dull and hardened whose hearts are not pained by grief and sorrow and who do not feel so ashamed that they shed tears. Therefore Scripture, after having convicted men of their crimes, exhorts them to put on "sackcloth and ashes" (Dan. 9:3; Jonah 3:6; Matt. 11:21).

FOR MEDITATION: As Calvin points out, more important than the presence or absence of physical tears is the presence of a repentant heart. Tears may impress others, but they will not fool God if they are tears of hypocrisy. He looks for a broken and contrite heart. By the Spirit's grace, let us devote ourselves today to cultivating deeply repentant hearts.

Repenting Too Late

Then Judas, which had betrayed him, when he saw that he was condemned, repented himself, and brought again the thirty pieces of silver to the chief priests and elders. Matthew 27:3
SUGGESTED FURTHER READING: Hebrews 12:14–29

True repentance is displeasure at sin, which, along with love and desire for righteousness, arises out of fear and reverence for God.

Wicked people are far from such feeling, for they desire to sin without intermission, and even, as far as lies in their power, endeavor to deceive both God and their own conscience. Notwithstanding their reluctance and opposition, they are tormented with blind horror by their conscience. So though they do not hate their sin, they still feel such sorrow and distress that it presses heavily and painfully upon them. Their grief is useless, though, for they do not cheerfully turn to God or even aim at doing better, but, being attached to their wicked desires, they pine away in the torment that they cannot escape.

In this way God punishes their obstinacy, for though his elect are drawn to him by severe chastisements, and, as it were, contrary to their will, yet in due time he heals the wounds that he has inflicted so that they come cheerfully to him, by whose hand they acknowledge that they are struck and by whose wrath they are alarmed. The wicked, who have no hatred of sin, not only dread but fly from the judgment of God. Having received an incurable wound, they perish in the midst of their sorrows.

If Judas had listened to the warning of Christ, there would still have been opportunity for repentance, but since he despised so gracious an offer of salvation, he is given up to the dominion of Satan, who may then throw him into despair.

FOR MEDITATION: The accounts of the false repentance of Judas, Esau, Ahab, and others in Scripture serve as warning beacons for us. What are the major marks of difference between true and false repentance? Do believers always exercise true repentance? How can we, by the Spirit's grace, cultivate more genuine repentance before God?

Trusting in God's Timing

He trusted in God, let him deliver him now, if he will have him: for he said, I am the Son of God. Matthew 27:43
SUGGESTED FURTHER READING: 2 Peter 3

Satan holds in his hand a very sharp arrow of temptation when he pretends that God has forgotten us because God does not relieve us speedily and at that very moment. For since God watches over the safety of his people and not only grants them seasonable aid but even anticipates their necessities (as Scripture everywhere teaches), he may appear not to love those whom he does not assist.

Satan attempts to drive us to despair by the logic that it is in vain for us to feel assured of the love of God when we do not clearly perceive his aid. As he suggests to our minds this kind of imposition, so he employs his agents, who contend that God has sold and abandoned our salvation because he delays in giving us his assistance.

We ought to reject as false the argument that God does not love those whom he appears to forsake for a time. Indeed, nothing is more unreasonable than to limit God's love to any point of time. God has, indeed, promised that he will be our deliverer, but if he sometimes appears to wink at our calamities, we ought to patiently endure the delay.

It is contrary to the nature of faith that the word *now* should be insisted on by those whom God is training by the cross and by adversity to obedience, and whom he entreats to pray and to call on his name, for these are rather the testimonies of his fatherly love, as the apostle tells us (Heb. 12:6). But consider this peculiarity, that though Christ was the "well-beloved Son" (Matt. 3:17; 17:5), yet he was not delivered from death until he had endured the punishment which we deserved, for that was the price by which our salvation was purchased.

FOR MEDITATION: Most of us live in a high-speed culture. Employers demand instant results, computer users demand instant response, and all of us demand instant gratification. Too often we demand instant responses from God as well, and we are filled with doubt and unbelief when he does not respond on our desired clock. How can we learn to submit to his plan and his schedule, trusting that he knows far better than we when to act?

Believing at the Last Hour

But the other answering rebuked him, saying, Dost not thou fear God, seeing thou art in the same condemnation? Luke 23:40
SUGGESTED FURTHER READING: Ephesians 2:1–10

In the thief on the cross, a most wicked man, a striking mirror of the unexpected and incredible grace of God is held out to us. The mirror shows how this man who is near death is suddenly changed into a new man and drawn from hell itself to heaven. It also shows how, having obtained in a moment the forgiveness of all the sins in which he has been plunged through his whole life, this man is admitted to heaven before the apostles and first-fruits of the new church.

This is a remarkable example of how the grace of God shines in the conversion of a man. For it is not by the natural movement of the flesh that this man lays aside his fierce cruelty and proud contempt of God and immediately repents. Rather, he is subdued by the hand of God, for all of Scripture shows that repentance is God's work.

This grace is much more excellent and goes far beyond the expectation of all. For who would ever have thought that this robber in the very throes of death would become not only a devout worshiper of God but also a distinguished teacher of faith and piety to the whole world, so that we, too, might receive from his mouth the rule of a true and proper confession?

The first proof the thief gives of his repentance is that he severely reproves and restrains the wicked forwardness of his companion, the other thief on the cross. He then adds a second proof by humbling himself in openly acknowledging his crimes and ascribing to Christ the praise due to his righteousness. Third, he displays astonishing faith by committing himself and his salvation to the protection of Christ, whom he sees hanging on the cross and near death.

FOR MEDITATION: This thief's acquaintances would never have believed he would become such a gospel preacher. But think how much gospel truth has been impressed upon hearts by this man's testimony preserved in Scripture. When the grace of God grips us, there is no telling what unexpected and miraculous things the Lord will do through us. Pray that you will be kept in the grip of that grace today, being used by God for those whose paths you providentially cross.

Waiting for the Kingdom

Joseph of Arimathaea, an honourable counsellor, which also waited for the kingdom of God, came, and went in boldly unto Pilate, and craved the body of Jesus. Mark 15:43

SUGGESTED FURTHER READING: 1 Thessalonians 4:13–18

Let us observe that, while salvation through Christ was promised indiscriminately to all the Jews and the promise of it was common to them all, the Holy Spirit testifies of only a very few what is said here of Joseph: *which also waited for the kingdom of God.*

Hence it is evident that nearly all of the people had buried in base forgetfulness the inestimable grace of God. All of them had on their lips the language of boasting in referring to the coming of Christ, which was approaching. But few had the covenant of God so fixed in their minds that they would rise by faith to spiritual renovation. That was indeed an awful insensibility. So we need not wonder if pure religion fell into decay when the faith of salvation was extinguished.

Would to God that a similar corruption does not prevail today, in this unhappy age. Christ once appeared as a Redeemer to the Jews and to the whole world, as was declared in the predictions of the prophets. He set up the kingdom of God by restoring affairs from confusion and disorder to a regular and proper condition. He has assigned to us a period of warfare to exercise our patience till he comes again from heaven to complete his reign which he has begun.

How many aspire to this hope, even in a moderate degree? Do not almost all cleave to the earth, as if there were no promise of a resurrection? But while the greater part of people are forgetful of their end and fall away on all sides, let us remember that it is a virtue peculiar to believers to seek the things which are above, especially since the grace of God has shone upon us through the gospel.

FOR MEDITATION: To be characterized as one who waits for the kingdom of God would be a great honor. We all wait and hope for various things. Is the kingdom of God one of them? Is there anything preventing you from having this as your greatest hope and expectation?

Seeking the Resurrected Savior

He is not here: for he is risen, as he said. Come, see the place where the Lord lay. Matthew 28:6

SUGGESTED FURTHER READING: 1 Corinthians 15:1–20

We now come to the closing scene of our redemption. For the lively assurance of our reconciliation with God arises from Christ, having come from hell as the conqueror of death, to show that he has the power of a new life at his disposal.

Paul justly says there will be no gospel and the hope of salvation will be vain and fruitless unless we believe that Christ is risen from the dead (1 Cor. 15:14). For in this Christ obtained righteousness for us and opened our entrance into heaven. In short, our adoption was ratified when Christ rose from the dead, exerting the power of his Spirit and proving himself to be the Son of God.

Though Christ manifested his resurrection in a different manner from what our fleshly sense would have desired, still we ought to regard the method which he approved as also the best. First, he went out of the grave without a witness so that the emptiness of the place might be the earliest indication of his resurrection. Second, Christ chose to have the message that he was alive announced to the women by the angels. Third, he appeared to the women, and then to the apostles on various occasions.

It is an astonishing display of the goodness of Christ that he kindly and generously presented himself alive to the women who did him wrong in seeking him among the dead. If he had not permitted them to come in vain to his grave, we might conclude with certainty that those who now aspire to him by faith will not be disappointed, for the distance of places does not prevent believers from enjoying him who fills heaven and earth by the power of his Spirit.

FOR MEDITATION: What great grace that Jesus reveals himself to those who do not have everything figured out before they come to him! Even if we seek him in wrong ways or in the wrong places, yet he comes to us in mercy without holding those sins against us. We can attribute our finding Christ to nothing but his grace.

Needing Forgiveness

Whose soever sins ye remit, they are remitted unto them; and whose soever sins ye retain, they are retained. John 20:23

SUGGESTED FURTHER READING: Matthew 9:1–8

The principal design of preaching the gospel is that men may be reconciled to God. That is accomplished by the unconditional pardon of sins. It is what Paul informs us when he calls the gospel "the ministry of reconciliation" (2 Cor. 5:18).

Many other things undoubtedly are contained in the gospel, but the principal object that God intends to accomplish is to receive men into favor by not imputing their sins to them. If, therefore, we wish to show that we are faithful ministers of the gospel, we must give most earnest attention to this subject, for the chief difference between the gospel and heathen philosophy is that the gospel says the salvation of people consists of the forgiveness of sins through free grace.

This forgiveness is the source of the other blessings that God bestows, such as enlightening and regenerating us by his Spirit, forming us anew to his image, and arming us with unshaken firmness against the world and Satan. Thus the whole doctrine of godliness and the spiritual building of the church rest on the foundation that God, having acquitted us from all sins, adopts us as his children by free grace.

While Christ directs the apostles to forgive sins, he does not convey to them what is peculiar to himself in forgiving sins. He does not surrender this honor, which belongs peculiarly to himself, to the apostles, but directs them in his name to proclaim the forgiveness of sins so that through their agency he may reconcile men to God. In short, it is Christ alone who forgives sins through his apostles and ministers.

FOR MEDITATION: Real life begins with the forgiveness of sins. If sin still corrupts our relationship with God, no other spiritual blessings can follow. The gospel contains many blessings in so many areas of life, but all of those come back to this fundamental point: the forgiveness of sins. Are your sins forgiven? If so, is this the basis for all your joy in life?

Expecting Hardship

Verily, verily, I say unto thee, When thou wast young, thou girdest thyself, and walkedst whither thou wouldest: but when thou shalt be old, thou shalt stretch forth thy hands, and another shall gird thee, and carry thee whither thou wouldest not. John 21:18
SUGGESTED FURTHER READING: Matthew 13:1–23

Peter offers us a striking mirror of our ordinary condition. Many people have an easy and agreeable life before Christ calls them, but as soon as they have made profession of his name and have been received as his disciples, or, at least, some time afterward, they are led into distressing struggles, a troublesome life, great dangers, and sometimes death itself. These troubles, though hard, must be patiently endured.

The Lord moderates the cross by which he tries his servants, however. He spares them a little time until their strength has come to maturity, for he well knows their weakness and does not press them beyond the measure of it. Christ thus puts up with Peter, so long as he sees this apostle to be tender and weak. Let us therefore learn to devote ourselves to Christ to the last breath, knowing that he will supply us with strength.

In this respect, we behold base ingratitude in many people, for the more gently the Lord deals with them, the more thoroughly do they habituate themselves to softness and slothfulness. Thus we scarcely find one person in a hundred who does not murmur if, after having experienced long forbearance, he is then treated with some measure of severity. Rather, we ought to consider the goodness of God in sparing us for a time and to focus on Christ, who said that so long as he dwelt on earth he conversed cheerfully with his disciples, as if he had been present at a marriage, but that fasting and tears afterward awaited them (Matt. 9:15).

FOR MEDITATION: Some of us have undergone severe trials, but many of us have been largely spared. Isn't it true that we often thank God for his goodness but murmur when periods of peace and joy are interrupted by a trial? When trouble next looms on your horizon, praise God for his goodness and resolve to devote yourself to him, no matter what you may encounter.

Provoking Judgment

And Peter answered unto her, Tell me whether ye sold the land for so much? And she said, Yea, for so much. Acts 5:8
SUGGESTED FURTHER READING: Luke 13:1–9

We see that God does not immediately punish Sapphira. He first thoroughly tries the matter of her deception, lest he should send vengeance upon anyone except the obstinate and those who will not be pardoned. For though Sapphira knew that she was withholding the truth, she ought to have been as stricken with this question of Peter as if she had been cited to appear before the judgment seat of God.

She is granted time to repent; indeed, given a pleasant invitation to repent. But in holding on so carelessly to her lie, Sapphira declares that she is incurable because she is untouched by fearing God.

Here we are taught to diligently labor to bring sinners to the way of truth. For the Spirit of God patiently works with sinners, but when stubbornness and the stubborn contempt of God are added to the offense, it is high time for punishment. People are too arrogant when they are displeased with the severity of God. It is rather our duty to consider how we shall in time come to stand before the judgment seat of God. We will despise his holy power and majesty too much if we freely mock him without any punishment.

Moreover, many circumstances sufficiently prove that Ananias and Sapphira were not worthy of only one death. For, first, hypocrisy is of itself very abominable to God. Second, this couple was determined to lie to God, and this arose from great contempt, for they did not reverence and fear Christ, who was the chief governor of the people before whom Ananias and Sapphira came.

The greatness of the spiritual judgment on this couple (which is as yet hid) is set before us in the bodily punishment of two, as in a mirror. For if we consider what it means to be cast into eternal fire, we shall not judge that falling down dead before others is the greatest evil and punishment of all.

FOR MEDITATION: The Lord's striking punishment on Ananias and Sapphira should be very sobering—so many of us are guilty of the same sin. In God's mercy, we have not been struck dead for failing to tell the truth. How can this story serve to remind us of the greater punishment to come?

Persevering after Persecution

Go, stand and speak in the temple to the people all the words of this life.
Acts 5:20
SUGGESTED FURTHER READING: John 16

The apostles are delivered so they might employ themselves in bravely preaching the gospel and courageously provoking their enemies until they valiantly die. The apostles are eventually put to death when the hand of God ceases and they have finished their course. But for now the Lord opens the prison for them so they may be at liberty to fulfill their function.

This is worth noting because we see many people who, having escaped out of persecution, afterward keep silence, as if they have done their duty toward God and are no more to be troubled. Others escape further duty by denying Christ. The Lord does deliver his children to the end, not that they may cease from the course that they have begun, but rather that they might afterward be more zealous.

The apostles might have objected, saying it was better to keep silence for a time, because they could not speak one word without danger. If we are now apprehended for only one sermon, they might ask, how much more shall the fury of our enemies be inflamed if they see us make no end of speaking?

But because they knew that they were to live and to die to the Lord, the apostles did not refuse to do what the Lord commands. So we must always mark what function the Lord prescribes to us. We may be asked to do many things that may discourage us, unless we are content with the commandment of God alone and do our duty, committing the success to him.

FOR MEDITATION: We are quick to think that our hardships merit a time of peace and ease. But we can see from the apostles' example that this is not the case at all. Submitting to hardships is so often difficult; let us pray for God's grace so that we might be spurred on to new and radical obedience by the trials we face.

Declaring what is Clean

And the voice spake unto him again the second time, What God hath cleansed, that call not thou common. Acts 10:15

SUGGESTED FURTHER READING: Romans 14

The voice that speaks to Peter mentions clean and unclean meats, but this sentence must be extended to all parts of the life. It says, word for word, *What God hath cleansed, that call not thou common*, but its meaning is that we are not to allow or condemn anything because we stand and fall by the judgment of God alone, so is he judge of all things (Rom. 14:4).

In regard to clean or unclean meats, after the abrogating of the law, God pronounced that all meat was pure and clean. If, on the other hand, mortal man makes his own judgment, forbidding certain foods and allowing others, he takes unto himself the authority and power of God by sacrilegious boldness.

We must always ask for the mouth of the Lord, that we may thereby be assured of what we may lawfully do, for it was not lawful even for Peter to make something profane that was declared lawful by the Word of God.

Furthermore, it is of great importance here to destroy the obstinacy of people, which they too often use in perverse judgments. There is almost no one who does not grant liberty to himself to judge another person's doings. Now, since we are churlish and malicious, we lean more toward the worse part. In so doing, we take from God what is his. The voice that came to Peter ought to suffice in correcting such boldness, for it is not lawful for us to make this or that unclean. That power belongs to God alone.

These words are also given to us to understand that the Jews were not the holy people of the Lord because they excelled through their own worthiness, but only by reason of God's adoption. After God received the Gentiles into the society of the covenant, all people—Jew and Gentile alike—possess equal gospel rights.

FOR MEDITATION: Creating new laws and binding them upon others may be quick, clean, and easy, but it is not our place. Rather, we are to labor to understand God's will as it is revealed to us in his Word, and we are to equip ourselves and our brothers and sisters to apply that Word to our lives. If God has called something clean, it is sinful for us to call it unclean, no matter how upright our motives.

Praising God in Fetters

And when they had laid many stripes upon them, they cast them into prison, charging the jailor to keep them safely. Acts 16:23

SUGGESTED FURTHER READING: Psalm 5

Even when Paul and Silas lay bound with fetters, they lauded God in prayer. So it appears that neither the reproach they suffered, nor the stripes that made their flesh smart, nor the stink of the deep dungeon, nor the danger of death that was at hand, could hinder them from giving thanks to the Lord joyfully and with glad hearts.

We must note the general rule here that though we find it difficult to pray as we ought, we must praise God. For though the desire to pray arises from feeling our want and miseries, and therefore is, for the most part, joined with sorrow and carefulness, yet the faithful must so bridle their affections that they do not murmur against God. The right form of prayer, then, joins two affections: care and sorrow, by reason of the present necessity which keeps us down; and joyfulness, by reason of the obedience whereby we submit ourselves to God, and by reason of the hope which, showing us the haven nigh at hand, refreshes us even in the midst of shipwreck.

That is the form that Paul prescribes to us. He says to us, let your prayers be made known to God with thanksgiving (Phil. 4:6). But note the circumstances of this teaching. The pain of his stripes were grievous, prison was troublesome, and dangers were great, but in all this, Paul and Silas ceased not to praise God. We gather by this how greatly they were encouraged to bear the cross. So Luke reports that the apostles rejoiced because they were counted worthy to suffer reproach for the name of the Lord (Acts 5:41).

FOR MEDITATION: Isn't it true that our prayers in times of terrible suffering and trouble easily become little more than complaints? Rather than praising God and humbly asking that his will be done, we use prayer as a forum to air our grievances against him. Paul and Silas did otherwise. Though their sufferings are great, they praise him in prayer and song. Remember his example when you next turn to God during a particularly troublesome time.

Thanking God for Faith

First, I thank my God through Jesus Christ for you all, that your faith is spoken of throughout the whole world. Romans 1:8
SUGGESTED FURTHER READING: Romans 3:19–31

The first thing worthy of remark here is that Paul commends the faith of those in the church at Rome, saying that it has been received from God. We are thus taught that faith is God's gift, for thanksgiving acknowledges a benefit. He who gives thanks to God for faith confesses that faith comes from God.

Since the apostle always begins his congratulations with thanksgiving, let us be hereby reminded that all our blessings are God's free gifts. It is needful to become accustomed to such forms of speaking that we may be led more fully to rouse ourselves in the duty of acknowledging God as the giver of all our blessings and to stir up others to join us in the same acknowledgment.

If it is right to give thanks in little things, how much more we should thank God for faith, which is neither a small nor an indiscriminate gift of God. Furthermore, we have an example here that thanks ought to be given "through Christ," according to the apostle's command in Hebrews 13:15, since it is in Christ's name that we seek and obtain mercy from the Father.

I observe in the last place that the apostle calls God *my God*. This familiarity with God is the special privilege of the faithful, and on them alone God bestows this honor. There is indeed implied in this a mutual relationship, which is expressed in this promise: "I will be to them a God; they shall be to me a people" (Jer. 30:22).

At the same time, I prefer to confine this to the character that Paul sustains as an attestation of his obedience in the work of preaching the gospel. So Hezekiah called God the God of Isaiah, when he desired him to give him the testimony of a true and faithful prophet (Isa. 37:4).

FOR MEDITATION: Paul offered thanks to God for the truth that faith is a gift of God. We should respond in the same way with praise to God for such an amazing and undeserved gift! Without it, our condition would be hopeless.

Finding No Excuse

For when the Gentiles, which have not the law, do by nature the things contained in the law, these, having not the law, are a law unto themselves: which show the work of the law written in their hearts, their conscience also bearing witness, and their thoughts the mean while accusing or else excusing one another. Romans 2:14–15

SUGGESTED FURTHER READING: Romans 3:1–19

Paul did not think it enough to condemn us by mere assertion and to pronounce on us the just judgment of God. He proves the rightness of this by reasons to excite us to a greater desire for Christ and to a greater love toward Christ. Indeed, he shows that Gentiles in vain use ignorance as an excuse for failing to obey God's law, since they prove by their own deeds that they have some rule of righteousness in them. No nation is so lost to everything human that it does not keep within the limits of some laws.

Since, then, all nations, of themselves and without a monitor, are disposed to make laws for themselves, it is evident beyond all question that they have some notions of justice and rectitude, which the Greeks call preconceptions. These are implanted by nature in the hearts of men. Though they are without law, the Gentiles have a law, for though they have no written law, they are yet by no means wholly destitute of the knowledge of what is right and just, for they could not otherwise distinguish between vice and virtue. They restrain vice by punishment, and commend and manifest their approbation of virtue by honoring it with rewards.

The apostle sets nature in opposition to a written law, meaning that the Gentiles had the natural light of righteousness, which supplied the place of that law by which the Jews were instructed. So they were a law to themselves. For why else did they institute religious rites, unless they were convinced that God ought to be worshiped? Why were they ashamed of adultery and theft, unless they deemed them evils?

FOR MEDITATION: We can argue against it, but there is a law in the heart of mankind that is placed there by virtue of creation. This law is clear enough to condemn us all. None of us has kept God's revealed will and laws, but neither have we kept the law found in our hearts. Thus, we stand condemned before God and without excuse, no matter who we are. How should this change our understandings of ourselves and our hearts?

Learning from History

Now it was not written for his sake alone, that it was imputed to him.
Romans 4:23
SUGGESTED FURTHER READING: Hebrews 4

This passage reminds us of our duty to seek to profit from the examples recorded in Scripture. Heathens have said that history is the teacher of what life ought to be, but since that history has been handed down by them, no one can derive sound instruction from it. Scripture alone justly makes this claim. For in the first place, it prescribes general rules by which we may test all other history so as to render it serviceable to us. Second, it clearly points out what things we are to follow and what we are to avoid. But as to the special truth that it teaches, it possesses the peculiarity of clearly revealing the providence of God, his justice and goodness toward his own people, and his judgments on the wicked.

If we would make the right and proper use of sacred histories, we must remember to use them by drawing sound doctrine from them. In some parts they instruct us how to form our life; in others, how to strengthen faith; and in still others, how we are to be stirred up to serve the Lord. In forming our life, the example of the saints may be useful, for we may learn from them sobriety, chastity, love, patience, moderation, contempt of the world, and other virtues. What may serve to confirm faith is the help that God gave these saints, the protection that brought them comfort in adversity, and the paternal care that God always exercised over them.

The judgments of God and the punishments inflicted on the wicked will also help us, provided they fill us with the fear that imbues our hearts with reverence and devotion.

FOR MEDITATION: Those who do not learn from history are doomed to repeat it. The biblical narratives are not there simply for our information; they are meant for our instruction. That is, let us not simply learn *about* the heroes of faith, but also learn *from* them.

Standing Firm

*By whom also we have access by faith into this grace wherein we stand,
and rejoice in hope of the glory of God.* Romans 5:2
SUGGESTED FURTHER READING: Ephesians 2:11–22

Our reconciliation with God depends solely on Christ, for he alone is
the beloved Son, and we are by nature the children of wrath. This favor
is communicated to us by the gospel, for the gospel is the ministry of
reconciliation, by which we are in a manner brought into the kingdom
of God.

Rightly then does Paul set before our eyes in Christ a sure pledge of
God's favor, so that he might more easily draw us away from every
confidence in works. He teaches us by using the word *access* that
salvation begins with Christ. He therefore excludes those preparations by
which foolish men imagine that they can anticipate God's mercy. It is as
though he says, "Christ comes not to you, nor helps you, on account of
your merits."

He then immediately adds that it is through continuing the same favor
that our salvation becomes certain and sure, thereby intimating that
perseverance is not founded on our power and diligence, but on Christ.
At the same time, he says that we *stand,* indicating that the gospel ought
to strike such deep roots into the hearts of the godly that, strengthened
by its truth, they may stand firm against all the devices of Satan and of
the flesh. By the word *stand*, he also means that faith is not a changeable
persuasion which lasts only for a day, but it is immutable and sinks deep
into the heart so that it endures throughout life.

Therefore, it is not he who is led by a sudden impulse to believe, that
has faith, and is to be reckoned among the faithful; but he who
constantly, and, so to speak, with a firm and fixed foot, abides in that
place appointed to him by God so as to cleave always to Christ.

FOR MEDITATION: To stand in this grace of God is a great privilege and an
inestimable mercy. We only stand because of Christ and his work. That
leaves no room for boasting but only for rejoicing in the hope of the
glory of God. If you are standing in that grace today, praise him for that
mercy and rest in it as you face the day's temptations and trials.

Finding Glory in Tribulation

And not only so, but we glory in tribulations also: knowing that tribulation worketh patience. Romans 5:3
SUGGESTED FURTHER READING: Hebrews 12:1–14

By saying that the saints glory in tribulations, Paul is not saying they did not dread or avoid adversities, or were not distressed with their bitterness when they happened (for there is no patience when there is no feeling of bitterness). Rather, as in their grief and sorrow they were not without great consolation because they regarded that whatever they bore was dispensed to them for good by the hand of a most indulgent Father, they are justly said to glory, for whenever salvation is promoted, a reason for glorying is not wanting.

We are then taught here what the design of our tribulations is, if indeed we would prove ourselves to be the children of God. Tribulations ought to teach us patience. If they do not serve this purpose, the work of the Lord is rendered void and of no effect through our corruption. For how does he prove that adversities do not hinder the glorying of the faithful except than by the patience in enduring them, for is it not in them that they feel the help of God, which nourishes and confirms their hope?

Certainly, those who do not learn patience do not make good progress. Nor can we object to finding glory in suffering by saying that Scripture records some complaints of saints that are full of despondency, for the Lord sometimes so depresses and straitens his people that they can hardly breathe and can hardly remember any source of consolation. Yet in a moment God brings to life those whom he has nearly sunk in the darkness of death. So what Paul says about glory in tribulation is always accomplished: "We are in every way oppressed, but not made anxious; we are in danger, but we are not in despair; we suffer persecution, but we are not forsaken; we are cast down but we are not destroyed" (2 Cor. 4:8).

FOR MEDITATION: Most people would say that tribulation works exasperation, not patience! Patience amid tribulation can only be the fruit of a supernatural change of heart, brought about by God. Has this change been made in you? If so, how can Hebrews 12:1–14 assist you in continuing to be patient under tribulation?

Spreading the Love

And hope maketh not ashamed; because the love of God is shed abroad in our hearts by the Holy Ghost which is given unto us. Romans 5:5
SUGGESTED FURTHER READING: Titus 3:4–7

Hope regards salvation as most certain. It hence appears that the Lord tries us by adversities so that our salvation may thereby gradually advance. Those evils that do in a manner promote our happiness then cannot render us miserable. Thus is proved what the apostle Paul says, that the godly have reasons for glorying God in the midst of their afflictions (Rom. 5:3).

I therefore say that tribulations stimulate us to patience, and that patience experiences divine help by which we are more encouraged to entertain hope; for however we are pressed and seem to be nearly consumed, we do not yet cease to feel God's favor toward us. This affords the richest consolation, which is much more abundant than when all things prosper. For as that which appears to be happiness is misery itself when God is averse to and displeased with us, when he is gracious to us, even calamities themselves will surely be turned to a prosperous and joyful end.

Seeing that all things must serve the will of the Creator, who, in his paternal favor toward us overrules all the trials of the cross for our salvation, this knowledge of divine love toward us is instilled into our hearts by the Spirit of God. The good things which God has prepared for his servants are hid from the ears and the eyes and the minds of men; thus, only the Spirit can reveal them.

The words *shed abroad* are also very significant; for they mean that the revelation of divine love toward us is so abounding that it fills our hearts. Being thus spread through every part of us, it not only mitigates our sorrow in adversities, but also, like a sweet seasoning, helps us love even our tribulations.

FOR MEDITATION: Grace that can teach us patience in tribulation is certainly amazing. It is no wonder, then, that the love of God will be shed abroad in our hearts. Hearts that are so brimming with love should not be able to contain it but be compelled to share it with others. If you know this love, do not hoard it for yourself. How can you use it to minister to those around you who desperately need the grace of God?

Defining our Nature

For if by one man's offence death reigned by one; much more they which receive abundance of grace and of the gift of righteousness shall reign in life by one, Jesus Christ. Romans 5:17
SUGGESTED FURTHER READING: Genesis 3

It may be useful to note here the differences between Christ and Adam. First, by Adam's sin we are not condemned through imputation alone, as though we were punished only for the sin of another. Rather, we suffer his punishment because we ourselves are also guilty. As our nature is polluted in Adam, we are regarded by God as having committed sin. But through the righteousness of Christ, we are restored in a different way to salvation; for it is not accepted for us because it is in us, but because we possess Christ himself with all his blessings given to us through the bountiful kindness of the Father. Hence the gift of righteousness is not something that God endows us with, as some absurdly explain, but is a free imputation of righteousness. In this, the apostle plainly declares what he understands by the word *grace*.

Second, the benefit of Christ does not come to all men. Adam has involved his whole race in condemnation, the reason for which is indeed evident. As the curse we derive from Adam is conveyed to us by nature, it is no wonder that it includes all of humanity. But if we are to participate in the grace of Christ, we must be engrafted in him by faith. To partake of the miserable inheritance of sin, it is enough for us to be human, for sin dwells in all flesh and blood. But to enjoy the righteousness of Christ, it is necessary for us to become believers, for participation in him is attained only by faith.

FOR MEDITATION: Thomas Goodwin pictured two giants who represent mankind: one is Adam and one is Christ. Every single person is hooked to the belt of one of these two giants. By nature, we are all hooked onto the belt of the first Adam. His fall became our fall. Paul teaches us in Romans 5 that the guilt of Adam's sin is imputed to us and the pollution of his sin is inherited by us. By grace, the Holy Spirit unhooks us from the belt of the first Adam by regeneration and hooks us onto the belt of the Second Adam, Jesus Christ. Christ then becomes our representative head with the Father, and we, by grace, learn to live out of him. To whose belt are you hooked now?

Employed in his Service

Neither yield ye your members as instruments of unrighteousness unto sin: but yield yourselves unto God, as those that are alive from the dead, and your members as instruments of righteousness unto God. Romans 6:13

SUGGESTED FURTHER READING: 1 Corinthians 6:9–20

Once sin has obtained dominion in our soul, all our faculties are continually applied to its service. Paul describes the reign of sin by what follows it so that he might more clearly show what we must do to shake off its yoke.

Borrowing an image from the military, he calls our members weapons or arms, saying, in effect, "The soldier always has his arms ready so he may use them whenever ordered to do so by his general, but he never uses them except at his command. So Christians ought to regard all their faculties as weapons of spiritual warfare. If they use any of their members in the indulgence of depravity, they are in the service of sin. But they have made the oath of soldiers to God and to Christ, and by this are held bound, they must be far removed from any dealings with the camps of sin."

People ought to ask themselves by what right they proudly lay claim to the Christian name if they have prepared all their members to commit every kind of abomination, as though they were the prostitutes of Satan.

Paul bids us to wholly present ourselves to God so that we restrain our minds and hearts from all wanderings into which the lusts of the flesh may draw us. We may then only regard the will of God which readies us to receive his commands and prepare to execute his orders, so that our members may be devoted and consecrated to his will, and so that all the faculties of our souls and our bodies may aspire after nothing but his glory. The reason for this is that the Lord, having destroyed our former life, has not in vain created us for another, which ought to be accompanied with suitable actions.

FOR MEDITATION: What could be more blessed than to be totally employed, with all our members, in the service of God, our Creator and Redeemer? If we have been brought forth from the dead, do we not owe him everything? He who raised us can also give us the strength we need to employ our members in his service. What habits in your life should change in order to do so?

Freed from Bondage

For sin shall not have dominion over you: for ye are not under the law, but under grace. Romans 6:14

SUGGESTED FURTHER READING: Galatians 3

The yoke of the law can only tear and bruise those who carry it. It hence follows that the faithful must flee to Christ and implore him to defend their freedom. As such Christ exhibits himself, for he himself went under the bondage of the law, to which he was himself no debtor, so that he might, as the apostle says, redeem those who were under the law.

To be no longer under the law means that we are freed from the letter that prescribes what makes us guilty, since we are not able to perform it. It also means that we are no longer subject to the law, which requires perfect righteousness and pronounces death on all who deviate in any part from it. Likewise, by *grace*, we may understand both parts of redemption: the remission of sins, by which God imputes righteousness to us; and the sanctification of the Spirit, by which he forms us anew unto good works. It is as if Paul says, "We who are under grace are not therefore under the law."

The intent of this verse is now clear; for the apostle intends to comfort us, lest we should become weary in mind while striving to do what is right because we still find many imperfections in ourselves. For however much we may be harassed by the stings of sin, it cannot yet overcome us. The Spirit of God enables us to conquer sin. Then, being under grace, we are freed from the rigorous requirements of the law.

We must further understand the apostle assumes that all who are without the grace of God and are yet bound under the yoke of the law are under condemnation. We may conclude that, as long as they are under the law, they are subject to the dominion of sin.

FOR MEDITATION: The glorious realization that those who are in Christ are free from the law should not encourage us to indulge in sin. Rather, the exhilaration of this freedom motivates us to live all the more for God. We should respond out of thankfulness for so great a deliverance. If you are free today, marvel at that freedom and let it motivate you to loving sacrifice.

Divided against Sin

For that which I do I allow not: for what I would, that do I not; but what I hate, that do I. Romans 7:15

SUGGESTED FURTHER READING: Galatians 5:16–26

Here the apostle teaches us a critical difference between the ungodly and the faithful. The ungodly are never so blinded and hardened that, when they are reminded of their crimes, they condemn them in their own conscience. Knowledge is not so utterly extinguished in them, for they still retain the difference between right and wrong. Sometimes they are shaken with such dread because of their sin that they suffer a kind of condemnation even in this life. Nevertheless they approve of sin with all their heart and give themselves up to it without any feeling of genuine hatred, for those stings of conscience by which they are harassed proceed from opposition in judgment rather than from any contrary inclination in the will.

By contrast, the godly, in whom the regeneration of God has begun, are divided, for the chief desire of their heart is to aspire to God, seek celestial righteousness, and hate sin. Yet they are drawn down to the earth by the remnants of their flesh. Thus, while pulled in two ways, they fight against their own nature, and nature fights against them; they condemn their sins, not only by being constrained by the judgment of reason, but because they truly abominate sins in their hearts and loathe themselves on their account. This is the Christian conflict between the flesh and the spirit of which Paul speaks in Galatians 5:17.

It has therefore been justly said that the carnal man runs headlong into sin with the approbation and consent of the whole soul, but a division immediately begins for the first time when a person is called by the Lord and renewed by the Spirit.

FOR MEDITATION: When God's grace works salvation in a person's heart, he is no longer able to sin as he did before. Though his heart loved to sin, even while fearing for his soul, now he cannot find the same pleasure in sin because he relishes the things of God. This is an excellent mirror for self-examination. Do you hate sin? Has it lost its luster in your eyes?

Quickening Life in Us

And if Christ be in you, the body is dead because of sin; but the Spirit is life because of righteousness. Romans 8:10

SUGGESTED FURTHER READING: John 6:60–71

What Paul before said of the Spirit he now says of Christ to show the manner of Christ's dwelling in us, for as by the Spirit Christ consecrates us as temples to himself, so by the Spirit he also dwells in us.

Paul more fully explains that the children of God are accounted spiritual, not on the ground of a full and complete perfection, but on account of the newness of life that has begun in them. He anticipates here an opportunity for doubt that might disturb us, namely, that though the Spirit possesses a part of us, another part is still under the power of death. The apostle addresses this doubt by answering that the power of quickening is in the Spirit of Christ, which will become more and more effectual in swallowing up our mortality. We must thus patiently wait until the relics of sin are entirely abolished in us.

The word *Spirit* does not refer to the soul but to the Spirit of regeneration. Paul calls the Spirit *life* here, not only because the Spirit lives and reigns in us, but also because he quickens us by his power until at length, having destroyed our mortal flesh, he perfectly renews us.

On the other hand, the word *body* refers to that polluted mass which is not yet purified by the Spirit of God from earthly dregs and delights in nothing but what is corrupt; for it would be otherwise absurd to ascribe the fault of sin to the body. Besides, the soul is so far from being life that it does not of itself live. So what Paul says here is that, though we merit death as long as the corruption of our first nature remains in us, yet the Spirit of God conquers sin. What is more, it is no hindrance that we are only favored with the first-fruits, for even one spark of the Spirit is the seed of life in us.

FOR MEDITATION: It is a great comfort to know that we who are believers are alive because of the Spirit rather than our perfection. Though we continue to struggle with remaining corruptions, we can be sure that these corruptions are not an indication that we are still dead in sin. We are alive in the Spirit and on our way to perfectly sanctified life eternal. Let this encourage you when disappointed with your shortcomings and sin.

Shining in Affliction

Who shall separate us from the love of Christ? Shall tribulation, or distress, or persecution, or famine, or nakedness, or peril, or sword?
Romans 8:35
SUGGESTED FURTHER READING: Daniel 1

Those who are persuaded of God's kindness toward them are able to stand firm in the heaviest afflictions. But people are also harassed by afflictions in no small degree for various reasons; some interpret afflictions as tokens of God's wrath, while some think afflictions prove they are forsaken by God. Some see no end to trials and neglect to meditate on a better life. When the mind is purged from such mistakes, it becomes calm and quietly rests.

The meaning of this text is that, whatever happens, we ought to stand firm in believing that God, who having once embraced us in love, never ceases to care for us. The apostle does not simply say that nothing can tear God away from loving us, but that the knowledge and lively sense of God's love is so vigorous in our hearts that it shines in the darkness of afflictions. For as clouds may obscure the clear brightness of the sun, yet do not yet wholly deprive us of its light, so God sends forth through the darkness of adversities the rays of his favor lest temptations should overwhelm us with despair. Indeed, our faith, supported by God's promises, as if by wings, makes its way upward to heaven through all intervening obstacles.

It is true that adversities are tokens of God's wrath when viewed in themselves, but when pardon and reconciliation precede them, we may be assured that though God chastises us, he never forgets his mercy. Adversity reminds us of what we have deserved, yet it also testifies that our salvation is the object of God's care, which he extends to us while he leads us to repentance.

FOR MEDITATION: What would we be like if we never encountered affliction? We would all be like spoiled children. In affliction, God takes us into his gymnasium to firm and fit us for his fellowship and kingdom. Think back to the greatest afflictions in your life. How has God used these afflictions to your spiritual profit?

Living as an Acceptable Sacrifice

I beseech you therefore, brethren, by the mercies of God, that ye present your bodies a living sacrifice, holy, acceptable unto God, which is your reasonable service. Romans 12:1

SUGGESTED FURTHER READING: Leviticus 22:17–20

The beginning of a right course in good works teaches us that we are consecrated to the Lord. It follows that we must cease to live to ourselves so that we may devote all of the actions of our life to his service.

Two things should be considered here: first, that we are the Lord's; and second, that on this account we are to be holy, for it is an indignity to God's holiness that anything that is not first consecrated should be offered to God. Having admitted those two things, we then must realize that holiness is to be practiced throughout life. We are guilty of a kind of sacrilege when we relapse into uncleanness, for it is nothing else than profaning what is consecrated.

This text offers expressions that are especially suitable for teaching these truths. The apostle says, first, that our *body* ought to be offered as a sacrifice to God. By this he means that we are not our own but have entirely given our body away to become the property of God. We cannot do this unless we renounce and deny ourselves.

Second, by adding two adjectives, Paul shows us what kind of sacrifice this ought to be. By calling it a *living* sacrifice, he teaches that we are to be continually sacrificed to the Lord so that our former life will be destroyed in us and we may be raised up to a new life. By the term *holy*, he notes what necessarily belongs to a sacrifice, for a victim of sacrifice is only approved when it has been made holy. With the third word, *acceptable*, Paul reminds us that our life is rightly ordered as a sacrifice when it is made pleasing to God.

The apostle brings to us no common consolation in this text, for he teaches us that our work is pleasing and acceptable to God when we devote ourselves to purity and holiness.

FOR MEDITATION: The theology of Romans 1–11 creates a radically different lifestyle. Thinking of ourselves as "living sacrifices, holy and acceptable to God" is a powerful way to retain our focus and a great aid to spur us on to new obedience.

Honoring Christ above All

Now this I say, that every one of you saith, I am of Paul; and I of Apollos; and I of Cephas; and I of Christ. 1 Corinthians 1:12
SUGGESTED FURTHER READING: 2 Timothy 4:1–5

Paul's objective here is to maintain Christ's exclusive authority in the church, so that we may all exercise dependence upon him, that he alone may be recognized as Lord and Master, and that the name of no individual will be set in opposition to his.

The apostle condemns as most destructive those enemies of our faith who draw disciples after them (Acts 20:30) and split the church into parties. No man may have such preeminence in the church that he usurps Christ's supremacy. No one may be held in such honor that he undermines, even in the slightest degree, the dignity of Christ.

It is true that a certain degree of honor is due to Christ's ministers, who are masters in their own place, but we must always keep in view that Christ must have what belongs to him without any infringement. He shall be the sole Master and looked upon as such. Hence the aim of good ministers must be to serve Christ together and claim for him exclusive power, authority, and glory. They must fight under Christ's banner, obey him alone, and bring others in subjection to him. If someone is influenced by ambition, that man gathers disciples to himself, not to Christ.

The fountain of all evils, the most hurtful of all plagues, the deadliest poison of all churches is a minister who seeks his own interests rather than those of Christ. In short, the unity of the church consists of dependence on Christ alone. Men occupy an inferior place to Christ and may not detract in any degree from his preeminence.

FOR MEDITATION: Many of us are tempted to think too highly of ourselves—and we usually want others to think the same. We can easily be more concerned that others agree with us on a particular subject than that they follow Christ in all things. If you are struggling in this area, repent and ask for the grace to practice humility and to put others ahead of yourself.

Becoming Servant Ministers

Let a man so account of us, as of the ministers of Christ, and stewards of the mysteries of God. 1 Corinthians 4:1

SUGGESTED FURTHER READING: Hebrews 3:1–6

It was a matter of no little importance to see the church torn by corrupt factions resulting from the likes or dislikes people had toward various leaders. Paul thus enters into a lengthy discussion about the ministry of the Word.

He offers three basic considerations. First, Paul describes the office of the minister of the church. Second, he shows it is not enough for anyone to have a title or even to undertake a duty; faithful administration of the office is required. Third, as the judgment formed of him by the Corinthians was preposterous, Paul brings himself and his critics to the judgment seat of Christ.

First, then, he teaches how every teacher in the church ought to be regarded. In this regard he modifies his discourse in such a manner that he neither lowers the value of the ministry nor assigns to a man more value than is necessary. Both extremes are dangerous because when ministers are poorly esteemed, contempt of the Word arises. On the other hand, if ministers are extolled beyond measure, they may abuse their liberty and become "wanton against the Lord" (1 Tim. 5:11).

Paul calls teachers *ministers of Christ*, meaning they ought to apply themselves not to their own work but to that of the Lord, who has hired them as his servants. They are not appointed to rule the church in an authoritative manner but are subject to Christ's authority. In short, they are servants, not masters, of the church.

FOR MEDITATION: Ministers of the Word have often been esteemed far above what is suitable for a mere sinner in the service of the Lord; but they have equally often been held in extremely low esteem. As Calvin points out, neither situation is healthy. We must strive to treat our shepherds with proper respect, not placing them on a pedestal nor demeaning and criticizing them. How do you treat your pastor?

Serving as Asked

For who maketh thee to differ from another? And what hast thou that thou didst not receive? Now if thou didst receive it, why dost thou glory, as if thou hadst not received it? 1 Corinthians 4:7

SUGGESTED FURTHER READING: Lamentations 3:22–33

The meaning of this verse may be stated: "Let that man come forward, whosoever he be, that is desirous of distinction, and troubles the church by his ambition. I will demand of him, who makes him superior to others? Who has conferred upon him the privilege of being taken out of the rank of the others and made superior to others?"

The reasoning in this is dependent on the order that the Lord has appointed in his church so that the members of Christ's body may be united together, and everyone may rest satisfied with his own place, his own rank, his own office, and his own honor. If one member desires to leave his place so he may leap into the place of another and invade his office, what will become of the entire body?

Let us know that the Lord has placed each of us in the church and assigned to each one his own station, so that, being under one head, we may be mutually helpful to each other. Let us also know that we have been endowed with a diversity of gifts so that we may serve the Lord with modesty and humility, and so we may endeavor to promote the glory of him who has conferred upon us everything that we have.

The best remedy for correcting the ambition of those who desire distinction is to call them back to God so they might acknowledge that they were not placed in a high or low station according to anyone's pleasure. Rather, this decision belongs to God alone. God does not confer gifts upon anyone to elevate him to the place of the head but distributes his gifts so that God alone is glorified in all things.

FOR MEDITATION: Some parts of the body of Christ are more noticeable and more appreciated than others. But Paul points out that prominent members of the church are nothing more than what God has made. They have no reason to boast. In the same way, less prominent members are nothing less than what God has made, so they have no reason to complain or be discontent. Are you filled with pride because of your position? Or do you covet another person's position? Both sins must be humbly repented of.

Offering Godly Correction

I write not these things to shame you, but as my beloved sons I warn you.
1 Corinthians 4:14
SUGGESTED FURTHER READING: Colossians 3:12–17

A man with a malevolent disposition may inflict disgrace upon someone, reproving him and his faults in such a manner that the sinner is held up to the reproach of all. Though accused, Paul does not do that. He simply affirms that what he has said was done without malice, not to upbraid or to hurt the reputation of Corinthian believers, but with a paternal affection he admonished them about what he saw as defective in them.

What was the purpose of this admonition? It was that the Corinthians, who were puffed up with mere empty notions, might learn to glory in the abasement of the cross, as Paul did, and might no longer despise Paul for those grounds on which he was deservedly honorable in the sight of God and angels. In effect, they should lay aside their accustomed haughtiness so they might set a higher value on those marks of Christ (Gal. 6:17) that were upon Paul rather than on the empty and counterfeit show of false apostles.

Let teachers learn from this that, in reproving others, they must always use such moderation as not to wound men's minds with excessive severity. In agreement with the well-known proverb, they must mix honey or oil with vinegar so that they might above all things take care not to appear to triumph over those whom they reprove or take delight in their disgrace. Indeed, they must endeavor to make clear that they seek nothing but to promote the welfare of others. For what good will the teacher do with a reprimand if he does not season his reproof with that moderation of which I have spoken?

Hence if we desire to do any good by *correcting* men's faults, we must distinctly let them know that our reproofs proceed from a friendly disposition.

FOR MEDITATION: Aware that he would be nothing without the grace of God toward him, the Christian is to reprove with great humility and love. Sadly, many of us forget our debt to God and proudly reprimand others so we appear far better. This is foolish, damaging to their souls, and usually breeds resentment rather than repentance.

Mourning One Person's Sin

And ye are puffed up, and have not rather mourned, that he that hath done this deed might be taken away from among you. 1 Corinthians 5:2
SUGGESTED FURTHER READING: Matthew 18:15–20

Why should the Corinthians *mourn* over one man's sin? For two reasons: first, as a consequence of the communion that exists among the members of the church, it is becoming that all should feel hurt at so deadly a fall of one of their number. Second, when such an enormous sin is perpetrated in a particular church, the perpetrator is an offender in such a manner that he pollutes the whole society.

For as God humbles the father of a family in the disgrace of his wife or of his children, and a whole kindred in the disgrace of one of their number, so every church ought to consider itself stained with disgrace when any base crime is perpetrated in it. Furthermore, we have seen how the anger of God was kindled against the entire nation of Israel because of the sacrilege of one individual, Achan (Josh. 7:1).

God was not cruel in taking vengeance on the innocent for one man's crime. Rather, since there is already some token of God's anger when anything of this nature has occurred among a people, so by correcting a community for the fault of one individual, God distinctly teaches that the whole body is infected and polluted with the contagion of the offense.

Hence we readily infer that the duty of every church is to *mourn* over the faults of individual members because domestic calamities belong to the entire body. Assuredly a pious and dutiful correction arises when we are inflamed with holy zeal through displeasure at the offense, for otherwise the severity of the correction will be bitter.

FOR MEDITATION: Corruption in one place will affect the entire body. The church is a body also; thus, the effect of one person's sin will be felt by all. Corruption must be cured as fast as possible before it spreads and worse damage is done. If the corruption cannot be cured, it must be excised. Though that process it painful and difficult, it must be done if the rest of the body is to be saved. Is there any form of corruption that you are contributing to the body? Is there any elsewhere that you should pray for and humbly confront?

Providing a Way of Escape

There hath no temptation taken you but such as is common to man: but God is faithful, who will not suffer you to be tempted above that ye are able; but will with the temptation also make a way to escape, that ye may be able to bear it. 1 Corinthians 10:13

SUGGESTED FURTHER READING: James 1:12–18

As Paul taught believers to be of good courage in the past so that he might stir them to repentance, so he also comforts them for the future with the sure hope that God will not suffer them to be tempted beyond their strength. However, he adds the warning to look to the Lord, because a temptation, however slight, may quickly overcome us, and we will certainly fall if we rely upon our own strength.

Paul speaks of the Lord as *faithful*, not merely because God is true to his promises, but also, as he appears to say, "The Lord is the sure guardian of his people, under whose protection you are safe, for he never leaves his people destitute. Accordingly, when he has received you under his protection, you will have no cause to fear, provided you depend entirely upon him. For certainly this would be a kind of deception if he were to withdraw his aid in the time of need, or if upon seeing us weak and ready to sink under the load, he were to lengthen our trials."

The term *temptation* here denotes, in a general way, everything that lures us. So that we may not be overcome by temptation, God helps us in two ways: he supplies us with strength, and he sets limits to temptation. The apostle chiefly speaks of this second help here. At the same time, he does not exclude the promise that God alleviates temptations so they do not overpower us by their weight. For he knows the measure of our power, which he himself has conferred, and regulates our temptations accordingly.

FOR MEDITATION: This text offers great encouragement for weary saints. We need not constantly lose the battle against temptation, for God promises deliverance. Victory *is* possible, in the faithful strength and wisdom of God, no matter how long we have known defeat. If he provides the way of escape, why should we not take heart? Ask him for grace that his provision may be stronger than your corruption.

Dealing with Needless Contention

But if any man seem to be contentious, we have no such custom, neither the churches of God. 1 Corinthians 11:16
SUGGESTED FURTHER READING: 1 Timothy 6:1–12

A *contentious* person is inclined to stir up disputes and does not care what becomes of the truth. This description is of all who, without any need, abolish good and useful customs, raise disputes respecting matters that are not doubtful, do not yield to reason, and cannot endure anyone being above them.

This description also includes people who, from foolish affectation, aim at acting in some new and unusual way. Paul does not reckon such people worthy of response, because contention is a pernicious thing and ought to be banished from churches.

He teaches us that those who are obstinate and fond of quarreling should be restrained by authority rather than debated in lengthy disputations. For you will never end contention if you are disposed to contend with a combative person until you have defeated him. And if he were defeated a hundred times, he would still argue.

Let us therefore carefully note this passage so we do not allow ourselves to be carried away with needless disputations. At the same time, we should understand how to distinguish contentious persons. For we must not always reckon as contentious the man who does not acquiesce in our decisions or who ventures to contradict us, but when temper and obstinacy show themselves, let us then say with Paul that those contentions are at variance with the custom of the church.

FOR MEDITATION: Contending for the truth against error is the noble duty of the church, but some people contend for their own opinions on obscure subjects simply because they love contention, not because they love truth. This behavior is not acceptable in the church and is entirely against the Spirit of Christ. Many of us have pet peeves. Are we creating needless contention by repeatedly raising non-essential issues?

Blessing from Heresy

For there must be also heresies among you, that they which are approved may be made manifest among you. 1 Corinthians 11:19
SUGGESTED FURTHER READING: 1 Timothy 4

It is true that the church can be torn asunder by false doctrine and that heresy is the root and origin of schism. It is also true that envy or pride is the mother of almost all heresies. At the same time, it is helpful to distinguish between heresies and schisms.

Schisms are secret grudges that are at work in breaking down the agreement that ought to subsist among the pious because inclinations are at variance with each other. Or they are disagreements that arise when everyone is mightily pleased with his own way and finds fault with everything done by others. Heresies occur in the church when evil proceeds to such a pitch that it breaks into open hostility, and people deliberately divide themselves into opposite parties.

So that believers might not feel discouraged on seeing the Corinthians torn by divisions, the apostle turns this occasion of offense in an opposite direction, saying that the Lord uses such trials to prove his people's constancy. What a lovely consolation! He seems to say, "We should be far from being troubled or cast down when we do not see complete unity in the church. On the contrary, we ought to remain firm and constant under threats of separation due to the lack of proper agreement, even if sects should arise. For in this way hypocrites are detected, and the sincerity of believers is tried. As disagreements give occasion for discovering the fickleness of those who are not rooted in the Lord's Word and for seeing the wickedness of those who have assumed the appearance of good men, so the good of believers affords a more single manifestation of their constancy and sincerity."

FOR MEDITATION: This is certainly a fresh perspective on church division. Though strife itself does not bring glory to God, it does serve to sift the church and expose those who are not rooted in the Lord. If we find ourselves in the middle of such strife, we should examine ourselves and our motivations. Having done that, we should pray that God would purify his church through this difficult time.

Drawn to Evil

For there must be also heresies among you, that they which are approved may be made manifest among you. 1 Corinthians 11:19

SUGGESTED FURTHER READING: Titus 3:9–15

Observe what Paul says here: there *must be* heresies. By this he teaches that heresies do not happen by chance but by the sure providence of God. That is because God has it in view to try his people as gold in the furnace. If using heresy for that is agreeable to the mind of God, it is consequently expedient.

At the same time, we must not enter into thorny disputes or into labyrinths of despair as if heresy were our fate. We know there never will be a time when reprobates do not exist. We know that reprobates are governed by the spirit of Satan and are effectually drawn to what is evil. We also know that Satan actively leaves no stone unturned in trying to break up the unity of the church. From this—not from fate—comes the necessity for heresy that Paul mentions.

We also know that the Lord, by his admirable wisdom, turns Satan's deadly machinations to promote the salvation of believers. Hence comes the purpose of which Paul speaks, that God allows heresies so that the good may shine forth more conspicuously. For we should not ascribe the advantage to *heresies*, which, being evil, can produce nothing but what is evil. Rather, the advantage belongs to God, who, by his infinite goodness, changes the nature of things so that even those things which have been contrived for the ruin of the elect become salutary to them.

In the end, the wicked are impelled by Satan in such a manner that they both act and are acted upon with the consent of their wills. Hence they are without excuse for their wickedness.

FOR MEDITATION: Given human depravity, we ought not be surprised that heresies surface in the world and even in our own families and churches. As we lovingly yet firmly confront those who depart from Scripture, let us be encouraged that God will bring good out of evil and reward us for our faithfulness in dealing with this unpleasant and sinful reality. Do you walk with integrity before heretics, striving to correct them and lovingly show them their error?

Guilty of the Body and Blood

*Wherefore whosoever shall eat this bread, and drink this cup of the Lord,
unworthily, shall be guilty of the body and blood of the Lord.*
1 Corinthians 11:27
SUGGESTED FURTHER READING: 2 Corinthians 13

If the Lord requires our gratitude in receiving this sacrament, and he
would have us acknowledge his grace with the heart and publish it with
the mouth, that person will not go unpunished who has put insult upon
Christ rather than honor, for the Lord will not allow his commandment
to be despised.

Now, if we would catch the meaning of this declaration, we must
know what it is to *eat unworthily.* Some restrict that to the Corinthians
and the abuse of the Lord's Supper that has crept in among them, but I
believe that Paul, according to his usual manner, passes here from a
particular case to a general statement, or from one instance to an entire
class. One fault prevails among the Corinthians. Paul uses this to speak
of every kind of faulty administration or reception of the Lord's Supper.
"God will not allow this sacrament to be profaned without punishing it
severely," he writes.

To *eat unworthily,* then, is to pervert the pure and right use of the
Lord's Supper by our abuse of it. There are various degrees of this
unworthiness, and some offend more grievously, while others less so.
Some fornicator, perhaps, or perjurer, or drunkard, or cheat (1 Cor.
5:11) intrudes on the Supper without repentance. As such downright
contempt is a token of wanton insult against Christ, there can be no
doubt that such a person receives the Supper to his own destruction.
Another, perhaps, who is not addicted to any open or flagrant vice,
comes forward to the Supper. But he is not prepared in heart to receive
Communion. Since this carelessness or negligence is a sign of irreverence,
it also deserves punishment from God. As there are various degrees of
unworthy participation, the Lord punishes some slightly, while on others
he inflicts more severe punishment.

FOR MEDITATION: It is a terrifying prospect to be guilty of the body and
blood of the Lord. Let Paul's warning drive you to make sure that you
never attend the Table unworthily. You will always attend as a sinner,
but come as a sinner saved by grace and be prepared in your heart to
remember him.

Examining Ourselves for the Supper

But let a man examine himself, and so let him eat of that bread, and drink of that cup. 1 Corinthians 11:28

SUGGESTED FURTHER READING: 1 Peter 1:3–11

This teaching is drawn from the foregoing warning: "If those that *eat unworthily* are *guilty of the body and blood of the Lord*, then let no man approach who is not properly and duly prepared. Let every one, therefore, take heed that he may not fall into this sacrilege through idleness or carelessness." Now Paul exhorts us to an examination of another sort that may accord with the legitimate use of the sacred Supper.

You see here a method that is most easily understood. If you wish to rightly use the benefit afforded by Christ, bring to it faith and repentance. Trial must be made of these two things if you would come duly prepared. Under repentance I include love, for the person who has learned to so renounce himself that he gives himself wholly to Christ and his service will also, without doubt, carefully maintain that unity which Christ has directed.

At the same time, the faith or repentance that is required is not perfect, for some, by urging beyond due bounds a perfection that can nowhere be found, would forever shut out every individual from the Supper. If, however, you seek after the righteousness of God with the earnest desire of your mind, and, humbled by a view of your misery, do wholly lean upon Christ's grace, you may rest upon it, knowing that through him you are a worthy guest to approach the Table. You are worthy in this respect, that the Lord does not exclude you, even though from another point of view something in you is not what it ought to be. For faith, even when it is just begun, makes worthy those who were unworthy.

FOR MEDITATION: The Lord's Supper is not for those who are perfect. It is for those who are sinners but who have repented of their sin and believe in the Lord Jesus Christ alone for salvation. Thus, examination for Communion is not a search for perfection but a search for a living relationship with Christ; only through his merits may we attend his Supper. Do you practice such examination before Communion?

Being One in Christ

Now ye are the body of Christ, and members in particular. 1 Corinthians 12:27

SUGGESTED FURTHER READING: Philippians 2

What has been said about the nature and condition of the human body must be applied to us; for we are not merely a civil society, but, having been engrafted into Christ's body, are truly members of one another.

Therefore, we should know that whatever any one of us has, it has been given to us for the edification of our fellow believers. Accordingly, let us bring forward what we have and not keep it back, buried, as it were, within self, or only for our own use. Let not the person who is endowed with superior gifts be puffed up with pride and despise others; rather, let him consider nothing is so diminutive as to be of no use. For in truth, even the least among the pious brings forth fruit according to his slender capacity, so there is no useless member in the church.

Those who are not endowed with much honor should not envy those above them or refuse to do their duty to them, but they should maintain the station in which they have been placed. Let there be mutual affection, mutual fellow feeling, mutual concern. Let us have regard for the advantage of all, so that we may not destroy the church by maligning, or envy, or pride, or any disagreement. On the contrary, let every one of us strive to preserve the church to the utmost of our power.

This is a large and magnificent subject, but I content myself with having pointed out one way in which the above text must be applied to the church.

FOR MEDITATION: The church being one in Jesus Christ implies that each member of the church has particular tasks to do, just as families share tasks in their home. Some of these tasks are prominent; others, more mundane. Paul is directing every member of the church to use his or her gifts for the health and well-being of the church and their fellow members. If you are a believer, what gifts has the Spirit given you to use for the upbuilding of the church? Are you using those gifts now? How could you use them more effectively?

Seeking Selfless Love

... doth not behave itself unseemly, seeketh not her own, is not easily provoked, thinketh no evil. 1 Corinthians 13:5
SUGGESTED FURTHER READING: 1 Corinthians 12:12–31

Love does not exult in foolish showiness, nor does it bluster, but it observes moderation and propriety in all things. Paul thus indirectly reproves the Corinthians for shamefully putting aside all propriety by unseemly haughtiness.

The apostle says true love *seeketh not her own.* From this we infer how very far we are from having love implanted in us by nature, for we are naturally prone to love and care for ourselves and aim at our own advantage. To speak more correctly, we rush headlong into activity that promotes self. The remedy for so perverse an inclination is *love,* which helps us to stop caring only for ourselves and to be concerned for our neighbors by loving them and being concerned for their welfare.

What is more, to seek one's own things is to be devoted to self and to be wholly taken up with concern for one's own advantage. This definition of love solves the question about whether it is lawful for a Christian to be concerned for his own advantage. Paul does not here reprove every kind of care or concern for self, but the excess of it, which proceeds from an immoderate and blind attachment to self.

Excess self-concern is thinking of ourselves to the neglect of others, or so desiring our personal advantage that we let go of the concern that God commands us to have for our neighbors. Paul says *love* is also a bridle to repress quarrels. This follows the first two statements; for where there is gentleness and forbearance, people do not suddenly become angry and are not easily stirred up to disputes and contests.

FOR MEDITATION: The kind of love that Paul speaks about here is unconditional and sacrificial. Such love does not seek to serve itself; it seeks the good of others and the honor of God. If such love brings rewards, these are to be rejoiced in, but they are never to be the goal. How much of our love seeks its own? How can we love more unconditionally today?

Bearing the Marks of Christ

Always bearing about in the body the dying of the Lord Jesus, that the life also of Jesus might be made manifest in our body. 2 Corinthians 4:10
SUGGESTED FURTHER READING: Romans 8:28–39

The word *mortification* translated as *dying,* means something different here than it does in many passages of Scripture. Often mortification means self-denial, or renouncing the lusts of the flesh and being renewed unto obedience to God. In this verse, however, it means the afflictions by which we are stirred up to meditate on the termination of the present life.

To make it more plain, let us call the former usage "inward mortification" and the latter one "outward mortification." Both kinds of mortification conform us to Christ; one directly, and the other indirectly, so to speak. Paul speaks of inward mortification in Colossians 3:5 and in Romans 6:6, where he teaches that our old man is crucified so that we may walk in newness of life. He speaks of outward mortification in Romans 8:29, where he teaches that we were predestinated by God so that we might be conformed to the image of his Son.

However, this mortification of Christ is only so for believers, because the wicked, in enduring the afflictions of this present life, share those with Adam, but the elect participate in sufferings with the Son of God, so that all those miseries that by nature are accursed are helpful to their salvation. It is true that all the sons of God have in common bearing about the mortification of Christ. But as one is distinguished from another by a larger measure of gifts, he in that proportion comes closer to conforming with Christ in this respect.

Paul adds, *that the life also of Jesus might be made manifest in our body.* Here is the best antidote to adversity; as Christ's death is the gate of life, so we know that a blessed resurrection will terminate all our miseries. Christ has associated us with himself so that if we submit to die with him, we shall also be partakers of life with him.

FOR MEDITATION: Afflictions can be a great blessing for us. John Bunyan said that believers "are like bells; the harder they are hit, the better they sound." This "better sound" derives from being and sounding more like Christ. How have your afflictions brought you closer to Christ and made you more like him? What can we do to further this process of sanctification amid our afflictions?

Finding Blessing in Death

We are confident, I say, and willing rather to be absent from the body, and to be present with the Lord. 2 Corinthians 5:8
SUGGESTED FURTHER READING: Revelation 21:1–9

Paul here repeats what he has said respecting the confidence of the pious; they are far from breaking down under the severity of the cross and from being disheartened by afflictions. Rather, in those they are made more courageous. For the worst of evils is death, yet believers long to attain death as the commencement of perfect blessedness.

The word *and* in this verse may be regarded as equivalent to *because*, thus reading, "Nothing can befall us that can shake our confidence and courage, since death (which others so much dread) is to us *great gain* (Phil. 1:21). For nothing is better than leaving the body, for in it we may attain close fellowship with God and may truly and openly enjoy his presence. In the decay of the body, we lose nothing that belongs to us."

Observe here that true faith begets not merely contempt of death but even desire for it. On the other hand, a token of unbelief is when the dread of death predominates in us above the joy and consolation of hope. True believers desire death, not as if they would by an importunate desire anticipate their Lord's day, for they willingly retain footing in their earthly station so long as their Lord may see it good for them. They would rather live to the glory of Christ and "die to themselves" (Rom. 14:7) than live for their own advantage. The desire for death, of which Paul speaks, springs forth from faith. It is not at all in variance with the will of God.

We may also gather from these words of Paul that souls, when released from the body, live in the presence of God. For if by being *absent from the body* they have God *present* with them, they surely live with him.

FOR MEDITATION: The Bible does not speak much about the intermediate state of man—that is, our state between death and when Christ resurrects our bodies at his Second Coming. But Paul confirms for us that our souls shall indeed be present with the Lord. That means more to believers than anything else. To be with the Lord, without the conflict of sin, ought to be our crowning desire. It ought to make us welcome death. Today, meditate on what this entails, and thank God for the intermediate state even as we long for the day when our entire man— soul and body—shall serve the Lord in perfection forever.

Knowing Godly Sorrow

*For godly sorrow worketh repentance to salvation not to be repented of:
but the sorrow of the world worketh death.* 2 Corinthians 7:10
SUGGESTED FURTHER READING: Psalm 51

To understand what is meant by *godly sorrow*, we must observe that
godly sorrow is contrasted here with *sorrow of the world*. There is also a
contrast between two kinds of joy. The joy of the world is when men
foolishly and without the fear of the Lord exult in vanity, that is, with
the world. Intoxicated with a transient happiness, they look no higher
than the earth. True joy is when men place all their happiness in God
and take satisfaction in his grace. They show this joy in contempt of the
world, regarding earthly prosperity as if it is of no use to them and being
joyful in the midst of adversity.

So, the *sorrow of the world* is when men despair as a *consequence* of
earthly afflictions and are overwhelmed with grief. *Godly sorrow* has
an eye to God; those who have it reckon it misery to have lost the favor
of God. Impressed with the fear of God's judgment, they mourn over
their sins.

Paul says godly sorrow is the cause and origin of repentance. It is to be
carefully observed, for unless the sinner is dissatisfied with himself,
detests his manner of life, and is thoroughly grieved by an apprehension
of sin, he will never betake himself to the Lord. On the other hand, it is
impossible for a person to experience sorrow of this kind without giving
birth to a new heart.

Hence repentance arises in grief, for the reason that I have mentioned.
No one can return to the right way unless he hates sin. Where there is
hatred of sin, there is grief and dissatisfaction with self.

FOR MEDITATION: There are many sorrows in this world, and none of
them are pleasant. Godly sorrow is not pleasant, either, and thus it is
avoided by most. But it is a sorrow that leads to the great joy of
salvation. It is not to be regretted, for it leads to repentance and life.
Have you experienced godly sorrow? Think of the joy that it has brought
about.

Hoarding Manna

As it is written, He that had gathered much had nothing over; and he that had gathered little had no lack. 2 Corinthians 8:15
SUGGESTED FURTHER READING: Exodus 16

The Lord has not prescribed to us a homer or any other measure by which the food of each day is to be regulated, but he has imposed upon us frugality and temperance, and has forbidden that anyone should go to excess, taking advantage of his abundance.

So let those who have riches, whether left by inheritance or procured by industry and efforts, consider that their abundance is not intended to be exhibited in intemperance or excess but to relieve the necessities of their brethren. For whatever we have is *manna*, regardless of where it comes from, provided it is really ours. Riches acquired by fraud and unlawful strategies are unworthy to be called manna, but are rather *quails* sent by the anger of God (Num. 11:31).

As in hoarding manna, either from excessive greed or from distrust, what is saved immediately putrefies, so we need not doubt that the riches that are heaped up at the expense of other people are also accursed and will soon perish. Furthermore, that happens in connection with the ruin of the owner. So we are not to think that the way to increase our possessions is to work toward our own advantage for a long time while defrauding those who are poor of the beneficence that we owe them.

I acknowledge, indeed, that equality is not imposed upon us to make it unlawful for the rich to live in greater elegance than the poor, but equality is to be observed in such a way that no one is allowed to starve, and no one hoards his abundance at the expense of defrauding others.

FOR MEDITATION: Thinking of our money as manna is an excellent way to remember its origin and its intent. Hoarding will bring no gain. If the Lord has blessed us with great gifts, we should determine how we can best use them in his service and for the poor in our fellowship. If we have little, we should not be anxious but trust that the Lord will move the hearts of those who have more than us to help us.

Asking without Receiving

For this thing I besought the Lord thrice, that it might depart from me.
2 Corinthians 12:8
SUGGESTED FURTHER READING: Mark 14:32–42

It may seem from this text that Paul has not prayed in faith, for we read everywhere in Scripture that we shall obtain whatever we ask in faith. Paul prays, and does not obtain what he asks for.

I address this problem by saying that as there are different ways of asking, so there are different ways of obtaining. We ask in simple terms for those things for which we have an express promise. For example, we ask for the perfecting of God's kingdom, the hallowing of his name (Matt. 6:9), the remission of our sins, and everything that is advantageous to us. But when we think that the kingdom of God *can*, indeed, *must* be advanced in this particular manner or in that, and what is necessary for the hallowing of his name, we are often mistaken in our opinion.

In like manner, we often commit a serious mistake about asking for what tends to promote our own welfare. We ask for things confidently and without reservation, while we do not have the right to prescribe the means for receiving them. If, however, we specify the means, we always have an implied condition, even though we don't express it.

Paul was not ignorant about this. Hence, as to the *object* of his prayer, there can be no doubt that he was heard, though he met with a refusal as to the express form of that answer. By this we are admonished not to give way to despondency in thinking our prayers are lost labor when God does not gratify or comply with our wishes. Rather, we must be satisfied with his grace in not forsaking us. For the reason why God sometimes mercifully refuses to give his own people what in his wrath he grants to the wicked is that he better foresees what is expedient for us than our understanding is able to apprehend.

FOR MEDITATION: Even with the knowledge that God knows best, it is difficult to submit to his will when our prayers seem to go unanswered. We must pray for the grace to will what God wills and to leave it to his wisdom how he brings his will about. Are you trusting him with all your current concerns?

Putting on Christ

For as many of you as have been baptized into Christ have put on Christ.
Galatians 3:27
SUGGESTED FURTHER READING: Romans 6:1–14

Paul explains in a few words what it means to be united or made one with the Son of God. He uses the metaphor of putting on a garment in saying that the Galatians *have put on Christ*; meaning that these believers are so closely united with Christ that in the presence of God they so bear the name and character of Christ that they are viewed in him rather than in themselves. This metaphor of taking on garments occurs frequently in Scripture.

The argument that, because they have been baptized, they have put on Christ, appears weak, however; for how far is baptism from being efficacious in all people? Is it reasonable that the grace of the Holy Spirit should be so closely linked to an external symbol? Does not the uniform doctrine of Scripture as well as experience appear to confute this statement?

I answer this objection by saying it is customary for Paul to treat the sacraments from two points of view. When he is dealing with hypocrites, in whom a mere symbol awakens pride, he loudly proclaims the emptiness and worthlessness of the outward symbol. He also denounces, in strong terms, their foolish confidence in this symbol. In such cases he contemplates not the ordinance of God but the corruption of wicked men.

On the other hand, he addresses believers who make proper use of the symbols by viewing them in connection with the truth that they represent. In this case, Paul makes no boast of any false splendor that comes from the sacraments but calls our attention to the actual fact represented by the outward ceremony. Thus, in agreement with the divine appointment, the truth comes to be associated with the symbols.

FOR MEDITATION: Living as one who has put on Christ by faith is one of the Christian's greatest privileges. By the Spirit's grace, how can you put into practice today that you have put on Christ? How can the sacraments assist you in this task?

Forming Christ in You

My little children, of whom I travail in birth again until Christ be formed in you. Galatians 4:19

SUGGESTED FURTHER READING: 1 John 2:12–29

In this text Paul soothes the anger of the Galatians. He does not set aside as useless their former birth but says that they must be nourished again in the womb, for they have not yet been fully formed.

Christ being formed in us is the same thing as our being formed in Christ, for we are born to become new creatures in him. He, on the other hand, is born in us so that we may live in him. Since the true image of Christ was defaced by the superstitions introduced by the false apostles, Paul labors to restore that image in all its perfection and brightness. This is done by the ministers of the gospel when they give milk to babes and strong meat to those who are of full age (Heb. 5:13, 14). In short, this is to be their goal in all of their preaching.

Paul here compares himself to a woman in labor, because the Galatians have not yet been completely born. This is a remarkable passage for illustrating the efficacy of the Christian ministry. True, we are "born of God" (1 John 3:9), but God uses a minister and preaching as his instruments for that purpose. So he is pleased to ascribe to them that work which he himself performs through the power of his Spirit in co-operation with the labors of man.

Let us always pay attention to the distinction that, when a minister is contrasted with God, he is nothing and can do nothing and is utterly useless. But because the Holy Spirit works efficaciously by means of the minister, the minister comes to be regarded and praised as an agent. Still, it is not what he can do in himself or apart from God but what God does by him that is here described. If ministers wish to do anything, let them labor to form Christ, not to form themselves, in their listeners.

FOR MEDITATION: How often don't we try to form ourselves, rather than Christ, in others? If someone should become like us and hold the same opinions as us, we would be quite satisfied with ourselves. But we should be laboring to form Christ in others so they might quickly surpass us in godliness and spur us on to have Christ formed in us more and more.

Being Gentle in Correction

Brethren, if a man be overtaken in a fault, ye which are spiritual, restore such an one in the spirit of meekness; considering thyself, lest thou also be tempted. Galatians 6:1

SUGGESTED FURTHER READING: Jeremiah 30:1–17

We are taught here to correct the faults of others in a mild manner, considering no rebuke to have a religious and Christian character that does not breathe the spirit of meekness. To this end, Paul explains the goal of pious reproof, which is to *restore* a person who has fallen and to place him back in his former condition. That goal will never be accomplished by violence, by a disposition to accuse, or by fierceness of manner or language. Consequently, we must display a gentle and meek spirit if we are to heal a fellow believer. Lest any one should satisfy himself by simply assuming the outward form of meekness, the apostle demands *the spirit of meekness,* for no person is prepared to chastise a brother till he has succeeded in acquiring a gentle spirit.

Another argument for gentleness in correcting others is the expression *if a man be overtaken in a fault.* If a person has been carried away through want of consideration or through the cunning art of a deceiver, it would be cruel to treat such a person with harshness. We know that the devil is always lying in wait and has a thousand ways of leading us astray. When we perceive that a believer has transgressed, let us consider that he has fallen into the snares of Satan. Let us then be moved with compassion and prepare our minds to exercise forgiveness.

Offenses and falls of this description must undoubtedly be distinguished from deep-seated crimes that are accompanied by deliberate and obstinate disregard of the authority of God. Such displays of wicked and perverse disobedience to God must be treated with greater severity, for what advantage would be gained by gentle treatment? The word *also* implies that not only the weak who have been tempted but also those who have yielded to temptation shall be treated with forbearance.

FOR MEDITATION: It can be difficult to react with gentleness and meekness to the faults we find in others. If we ourselves do not particularly struggle with the same sin, how easily we condemn their behavior and deeply wound them in the process. We should keep in mind that only God's grace keeps us from easily falling into the same temptation.

Considering our Weakness

Brethren, if a man be overtaken in a fault, ye which are spiritual, restore such an one in the spirit of meekness; considering thyself, lest thou also be tempted. Galatians 6:1
SUGGESTED FURTHER READING: 1 Peter 4:7–19

Not without reason, Paul passes from the plural to the singular number in this verse in saying, *Considering thyself, lest thou also be tempted.* He gives weight to his admonition when he addresses each person individually and bids him to look carefully at himself. "Whoever thou art that takest upon thee the office of reproving others, look to thyself," he seems to say.

Nothing is more difficult for us than to acknowledge or examine our own weaknesses. However acute we are in detecting the faults of others, it is more difficult, as the saying goes, to see "the deformity that hangs behind our own back." Therefore, to rouse us to greater activity, Paul uses the singular number.

His words have two implications. As we acknowledge that we are liable to sin, we will more willingly grant forgiveness to others, which, in turn, we can expect will be extended to us. Some restate the meaning of these words as: "Thou who art a sinner, and needest the compassion of thy brethren, oughtest not to show thyself fierce and implacable to others." I would rather choose to say these words are offered as a warning that, in correcting others, we should not ourselves commit sin.

There is a danger here that deserves our most careful attention and against which it is difficult to guard, for nothing is easier than to exceed proper limits. The word *tempt*, however, may very properly be taken in this passage as extending to the whole life. Whenever we have occasion to pronounce censure on another, let us begin by examining ourselves. Then, remembering our own weakness, let us be indulgent to others.

FOR MEDITATION: We should be careful not to compound the sinful nature of a situation by adding sin to sin. If we are rebuking sin, we should make sure that our rebukes are as free from sin as possible. We must restore others with a spirit of meekness, not haughtiness.

Bearing Others' Burdens

Bear ye one another's burdens, and so fulfil the law of Christ. Galatians 6:2

SUGGESTED FURTHER READING: 1 Corinthians 13

The weaknesses or sins under which we groan are called *burdens.* "Bearing another's burdens" is singularly appropriate in a teaching recommending kind behavior, for nature tells us that those who bend under a burden ought to be relieved.

Paul orders us to *bear* the burdens of others. We must not indulge or overlook the sins by which our brethren are pressed down, but relieve them, and that can only be done by mild and friendly correction. Many adulterers, thieves, wicked, and abandoned characters of every description would willingly make Christ an accomplice in their crimes. All would choose to lay upon believers the task of bearing their burdens. But as the apostle has just exhorted us to *restore* a brother, the manner in which Christians are required to *bear one another's burdens* cannot be mistaken.

The word *law*, when applied here to Christ, serves the place of an argument. There is an implied contrast between the law of Christ and the law of Moses. It is as if Paul says, "If you are very desirous to keep a law, Christ enjoins on you a law which you are bound to prefer to all others, which is to cherish kindness toward each other." He who has no kindness has nothing.

On the other hand, the apostle tells us that, whenever someone compassionately assists his neighbor, the law of Christ is *fulfilled.* He thereby intimates that everything that does not proceed from love is superfluous, for the Greek word he uses here conveys the idea of what is absolutely perfect. But since no one performs in every respect what Paul requires, we are still at a distance from perfection. He who comes closest to it in regarding others is yet far distant with respect to God.

FOR MEDITATION: Sadly, we grow accustomed to living with selfish hearts in a selfish society, seldom realizing that true joy flows from a life of service in which we bear the burdens of others. Yet God is patient with us, continually putting the needy on our life's path. What needy people has Providence placed on your path at the present time? Are you bearing their burdens in love by praying for them, sympathizing with them, and acting for them? What concrete actions could you take this week to help bear someone else's burdens?

Sealed with the Holy Spirit

In whom ye also trusted, after that ye heard the word of truth, the gospel of your salvation: in whom also after that ye believed, ye were sealed with that holy Spirit of promise. Ephesians 1:13
SUGGESTED FURTHER READING: Galatians 4:1–7

Satan attempts nothing more earnestly than leading us to doubt or despise the gospel. Paul therefore furnishes us with two shields to repel both temptations. In opposition to every doubt, let us bring forward the testimony that the gospel is certain truth, which cannot deceive, and is also *the word of truth*, as if there were no truth but itself.

Happy are those who have embraced the gospel and whose attachment to it is steadfast, for beyond all doubt, this is truth and life.

Having maintained that the gospel is certain, Paul now comes to the proof: *in whom also after that ye believed.* What higher surety can be found than the Holy Spirit? "For you have the testimony of the Spirit of God himself, who seals the truth of it in your hearts," Paul says.

Seals give validity to charters and to testaments. In ancient times, seals were the principal means by which the writer of a letter could be known. In short, a seal distinguishes what is true and certain from what is false and spurious. This is the office the apostle ascribes to the Holy Spirit.

Our minds cannot become so firmly established in the truth of God that they resist the temptations of Satan until we have been confirmed in it by the Holy Spirit. The conviction of truth that believers have of the Word of God, their own salvation, and religion in general does not spring from the judgment of the flesh or from human and philosophical arguments but from the seal of the Spirit, who imparts to consciences such certainty as to remove all doubt.

The foundation of faith would be frail and unsteady if it rested on human wisdom. Therefore, as preaching is the instrument of faith, so the Holy Spirit makes preaching efficacious.

FOR MEDITATION: We live in a world that constantly attacks the truth of the Bible. In these conditions, it is easy for doubts to creep into our minds. Is the Bible really true? Paul was convinced it was the word of truth. Though rational arguments can never lay every doubt finally to rest, the supernatural witness of the Holy Spirit can. Believers know, in the face of all opposition, that the Word is true and that they are building on the rock.

Satan's Limited Power

Wherein in time past ye walked according to the course of this world, according to the prince of the power of the air, the spirit that now worketh in the children of disobedience. Ephesians 2:2
SUGGESTED FURTHER READING: 2 Timothy 2:20–26

In accordance with the practice of the inspired writers, the devil is mentioned as a singular being. As the children of God have one head, so have the wicked; for each of these groups forms a distinct body.

By assigning to Satan dominion over all wicked beings, ungodliness is represented as an unbroken mass. As to Paul's attributing to the devil power over the air, that will be covered when we discuss the sixth chapter. At present, we shall merely refer to the strange absurdity of the Manicheans in trying to prove from this passage the existence of two principles, as if Satan could do anything without divine permission.

Paul does not allow Satan the highest authority, for that is the will of God alone, but he does say the devil has a tyranny that God permits him to exercise. What is Satan but God's executioner to punish man's ingratitude? This is implied in Paul's language when he represents the success of Satan as confined to unbelievers, for the children of God are exempt from his power. If this is true, it follows that Satan does nothing but what is under the control of a superior, and is not an unlimited monarch.

We may now draw from it the truth that ungodly men have no excuse in being driven by Satan to commit all sorts of crimes. How can they be subject to the devil's tyranny unless they are rebels against God? If none are the slaves of Satan but those who have renounced the service and authority of God, let them blame themselves for having so cruel a master.

FOR MEDITATION: Christ brings release to captives, so there is no reason to remain in Satan's service. If you call out to God, there is nothing Satan can do to prevent your leaving his clutches and entering the kingdom of light. Are you in bondage to Satan? You need not remain in such a state. Call out to God!

Finding True Peace and Access

And came and preached peace to you which were afar off, and to them that were nigh. For through him we both have access by one Spirit unto the Father. Ephesians 2:17–18

SUGGESTED FURTHER READING: John 14

Observe here that the gospel is the message of *peace* by which God declares himself reconciled to us and makes known his paternal love. Take away the gospel, and war and enmity continue to exist between God and men. On the other hand, the native tendency of the gospel is to give peace and calmness to the conscience, which otherwise would be tormented by distressing alarm.

For through him we both have access. This is an argument based on the fact that we are permitted to draw near to God. But it may also be viewed as an announcement of peace; for wicked men, lulled into a profound sleep, sometimes deceive themselves with false notions of peace. They think they are at rest when they have learned to forget divine judgment and to keep themselves at the greatest possible distance from God.

It is necessary to explain the nature of true peace, for it is widely different from a stupefied conscience, from false confidence, from proud boasting, and from ignorance of our own wretchedness. It is a settled composure which leads us not to dread but to desire and seek the feet of God. Now, Christ opens the door to us, yes, he is himself the door (John 10:9). As this is a double door thrown open to admit both Jews and Gentiles, we are led to view God exhibiting his fatherly kindness to both.

Paul adds that we have access to God *by one Spirit*, who leads and guides us to Christ and "by whom we cry, Abba, Father" (Rom. 8:15). From this arises our boldness of approach. Jews had various means of drawing near to God, but now Jews and Gentiles have but one way: to be led by the Spirit of God.

FOR MEDITATION: Peace and access summarize the gospel of Jesus Christ. Peace may only be gained by access to God; apart from Christ, access to God brings anything but peace. Let us praise him, then, for granting us these two great blessings, which together comprise the greatest blessing of all.

Walking Worthy in Humility

I therefore, the prisoner of the Lord, beseech you that ye walk worthy of the vocation wherewith ye are called, with all lowliness and meekness, with long-suffering, forbearing one another in love. Ephesians 4:1–2

SUGGESTED FURTHER READING: Luke 14:7–11

That ye walk worthy is a general sentiment, or preface, on which the following statements are founded. Paul formerly had described the vocation to which the Ephesians were called. He now reminds them that they must live in obedience to God so that they may not be unworthy of such distinguished grace.

He says they are to do this *with all lowliness.* He then proceeds to particulars, beginning with humility. The reason why he begins with humility is that it is the first step to unity, which he is about to discuss. Humility produces *meekness*, which disposes us to bear with our brethren and thus to preserve that unity which otherwise would be broken a hundred times a day.

Let us remember, therefore, that in cultivating kindness toward others, we must begin with humility. Where do rudeness, pride, and disdainful language toward others arise? Where do quarrels, insults, and reproaches originate? Are they not what results when people carry love of self and their own interests to excess?

By laying aside haughtiness and the desire of pleasing ourselves, we shall become meek and gentle and acquire that moderation of temper that will overlook and forgive many things in the conduct of others. Let us carefully observe the order and arrangement of this teaching. It is of no use to inculcate forbearance until our natural fierceness has been subdued and we have acquired mildness. Likewise, it will be equally useless to seek *meekness* unless we begin with humility.

FOR MEDITATION: Church unity begins with humility. As long as we are haughty and proud, we will make no progress, no matter how many ecumenical conferences are held. For the church to be humble, each of its members must be humble. Out of that humility will flow the meekness, long-suffering, and forbearance needed to achieve unity. Examine yourself for this type of humility.

Controlling Anger

Be ye angry, and sin not: let not the sun go down upon your wrath.
Ephesians 4:26
SUGGESTED FURTHER READING: Psalm 37:1–11

We offend God in three ways when we are angry. The first is allowing our anger to arise from slight causes, often from no cause whatever, or at least from private injuries or offenses. The second is carrying anger beyond proper bounds and rushing into intemperate excesses. The third is directing anger, which should have been directed against ourselves or against our sins, against others.

Paul, in wishing to describe the proper limitation of anger, most appropriately uses the well-known text, *Be ye angry, and sin not.* We comply with this injunction if our anger is not directed at others but at ourselves, and if we pour out indignation against our own faults. With respect to others, we ought to be angry, not at their persons, but at their faults. Nor should we be moved to anger by offenses against ourselves, but out of zeal for the glory of the Lord. Lastly, our anger ought to subside after a reasonable time without mixing itself with the violence of carnal passions.

Next Paul says, *let not the sun go down upon your wrath.* So strong is the tendency of the human mind to do what is evil that we sometimes give way to improper and sinful passion. Paul therefore suggests that we should quickly suppress our anger and not allow it to gather strength by continuing it. The first remedy for anger is *be ye angry, and sin not,* but since the great weakness of human nature renders this exceedingly difficult, the next step is to not cherish wrath too long in our minds or allow it sufficient time to become strong. Paul thus says, *let not the sun go down upon your wrath.* If at any time we are angry, let us endeavor to be appeased before the sun has set.

FOR MEDITATION: If we examine our anger and its causes, we usually find no justification for it. Even worse, we often let this anger fester and ruin many other parts of our lives. Who has not let anger about some trivial thing ruin the entire day, a day full of blessings from God? We must repent of this and seek to follow Paul's instruction.

Grieving the Holy Spirit

And grieve not the holy Spirit of God, whereby ye are sealed unto the day of redemption. Ephesians 4:30
SUGGESTED FURTHER READING: 1 Corinthians 3:13–23

Because the Holy Spirit dwells in us, every part of our soul and our body ought to be devoted to him. If we give ourselves up to anything that is impure, we may rightly be said to be driving him away from making his abode with us. To express this in more familiar terms, human affections such as joy and grief are ascribed to the Holy Spirit. So we are to endeavor that the Holy Spirit may dwell cheerfully with us, as in a pleasant and joyful dwelling, and give him no occasion for grief.

We are sealed by the Spirit, Paul says. Because God has sealed us by his Spirit, we grieve him when we do not follow his guidance and pollute ourselves by wicked passions. No language can adequately express this solemn truth that the Holy Spirit rejoices and is glad on our account when we are obedient to him in all things and do not think nor speak anything but what is pure and holy. On the other hand, he is grieved when we admit anything into our minds that is unworthy of our calling.

Now, let us reflect what shocking wickedness there must be in grieving the Holy Spirit to such a degree that it compels him to withdraw from us. The same truth is expressed by the prophet Isaiah, but in a different sense, for he says people "vexed his Holy Spirit" (Isa. 63:10) in the same sense in which we are accustomed to speak of vexing the mind of a man.

The Spirit of God is the seal by which we are distinguished from the wicked. It is impressed on our hearts as a sure evidence of adoption.

FOR MEDITATION: Several minutes of quiet reflection on the dreadfulness of grieving God Almighty should be a great impetus to new obedience. In what ways could you be grieving the Holy Spirit at the present time? What should you do about this?

Following Christ as Children

Be ye therefore followers of God, as dear children; and walk in love, as Christ also hath loved us, and hath given himself for us an offering and a sacrifice to God for a sweet-smelling savor. Ephesians 5:1–2

SUGGESTED FURTHER READING: Romans 8:12–17

Children ought to be like their father. The same principle is followed out and enforced by the consideration that we are children of God, Paul says. So, as much as possible, we ought to resemble God in acts of kindness.

It is impossible not to see that the division of chapters here is particularly unwise, since it separates parts of a subject which are very closely related. But let us go on. Paul is saying that, if we are the children of God, we ought to be *followers of God*. Christ declares that, unless we show kindness to the unworthy, we cannot be the children of our heavenly Father: "Love your enemies, bless them that curse you, do good to them that hate you, and pray for them which despitefully use you and persecute you; that ye may be the children of your Father which is in heaven; for he maketh his sun to rise on the evil and on the good, and sendeth rain on the just and on the unjust" (Matt. 5:44–45).

Paul further admonishes us to *walk in love, as Christ also hath loved us*. Having called us to imitate God, he now calls us to imitate Christ, who is our true model. We should embrace each other with the love with which Christ has embraced us, for what we perceive in Christ is our true guide.

What is more, he *gave himself for us*. This is remarkable proof of the highest love. Seemingly forgetful of himself, Christ did not spare his own life so that he might redeem us from death. If we want to be partakers of this benefit, we must cultivate similar love toward our neighbor. None of us has reached such high perfection, but all must aim and strive according to the measure of their ability.

FOR MEDITATION: With so awesome a heavenly Father, shouldn't we be dear children to him, following him in everything and seeking to be a delight to him rather than a grief? We should look to our older brother, Christ, for the grace and strength to follow his example in being a faithful child of the Father.

Becoming One Flesh

For this cause shall a man leave his father and mother, and shall be joined unto his wife, and they two shall be one flesh. Ephesians 5:31
SUGGESTED FURTHER READING: Genesis 2:18–25

He *shall leave his father and mother*, Paul says. It is as if he admonishes, "Let him rather *leave his father and mother* than not cleave to his wife."

Marriage does not set aside the other duties of mankind, nor are the commandments of God so inconsistent with each other that a man cannot be a good and faithful husband without ceasing to be a dutiful son. It is rather a question of degree. Moses draws the comparison between marriage and duty to one's parents so he can more strongly express the close and sacred union that exists between husband and wife. A son is bound by an inviolable law of nature to perform his duties toward his father. While the obligations of a husband toward his wife are declared to be stronger than that of a son toward his father, their force is better understood in the comparison. He who resolves to be a good husband will not fail to perform his filial duties but will regard marriage as more sacred than all other ties.

And they two shall be one flesh means they shall be one man, or, to use a common phrase, they shall become one person; which certainly would not hold true in any other kind of relationship. Everything depends on this, that the wife was formed of the flesh and bones of her husband. Such is the union between us and Christ, who makes us partakers of his substance. "We are bone of his bone, and flesh of his flesh" (Gen. 2:23), not because he has a human nature like ours, but because, by the power of his Spirit, he makes us part of his body, and from him we derive life.

FOR MEDITATION: In the gospel, we find the pattern for how marriage ought to be conducted. When a husband and wife are careful to exemplify the roles of Christ and the church, many dreadful and burdensome evils are avoided. Is there an area of marriage in which you should be more careful to do so? Let us remember that the grace to conduct marriage in that way is only available through the cross, under which husband and wife can meet for forgiveness.

Obeying Parents in the Lord

Children, obey your parents in the Lord: for this is right. Ephesians 6:1
SUGGESTED FURTHER READING: Colossians 3:18–25

Why does the apostle use the word *obey* instead of *honor*, which has a greater scope of meaning? It is because obedience is evidence of the honor which children owe to their parents and is therefore more earnestly enforced.

Obedience is also more difficult, for the human mind recoils from the idea of subjection and with difficulty allows itself to be placed under the control of another. Experience shows how rare this virtue is, for do we find even one among a thousand who is obedient to his parents? By a figure of speech, a part is here put for the whole, but it is the most important part and is necessarily accompanied by all the others.

Children are to obey their parents *in the Lord*. Besides the law of nature, which is acknowledged by all nations, the authority of God enforces the obedience of children. Hence it follows that parents are to be obeyed so far as is consistent with piety to God, which comes first. If the command of God is the rule by which the submission of children is to be regulated, it would be foolish to suppose that the performance of this duty could lead away from obeying God himself.

For this is right is added to restrain the fierceness which, as we have already said, appears to be natural to almost all people. It is *right*, because God has commanded it. We are not at liberty to dispute or call in question the appointment of him whose will is the unerring rule of goodness and righteousness. That this honor should be represented as including obedience is not surprising, for mere ceremony is of no value in the sight of God. The precept *honor thy father and mother* includes all the duties by which children can express sincere affection and respect to their parents.

FOR MEDITATION: Are you showing due respect to your parents, even as an adult? How do the principles Calvin has outlined here apply to us in other areas of life in which we are subject to divinely appointed authority?

The Promise of Honoring Parents

Honour thy father and mother, which is the first commandment with promise; that it may be well with thee, and thou mayest live long on the earth. Ephesians 6:2–3
SUGGESTED FURTHER READING: Deuteronomy 5:1–21

The promises annexed to the commandments are intended to excite our hopes and to impart a greater cheerfulness to our obedience. Therefore Paul includes promise as a kind of seasoning to render more pleasant and agreeable the submission that he requires of children.

He does not merely say that God offers a reward to one who obeys his father and mother, but also that such a reward is peculiar to this commandment. If each of the commandments had its own promise, there would be no ground for the commendation bestowed with this commandment. But this is *the first commandment*, Paul tells us, that God has been pleased, as it were, to seal with a remarkable promise.

There is some difficulty here, for the second commandment likewise contains a promise: "I am the LORD thy God, ... showing mercy unto thousands of them that love me, and keep my commandments" (Exod. 20:5–6). But this promise is applied indiscriminately to the whole law and cannot be said to be annexed to a particular commandment. Paul's assertion still holds true, that no other commandment but the one requiring the obedience of children to their parents is distinguished by a promise.

That it may be well with thee is promised; so is a long life. From this we understand that the present life is not to be overlooked among the gifts of God. The reward promised to obedient children is highly appropriate. Those who show kindness to their parents, from whom they derived life, are assured by God that life will go well for them while on this earth.

FOR MEDITATION: Obedience to God's commandments can only result in blessing because they are given for our own good. In addition to the good that results from simple obedience to God's commands, God provides promises of good will and blessing. His intent in giving laws is not to hold us in bondage but to save us from evil and bless us. Give him praise today for this love.

Esteeming Others before Self

Let nothing be done through strife or vainglory; but in lowliness of mind let each esteem other better than themselves. Philippians 2:3
SUGGESTED FURTHER READING: Matthew 7:1–5

Paul here defines true humility, which is to esteem others more than self. Now, if anything in life is difficult, it is humility. Hence it is not surprising that humility is a rare virtue.

It is said, "Everyone has the mind of a king by claiming everything for himself." This is pride. From such foolish admiration of ourselves rises contempt of others. We are far from what Paul teaches here, for we can hardly endure others to be on a level with ourselves, much less allow them to have superiority.

But how is it possible that one who truly is distinguished above others can reckon those to be superior to him whom he knows are greatly beneath him? I answer that this altogether depends on a right estimate of God's gifts and our own infirmities. For however anyone is distinguished by illustrious gifts, he ought to consider that they have not been conferred upon him that he might be self-complacent, that he might exalt himself, or even that he might hold himself in esteem. Instead, let him be active in correcting and detecting his faults, and he will have abundant occasion for humility.

On the other hand, he will regard with honor those in whom there is excellence and will in love bury their faults. The man who observes this rule will not find it difficult to prefer others before self. This, too, Paul meant when he added that they ought not to have everyone a regard to themselves but to their neighbors, or that they ought not to be devoted to themselves. Hence it is quite possible that a pious man, even though aware that he is superior, may nevertheless hold others in greater esteem.

FOR MEDITATION: Considering others before self is so contrary to our nature that only the grace of God can bring it about. Yet what glorious release from pride and selfishness it offers! To focus on the good in others and keep ourselves from glossing over our own faults is necessary if we are to remain humble.

Bound to Serve

For all seek their own, not the things which are Jesus Christ's.
Philippians 2:21
SUGGESTED FURTHER READING: Matthew 16:21–28

How great a hindrance it is for Christ's ministers to seek their own interests. Nor is there any merit in these excuses: "I do harm to no one," "I must also have regard for my own advantage," or "I am not so devoid of feeling as not to be prompted by a regard for my own advantage." For you must give up your rights if you would discharge your duty; a regard to your own interests must not be preferred to Christ's glory or even placed on a level with it.

Wherever Christ calls you, you must promptly go, leaving all else. You ought to regard your calling in such a way that you turn away your powers of perception from everything that would impede you. You might have the power to live elsewhere in greater opulence, but God has bound you to the church, which affords you a very moderate sustenance. You might gain more honor elsewhere, but God has assigned you a situation in which you must live in a humble style. You might have a more favorable climate elsewhere or a more delightful region, but it is here that you are asked to be.

You might wish to deal with more humane people, feeling offended by people now who show ingratitude or incivility or pride. In short, you have no sympathy with the disposition or the manners of the nation in which you are asked to serve. But you must struggle with yourself and suppress the opposing inclinations that you keep of the profession to which you are called, for you are not free or at your own disposal. In conclusion, forget yourself if you would serve God.

FOR MEDITATION: It is easy to develop romantic notions about what it means to follow God. But when we realize the crosses we must bear, our hearts may rebel against God's plan for us. We must not seek our own things, however, but the things of Christ, no matter what situations he places us in. We live not for ourselves, but for him.

Sorrowing unto Death

For indeed he was sick nigh unto death: but God had mercy on him; and not on him only, but on me also, lest I should have sorrow upon sorrow.
Philippians 2:27
SUGGESTED FURTHER READING: 2 Kings 4:8–37

Observe two things here: first, the dispositions of grief that God originally implanted in our nature are not evil in themselves. They are not the fault of corrupt nature but come forth from God as their author. This kind of grief is felt on the occasion of the death of friends. Second, notice that Paul had many other reasons for regret in connection with the death of Epaphroditus. These regrets were not merely excusable; they were altogether necessary.

Grief is inevitable in the case of all believers, for on the occasion of the death of anyone, we are reminded of the anger of God against sin. But Paul in his grief was more affected with the loss sustained by the church, which he saw would be deprived of a singularly good pastor at a time when good leaders were so few in number.

However, because of the depravity of our nature, everything in us is so perverted that no matter in what direction our minds are bent, our feelings always tend to go beyond bounds. Hence nothing is so pure or right in itself as not to bring with it some contagion. Indeed, Paul, being a man, would no doubt have experienced something of human error in his grief, for he was subject to infirmity. He needed to be tried with temptations so he might have the opportunity of victory by striving and resisting.

FOR MEDITATION: The loss of a loved one hurts deeply. We need to mourn when we suffer loss; that is how God has constituted us. Yet, if our loved ones have gone to be with the Lord, we need not sorrow as those without hope. Nor should we wish them back, for their sake. How can meditating on their eternal abode remove a great part of our sorrow?

The Fellowship of Suffering

That I may know him, and the power of his resurrection, and the fellowship of his sufferings, being made comformable unto his death.
Philippians 3:10
SUGGESTED FURTHER READING: Galatians 2:11–21

Having spoken of the freely conferred righteousness procured for us through the resurrection of Christ and obtained by us through faith, Paul proceeds to discuss *the fellowship of his sufferings*, or the exercises of the pious, so that it might not seem as though he introduces an inactive faith that produces no effects in this life.

Indirectly, he also implies that these are the exercises that the Lord would have his people use rather than the useless elements of ceremonies that the false apostles press upon believers. So, let every one who has by faith become a partaker of all Christ's benefits acknowledge that the condition of these benefits is that his whole life be conformed to Christ's death.

There is both participation and fellowship in the death of Christ. One exercise is inward; it is what the Scripture tends to call the mortification of the flesh or the crucifixion of the old man. It is what Paul describes in Romans 6. The other is outward; Scripture terms this the mortification of the outward man. This endurance of the cross is what Paul describes in Romans 8 and also in Philippians 3:10, if I am not mistaken. For after introducing the *power of his resurrection*, Christ crucified is set before us, that we may follow him through tribulations and distresses. The resurrection of the dead is expressly mentioned so we know that we must die before we live. Believers must make this a continued subject of meditation as long as they sojourn in this world.

This is a choice consolation: if we are his members, we are partakers of Christ's cross, and that, through afflictions, the way to everlasting blessedness is open to us.

FOR MEDITATION: Believers in principle are sanctified and delivered from the bondage of sin. But as long as they remain in this life, they must continue to struggle with remaining sin and the old inclinations that governed them before they knew grace. Thus this prayer of Paul's is very appropriate for every believer: that they might know the power of his resurrection and the fellowship of his sufferings in conforming to his death.

Running to the Goal

Brethren, I count not myself to have apprehended: but this one thing I do, forgetting those things which are behind, and reaching forth unto those things which are before. Philippians 3:13

SUGGESTED FURTHER READING: Hebrews 11:32–12:2

Paul does not question the certainty of his salvation here, as though that were still in suspense. He merely repeats what he has said before—that he aims to make further progress because he has not yet attained the goal of his calling. He asserts this immediately afterward by saying that he is intent on this one thing and leaves off everything else.

For now, he compares our life to a racecourse on which God has marked the limits for us to run. It would profit the runner nothing to leave the starting point unless he went forward to reach the goal. Likewise, we must pursue the course of our calling until death and must not cease to run until we have obtained what we seek.

Furthermore, the way is marked for the runner so he may not purposely tire himself by wandering off in this direction or that. A goal is set before us, towards which we ought to undeviatingly direct our course, and God does not permit us to wander about heedlessly.

Third, as the runner must be free from entanglement and not stop running because of any impediment, continuing his course and surmounting every obstacle, so we must take heed that we do not apply our mind or heart to anything that may divert our attention. On the contrary, we must endeavor to be free of every distraction so we may exclusively apply the whole bent of our mind to God's calling.

These things Paul comprehends in one statement. When he says he does *this one thing* and forgets all *those things which are behind*, he refers to his diligence and excludes everything that is a distraction.

FOR MEDITATION: Regeneration and justification are only the beginning of the Christian life. The believer's legal status before God will never change from that point on, but there is still much running to be done. Sanctification must flow out of justification. Paul knows that he must strive to progress. We too must not be content to stop and relax where we are; we must press on toward the goal of complete salvation in Jesus. Take encouragement from Calvin's words that "God does not permit us to wander about heedlessly," and press on.

The Grace to Rejoice

Rejoice in the Lord always: and again I say, Rejoice. Philippians 4:4
SUGGESTED FURTHER READING: Acts 16:16–25

Paul's exhortation to rejoice is well suited to the times. The condition of believers was exceedingly difficult, and dangers threatened them on every side, so it was possible that they might be overcome by grief or impatience. Hence the apostle tells them that, even in the midst of hostility and disturbance, they should *rejoice in the Lord*. For assuredly those spiritual consolations that the Lord uses to refresh and gladden us ought to show their efficacy most of all when the whole world tempts us to despair.

Considering the circumstances of the time, let us examine what might have been the effect of the command to rejoice, uttered by the mouth of Paul, who himself had special occasion to sorrow. For believers who are appalled by persecutions, or imprisonments, or exile, or death, here is the apostle, who, amid imprisonments, in the very heat of persecution, and amid apprehensions of death, is not merely joyful but even stirs up others to joy. In sum, no matter what comes our way, those who have the Lord on their side have ample and sufficient grounds for joy.

The repetition of the exhortation gives it greater force. Paul says, let your strength and stability be to *rejoice in the Lord*, not for a mere moment, but so that your joy in him may be perpetuated. For, unquestionably, being joyful in the Lord differs from the joy of the world. We know from experience that the joy of the world is deceptive, frail, and fading. Christ even pronounces it accursed (Luke 6:25). But the joy we have in God is settled and is never taken away from us.

FOR MEDITATION: These words of Paul, written from a Roman dungeon, should be an impetus to rejoice and a rebuke against our failure to rejoice. If Paul knew the grace that caused him to rejoice in such a dire situation, why are we so quick to stop rejoicing during trials? Do we not know the same grace?

Perishing under Man-Made Law

Touch not; taste not; handle not; which all are to perish with the using; after the commandments and doctrines of men. Colossians 2:21–22

SUGGESTED FURTHER READING: Matthew 15:1–20

Paul points out to what length the waywardness of those who bind consciences by their laws is likely to go. From the very beginning they are unduly severe; hence Paul begins with their prohibitions not simply against eating but even against slightly partaking.

After they have obtained what they wish, they go even further than the command, declaring it unlawful even to taste what they do not wish should be eaten. At length they make it criminal even to touch such food. In short, once leaders have taken upon themselves the right to tyrannize people's souls, there is no end of daily adding new laws to old ones and starting up new enactments from time to time. Hence Paul admirably admonishes us that human traditions are a labyrinth in which consciences are more and more entangled; nay, more, they are snares, which from the beginning bind people in such a way that in time they are strangled.

In sum, the worship of God, true piety, and the holiness of Christians do not consist of what they drink and eat and wear, for those things are transient, liable to corruption, and perish by abuse.

Second, Paul adds that such observances originate with men and not with God, who, by his thunderbolt prostrates and swallows up all traditions of men. Paul says God does this because "Those who bring consciences into bondage do injury to Christ, and make void his death. For whatever is of human invention does not bind conscience."

FOR MEDITATION: In the church today, we create many laws and think that obeying them recommends us to God. We even bind them upon the consciences of others. But some of those laws are simply the creations of men and cannot gain us favor in God's sight. Such favor can only come through the Son, Jesus Christ. Man-made laws often hinder people in pursuing salvation.

Trusting that Jesus Will Return

When the Lord Jesus shall be revealed from heaven with his mighty angels, in flaming fire taking vengeance on them that know not God, and that obey not the gospel of our Lord Jesus Christ. 2 Thessalonians 1:7–8
SUGGESTED FURTHER READING: Matthew 25:1–13

One of the articles of our faith is that Christ will come again to earth from heaven. He will not come in vain, so in faith we ought to seek the purpose of his coming, which is to come as Redeemer to his own people and to judge the whole world.

The description in our text is given so the pious may understand that God is much more concerned about their afflictions than he is about the dreadfulness of the judgment that awaits his enemies.

One chief occasion of our grief and distress is that we think God is only lightly affected with our calamities. We see how David breaks forth in complaints from time to time when he is consumed by the pride and insolence of his enemies. Hence the apostle brings forward this description of heaven for the consolation of believers. He represents the tribunal of Christ as full of horror so believers may not be disheartened by their present condition of oppression, in which they are proudly and disdainfully trampled upon by the wicked.

What is to be the nature of that *flaming fire*, and of what materials, I leave to the disputations of people with foolish curiosity. I am content with affirming what Paul had in view to teach: that Christ will be a most strict avenger of the injuries that the wicked inflict upon us. The metaphor of *flame* and *fire* (verse 8), however, is abundantly common in Scripture in describing the anger of God.

By *mighty angels*, Paul means those in whom Christ will exercise his power, for he will bring angels with him to display the glory of his kingdom. Hence, they are elsewhere called the angels of his majesty.

FOR MEDITATION: Though some believers are overly fascinated with the details of the Lord's Second Coming, many pay little attention to it and live as if it will not happen. Many people already in New Testament times voiced doubts. Why hadn't Jesus returned as he said he would? they asked. Yet the Second Coming is one of the articles of our faith and we must wait for it, patiently praying that he will come quickly.

Predicting Apostasy

Let no man deceive you by any means: for that day shall not come, except there come a falling away first, and that man of sin be revealed, the son of perdition. 2 Thessalonians 2:3

SUGGESTED FURTHER READING: 1 John 2:18–25

So that the Thessalonians do not groundlessly promise themselves the joyful day of redemption in a short time, Paul offers them a melancholy prediction about the scattering of the church, declaring that believers must exercise warfare for a long period before gaining a triumph.

We have here a remarkable passage, and one that is worthy of observation in the highest degree. A grievous and dangerous temptation that might shake even the most confirmed believers and make them lose their footing would be to see the church, which had been raised up gradually and with difficulty and with much labor to some considerable standing, suddenly fall down, as if torn down by a tempest. Accordingly, Paul fortifies the minds, not merely of the Thessalonians but of all the pious, in advance, so that when the church does scatter, believers might not be alarmed as though it were a thing that was new and unpredicted.

Paul says that the day of Christ will not come until the world has fallen into apostasy and the reign of the antichrist has obtained a footing in the church. He uses the term *falling away* or *apostasy* to mean a treacherous departure from God, not just on the part of one or a few people, but a large multitude of persons. For when apostasy is mentioned without adding anything else, it cannot be restricted to a few.

Now, no one can be termed *apostate* unless he has previously made a profession of faith in Christ and the gospel. Paul therefore predicts a certain general revolt of the visible church. He says, "The church must be reduced to an unsightly and dreadful state of ruin, before its full restoration is effected."

FOR MEDITATION: God *will* establish his reign and kingdom; those plans cannot and will not be foiled. In light of this, we can know that whatever apostasies rock the church, she will not be destroyed. There is no reason for despair, and there is great reason for hope, because God—not the man of sin—is in control.

Exposing Heresy

Holding faith, and a good conscience; which some having put away concerning faith have made shipwreck. 1 Timothy 1:19
SUGGESTED FURTHER READING: Jude

This verse teaches us two lessons. First, teachers and ministers of the gospel, and through them the churches, are taught the horror with which they are to regard a hypocritical and deceitful profession of true doctrine and which is severely punished.

Second, this passage removes the reason why so many people are greatly distressed when they perceive that some who formerly professed their attachment to Christ and to the gospel not only fall back into their former superstitions but (which is far worse) are also bewildered and captivated by monstrous errors. By such examples, God openly supports the majesty of the gospel and openly shows that he cannot endure the profaning of it.

Experience has taught us in every age that all the errors that have existed in the Christian church from the beginning proceeded from the source, which, in some persons was ambition, and in others, covetousness, and which extinguished the true fear of God. A bad conscience is therefore the mother of all heresies. We see that a vast number of people who have not sincerely and honestly embraced the faith are hurried along like brute beasts so that their hypocrisy is eventually exposed.

In addition, contempt of God is universally prevalent. The licentious and disgraceful lives of almost all ranks show that there is either none at all or the smallest possible portion of integrity in the world. So there is very great reason to fear lest the light which has been kindled may be speedily extinguished and God may leave the pure understanding of the gospel to be possessed by very few.

FOR MEDITATION: How critical it is for us to maintain an attitude of faith and a good conscience before God! Without these gifts from him, we will certainly make shipwreck. How can the very fear of making shipwreck help us maintain faith and a good conscience before him and before fellow man? How should we treat those who have made shipwreck concerning faith? Do you ever reach out to them?

Divided to the Quick

For the word of God is quick, and powerful, and sharper than any twoedged sword, piercing even to the dividing asunder of soul and spirit, and of the joints and marrow, and is a discerner of the thoughts and intents of the heart. Hebrews 4:12
SUGGESTED FURTHER READING: Acts 2:14–41

It appears from this verse that the Word of God is not equally efficacious in all. In the elect the Word is quick and powerful, for when they are humbled by a true knowledge of themselves, the elect flee to the grace of Christ. This is never the case, except when the Word penetrates the innermost heart.

Hypocrisy, which has marvelous and extremely winding recesses in the hearts of men, must be sifted out. We must not be slightly pricked or torn but thoroughly wounded so that, prostrate under a sense of eternal death, we are taught to die to ourselves. In short, we shall never be renewed in the whole mind (Eph. 4:23) until our old man is slain by the edge of the spiritual sword. Hence Paul says that the faithful are offered as a sacrifice to God by the gospel (Phil. 2:17), for they cannot otherwise be brought to obey God than by having, as it were, their own will slain. Nor can they receive the light of God's wisdom in any other way than by first having the wisdom of the flesh destroyed in them.

Nothing of this kind is found in the reprobate, for they will either carelessly disregard God speaking to them, and thus mock him, or they will clamor against his truth and obstinately resist it. In short, as the Word of God is a hammer, so is the heart of a reprobate like an anvil, which in its hardness repels the hammer's strokes, however powerful they may be. The Word of God is far from being so efficacious toward them as to penetrate them to *the dividing asunder of soul and spirit*. Hence it appears that this character of the Word is to be confined to the faithful only, as they alone are thus searched to the quick.

FOR MEDITATION: Has the Holy Spirit ever used the Word to penetrate the depths of your heart, expose your sin, discern your thoughts, and cause you to cry out for mercy? After having found the Lord Jesus Christ as a needy sinner, is this convicting ministry of the Word and Spirit continuing in your life in a sanctifying way?

Coming Boldly to the Throne

Let us therefore come boldly unto the throne of grace, that we may obtain mercy, and find grace to help in time of need. Hebrews 4:16
SUGGESTED FURTHER READING: Ephesians 3:11–21

The ground of the assurance to come boldly to God is that the throne of God is adorned with a new name, *grace*, which ought to be remembered whenever we shun the presence of God. For the glory of God, when contemplated by itself, can produce no other effect than to fill us with despair. So awful is his throne.

To remedy our reluctance and free our minds from all fear and trembling, the apostle adorns the throne of God with *grace*. He gives it a name that can allure us by its sweetness, as if to say, "Since God has affirmed to his throne, as it were, the banner of grace and of his paternal love toward us, there are no reasons why his majesty should drive us away."

The effect of this is that we may call upon God without fear, since we know that he is gracious to us; for when Christ receives us under his protection and patronage, he covers us with his goodness, and the majesty of God, which otherwise would be terrible to us, is replaced by grace and paternal favor.

He does this so that we may obtain mercy, the apostle says. This assurance is not added without great reason. Rather, it is given to encourage those who feel the need of mercy, lest anyone should be cast down by the sense of his misery and close up the way by his own reluctance. The expression *that we may obtain mercy* contains the most delightful truth that all who in reliance on the advocacy of Christ pray to God are certain to obtain mercy. On the other hand, the apostle indirectly, or by implication, holds out a threat to all who do not take this way, saying that God will be inexorable to them because they disregard the only true way of being reconciled to him.

FOR MEDITATION: It is good to be reminded of the simple yet ultimate truth that there can be no access to the Father except through the Son. A bold approach to the throne without the pardon obtained by the Son would be sheer suicide. We would find neither mercy nor grace there; we would find unmitigated divine wrath. Are you coming to the throne of grace freely and daily with your every need, through Jesus Christ, for mercy and grace?

Tasting the Heavenly Gift

For it is impossible for those who were once enlightened, and have tasted of the heavenly gift, and were made partakers of the Holy Ghost, and have tasted the good word of God, and the powers of the world to come ... Hebrews 6:4–5
SUGGESTED FURTHER READING: Jeremiah 15:16–21

We must note in passing the names by which this verse signals knowledge of the gospel. The writer calls it *enlightened*; hence people are blind until Christ, the light of the world, enlightens them. It is *a tasting of the heavenly gift*, intimating that the things which Christ confers on us are above nature and the world, yet may be tasted by faith. We are *partakers of the Holy Ghost* for he distributes to those he wills all the light and knowledge that we can have. Without him no one can say that Jesus is Lord (1 Cor. 12:3), for he opens the eyes of our minds and reveals to us the secret things of God.

Knowing the gospel is a *tasting of the good word of God*, by which he means that the will of God is therein revealed, not in any common way, but in such a way as sweetly delights us. In short, this title points out the difference between the law and the gospel; for the law offers nothing but severity and condemnation, whereas the gospel is a sweet testimony of God's love and fatherly kindness toward us.

Lastly, he calls it a *tasting of the powers of the world to come*, by which he intimates that we are admitted by faith into the kingdom of heaven so that we see in spirit that blessed immortality which is hid from our senses.

Let us then know that the gospel cannot be rightly known in any other way than by the illumination of the Spirit. Thus, in being thus drawn away from the world, we are raised up to heaven, and in knowing the goodness of God, we rely on his Word.

FOR MEDITATION: The author of Hebrews speaks of spiritual tasting— tasting "of the heavenly gift," tasting of "the good word of God," and tasting of "the powers of the world to come." Have you experienced these spiritual tastes? Can you say with Jeremiah that you did "eat" God's Word spiritually, by faith and in truth, and, without falling away, found it to be "the joy and rejoicing" of your heart (15:16)?

Recompensing Good Works

For God is not unrighteous to forget your work and labour of love, which ye have showed toward his name, in that ye have ministered to the saints, and do minister. Hebrews 6:10

SUGGESTED FURTHER READING: James 1:19–27

In this text the author seems to build salvation on works and to make God a debtor to them. But the apostle does not speak here of the cause of our salvation. Everywhere else, Scripture shows there is no other fountain of salvation but the gratuitous mercy of God. Thus when God promises reward for works, that depends on the gratuitous promise by which he adopts us as his children and reconciles us to himself by not imputing our sins. Reward is reserved for works, not through merit, but through the free bounty of God alone. Yet even this free reward of works does not take place unless we are first received into favor through the kind mediation of Christ.

We hence conclude that God does not pay us a debt but performs what he has freely promised. He performs it inasmuch as he pardons us and our works; nay, he looks not so much on our works as on his grace in our works. On this account he does not forget our works because he recognizes himself and the work of his Spirit in them. He is *not unrighteous*, as the apostle says, for he cannot deny himself.

This passage, then, corresponds with Paul's saying: "He which hath begun in you a good work will perform it" (Phil. 1:6). For what can God find in us to induce him to love us except what he has first conferred on us? God so regards himself and his own gifts that he carries to the end that of his own good will he has begun in us. This is not an inducement from anything we do; rather, God is righteous in recompensing works because he is true and faithful and has made himself a debtor to us, not by receiving anything from us, but, as Augustine says, by freely promising all things.

FOR MEDITATION: As Calvin explains here, good works are the fruit of salvation which is wrought entirely of grace based on the merits of Christ. The good works that flow out of this salvation do not gain or retain our favor with God. Those things depend on Christ's righteousness, not our own. Nevertheless, God delights in the obedience and good works of his children and promises to reward them. How should God's promised rewards motivate us?

Our Interceding Priest

Wherefore he is able also to save them to the uttermost that come unto God by him, seeing he ever liveth to make intercession for them. Hebrews 7:25
SUGGESTED FURTHER READING: 1 John 2:1–11

The chief good of man is to be united to God, who is the fountain of life and of all blessings, but man's own unworthiness drives him away from any access to God.

The particular office of a mediator is to help us in this respect; to stretch out his hand that he may lead us to heaven. The writer of Hebrews alludes to the ancient shadows of the law, for though the high priest carried the names of the twelve tribes on his shoulders and symbols of the tribes on his breast, yet he alone entered the sanctuary of God while the people stood in the court. Today, in reliance on Christ the Mediator, we enter by faith into heaven, for no longer does any veil intervene between us and God. God openly appears to us and lovingly invites us to come to him.

The text goes on to assure us: *Seeing he ever liveth.* What a pledge this is, and how great is Christ's love toward us! Christ lives for us, not for himself. He was received into a blessed immortality to reign in heaven for our sake, as the apostle declares. The life, the kingdom, and the glory of Christ were all destined for our salvation. Christ has nothing that may not be applied to our benefit, for he has been given to us by the Father once for all and on the condition that everything of his should be ours.

At the same time, this text teaches us that Christ performs this office as a priest, for only a priest may *intercede* for the people so they may obtain favor with God. This is what Christ is ever doing, for it was for this purpose that he rose from the dead. Through his continual intercession, he claims for himself the office of priest.

FOR MEDITATION: The intercession of Christ is a glorious doctrine that, to our detriment, is seldom addressed today. Yet it is one of the most comforting truths in all the Bible. To know that Christ is praying for us every moment—also in times of such affliction and pain that we can scarcely pray—can give us strength to carry the heaviest of burdens. Are you relying on Christ's intercession on a regular basis? How can you get more comfort from this doctrine?

Drawing Near to God

Let us draw near with a true heart in full assurance of faith, having our hearts sprinkled from an evil conscience, and our bodies washed with pure water. Hebrews 10:22

SUGGESTED FURTHER READING: 1 John 3:14–24

The writer of Hebrews tells us that in Christ and his sacrifice is nothing but what is spiritual or heavenly. So we must do our part to correspond with this great sacrifice.

The Jews formerly cleansed themselves by various washings to prepare themselves for service to God. The priest, being a mortal, was chosen from among sinners to perform sacred things for a time. He was adorned with precious vestments of this world that he might stand in the presence of God. Yet he alone came near the ark of the covenant. To sanctify his entrance, the priest borrowed a brute animal either from the herd or the flock for a sacrifice.

In Christ, our heavenly priest, all these things are far superior. He is not only pure and innocent, but he is the fountain of all holiness and righteousness. He was consecrated as a priest by a heavenly oracle, not for the short period of a mortal life, but forever. To sanction his appointment, an oath was interposed. He came forth adorned with all the gifts of the Holy Spirit in the highest perfection, he propitiated God by his own blood and reconciled him to men, he ascended above all the heavens to appear before God as our mediator.

Nothing is to be brought on our part but what corresponds with all this, as there ought to be a mutual agreement or concord between the priest and the people. We can do away, then, with all the external washings of the flesh. We may cease the whole apparatus of ceremonies, for the apostle sets in opposition to these external rites a *true heart*, the certainty of faith, and a cleansing from all vices. Hence we learn what the condition of our hearts must be so that we may enjoy the benefits conferred by Christ. We cannot come to him without an upright or true heart, a sure faith, and a pure conscience.

FOR MEDITATION: Assurance in Christ and a good conscience in the believer ride in tandem in the believer's life. We cannot persist in high levels of assurance if we persist in low levels of obedience. Why is this so? How can we foster greater measures of obedience in our lives without falling into legalism or justification by works?

Joining Together

Not forsaking the assembling of ourselves together, as the manner of some is; but exhorting one another: and so much the more, as ye see the day approaching. Hebrews 10:25

SUGGESTED FURTHER READING: John 17

We may gather from this passage a general teaching that evil prevails everywhere among mankind. One evil is that everyone sets himself above others. Another is that those who seem to excel in anything cannot tolerate inferiors to be equal with themselves. There is so much ill temper in almost all of us that individuals would gladly make churches for themselves, if they could, for they find it difficult to accommodate themselves to the ways and habits of others.

The rich envy one another, and hardly one in a hundred can be found among them who will allow the poor to be called brothers. Unless similarity of habits or some allurements or advantages draw us together, we find it very difficult to maintain continual concord among ourselves.

What we all extremely need to hear, therefore, is the admonition to love and not to envy. We should not separate ourselves from those to whom God has joined us but embrace with brotherly kindness all who are united to us in faith. Surely it behooves us even more earnestly to cultivate unity, since the goal of the more eagerly watchful Satan is either to tear us by any means from the church or stealthily to seduce us from it.

The effect would be happy if no one were to please himself too much, we preserved the one object of mutually provoking one another to love, and we allowed no emulation among ourselves but that of doing good works. For doubtless the contempt of the brethren, moroseness, envy, immoderate estimate of self, and other sinful impulses clearly show that our love is either very cold or does not exist at all.

FOR MEDITATION: The multiplication of denominations since the time of the Reformation validates Calvin's observations. Many of us find it very difficult to humble ourselves and take a servant role in church. We dispute and cause divisions and split the body of Christ, each thinking ours is the only way. We should rather thank God for the command to join together, without which we would probably have many more divisions than we already do.

Counting Trials as Joy

My brethren, count it all joy when ye fall into divers temptations. James 1:2

SUGGESTED FURTHER READING: 1 Peter 4:12–19

To know more fully what James means, we must understand that *temptations* or trials include all adverse things. They are called temptations because they are tests of our obedience to God. He asks the faithful to rejoice, not only when they fall into one temptation but into many, and not only into one kind of temptation but various kinds. Doubtless, since temptations serve to mortify our flesh as the vices of the flesh continually rise up in us, so this command must be often repeated.

As we labor under diseases, different remedies are applied to remove them. So the Lord afflicts us in various ways because ambition, avarice, envy, gluttony, intemperance, excessive love of the world, and the innumerable lusts in which we abound cannot be cured by the same medicine.

When he bids us to *count it all joy*, it is as though he says temptations ought to be deemed as gain and thus should be regarded as occasions of joy. In short, he means that nothing in afflictions ought to disturb our joy. So he not only commands us to bear adversities calmly and with an even mind, but shows us that this joy is the reason why the faithful should rejoice when pressed down by afflictions.

Certainly, the senses of our nature are so formed that every trial produces in us grief and sorrow. Not one of us can so far divest himself of his nature as not to grieve or be sorrowful whenever he feels evil. But this does not prevent the children of God from rising up by the guidance of the Spirit above the sorrow of the flesh. Hence, in the midst of trouble, we cease not to rejoice.

FOR MEDITATION: To joy in affliction goes against our natures. The Buddhist may be able to empty himself of passions so that he can face affliction without sorrow, but he cannot face afflictions with joy. This is something only the believer can do through the power of the Holy Spirit. Are you rejoicing, by the Spirit's grace, in any affliction you may be facing? How can you regain the joy that you may have lost?

Taming the Tongue

Therewith bless we God, even the Father; and therewith curse we men, which are made after the similitude of God. James 3:9
SUGGESTED FURTHER READING: Psalm 140

A clear example of the tongue's deadly poison is that it can transform itself through appalling inconstancy; for when it pretends to bless God, it immediately curses him in his own image by cursing men. Since God should be blessed in all his works, he ought to be especially blessed by men in whom his image and glory peculiarly shine forth.

It is unbearable hypocrisy for man to use the same tongue in blessing God that he uses in cursing men. When such evil speaking prevails, there can be no calling on God. His praises must necessarily cease. For it is impious profanation of God's name when the tongue is hostile toward our brethren and pretends only to praise God. Therefore, if we would rightly praise God, we must especially correct the vice of speaking evil to our neighbor.

This particular truth ought to be kept in mind that severe critics display their own hostility, when, after offering praises in sweet strains to God, they suddenly vomit forth against their brethren whatever curses they can imagine. Were anyone to object and say that the image of God in human nature has been blotted out by the sin of Adam, we must, indeed, confess that it has been miserably deformed, but in such a way that some of its original features still appear. Righteousness and rectitude and the freedom of choosing what is good have been lost, but many excellent endowments by which we excel the brutes still remain. He, then, who truly worships and honors God will be afraid to speak slanderously of man.

FOR MEDITATION: How easy it is to use the same mouth for both righteous and evil ends! Our words can produce evil just as easily as good, and our sinful hearts are constantly inclined toward sin. When tempted to say slanderous or inappropriate things, we should remember that we use the same mouth to praise God. This is an excellent way of discerning whether the words we are about to say are proper.

Refraining from Slander

Speak not evil one of another, brethren. He that speaketh evil of his brother, and judgeth his brother, speaketh evil of the law, and judgeth the law: but if thou judge the law, thou art not a doer of the law, but a judge. James 4:11
SUGGESTED FURTHER READING: 1 Peter 2:1–10

Another disease innate in human nature is thinking that others should live according to our own will or fancy. James suitably condemns such presumption in this passage because with such presumption we dare to impose on others our rule of life.

He then defines *detraction* as the calumnies and suspicious works that flow out of a malignant and perverted judgment. The evil of slandering includes a wide range of deeds, but here James properly refers to that kind of slandering in which we superciliously judge the deeds and sayings of others as though our own morality were the law in confidently condemning whatever displeases us.

That this presumption is here reproved is evident in the reasons that are immediately added: *he that speaketh evil of*, or *judgeth, his brother, speaketh evil of*, or *judgeth, the law*. James suggests that much is taken away from the law when one claims authority over others. Detraction against the law is opposed to the reverence we owe to God's law.

He then reminds us that there is but one Lord, according to whose will all must stand or fall, and at whose tribunal we must all appear. Hence he concludes that the person who judges others according to his own view of things assumes for himself what peculiarly belongs to God. James reproves those who under the pretense of sanctity condemn others and therefore set up their own morality in the place of divine law.

James uses the same reason that Paul does: that we act presumptuously when we assume authority over others, while the law of God subordinates all of us to itself without exception. Let us then learn that we are not to judge others except according to God's law.

FOR MEDITATION: Our tendency is to set up our own opinions as law. We judge those who do not conform to them, and we easily give way to slandering them. This is a great danger, especially if we think we are upholding God's standards and do not see that we are simply holding our opinions up as the standard by which others must live. Is there an area where you are guilty of this right now and should repent?

Honoring the Weaker Vessel

Likewise, ye husbands, dwell with them according to knowledge, giving honor unto the wife, as unto the weaker vessel, and as being heirs together of the grace of life; that your prayers be not hindered. 1 Peter 3:7
SUGGESTED FURTHER READING: Ephesians 5:22–33

Let husbands remember that they need prudence to rightly do their duty. Doubtless they may endure many foolish things and bear many unpleasant things, but at the same time, they must beware lest their indulgence fosters folly. The admonition of Peter is not in vain that a husband ought to cohabit with his wife as with a *weaker vessel*. Part of prudence is that a husband should honor his wife. Nothing destroys the friendship of life more than contempt, nor can we really love anyone but those whom we esteem. Love must be joined with respect.

Moreover, Peter uses a twofold argument to persuade husbands to treat their wives honorably and kindly. The first is derived from the weakness of the sex; the other, from the honor with which God favors them. These things indeed seem to be somewhat contrary—that honor should be given to wives because they are weak and because they excel— but these things well agree with each other where love exists.

God is despised in his gifts unless we honor those on whom he has conferred any excellence. But when we consider that we are members of the same body, we learn to bear with one another and to mutually cover our infirmities. This is what Paul means when he says that greater honor is given to the weaker members (1 Cor. 12:23) so that we are more careful in protecting them from shame.

Peter does not without reason command that women should be cared for and be honored with kind treatment because they are weak. As we more easily forgive children when they offend us through inexperience of age, so the weakness of women ought to make us less rigid and severe toward our wives.

FOR MEDITATION: How critical it is for husbands to truly understand their wives! The art of understanding one's mate and responding to him or her with wisdom and patience is a key ingredient to marital happiness. Have you learned to love your wife for ways in which she is different from you? Do you respond to those differences in a kind manner, remembering that you are both—if you are believers—heirs together of the grace of life?

Why God Waits

The Lord is not slack concerning his promise, as some men count slackness: but is longsuffering to us-ward, not willing that any should perish, but that all should come to repentance. 2 Peter 3:9
SUGGESTED FURTHER READING: Deuteronomy 29:25–29

Peter checks extreme and unreasonable haste for the day of resurrection by saying that the Lord defers his coming so that he might invite all mankind to repentance. When we hear that the Lord in delaying shows concern for our salvation and defers the time because he cares for us, there is no reason why we should continue to complain of his tardiness.

There is no tardiness in God, who regulates time in the best manner to promote our salvation. As to the duration of the whole world, we must think the same of the life of every individual, for God, by prolonging time, sustains each person so he may repent. God refrains from hastening the end of the world so that all are given time to repent.

This is a very necessary admonition given to us so that we may learn to rightly use time, for otherwise we shall suffer a just punishment for our idleness.

He is *not willing that any should perish*, Peter tells us. So wonderful is his love toward mankind that God would have them all saved and is himself prepared to bestow salvation on the lost. But we are to notice that God is ready to receive all to repentance so that none may perish. Therefore, everyone who is desirous of salvation must learn to enter in by this way.

Some may ask, if God wishes none to perish, why do so many perish? To this I answer that no mention is made here of the hidden purpose of God, according to which the reprobate are doomed to their own ruin, but only of God's will made known to us in the gospel. For God stretches forth his hand to all, but lays hold only of his own to lead those to himself whom he has chosen before the foundation of the world.

FOR MEDITATION: Many people have been caught up by the thorny question raised by Calvin in the last paragraph. Rather than submitting to the revealed will of God, they refuse to bow to Christ until they have plumbed the depths of God's hidden will, which they can never do. God says he desires all to come to repentance; therefore, we should not have the audacity to retort that he does not.

Trusting the Gospel

Blessed be the God and Father of our Lord Jesus Christ, who hath blessed us with all spiritual blessings in heavenly places in Christ. Ephesians 1:3

SUGGESTED FURTHER READING: 2 Timothy 3:10–17

This verse warns us, first, to keep the pure doctrine which we know proceeds from God, for we cannot go wrong if we follow that rule. Also, seeing that in our Lord Jesus Christ we have the performance of all that is requisite and needful for our instruction, we have no need to doubt whether we must keep to the gospel or add something to it. So let us be content to take the Son of God as our master, especially as he condescends to stoop so low as to take that charge upon him. He also testifies that if we have profited well by his doctrine, we shall come to the true purpose for which we make our way.

You see, then, that the first lesson we gather from this passage is that our faith must not waver one way or another but rest on a sure and immovable foundation, namely, God's truth as contained in the gospel. Seeing that we sufficiently acknowledge what Paul says to us here, let us not doubt that God's Spirit speaks to us today by his mouth. Let us not hear the doctrine as if it were subject to our judgment, but let us subject our own understanding and minds to it and receive it without calling it in question, for otherwise we will willfully make war against God and lift up ourselves above him. This is one of the things we should note from this passage.

FOR MEDITATION: As Calvin says, we must let revelation reign over our reason, not the other way around, as if we are the judges of whether or not what God says is true. With this right attitude, faith in the certain Word of God can flourish, and we can know that we stand on a sure foundation. Are you submitting your reason to the Word of God?

God's Electing Choice

According as he hath chosen us in him before the foundation of the world, that we should be holy and without blame before him in love.
Ephesians 1:4
SUGGESTED FURTHER READING: Romans 9:6–21

We see how God's goodness shines forth to us in the preaching of the gospel to us, for in it we have, as it were, a token that he pities us, loves us, calls us, and attracts us to him. But we also see how receiving the doctrine preached to us with heart and affection is a further and more special token by which we perceive that God intends to be our Father and has adopted us to be his children.

Not without reason, then, Paul says in this passage that we are blessed by God even before the foundation of the world, according to his election. For that does not happen because we have come to him or sought him. But to fulfill in every respect what the prophet Isaiah says (Isa. 65:1), God shows himself to those who did not seek him and were far off, yet saw him near at hand. He says to them, "Here I am, here I am. Although you have despised me, yet I condescend to come to you because I care for your salvation." This is what Paul is aiming at in this passage.

How, then, do we come to God? How do we obey him? How do we have a quiet mind that yields itself to him in accordance with faith? As all these things come from him, so it follows that he must do everything himself. Wherefore let us observe that, in saying that God elected us before the creation of the world, Paul presupposes what is true, namely, that God could not see anything in us except the evil that was there, for there was not one drop of goodness for him to find. Seeing that he has elected us, we must regard this as a very clear token of his free grace.

FOR MEDITATION: God did not need to tell us that he chose us before the foundation of the world, and yet he did reveal that. We should glory in this truth, not be ashamed of it. That he knew us and loved us before we existed is a wonder beyond description. Let us thank him for that, for there is no other way that we could have been saved except that he chose us.

Moving Forward with Confidence

Having predestinated us unto the adoption of children by Jesus Christ to himself, according to the good pleasure of his will, to the praise of the glory of his grace, wherein he hath made us accepted in the beloved. Ephesians 1:5–6
SUGGESTED FURTHER READING: 1 John 3:1–10

When we have adoption engraved on our hearts, we have a good and infallible pledge that God will guide us to the end. Since he has begun leading us into the way of salvation, he will bring us to the perfection to which he calls us, because, in truth, without him we could not continue so much as a single day.

So now let us fall down before the majesty of our good God by acknowledging our faults, asking him to make us perceive them more and more, and that, by being utterly ashamed of them, we may hate our vices and our life in every part as is evil and perverse. Let us resort to him who alone is able to give the remedy, and let us not swerve one way or another from him as he communicates himself to us in our Lord Jesus Christ.

Let us keep moving straight to him, acknowledging that we are chosen in him, that we are sustained and preserved for his sake, and that he will exert his power more and more in us until we have finished our race and come to the heavenly heritage where we are going. Though we are yet far from it, yet he will assuredly give us steady and invincible strength to continually hold out till we have fully renounced the world.

Being abased in ourselves, let us seek to be so renewed in the image of God that he may shine perfectly in us till we are made partakers of the glorious immortality which he has so dearly bought for us. Let us also pray that it may please him to grant this grace, not only to us but also to all people and nations.

FOR MEDITATION: If we are adopted as God's children, we should strive to be conformed to the image of Christ, the perfect Son of God. Our place in the family is assured, not by our merits, but by Christ's; yet we should strive to live as he lived so we become children who bring glory to our Father through obedience. How can you better live today as Christ lived?

Our Ministering Angels

That in the dispensation of the fulness of times he might gather together in one all things in Christ, both which are in heaven, and which are on earth; even in him. Ephesians 1:10

SUGGESTED FURTHER READING: Hebrews 1

In this text you see why, in Jacob's dream, God stood on top of a ladder that stretched from heaven to earth and the angels went up and down on it (Gen. 28:12). As that ladder, the Lord Jesus Christ is the true living and eternal God who touches both heaven and earth, because in Christ God has joined together his own divine essence and the nature of man.

You see that heaven is opened so that the angels may begin to acquaint themselves with us, even becoming our servants, for as Hebrews 1:14 says, the care of our souls is committed to them. So also Psalm 34 says, they encamp about us and watch us and are our guardians.

You also see how our Lord Jesus Christ once more unites us with the angels of paradise. That is why Christ says, "From henceforth you shall see the heavens open and the Son of Man coming down in his majesty with his angels" (John 1:51). By this we understand that heaven was formerly shut against us, and we were unworthy to find any favor at God's hand, but now Christ has come to be our head and has made atonement between his Father and us. He has taken the office of mediator and has become the head, not only of the faithful, but also of the angels, and has gathered all together in such a way that, whereas the devils make war against us and cease not to plot our destruction, the angels are armed with infinite power to uphold us (Col. 2:10).

Though we do not see these angels with our eyes, yet we may certainly believe that they watch us for our salvation.

FOR MEDITATION: The care that angels have for God's children is a subject about which we have little information in the Bible. Nevertheless, they do care for us, and we should not neglect to thank God for these messengers whom he sends. What a great comfort this offers!

Called to Faith and Love

Wherefore I also, after I heard of your faith in the Lord Jesus, and love unto all the saints, cease not to give thanks for you, making mention of you in my prayers. Ephesians 1:15–16
SUGGESTED FURTHER READING: Habakkuk 2:1–4

The heathen, of their own free will, believe they are under no obligation at all to God, except for good luck, as they call it, for they imagine they have earned all things by their own power and skill.

Here Paul shows us that wherever the church exists in the world, or where any people call upon God and are settled and grounded upon the beliefs of the gospel, God deserves all the glory. For there is so much rebellion in us that we are not only weak and feeble, as the papists imagine, but also utterly contrary to God until he has cleansed us. This is what God means by saying through his prophet Ezekiel that hearts which were formerly of stone shall be changed into hearts of flesh, indicating that he will soften them and cause them to bow in submission to him.

Furthermore, with the two words *faith* and *love*, Paul comprehends the whole perfection of Christians. The goal of the first table of the law is that we should worship one God only and cling to him for all things, acknowledging ourselves to be so indebted to him that we ought to flee to him alone for refuge and endeavor to spend our whole life in his service. That is the essence of the first table of the law.

The contents of the second are that we should live together in equity and uprightness, dealing with our neighbors in such a way that we strive to help all people without hurting anyone. We are certain that God has set forth such a good and perfect rule of good life in his law that nothing can be added to it.

FOR MEDITATION: Faith and love are the great goals we should be striving for and, by the grace of God, attaining. We will have neither perfect faith nor perfect love in this life, but we are still called to strive for them. When we finally achieve these in glory, it will not be because of our doing, but God's. And he will get all the glory. Let his glory urge you on today.

Given Wholly to Christ

And hath put all things under his feet, and gave him to be the head over all things to the church, which is his body, the fulness of him that filleth all in all. Ephesians 1:22–23
SUGGESTED FURTHER READING: 1 Corinthians 15:12–34

Let us learn to empty ourselves and to offer ourselves in sacrifice to God with true and genuine humility, yielding to him his deserved praise. Let none of us separate ourselves from him through ingratitude but give him such honor as to confess that we have everything from him and are joined to him by our Lord Jesus Christ, who is eternal God. We must also acknowledge that it is from Christ that all good things come; therefore, we must also yield and render to him all glory.

So let us cast ourselves down before the majesty of our good God with acknowledgment of our sins, praying that he will make us perceive them more and more and that this may cause us to have such dislike of ourselves that we may earnestly and heartily seek to give ourselves wholly to our Lord Jesus Christ.

Since Christ has already called us to himself by his gospel, let us fashion ourselves accordingly, renouncing all superstitions and assuring ourselves that all that we can ever imagine to bring us to the kingdom of heaven are but deceits of Satan. It is enough for us to make recourse to Jesus Christ.

Just as it was the Father's will to lift Christ on high so that all people should look to him, so also we must have our eyes fastened upon him and apply our minds to him in such a way that we may have no other way or preparation than by him alone. We must not swerve one way or another, but once we are brought into the right way, keep progressing continually toward our aim until we have fully come to perfection. We pray that it may please him to grant this grace, not only to us, but also to all people.

FOR MEDITATION: The essence of life lies in surrendering all that we are to the Lord Jesus Christ. What comfort we receive when we may do that! Then we can testify with the Heidelberg Catechism that our "only comfort in life and death" lies in belonging to Jesus Christ rather than to ourselves. Make it your daily prayer that you will be enabled to surrender all—your gifts, your dreams, your sins—to the only and all-sufficient Redeemer.

Quickened from the Dead

And you hath he quickened, who were dead in trespasses and sins.
Ephesians 2:1
SUGGESTED FURTHER READING: Romans 6:15–23

We see what the spiritual life of man is and where it lies, namely, in the
light of God's Word and in the working of the Holy Spirit. We are
fashioned anew according to the image that was lost and utterly defaced
in us by Adam's sin.

Is this new life found among worldly men who are most honored?
Certainly not! Not without reason does our Lord Jesus Christ say that
we are raised from death by means of the gospel. For no matter how
much we seem to flourish, no matter how splendid we appear before
men, and no matter how much we possess to invite the esteem of others,
yet we are only wretched, putrefying flesh. There is nothing but
rottenness and infection in us.

God thus loathes us. We are damned and lost before him, the angels
abhor us, all creatures curse and detest us, and all things demand
vengeance on us because we defile them. There is such corruption in us
that heaven and earth are infected with it until God brings about a
change (Rom. 8:19).

Our Lord Jesus Christ says that we are like dead men until we are
renewed by the gospel and by the faith that proceeds from it. There is
not one drop of life in us that deserves the name of life. In brief, we are
like corpses buried in the grave, and it is necessary for us to be drawn out
of that. We are cut off from God's kingdom; consequently, there is
nothing but filth in us. In spite of all this, God promises to be linked and
united with those who put their trust in him and his goodness. In this, we
are quickened to new life.

FOR MEDITATION: Until we realize that we are *dead* in sin while outside of
Christ, we entertain far greater thoughts of ourselves than is appropriate.
As Calvin vividly describes, we are disgusting in the sight of all that is
good and holy. This clear understanding of who we are apart from
Christ can only come by the grace of God. Pray that God would show
you who you were, before his renewal, and never let you forget it.

Quickened with Christ

But God, who is rich in mercy, for his great love wherewith he loved us, even when we were dead in sins, hath quickened us together with Christ (by grace ye are saved;) and hath raised us up together, and made us sit together in heavenly places in Christ Jesus. Ephesians 2:4–6
SUGGESTED FURTHER READING: Colossians 2

How necessary it is for us to understand what is spoken here about the different states of God's children after they are called to faith by the gospel. In passing, let us say we must not imagine an earthly paradise where we shall have neither trouble nor grief. We must realize that we shall never live at ease here on earth but by faith make room for that in the life to come.

Since the Holy Spirit assures us by the mouth of Paul that we shall one day be lifted up on high, we must meantime bow our heads and suffer ourselves to be oppressed by our enemies and to be dominated by them in all their pride. We must suffer these things and yet be fully persuaded and resolved of the promise that we shall not fail to inherit the kingdom of heaven. It is impossible for the head to be separated from the members, so our Lord Jesus Christ has not gone to heaven for his own sake alone. We must always come back to that principle that we are quickened together with Christ.

We confess that Jesus Christ has risen from the dead and gone up into heaven not only to glorify him in his own person. For first all knees must bow before him, and all creatures both in heaven and earth, and even in hell, must do him homage (Phil. 2:10). Nevertheless the union is fulfilled in this, that Jesus Christ, having gathered us into his body, has begun that thing in himself which he intends to perfect in us, verily, when the opportune time comes.

FOR MEDITATION: God does an amazing work in raising sinners from the dead spiritually and seating them with his Son in heavenly places. This great work of regeneration is described in the Canons of Dort as "a new creation: a resurrection from the dead, a making alive, which God works in us without our aid" (III–IV, 12). If you are a believer, meditate today on the magnitude and comprehensiveness of God's sovereign, saving grace shown to you. If you are not a believer, pray for that grace to shine upon you today, enabling you to repent and believe the gospel.

Regarding the Gift of God

For by grace are ye saved through faith; and that not of yourselves: it is the gift of God: not of works, lest any man should boast. Ephesians 2:8–9
SUGGESTED FURTHER READING: Acts 4:1–14

Let us humble ourselves before God, both for what is past and also for what is to come. For what is past, let us acknowledge that God has plucked us out of the pit of hell, and that though we were by nature damned, he has deigned to have us as his children. Let us glorify him as he deserves and assure ourselves that he has pulled us back from death so that the beginning, source, root, and only cause of our salvation is his free goodness and grace. In effect, it is a mark of true humility to give all the glory of our salvation to God.

For that which is to come, we should know that we cannot stir one of our little fingers to do any good unless we are governed by God and receive good works at his hand and from his Holy Spirit.

As often as we feel our own weakness, let us flee to him for refuge. When we have done any good, let us not be puffed up with any pride, but let us regard ourselves as so much more bound to God. He that is very weak must confess himself exceedingly indebted to God's mercy for supporting him, but he that excels above others and is a mirror of all holiness must confess that he is even more indebted to God.

Why? He has nothing of his own but holds all things from God. Therefore, let us throughout life walk in such a way that we may from year to year, from month to month, from day to day, from hour to hour, and from minute to minute continually acknowledge ourselves indebted to God for the goodness he has given us through his pure mercy. And let us know that we hold all things from him.

FOR MEDITATION: The essence of the Christian faith is to find salvation in another, namely, Jesus Christ. As soon as we cease to give all the glory to him, or begin to think that we had anything to contribute to our own salvation, we stray from the gospel. Sadly, our hearts are constantly inclined in this direction. But wonderfully, we cannot lose our salvation as a result of these thoughts, for we are saved by grace; yet we must fight against them today and pray daily that we may live to his glory alone.

Seeing God in his Gifts

That at that time ye were without Christ, being aliens from the commonwealth of Israel, and strangers from the covenants of promise, having no hope, and without God in the world. Ephesians 2:12
SUGGESTED FURTHER READING: Job 38

The Ephesians had enjoyed the light of the sun. All the elements had served them, and they had received many good things by God's gift in all his creatures. Yet they had not known Christ. And what is the world but an open stage on which God will have his majesty seen?

So, let us lift up our eyes. Do not the sun, the moon, and the stars lead us to him who gave the qualities we perceive in them? For behold, the sun is far away from us and yet always gives us light. It causes the earth to bring forth fruits. We see the double course it keeps; though it ranges now on one side and then on the other, it nevertheless continuously keeps its circuit and never forgets how far it ought to go on one side or the other, huge mass that it is. If a tennis ball were to be held up, it would need some help, but consider that the sun has nothing to hold it up but the secret power of God. Yet the sun is so huge and infinite a mass that it exceeds the whole earth. Whether it rises or goes down, turns or returns on one side or the other, yet it keeps its course every day and each year around the whole world. It does not fail in any of those things.

In short, when we behold the sky, we ought to be ravished with desire to go to God. Such should also be the case when we contemplate things that are closer to us, namely, the variety of good things that God bestows upon us. Finally, let us turn our eyes to ourselves. If we only look at one of our fingers, what workmanship and what goodness of God it shows!

FOR MEDITATION: Look at the sky. Look at your fingers. How unbelievable it is that so many men and women seem untroubled living without hope and without God! Our problem is deeper than a lack of evidence; it is a rebellious heart. Ask God to suppress all rebellion in you and in those around you, and that all may fall before God in adoration and humility.

Remitting or Retaining Sins

And came and preached peace to you which were afar off, and to them that were nigh. Ephesians 2:17

SUGGESTED FURTHER READING: Matthew 16:13–20

When we refuse to receive gospel peace, let us fear lest Jesus Christ change his voice, for it is certain that the gospel always promises damnation to those who do not conform themselves to God's will.

It is with good reason that the Scripture speaks of binding as well as loosing (Matt. 16:19), for our Lord Jesus Christ shows us that the very nature and office of the gospel is to pluck us out of the bondage and prison in which we are held until he sets us free. However, he also says bonds are prepared for those who do not take Christ as their Redeemer and do not allow themselves to be set free by him.

That is what Christ means by saying, "Whose soever sins ye remit, they are remitted unto them; and whose soever sins ye retain, they are retained" (John 20:23). He thereby shows that when we preach the gospel we must first of all declare the message of reconciliation. What we continually have to do is to show that God has been so kind to us as to reconcile himself to us in the person of his Son. He receives us to himself that we might be washed and cleansed from all our filthiness and be accepted as righteous before him. Look how wretched souls are released, how poor captives are let out of prison, and how those who were plunged in the shadows of death are brought to the light of life (Matt. 4:16).

On the other hand, we have a commission to "retain sins" by threatening despisers of the Word with God's dreadful wrath. We must tell people that when they refuse the Word and think they have escaped judgment, the doctrine they have heard will bind them like ropes and fetters.

FOR MEDITATION: The gospel of Jesus Christ draws a line right through all of humanity, separating all those who believe from all those who refuse to believe. There is no middle ground. If you have heard the gospel, you do not have the luxury of failing to respond. How did you respond? Are your sins remitted or retained?

Growing in the Word

In whom all the building fitly framed together groweth unto an holy temple in the Lord: in whom ye also are builded together for an habitation of God through the Spirit. Ephesians 2:21–22
SUGGESTED FURTHER READING: Psalm 119:9–24

Paul says here that it behooves all of us to be built and to grow like a building dedicated to God, through the Spirit.

In the first place, when he says we must be *builded*, he means to stir us up daily to grow more and more in faith. Second, he makes good use of the word *groweth*, meaning, in effect, that we must not think ourselves to be as perfect as we should be.

Some fanciful heads are so puffed up with pride that they imagine themselves to be so wise that they disdain to cast their eyes upon God's Word or to listen or be taught by it. How tragic is such a presumption! We cannot be disciples of our Lord Jesus Christ unless we know that we must be established in him and profit in him all our life.

God's Word is so great in height, breadth, and length (Eph. 3:18) that even if a person wholly busies himself in it, yet he would never know it all. We ought to study it throughout all of our life, knowing that God intends thereby to set us in the way. We must then go forward little by little, and keep at it continually in humility and modesty.

Paul shows us that to be established in our Lord Jesus Christ and to make progress in all the good things that he gives us, we must have his Word so we may be built upon it and grow more and more through it. To bring this about, we must be teachable. From day to day, we must labor to seek help in the Word to strengthen our faith, which shall not be perfect in this world, as we will discover by experience.

FOR MEDITATION: Bible study by yourself and with others is essential for spiritual maturation. Are you studying the Scriptures on a daily basis? Are the Scriptures your rule to walk and work by (Gal. 6:16), your food to nourish you (Job 23:12), and your sword to fight with (Eph. 6:17)—in short, the supreme means that you use to grow in the grace and knowledge of the Lord Jesus Christ? How do your study habits need improvement?

Assured of God's Will

How that by revelation he made known unto me the mystery; (as I wrote afore in few words, whereby, when ye read, ye may understand my knowledge in the mystery of Christ). Ephesians 3:3–4

SUGGESTED FURTHER READING: Hebrews 10:23–39

The Ephesians ought to have so well known the mystery or secret that had been revealed to them that they could be sure that Paul was ordained to declare the everlasting salvation of their souls to those that so far had been cut off and banished from the kingdom of heaven. In this verse we note that it is not enough to hear and understand what is preached to us concerning the gospel; we must go a little higher to know that God would have us assured of his good will by the witness of men.

Therefore let us know that when the gospel is preached and we are assembled together to be taught, this is not due to a policy or order of man but because of an ordinance of God. It is an abiding law, against which it is not lawful for us to attempt anything.

Since this is so, we ought to come together more soberly and advisedly, as to God's school and not as to man's school, to hear the Word being preached. It is true that we ought to examine the doctrine and not receive with indifference all things that are preached. But we must also so honor God's name that when the doctrine of the Holy Scripture is expounded to us, we may withdraw ourselves from the world and forsake our own reason. We may then submit ourselves with true obedience and humility to the things that we know have come from God.

When we come together with our minds so prepared, God will guide us by his Holy Spirit to the assurance that our faith comes from him and is grounded upon his power and does not come from men.

FOR MEDITATION: With this high regard for preaching, Calvin often stresses the importance of faithfully attending and listening to the Word preached. Do you attend God's preached Word faithfully? Do you pray for a blessing before you attend? Do you attend with a hearty appetite for God's Word? Do you listen with a loving, expectant faith and a tender, submissive conscience? Do you humbly and seriously examine yourself by what you hear, and strive to put sermons into practice by the grace of the Holy Spirit? Do you thank God for all that you receive from sermons?

Honoring God with Humility

Unto me, who am less than the least of all saints, is this grace given, that I should preach among the Gentiles the unsearchable riches of Christ. Ephesians 3:8

SUGGESTED FURTHER READING: Romans 12

Paul's example warns us that the more someone is exalted by God's hand, the more he should humble himself. Truly, even those who are most backward have reason enough to magnify God's goodness for his calling them into his church. For what a wonderful thing it is for us to be reckoned as God's children, heirs of his kingdom, and members of our Lord Jesus Christ to be partakers of the glory into which he is entered (Luke 24:26)!

The Christian who is supposedly inferior to others, is a nobody and a fool, and is contemptible in this world's eyes, is nevertheless adopted by God into the number of his children to be part of the body of our Lord Jesus Christ. Even the least of us has enough to glorify God's grace. Those who have advanced to any degree of honor then have less of an excuse if they do not honor God for what he has bestowed upon them above others.

For example, if a person has knowledge and grace to use in serving the church, he becomes doubly guilty if he does not acknowledge that he is even more indebted to God for these abilities. Also, those who by their strength or skill are able to do more than poor folk who have nothing more than what they need to look after themselves, ought to humble themselves before God and to stoop in such a way that there is no presumption or pride in them to puff them up.

In short, just as every person has received grace through God's goodness, so every person's aim always ought to be to honor God. We should confess that we are more indebted and bound to him because he has dealt so liberally with us.

FOR MEDITATION: Remembering that those who have been doubly gifted are doubly indebted to God is an excellent way to foster humility. Paul was greatly gifted by God and could easily have been consumed with pride. Yet he remembered where the gifts had come from and remained humble. We ought to do the same.

Understanding Mysteries

And to make all men see what is the fellowship of the mystery, which from the beginning of the world hath been hid in God, who created all things by Jesus Christ. Ephesians 3:9
SUGGESTED FURTHER READING: Isaiah 40

Scripture offers some rather mysterious teachings which are not easily understood. Have we perceived that? To understand, we must first humble ourselves and pray God to enlighten us by his Holy Spirit so we may profit from all his works and words. Moreover, let us yearn to learn the things that he shows us and be content with the understanding he gives us without yearning to know any more than what we learn in his school.

When we have such humility, our Lord will give us a sure resting place. Although his secrets are incomprehensible, and the teachings of the law and the gospel are mysteries above the grasp of the world, yet they are sufficient for our welfare and salvation. So that there is no muddle, no confusion, and no obscurity for us, God will guide us by his Holy Spirit, giving us the wisdom and discretion to know whatever he deems is for our profit.

But if we are unteachable and behave like runaway horses to search farther than we are allowed, God's wisdom will certainly prove elusive. There will be such a diversity of things and so many subjects that we will be at our wits' end. We shall remain utterly confused.

Even the faithful will clearly perceive what Paul says here so that they may ever be mindful to walk in awe and fear, not giving themselves too much rein or taking too much freedom to know more than our Lord wants them to know. Any doubt we might have entertained about how God will amaze us with his works is removed. Yet he will not have us wonder at those unless we allow ourselves to be taught by him.

FOR MEDITATION: It is foolish to presume that a creature should comprehend everything the Creator does. We think of ourselves far too highly if we rebel against the parts of God's Word that we cannot understand. Our hearts should be overtaken with awe, not rebellion. Be aware and in awe of God and his work today.

Asking with Boldness

In whom we have boldness and access with confidence by the faith of him. Ephesians 3:12

SUGGESTED FURTHER READING: Hebrews 4:12–16

We are admonished to go forward in faith until we are thoroughly persuaded that, in fighting against all the temptations that can assail us, we shall get the upper hand by means of faith. We may glory both against life and death and despise all distresses, knowing full well that nothing is able to separate us from the love that Jesus Christ has shown us and which God his Father has also displayed toward us in his person.

It follows that our prayers must be based upon full assurance of faith. For he who thinks he will obtain anything while doubting deceives himself. We must assure ourselves by the promises of the gospel that God is ready to receive us in mercy whenever we come to him. Thereby we perceive that Paul did not say in vain that if we have faith we must not seek anything more than Jesus Christ. He must be our entire treasure.

Let us, then, fall down before the majesty of our good God, acknowledging our sins, and praying that he so makes us feel them that we hate them more and more. Yet we must not cease to be happy that he has shown himself so compassionate toward us in the person of his only Son. He is willing to draw us out of the pit of hell to give us entrance into his kingdom. He grants us the grace to come to himself in true faith and to withdraw ourselves from all worldly enticements that turn us away from him so that we may forsake all vainglory. Since we are void of all goodness in ourselves, let us seek everything we lack in him who is the true fountain of all goodness and can never be drained dry.

Let it please him to grant this grace, not only to us, but to all people.

FOR MEDITATION: Boldness and confidence in the presence of God are completely misplaced if they are not in Christ. He is the only reason we can stand before a holy God; such boldness would otherwise be sheer arrogance and the height of stupidity. An arrogant sinner who approaches God will be immediately consumed by his wrath. All that we have, we have by virtue of a saving union with Christ. Praise him for this confidence today.

Measured Grace

But unto every one of us is given grace according to the measure of the gift of Christ. Ephesians 4:7
SUGGESTED FURTHER READING: 2 Thessalonians 1

Let each one of us look to himself, for we shall each give account of the benefits that God has bestowed upon us (Luke 16:2). The more a person has received, the more he will be blamed if he does not discharge his duty in serving his neighbors. The purpose of God's gifts is to edify one another so that God's temple may grow among us and be further built until it reaches full perfection.

You see, then, how we ought to use the spiritual gifts that we have received from God. For the same reason, those who know the gospel should show by the conduct of their whole life that they are the children of light, and not be like blind wretches that wander in darkness (Luke 16:8).

Let us learn to make God's gifts serviceable in such a way that he may be glorified in them. In that respect, we are told about the measure of those gifts so that we should not plead that this or that person fails to offer us a good example. For when it is a question of commendation, every one of us makes himself believe, and would persuade the entire world to believe, that he is most excellent. In the meanwhile, we do not consider that God has doubly bound us to him in promising to show us such bountifulness that he has set us higher than our neighbors.

Let us give better consideration to what we have done, both generally and particularly.

FOR MEDITATION: To whom much is given, much is required. It is a terrible travesty that many men and women whom God has gifted in extraordinary ways have used those gifts in rebellion against him. But how wonderful it is to see great gifts used in the service of God! Whether our gifts are greater or lesser than those of others, let us be sure to use them in God's service. How can you do so?

Building up the Body

From whom the whole body fitly joined together and compacted by that which every joint supplieth, according to the effectual working in the measure of every part, maketh increase of the body unto the edifying of itself in love. Ephesians 4:16
SUGGESTED FURTHER READING: Song of Solomon 5

Let us not forget to seek peace to the uttermost of our power, according to the text I referred to from Romans (Rom. 12:18). We should not willfully separate ourselves from the world, but, as it were, stretch our arms out to bring in all who yield themselves willingly to the obedience of God so that we may have one faith together. Let us work to bring this to pass.

Paul tells us that the faith and obedience that we yield to God are not meant to puff up our hearts with pride so that we reject other people. Each one of us is not to value and be content with himself but to follow the example of our heavenly Father, who attracts to himself those who are far off and are ready to be reconciled to their enemies.

Seeing that he has shown us that in our Lord Jesus Christ and given us such an excellent pledge of it, we must have the same doctrine of peace in our thoughts and in our hearts. We must try, as much as possible, to bring into the union of the gospel those who are yet separated from it. If those who have been, as it were, stark mad against God, then yield themselves as lambs and sheep of the flock, we must be ready to receive them.

Let us devote ourselves to peace, not to gain each person to profit us, but to assure ourselves that since God has joined us together and bound us to one another, each of us ought to work for the body to the uttermost of his ability. According to our own measure, we should draw our neighbors with us so that we may truly become one body, over which Jesus Christ may reign.

FOR MEDITATION: When the body of Christ acts like the body of Christ, others notice. But if we constantly attempt to tear each other out of the body, how can that attract others to Christ, our head? The way others perceive the church is how they perceive Christ. Are you making efforts to knit the body together in mutual love, thus making it beautiful to behold?

Growing in Goodness

This I say therefore, and testify in the Lord, that ye henceforth walk not as other Gentiles walk, in the vanity of their mind, having the understanding darkened, being alienated from the life of God through the ignorance that is in them, because of the blindness of their heart.
Ephesians 4:17–18
SUGGESTED FURTHER READING: 1 Corinthians 6

Let us learn to walk in the fear of God, noting what Paul sets down here about the consummation of all evil. He says this to show us the wages God will pay to all who do not yield to him in due time and place.

Let us quake at such threats, fearing that God will execute them upon us when we cannot bear to be rebuked for our vices. Let us urge ourselves forward and afflict ourselves for our vices. When we entertain vices, let us become so inwardly ashamed that we abase and condemn ourselves until God has relieved us of them in his mercy.

We must put this teaching of Paul's into practice so that once God has joined us to him through our Lord Jesus Christ and given us life, we may take heed that this new life is not obscured and quenched in us through our own malice and ingratitude.

In continuing this teaching, let us learn first of all to humble ourselves, for it is certain that humility will cause us to come to God. Second, let humility be joined with carefulness so that we are not so indifferent as to flatter ourselves. For through the same carefulness we must strive to the utmost to fight against our vices and lusts, waiting upon our Lord until he rids us completely of them.

In the meantime, let us always be gaining some victory, be it very little indeed, so that it may continually appear that our Lord Jesus Christ is working in us and making his grace prevail by causing us always to progress in goodness. May we be so much in love with goodness that we grow more and more in it until God takes us out of this world.

FOR MEDITATION: How important it is for believers to "walk the talk" of being a vital Christian. Many talk the talk but don't walk the walk, forgetting that, as has been said, our walk talks more than our talk talks. Are you prayerfully striving every day to be salt in the earth and light on the hill by having your talk and your walk be consistent in glorifying God?

Putting on the New Man

And that ye put on the new man, which after God is created in righteousness and true holiness. Ephesians 4:24
SUGGESTED FURTHER READING: John 3:1–16

Let us be fully resolved and persuaded that God will receive nothing from our hands but that which he knows to be his own. Without him, there is nothing but evil. His image was defaced in us by Adam's sin; therefore, we must be newly created in Jesus Christ.

Paul now shows us how that is done *in righteousness and true holiness.* By the word *righteousness,* he means soundness and uprightness. So we must live with our neighbors without deceit, without malice, and without mischief, giving to every person what is due to him. When such soundness reigns in us, we will show by our deeds that we are fashioned again in righteousness after God's image.

It is not enough for people to have what is due them, unless God also has his. For of what purpose is it for us not to steal from others while committing sacrilege against God? Or to abstain from taking our neighbor's goods, while robbing God of his honor? Righteousness must be linked with holiness, for the two tables of the law are inseparable. In the word *holiness,* Paul includes everything that belongs to the service of God.

A new life, therefore, is walking in purity before God, eschewing all corruption and uncleanness, and separating ourselves from all the defilements of the world so that we may offer ourselves in sacrifice to God. At the same time, we must walk in integrity and uprightness with our neighbors. Performing these two things is what is required for perfection in the Christian life.

FOR MEDITATION: Adam was created in righteousness and holiness, but his fall marred all his descendants. In Christ, we can be recreated into new men, made again in righteousness and holiness. This is an amazing truth! Many long to return to Eden, but they fail to realize that the crowning creation of Eden—righteous man—is being re-created all around them as God takes sinners and makes them new.

Working to Give

Let him that stole steal no more: but rather let him labour, working with his hands the thing which is good, that he may have to give to him that needeth. Ephesians 4:28

SUGGESTED FURTHER READING: 1 Thessalonians 4:9–12

Paul proceeds one step further regarding the change that he requires of the faithful. He tells them they must not only abstain from defrauding other people and from robbing them of their goods, but they must also try to help those in need.

The way the apostle teaches us to abstain from all evil seems to be very hard. Rather than living at our ease, as we have been accustomed to do, and having many goods, we should prepare to scratch our living out of the earth, work with great pain and travail, and in all of that to fare very harshly. Though this way seems very hard, we must go further. When we have the means to make a living without using wicked practices, we must spare something of what God gives us through his blessing and give it to relieve the needy.

Therefore, let us not regard our own inclinations, considering that of our own nature we are so perverse and wedded to our own profit that each one of us will always be well stocked. Since we have so little concern for others, even if they are members of the body of our Lord Jesus Christ, we must strive to force ourselves to do them good, for that striving will bring us together.

We must bear down upon our affections, then employ ourselves earnestly and sincerely until we confess that the bread we eat comes to us from God's hand. We are sustained by his goodness as by a father who gives a portion to his children. So let us labor to do good with the little we have and to help those who are in need.

FOR MEDITATION: We need Jesus to give us eyes to see the needs of others and hearts willing to work hard, not for our own gain, but for others. Giving to others is not our natural inclination, but Paul believes that the gospel is strong enough to turn even those who were thieves into compassionate and generous people. Is this evidenced in your life?

Edifying with the Tongue

Let no corrupt communication proceed out of your mouth, but that which is good to the use of edifying, that it may minister grace unto the hearers. Ephesians 4:29

SUGGESTED FURTHER READING: James 3:1–12

We must note in the first place that our Lord has given us tongues to communicate with one another. We should therefore use them to benefit our neighbors and wholly employ them to that end.

The tongue, which is the means of conveying our hearts and minds to others, ought to guide the rest of us, since it has superiority over all. On the other hand, the tongue is with good reason named our glory to show how we ought to use it and to what purpose, namely, to honor God (Ps. 16:9; 57:8). When we have given close attention to the order of nature, our hearts ought to be sufficiently impressed so that our words are beneficial and contribute to our neighbor's welfare and profit.

The first point, therefore, to bear in mind is that our Lord wills every part of us to be useful, especially the tongue, so that the drift of all our talk may be to edify. For example, one man needs counsel, another warning, another rebuking, and another to be reminded of something or else be taught because he is utterly ignorant.

The principal thing to keep in mind is to teach the ignorant and show them the way of salvation. If a person misbehaves or is negligent and slothful, he must be spurred on by good teachings. If he is unruly, he must be shamed (as much as is possible), that he may be brought back to serve God. Once we have come to that point, we should continually give ourselves to the benefit and profit of our neighbors in an infinite number of ways, both in respect to the body and the soul.

FOR MEDITATION: The tongue is so powerful that it must be handled with great care. Not only must it be kept from sin, it must be used for good. Some struggle to keep their tongue silent, while others struggle to get it moving. Whatever the case, we have the double duty to keep the tongue from evil and to employ it for good. Are your words a testimony to God's grace? Are you keeping your tongue from evil and using it for good?

Bearing Fruits of Righteousness

For the fruit of the Spirit is in all goodness and righteousness and truth.
Ephesians 5:9
SUGGESTED FURTHER READING: Galatians 5

Once our life is ordered after this manner, people will perceive that the light also bears fruit in us, that is to say, the light which God gives us is not idle but is given that we may apply ourselves to do the things that he commands and appoints. That is why Paul speaks of the fruit of righteousness.

The sun gives light to the world to be useful to us by guiding us in all our doings. That is the fruit and use of the sun. In the same way, the gospel is not a fruitless thing. The work of the gospel must show in our life, and this comes about when we are righteous, kind-hearted, and faithful.

In three words—*goodness, righteousness,* and *truth,* Paul includes all things that belong to the two tables of the law. For the manner of Holy Scripture, when speaking of serving God, is to send us back to our neighbors. If we love our neighbors as we ought to and live with them according to God's law, God will always have his sovereign right.

Until we are ruled by obedience to God, each one of us will love himself too much, desire to draw attention to himself, and glory in himself. In short, there will be nothing in us but pride, vainglory, covetousness, cruelty, and all manner of deceit until our Lord brings us under his yoke, and we have bowed in obedience to honor him and serve him and to bless his holy name. That will be done when we do our duty to other people, for the true trial and testimony is that we fear God.

FOR MEDITATION: Goodness. Righteousness. Truth. By the grace of God, are you striving to reflect the image of Christ through these qualities, as well as those listed in Galatians 5:22–23, to those around you? If so, you may know that the Spirit is at work within you, for these qualities represent the fruit of the Spirit. Give all praise to God for his own work within you.

Striving for Moderation

And be not drunk with wine, wherein is excess; but be filled with the Spirit. Ephesians 5:18
SUGGESTED FURTHER READING: 1 Peter 4:1–6

We learn from this passage that we must be sober and temperate in our eating and drinking. Though there may be an abundance of food and drink before us, we must be discreet in partaking so that meat and drink do not lead to trouble.

The heathen saw that very well, and it is no wonder. For we cannot wipe out the knowledge that we must eat and drink to live, not live to eat and drink. We eat food to strengthen us and make us able to perform our duties and not be useless. It is certain that bread and wine and meat are not given to make people downcast. But since without those people would become enfeebled by starvation, our Lord renews them and gives them strength, according to this saying of the psalm, that wine makes a man's heart glad, and bread strengthens it (Ps. 104:15). So you see what we should remember about eating and drinking.

If we cannot be as perfect as required, let us lament our faults and at all costs beware that we do not act like beasts in eating and drinking, so that God may be honored by us as he ought to be, not only by our doing homage to him for life but also by regarding our very food as a reason why we should come to him. Let us also understand that he now gives us a mere taste of his love so that in waiting for the full enjoyment of it, we may learn to forsake the world and serve him with a more willing mind, knowing that he is not only our Master with complete dominion over us, but also that he is our Father who seeks to win us by his goodness.

FOR MEDITATION: Moderation is the key to enjoying the wonderful blessings God has freely given to us without idolizing them and reaping the consequences of overindulgence. If moderation is difficult, Paul encourages us to turn our desires toward God and be filled with the Spirit rather than with wine. Do you struggle to moderate some of your desires? Find a way to sanctify that energy by directing it toward God and his service, and by remembering the reality of death, judgment, and eternity.

Giving Thanks for Everything

Giving thanks always for all things unto God and the Father in the name of our Lord Jesus Christ. Ephesians 5:20
SUGGESTED FURTHER READING: Psalm 100

Let us see if we do not have reason to bless God in all our adversities. First, whatever happens to us, he so supports us that if he should touch us in good earnest with a single finger of his hand, we should be overwhelmed at the first blow. Seeing that we keep going is a sign that he spares us. Have we not cause, then, to thank him for that?

Second, when he turns the chastisements that he sends us to our benefit, he purges us so we make continual progress to the kingdom of heaven. Similarly, he lifts us high because we are too much tied to the world, so that we shall be gathered together to come to the full perfection that is prepared for us in heaven. When we see all this, do we not have reason to praise our God, even if we are full of grief, care, fear, and doubts? It is indeed so, even if our own ingratitude hinders us. So much more, then, it behooves us to carefully note what Paul tells us here, namely, that we have reason to praise God without end and without ceasing.

If our mouth is sometimes stopped with grief, so that we seem to be barred from praising God and cannot apply ourselves freely to it, let us understand that God never shows himself so severe and rigorous toward us that he does not assuage all the bitterness that is in our afflictions so that he may draw us to himself and we might thank him and glorify him.

Since we receive no grace except by means of our Lord Jesus Christ, who also turns to our welfare the corrections that we have to suffer for our sins, therefore we should render thanks *unto God and the Father in the name of our Lord Jesus Christ.*

FOR MEDITATION: To give thanks always for all things is a great struggle for all believers and a great grace that God alone can grant. Meditate on how these thoughts can help us as believers to be more thankful in all things:

- All things that come upon us derive from the hand of our heavenly Father.
- Our heavenly Father makes no mistakes.
- If we are his children, all things shall work together for our good (Rom. 8:28).
- All that transpires in our lives serves to God's glory.

Dual Submission

Wives, submit yourselves unto your own husbands, as unto the Lord.
Ephesians 5:22
SUGGESTED FURTHER READING: Psalm 45

When Paul writes about wives owing subjection to their husbands, we should note that this subjection is twofold. Man was already the head of the woman before the sin and fall of Eve and Adam (1 Tim. 2:13). In showing that it was not fitting that the wife should rule in equal status with her husband, Paul says that the man did not come from the woman but the woman from the man; she is thus a part of his body.

God could have created Eve of the earth, as he did Adam, but that was not his will. Rather, he joined the man and the woman together in such a way that the man knew that his wife was his own substance and flesh and was thereby induced to love her. Likewise, the wife, knowing she was of no other being than the man, bore her subjection patiently and with voluntary affection.

If the hand, being a member of the body, should refuse to stay in its own place and should insist on settling itself upon the crown of the head, what would be the result? Thus, if we look back to the creation of the man and the woman, the husband ought to be induced to love and cherish his wife as himself; and the wife, seeing she was taken out of the substance of the man, ought to submit herself quietly to him as her head.

FOR MEDITATION: Before the fall, Eve gladly submitted to her husband and Adam gladly led her in love and righteousness. Today, because men and women are corrupted by sin, this order is often abused by men who do not love their wives as Christ loved the church. Nevertheless, wives are called to live in obedience as a display of God's mercy and long-suffering by submitting to their husbands in all that is lawful. Wives, are you living in submission to your husbands, under God?

Loving as Christ Loved

Husbands, love your wives, even as Christ also loved the church, and gave himself for it. Ephesians 5:25
SUGGESTED FURTHER READING: Matthew 19:1–12

Now let husbands consider well what they owe to their wives: that they should be as dear to them as their own lives. Even so, they will not reach the perfection of our Lord Jesus Christ but follow a great way behind him.

For their part, wives must bear in mind that since God's will is that marriage should be a type of the grace of our Lord Jesus Christ, they will be much too ungrateful if they do not submit themselves as God calls them to their husbands. At the same time, Paul means to magnify God's goodness toward us and the love that Jesus Christ has borne us in saying that he gave himself for us. Therefore, let us acknowledge that Christ's love comes to us by the free mercy of God his Father, and that our Lord Jesus Christ had respect to nothing but our miseries when he showed himself so merciful in helping us.

If we keep these things in mind, we shall be moved as husbands and wives to obey each other without disputing. Then, too, we shall be set afire to glorify God and acknowledge with our mouth and by our whole life how much we are indebted to him. In this we show that God not only has released us from condemnation and drawn us out of death but also has condescended to give us his well-beloved Son as a pledge of his love. Jesus Christ has willingly become the pledge and ransom to acquit us before God, so that the devil also might not have anything against us. For Satan is our adversary, and we are subject to him until our Redeemer sets us free from the devil's bondage.

FOR MEDITATION: If Christ has forgiven the sins of his people, how can they refuse to forgive the sins of others, especially of their spouses? Christian husbands must remember how much they have been forgiven, and be forgiving of their wives. In addition, they should be willing to sacrifice themselves for their wives, just as Christ did. A healthy marriage is founded in Christ. Husbands, are you reflecting Christ in your marriage by leading your wife in love and submitting to God?

Caring for Each Other

For no man ever yet hated his own flesh; but nourisheth it and cherisheth it, even as the Lord the church. Ephesians 5:29

SUGGESTED FURTHER READING: Isaiah 54

If we gave full attention to the prophet Isaiah's argument in Isaiah 54, we would be more moved by the exhortation that is set down here: *no man ever yet hated his own flesh; but nourisheth it and cherisheth it.*

Consider the care that each one of us has for himself; how tenderly we nourish all the parts of our body, even to the little toe of the foot (so to speak), how carefully we watch that nothing is lacking, and how prudent we are in every respect so that if any part of us is ill, we endeavor to find a remedy to keep ourselves in good health. Would that everyone of us really thought in that way, for it would surely be a means of teaching us to do likewise to our neighbors, or other people.

Much more this admonition ought to affect the attitude of fathers to their children, children to their fathers, husbands to their wives, wives to their husbands, and similarly we in the mutual relationships into which it has pleased our Lord to join us in a close bond.

If anyone responds to this, saying, "None of this applies to me," it necessarily follows that you do not belong to the family of mankind. For, as I said before, God has created and nourished us so we should all be like one lump. For though there are many fingers and sinews in a person's body, that does not stop them from being all one thing, nor is any one member hindered from nurturing another as well as himself.

FOR MEDITATION: Think about the amount of care you invest in yourself. How would your relationships with others (especially your husband or wife) change if you cared for them with the same care that you show yourself? If you get something in your eye, for example, you immediately work on relieving your discomfort. Do you treat your spouse this way, too, providing him or her immediate attention when trouble comes?

Joined Together by the Lord

Nevertheless let every one of you in particular so love his wife even as himself; and the wife see that she reverence her husband. Ephesians 5:33
SUGGESTED FURTHER READING: 1 Peter 3

Peter expressly says that when a man is too harsh and rigorous to his wife, and the wife becomes so cross that he cannot cope with her nor is she willing to submit herself as she ought, then their prayers are hindered (1 Peter 3:7). It is as if the apostle says, "Wretched people, what are you thinking? Are you not very miserable in seeing that the gate is shut against you and you cannot invoke God? What will become of you when you cannot put yourselves in the hands of your God?"

God loves concord between husbands and wives and bids them come to him. When a husband behaves peaceably toward his wife, and the wife also does her duty, the Lord says, "If you call upon me, I will give ear to you as if you prayed out of one mouth." Seeing that our Lord calls us to him for our good and for our salvation, commanding us to call upon him with a pure heart, must we not be possessed by the devil and take leave of our senses if we do not accept such a profitable condition?

Therefore let us note that, if a husband intends to discharge his duty, and the wife similarly, both of them must have an eye to God, accepting their marriage as from him, and assuring themselves that they did not meet by chance but were joined together by the Lord. For it was God's intent that the husband should be a companion to his wife and receive her as part of himself, and that the wife yield the degree of honor to her husband that belongs to him and submit herself to him as to her head.

FOR MEDITATION: Marriage is an ordinance of God, and every individual marriage is a part of God's plan. It is not something to be entered lightly. Great love and many prayers must grace the marriage if it is lived to the glory of God. When marital strife hinders prayer, it does not take much to start a downward spiral that can end only in shipwreck.

What condition is your marriage presently in? Are you arguing with your spouse more than you are complimenting him or her? If so, your downward spiral has already begun. Begin immediately to study your calling in marriage from Ephesians 5, and pray for grace to look at yourself rather than your spouse, asking, "How can I be a better husband?" or "How can I be a better wife?" Consider asking others for help. Don't let your marriage degenerate if you can possibly help it.

Praying Constantly

Praying always with all prayer and supplication in the Spirit, and watching thereunto with all perseverance and supplication for all saints. Ephesians 6:18
SUGGESTED FURTHER READING: Ezra 9

The more advanced we are in faith, the more earnest our zeal should be in calling upon our God, acknowledging and confessing that our salvation lies in his hand and that all good things come from him. Since we are so slothful in that respect, Paul sets before us two words, *prayer* and *supplication*, to express that we must not coldly go about this prayer but be touched to the quick to continue it with the kind of perseverance that does not grow weary.

It is true that God tells us through his prophet Isaiah (65:24) that he will hear us even before we cry out to him, and his hand will be ready to help us before we even have opened our mouth. But that is said to us not to encourage us to be slothful but to show us that God will not permit us to be kept waiting after we have called upon him, as though he were loath to help us. To prove that, he acts even before we call on him. We find that true by experience.

Nevertheless, he wants us to yield a true proof of our faith by praying to him. For the right way to show that his promises have been powerful in us is that, as soon as we are touched with any grief or affliction, we go straight to God and unburden our hearts to him. That is affirmed in other passages of Scripture, such as Psalms 50:15 and 62:8.

We see now how we must take advantage of God's Word, which assures us that God will never fail us. He assures us that by seeking him, we will certainly find what we ask for. So the prayers that we offer are keys to unlock the treasures that God reserves for us and will not keep from us. We must open the way to those treasures by praying.

FOR MEDITATION: Rather than engaging in protracted discussions of the necessity of prayer, we should humbly bow to the clear command and expectation of Scripture. We should pray often and always, knowing that prayer grounded in God's promises is the key that unlocks the way to God's treasures. If you are spiritually downcast or emotionally depressed, try using this key. For your encouragement, read the section in John Bunyan's *Pilgrim's Progress* that so beautifully tells how Christian escaped from the dungeon of Giant Despair.

Praying in the Spirit

Praying always with all prayer and supplication in the Spirit, and watching thereunto with all perseverance and supplication for all saints.
Ephesians 6:18
SUGGESTED FURTHER READING: John 16:17–28

Paul says we must pray at all times *in the Spirit*. That means all hypocrisy must be excluded in prayer.

We know that many people mumble when they come to God. It is their lips or the tips of their tongues that perform this duty, which is not the way that God wills us to pray and call upon him. He does not approve of such supplications; rather, he abhors them because when we pray senselessly to him in mere pretence, we commit a kind of sacrilege. It is necessary for our prayers not only to be made with our mouths but to come from the bottom of our hearts.

We do not have the power to pray rightly in ourselves, so it is necessary for the Holy Spirit to work in us. Therefore Paul uses the word *Spirit* to show that we must beseech God to govern us in such a way that he may thoroughly touch us so we may pray to him as we ought. He will accept our prayers when he sees in them the signs of his Holy Spirit.

We must always remember what Romans teaches, that we do not know what to pray for (Rom. 8:26), for it is something that exceeds our understanding. Though most of us fail in that respect, some imagine they perfectly know how and what to pray to God. Such opinion only shuts the door upon us unless we know our faults and infirmities and immediately resort to the remedy. Therefore it is most certain that we shall never be earnestly disposed to pray to God unless he governs us by his Holy Spirit.

FOR MEDITATION: Our prayers are so imperfect that it is a great comfort to know that Christ is beside the throne, sanctifying our words and interceding for us. As Calvin says, we often pray with our lips and not our hearts. Oh, that God's people would pray in the Spirit! Imagine what could happen with such a chorus of prayer like that.

Extending Salvation to All People

For this is good and acceptable in the sight of God our Saviour; who will have all men to be saved, and to come unto the knowledge of the truth.
1 Timothy 2:3–4
SUGGESTED FURTHER READING: Matthew 11:20–30

To understand this text, we must observe the condition of the world in the days of Paul. It was new and strange to have the gospel published to Gentiles in those days, for it had been apparent that God had chosen the descendents of Abraham, and the rest of the world was therefore deprived of all hope of salvation.

Indeed, we see how Holy Scripture makes clear the adoption of God's people. But Paul commands us to pray for the entire world, not without cause, for he adds the reason: *God will have all men to be saved.* It is as if he says, "My friends, it is reasonable that we should observe what the will of God is and his purpose: that every one of us may employ himself in rightly serving him."

Seeing it is the will of God that all men should partake of the salvation that he has sent in the person of his only begotten Son, we must endeavor to attract poor, silly, ignorant creatures to us, that we may together come to the inheritance of the kingdom of heaven that has been promised us.

But we must also observe that Paul speaks not of each person, but of all kinds of people. Therefore, when he says God wills all people to be saved, we must not think that he speaks of them individually. Rather, his meaning is that, though in times past God chose a certain people to be his own, he now shows mercy to all the world, even to those who seem to be shut off from the hope of salvation.

FOR MEDITATION: The glorious grace of God displayed in the new covenant should bring us to our knees. Most believers today are Gentiles, whose distant ancestors had little or no access to the great redemption God was working in Israel. This composition of the church is evidence that God desires that all kinds of people should come to faith. How does this truth serve as a spur for evangelistic and mission work?

Easing Doubt of Salvation

Who will have all men to be saved, and to come unto the knowledge of the truth. 1 Timothy 2:4

SUGGESTED FURTHER READING: 2 Corinthians 7

When it pleased God to draw us out of the darkness of unbelief and to give us the light of the gospel, he did not look at any service we performed or at any virtue we possessed. Rather, he called us, having chosen us before all time.

Paul says in Romans 8 that in knowing God, we must not take the glory for it, for the calling of the faithful rests upon the counsel of God. We see how far the Lord makes known to us what he decreed before we were born. He touches us with his Holy Spirit, and we are engrafted into the body of our Lord Jesus Christ. This is the proof of our adoption, the pledge given us to erase any doubt that God takes and holds us as his children. For by faith we are made one with Jesus Christ, who is the only begotten Son of God, unto whom belongs the inheritance of life.

When we know that according to his unchangeable election God has called us to himself, we are eased of any doubt of our salvation. Jesus Christ says that no man takes from him those whom the Father has given him (John 10:28). What has the Father given to Jesus Christ but those whom he has chosen and whom he knows are his?

Seeing that God has given us to his Son, to be kept and defended by him, and that Jesus Christ promises that none of us shall be lost, and he will exercise all the might and power of the Godhead to save and defend us, is not this a comfort surpassing all the treasures of the world? Is not this the true ground upon which all the assurance and certainty of our salvation is settled?

FOR MEDITATION: The famous Westminster Assembly of the 1640s concluded that there are three grounds of assurance of personal faith: one primary ground—the promises of God; and two secondary grounds—evidences of grace and the witness of the Spirit. What an encouragement it is that God's promises in Jesus Christ are the richest and fullest ground of assurance! What use do you make of God's promises in coming to assurance of the truth and of your own salvation?

Offering Ransom for All

Who gave himself a ransom for all, to be testified in due time. 1 Timothy 2:6

SUGGESTED FURTHER READING: Revelation 7:9–17

Jesus Christ has not only proclaimed glad tidings but has also sent forth his apostles and ministers to preach and publish peace to the entire world. He has done this to assemble the Jews, who were near to God by reason of the covenant and the solemn pledge made to their fathers, but who still needed reconciliation through Jesus Christ the Redeemer.

These glad tidings were afterward directed to those who were afar off, even to the poor Gentiles. They also received the message of salvation and the peace of God, and were assured that God so loved them that he forgave all their sins. Thus the wall of partition was broken down and the ceremonies destroyed by which God had differentiated between the Jews and the Gentiles. Why did this happen? Because this salvation belongs to the entire world without exception.

We therefore have this clear teaching that it was necessary for our Lord Jesus Christ to make atonement for our sins and that by his death he has purchased our redemption. We must, then, come to the truth set forth in the gospel so we may enjoy the blessings contained therein. We may not say that God is changeable because it pleased him to hide the witness of his gospel from the Gentiles for a while, and afterward preached it throughout the world, for he had already determined this in the counsel of his own will.

Let us therefore be convinced that it is our duty to worship and reverence him with all humility, for this is the greatest wisdom we can possess.

FOR MEDITATION: What an amazing reach the gospel has, laying hold of the ends of the earth! And what a blessing that, on the Last Day, people shall bow before Jesus from every tribe, nation, and race! Does the glorious catholicity and universality of the church move you to praise God? Does the love of Christ who gave himself as a ransom move you to pursue and support mission work? In what ways are you presently reaching out to others, far and near?

Praying with Holy Hands

I will therefore that men pray every where, lifting up holy hands, without wrath and doubting. 1 Timothy 2:8
SUGGESTED FURTHER READING: Ephesians 3:14–21

When we pray, let us learn to renounce everything that God does not allow, knowing that our salvation is in him alone. Let us put all our trust in him, believing that he will aid and assist us in all our troubles and afflictions, for if we do not pray in faith, although the ceremony may be good in itself, the prayer will be vain and superfluous.

Those who lift up their hands to heaven while remaining fastened to things on earth, condemn themselves; for they come before God solemnly declaring that they seek him, while at the same time remain attached to things below. They say they put their trust in him, but at the same time trust in themselves or some other creature; they pretend to be lifted up to heaven by faith, even as they drown in earthly pleasures.

Let us therefore learn that, when we pray to God, we must be void of all earthly cares and wicked affections, knowing there are many things that hinder us from coming to God. When we lift up our hands to heaven, it must be for the purpose of seeking God by faith. We cannot pray rightly unless we withdraw ourselves from the cares and wicked affections of the flesh.

Now let us fall down before the face of our good God, confessing our faults and praying that he will forget them and we may be received by him. Let us also pray that he will strengthen us and sanctify us from day to day by his Holy Spirit until we may wholly cast off all our imperfections and sins. Since this cannot be done as long as we live as mortals, let us pray that he will bear with our infirmities until he has utterly put them away.

FOR MEDITATION: Praying by faith is the thermometer of our spiritual life. How sad that we often find prayer such hard work! Let us ask God to forgive all our prayerlessness and strive to remember that prayer is an extraordinary and merciful gift of God. Consider William Bridge's words: "It is a mercy to pray, even though I never receive the mercy prayed for." But if unanswered prayer can be sweet, how much more answered petitions! Joseph Hall quipped, "Good prayers never come weeping back, for I am sure I shall receive either what I ask or what I should have been asking for."

Living in the House of God

But if I tarry long, that thou mayest know how thou oughtest to behave thyself in the house of God, which is the church of the living God, the pillar and ground of the truth. 1 Timothy 3:15

SUGGESTED FURTHER READING: Ephesians 4:1–16

Let those who are appointed as ministers of the Word of God know that they not only deal with people but are accountable to him who has called them to this high office. Let them not be puffed up with the honor and dignity of their position but know that they shall be so much less able to excuse themselves if they fail to walk uprightly. If they fail to serve him as they ought, they will commit horrible sacrilege and have a fearful vengeance of God prepared for them.

First, we are taught to do our duty. Because God has honored us in our unworthiness, we ought to labor to fill the office to which we are called. The church is called the house of the living God. That ought to awaken us to walk rightly. Why, then, do we sleep in our sins? Why do we run into wickedness? Do we think that God does not see us? Do we think we are far out of his sight and from the presence of our Lord Jesus Christ?

Let us remember that the Word of God is preached to us, that God dwells among us, and that he is present with us. As our Lord Jesus Christ says, "Where two or three are gathered together in my name, there am I in the midst of them" (Matt. 18:20). We also are told, "In him dwelleth all the fulness of the Godhead bodily" (Col. 2:9).

So then, however often the devil attempts to rock us to sleep, to tie us to the vanities of this world, or to tempt us with wicked lusts, we ought to remember and set before our eyes that God dwells in the midst of us and that we are his house.

FOR MEDITATION: Those who labor in gospel ministry are held by God to the highest standards, for they are ambassadors of God. They should tremble at the responsibility they hold and look to Christ for the strength to be faithful in their work and life. If you are a minister, you should think long and hard about these things. If you are not, you should pray long and hard for those who are called to minister to you.

Receiving Christ in the Supper

But if I tarry long, that thou mayest know how thou oughtest to behave thyself in the house of God, which is the church of the living God, the pillar and ground of the truth. 1 Timothy 3:15

SUGGESTED FURTHER READING: 1 Corinthians 11:17–34

When the apostle tells us to withdraw from all wicked affections, he calls us to our Savior, Jesus Christ. Must not we then take pains to come unto him in the Holy Supper? Let us solemnly meditate upon this subject.

Let us see how we are disposed, for God will not have us come to him in the Holy Supper as liars and deceivers. Let us see if we are disposed to receive God, not as a guest that travels by the way, but as one who has forever chosen us for his dwelling place, and as one who has dedicated us to himself as his temples so that we may be like a house built upon a rock. We must receive God by faith and as those who have been made truly one with our Lord Jesus Christ.

We should so examine and cleanse ourselves that when we receive the Supper of our Lord Jesus Christ, we may be more and more confirmed in his grace, that we may be engrafted into his body and truly be made one with him, and that all the promises we perceive in the gospel may better be confirmed in us. We must know that we live in him as he dwells in us, and that God owns us and takes us for his children.

We should be most earnest to call upon him and trust in his goodness, so he may so govern us by his Holy Spirit, and that poor ignorant creatures may through our example be brought to the right way. For today we see many people who are walking in the way of destruction. May we pay attention to what God has confirmed to us; that he would be pleased to show his grace, not only to one city or a little handful of people, but to reign over all the world so that everyone may serve and worship him in spirit and in truth.

FOR MEDITATION: How do you receive Christ in the Holy Supper? Do you focus by faith on the Lord Jesus Christ and his death and resurrection? How do you continue to grow in Christ after the Supper has been administered?

Called to Suffer

Be not thou therefore ashamed of the testimony of our Lord, nor of me his prisoner: but be thou partaker of the afflictions of the gospel according to the power of God. 2 Timothy 1:8
SUGGESTED FURTHER READING: Acts 5:17–42

Let us not deceive Jesus Christ in the testimony we owe him by closing our mouths when it is needful to maintain his honor and the authority of his gospel. When we see people afflicted for the cause of God, let us join with them and help them in their affliction. Let us not be shaken by the tempests that arise, but let us always remain constant in our purpose and stand as witnesses for the Son of God, seeing he is so gracious to use us in such a good cause.

Let us mark well whether men suffer for their sins or for the truth of God. When we see those who are oppressed, we must not despise them lest we do injury to God, but we must ascertain for what cause they suffer. If they have walked in good conscience and are blamed and tormented because they serve God, this is enough to remove whatever the wicked world can say against them. Therefore Paul says, *Be thou partaker of the afflictions of the gospel.*

No person would not willingly escape affliction, for this is human nature. Though we confess without pretense that God bestows a singular grace when he enables men to bear affliction and maintain his cause, yet not one of us would not willingly draw his neck out of persecution. For we must look at the lesson given by Paul, who says that the gospel brings troubles. Jesus Christ was crucified and his teaching is joined with many miseries. He could, if it pleased him, cause his teaching to be received without any resistance. But the Scripture must be fulfilled: "Rule thou in the midst of thine enemies" (Ps. 110).

FOR MEDITATION: We are called to be witnesses of Jesus Christ in this world, no matter what the cost. This can be very difficult to incorporate into our Christian life, but it is necessary if we are to take up our cross and follow him. In what ways has God made you "partaker of the afflictions of the gospel"?

Called to his Holy Purpose

Who hath saved us, and called us with an holy calling, not according to our works, but according to his own purpose and grace, which was given us in Christ Jesus before the world began. 2 Timothy 1:9

SUGGESTED FURTHER READING: Haggai 1

When God gives us a token of his goodness, it is so that we should hope for more from his hands and wait till he brings to pass what he has begun in us. If God has saved us and called us with a holy calling, do we think that he will leave us midway in the execution of it? When he has showed us our salvation and given us his gospel, whereby he calls us to his kingdom and opens the gates for us, do we think he will leave us here, and mock us, and deprive us of his grace, or make it unprofitable? No, no; rather, let us hope that he will bring his work to a perfect end.

Let us proceed with good courage, for God has already displayed his power toward us. Let us not doubt that he will continue it; that we shall have perfect victory over Satan and our enemies; that God the Father has given all power into the hands of Jesus Christ, who is our head and captain; and that we may be partakers of it. Thus we see Paul's meaning here. God has witnessed, and we know by experience, that he will never fail us in a time of need. Why is that? He has already saved us in calling us to the gospel and redeeming us from sin.

That we may profit by this doctrine, let us first know that, whereas God has given us the knowledge of his truth, it is as if he had already shown us that we belonged to his heavenly inheritance and that we were of his flock. If we are persuaded of this and resolved of it, we shall go forward in the cause, knowing that we are under his protection. He has sufficient strength to overcome all our enemies, which makes our salvation sure.

FOR MEDITATION: If you are his child, God has called you to some type of service in his kingdom. Whatever that calling is, it will not always be easy, no matter how much passion you have for it. When you realize that you cannot go forward on your own, you need not fear that God will abandon you. He called you according to his purpose and grace, and he will sustain you with that grace. Do not be discouraged; he will see you through.

Shunning Vain Babbling

But shun profane and vain babblings: for they will increase unto more ungodliness. 2 Timothy 2:16

SUGGESTED FURTHER READING: 2 Peter 2

When Paul speaks of vain babbling, he means talk that impresses curious men. We see many who take great pleasure in vain questions and seem to be ravished by them. These babblers do not openly speak against the truth, but they despise it as something too common and base, as a thing for children and fools. As for them, they think they know some higher and more profound matter. They are at variance with what would be profitable for them.

Therefore, let us weigh well the words of Paul. He says to shun *vain babblings*, for they offer nothing but fine rhetoric and exquisite words to give credit to him that speaks and to show that he is well learned. None of this should be received into the church; it must be banished.

God will have his people edified, so he has appointed his Word for that purpose. Therefore, if our purpose is the salvation of people that they may receive nourishment by the doctrine that is taught them, it is sacrilege to do otherwise, for in that we pervert the pure use of the Word of God. The word *profane* is set against that which is holy and dedicated to God. Whatever is holy pertains to the magnification of God and increases our knowledge of his majesty whereby we may worship him. It draws us to the kingdom of heaven or takes our affections from the world, and leads us to Jesus Christ so that we may be grafted into his body.

On the contrary, when we do not feel the glory of God, when we do not desire to submit ourselves to him, when we do not know the riches of the kingdom of heaven, when we are not drawn into his service to live in pureness of conscience, when we do not know what the salvation means that was purchased by our Lord Jesus Christ, we belong to the world and are *profane*.

FOR MEDITATION: Trends and fashions come and go, and the desire for anything new is always powerful. Preachers are not exempt from this temptation. When preaching from a book that has been read and preached for thousands of years, we are tempted to find something novel to say, and, in the pursuit of that goal, to veer into vain babbling. Let us lift up prayer for our preachers that they might be kept from this and would bring us the full, unadulterated, timeless Word of God.

Taking the Name of Christ

Nevertheless the foundation of God standeth sure, having this seal, The Lord knoweth them that are his. And, let every one that nameth the name of Christ depart from iniquity. 2 Timothy 2:19
SUGGESTED FURTHER READING: John 10:1–21

We cannot take the name *Christian* upon us, we cannot say that we belong to the children of God and are of his church, unless we have been delivered from our filthiness.

If a person calls himself the servant of a prince and yet is a thief, shouldn't he be doubly punished because he abused the title that did not truly belong to him? Behold the Son of God, who is the fountain of all holiness and righteousness! If we try to hide ourselves and cover all our filthiness, is not it so much more shameful if we do so under his name? Does not this horrible sacrilege deserve the most severe punishment?

It is true that, whatever pains we may take to serve God in pureness, we do not cease to be wretched sinners, full of blemishes, and to have many wicked imperfections in us. But it is a right affection if we desire to do well; if we hate sin, though we falter, seeing our purpose is good; and if we strive to go forward in the fear of God and in obedience to his will. Jesus Christ then accounts us as though we were just; he frees us from all our faults and does not charge them to our account. The faithful, though they are not entirely perfect and though they have many sins, are considered to be God's children. Jesus Christ considers it no dishonor that they are called by his name, for he causes the goodness that is in them and through his grace makes them acceptable to God.

Let us, then, mark well what the word *Christian* means, for those who claim that title are members of the Son of God! Christ was pleased to accept us, so we must cleave to him in all righteousness, for he has received all fullness that he might make us partakers of his grace.

FOR MEDITATION: Departing from iniquity is the lifelong calling and pursuit of true Christians. Are you intimately involved in this pursuit? Do you long and strive to walk in the King's highway of holiness on a daily basis?

Walking Unworthily in the Church

But in a great house there are not only vessels of gold and of silver, but also of wood and of earth; and some to honour, and some to dishonour.
2 Timothy 2:20
SUGGESTED FURTHER READING: Obadiah

Here Paul tells us we ought to be earnest and zealous in endeavoring to put away all stumbling blocks to worshiping God in his house. If we see evil in the church, it must be purged; it must be quickly cut off and not allowed to grow. We must earnestly want the temple of God to remain pure and clean. Nevertheless, we may need to suffer some things to remain which cannot be taken away. When we cannot remedy such wrongs, we must mourn them.

However the world may go, we ought not to distance ourselves from the church of God under the pretense that people in it do not walk as they ought. Therefore, when we see inferior vessels in the church of God, let us not grieve and cite them as a reason to withdraw ourselves from church. Rather, let us persevere.

Paul shows us that, though the wicked strive to bring the name of God into reproach and dishonor, they will not cease to serve his glory, for God will turn their wickedness into goodness. When we look at the wicked, we see they were made to dishonor God, to destroy the reputation of his majesty, to abolish his justice, and to turn things upside down so that the world may have no more knowledge of him.

That is their goal, and the devil pushes them forward, but they do not cease to be vessels in God's house. That is to say, God will find a way to use them in such a manner that he will be glorified by them. This does not excuse their wickedness or allow them to cloak themselves with a mantle as though serving him, for he well knows this was not their wish or intention.

FOR MEDITATION: Some people will stick with a church no matter how far it strays from the truths of Scripture. Others will abandon a church because the people let them down or because of more minute issues. When we consider our local church, we must find a balance between these extremes. We must not expect ministers, elders, deacons, and other church folk to be free from sin. Let's not judge the church by imperfect sinners, but by its perfect head, Jesus Christ. When church members implement this, sound churches will have much more peace in their ranks.

Used by the Lord

But in a great house there are not only vessels of gold and of silver, but also of wood and of earth; and some to honour, and some to dishonour.
2 Timothy 2:20

SUGGESTED FURTHER READING: 3 John

Let us submit ourselves to God's providence in the church, for if we become angry and peevish and say everything is out of order, we shall not be excused. Let us be fully resolved that, despite Satan, God will be glorified. Moreover, let us learn to practice this doctrine so that when we see nothing but blemishes among us, stumbling blocks are not removed as they ought to be, there is not as much honesty as there should be, people shut their eyes for fear of seeing the light while pretending they do, and when there is not enough rigor and severity used to keep them in order, we should mourn, and, if possible, correct such irregularities.

We must not think that, because we see these disorders in the church of God, it is utterly destroyed and our Lord Jesus Christ is unable to do anything. Rather, we must consider that, though the wicked disfigure the beauty of the church, though they defile and pollute it, yet God will still be glorified. After they have troubled the church long enough, God will bring them to an end and show himself as their judge.

Therefore, let us be patient, knowing that we have a wonderful God who works by such means that he causes even the devil and wicked men to praise him. It is true that the devil will always show himself as a deadly enemy to God's glory and will endeavor by all means to tread it underfoot, but in all of this, God will turn wickedness into good.

So it goes with the wicked who try to bring all things into disorder and to take charge of the kingdom of God among us, razing out the remembrance of God's name. When they have done all they can, they will still remain vessels.

FOR MEDITATION: You may be familiar with George Herbert's words: "No sooner is a temple built to God, but the devil builds a chapel hard by." If the Holy Spirit is working in our churches, we ought to expect opposition. To face no opposition from Satan and his seed is a bad sign. How can you more effectively respond to opposition in your church as well as persecution in your personal life in a way that glorifies God?

Reproved by the Word

All scripture is given by inspiration of God, and is profitable for doctrine, for reproof, for correction, for instruction in righteousness.
2 Timothy 3:16
SUGGESTED FURTHER READING: Ezekiel 18:19–32

Let us understand what Paul means by saying that Scripture is given to us *for reproof*. If we would be well instructed in the school of God, we must confess our guilt, be pricked to the heart, and be reproved for our faults.

When the Word of God is rightly expounded, the faithful are edified, but if an unbeliever comes into the church and hears the doctrine of God, he is reproved and judged. Though the unbeliever is wrapped in darkness and is pleased with his own ignorance, God so enlightens him in Scripture that the unbeliever sees the misery and wickedness in which he has lived. He sees his deplorable situation by hearing the Word of God. He sees the heavens open and realizes that he was not made for this life only but to be exalted to a higher station. Thus unbelievers are convicted by God's Word.

To make this more clear, Paul says the secrets of the heart are disclosed by Scripture. We know that when the Word of God is buried, no one takes heed of it or applies it to himself; our hearts remain in darkness. What, then, must we do? We must apply the Word of God to ourselves and be awakened out of sleep. We must no longer forget God or the salvation of our souls. Rather, we must search the very depth of our hearts and examine our entire lives so we may be ashamed of our filthiness and become our own judges. In that way we may avoid the condemnation that God has prepared by his own hand for us.

That is what Paul means by the word *reproof*.

FOR MEDITATION: Though an unbeliever may realize he is less than perfect, he has no idea of the extent to which he has rebelled against the Creator. Only when the Word of God is applied to a person's life does he realize how deep and wide is his corruption. We must not shrink from this reproof, painful though it may be. Let the Word reprove you and drive you to Christ for salvation.

Instructed in Righteousness

All scripture is given by inspiration of God, and is profitable for doctrine, for reproof, for correction, for instruction in righteousness.
2 Timothy 3:16
SUGGESTED FURTHER READING: Matthew 15:1–9

If we regulate our lives by the instructions contained in Holy Scripture, we will be justified. But the doctrine of men is but folly and an abomination to God. So it is not without cause that Paul says Scripture is given *for instruction in righteousness.*

He says that to be good divines, we must live holy lives. The Word of God is not given to teach us how to be eloquent and subtle, but to reform our lives so that the world may know we are servants of God. If we wish to know whether a person is profiting by the gospel, examine his life. A man may know how to talk and may make a fair profession of godliness, yet his life reveals that he does not live in accordance with the written Word of God.

Paul tells us that we must make the Word of God our counselor so that we may walk aright and form our lives by it. Thus, he says, "the man of God may be perfect, and thoroughly furnished unto all good works" (2 Tim. 3:17). So we must be instructed in righteousness and reject the invention of men, for God is not pleased with that. Men wish to serve God according to their own notions and bring their own works into account, but God will not allow that.

Seeing such impudent boldness in men that they cannot keep themselves within the bounds that God has set for them, Paul points out the disease so that it may be healed. He says that, if we have the Word of God in our hearts, we shall be upright in life and equipped unto all good works.

FOR MEDITATION: Righteousness is defined by God. The only way to learn righteousness is to listen to God's Word rather than the ideas of men. We are constantly surmising what would be the right thing to do or say without consulting Scripture. This should not be so. We must bring the Word to bear on everything we do and let it show us what righteousness is. How can you practice this today?

Enjoying God's Blessings

Unto the pure all things are pure: but unto them that are defiled and unbelieving is nothing pure; but even their mind and conscience is defiled. Titus 1:15

SUGGESTED FURTHER READING: Revelation 14:1–5

We must be faithful and stand fast in our liberty. We must follow the rule given to us in the Word of God and not suffer our souls to be brought into slavery by new laws forged by men. A hellish tyranny lessens God's authority and mixes the truth of the gospel with legalisms to pervert and corrupt the true service of God, which ought to be spiritual.

Therefore, let us consider how precious the privilege is to give thanks to God with quietness of conscience, being assured that his will and pleasure is that we should enjoy his blessings. To do so, let us not entangle ourselves with the superstitions of men but be content with what is contained in the pure, simple gospel. Then, as we have shown in the first part of our text, "unto them that are pure, all things will be pure."

When we have received the Lord Jesus Christ, we shall be cleansed from our filthiness and blemishes, for by his grace we are made partakers of God's benefits and are taken as his children, even though there is nothing but vanity in us.

Paul goes on to say, *But unto them that are defiled and unbelieving is nothing pure.* By this he means that whatever proceeds from those who are defiled and unbelieving is not acceptable to God but is full of infection.

Therefore, all the rules and laws they make are nothing but vanity, for God dislikes whatever they do. Indeed, he utterly abhors their ways. These things ought to be evident to us, yet hypocrisy is so rooted in us that we are apt to neglect them. We should readily confess that we cannot please God by serving him until our hearts are rid of wickedness.

FOR MEDITATION: The wicked cannot please God because everything they do is defiled and abhorrent in his sight. The righteous, on the other hand, are pleasing to God; their righteousness is not their own, but Christ's, and he washes all they do to make it pure in God's sight. If you are a believer, thank God for the righteousness of Christ and the purity that it engenders. If you are not a believer, pray that God would show you your unrighteousness and impurity, and drive you to his Son for righteousness and purity.

Living our Doctrine

In all things showing thyself a pattern of good works: in doctrine showing uncorruptness, gravity, sincerity. Titus 2:7
SUGGESTED FURTHER READING: Titus 1

When we teach others, we must also be willing to be taught, for if we are not willing to learn so that others may profit by our instruction, we shall never be able to do our duty. Therefore, he whom God has placed as teacher in his house must himself be ready and willing to receive doctrine and good instruction. We must listen when other men give counsel and be willing to receive information. Thus we have the meaning of Paul in few words; namely, those who are called to preach the Word of God must take heed that they are not self-willed but willing to be taught; be meek and quiet spirited, not puffed up with pride but endeavoring to edify others; must not think they know all things but desire to learn continually; and be gentle in their behavior. They must not be like those who are lofty in spirit and self-willed, for those often become schismatic; that is to say, they trouble the church of God and divide it into sects.

The meaning of this text is not only confined to ministers, for in exhorting them to beware of intemperance, covetousness and pride, and to be courteous, just, sober, and chaste, Paul expects by their example that all Christians should behave themselves in such a manner that soberness, justice, holiness, modesty, and all the virtues he speaks of may be common among them. If we wish to be children of God, let us correct the faults which here are condemned by Paul and endeavor to follow the virtues that he recommends.

FOR MEDITATION: Note how Paul unites good works and doctrine in this text. A Christian—especially a church leader—who is lacking in any of these areas can be very dangerous. The lives of leaders must become a pattern of good works for those whom they shepherd. They also must be careful to guard the true doctrine of God's Word. If either of these slip, the consequences will be dire. Pray for your leaders, that they will remain steadfast in these areas.

Seeking the Good of Others

And David lamented with this lamentation over Saul and over Jonathan his son. 2 Samuel 1:17

SUGGESTED FURTHER READING: 1 Samuel 26

We are not to obscure the commands of God to excuse ourselves. On the contrary, knowing very well that God condemns all vengeance, we must loathe it. Whenever we are tempted to give way, let us run to God, who controlled his servant David and bestowed on him the grace of stamping on those violent passions that could have moved him to hatred and bitterness toward Saul. This is the first point of this text.

Second, let us learn from David to seek the common good of those with whom we live. Let us seek to maintain and preserve peace in the community so that our personal profit and loss does not influence us when we confront a question of the public good. People should not just look after themselves but after others.

David shows us the way. Because he was a frail man like ourselves and did not lack feelings, he was in the same condition that we are in; nevertheless, he put other things before his personal concerns. They were nothing compared to the salvation and preservation of the people of Israel. That is why he mourned over Saul.

This seems strange at first glance, but it is certain that David's burning zeal for the good of the people over which God had placed him as king made him forget everything else. So he fought against himself and submitted to the will of God in proclaiming Saul's good characteristics.

As for the rest, there is no doubt that the lamentation recorded here was published all over the country so everyone would realize that David was not cut off from the people of Israel. They would take him as a faithful member, recognizing that he had always pursued the welfare and safety of the people and was still seeking that goal.

FOR MEDITATION: Our own personal struggles should not cloud how we conduct ourselves in the community, for we must contribute to its health, not adversely affect it. In what areas of your life are you presently putting your welfare before the welfare of those around you? Ask God for grace to repent in these areas, so that you put him first, others second, and yourself third in every area of life.

Trusting God in Loss

Saul and Jonathan were lovely and pleasant in their lives, and in their death they were not divided: they were swifter than eagles, they were stronger than lions. 2 Samuel 1:23

SUGGESTED FURTHER READING: Genesis 23

David shows here that his love for Jonathan was very remarkable, for he experienced great distress over his death. It is true that David's expression of emotion was too vehement. It was not right for him to sink as he did into the depths of sorrow. Although his emotion was not perfect, the basis of it was good.

Let us note that the children of God are not insensitive. They are saddened by the death of their neighbors and friends, and they feel even more regret, bitterness, and pain over the loss of those whom God has bound very closely to them. This kind of loss will happen to the children of God, but the point is that we must control our feelings and hold them captive to God.

When we are told to patiently accept the death of our relatives and friends, that does not mean we should not feel the loss or that we must respond like blocks of wood, for God does not take away our natural feelings. But even as we are sad, we must not fail to continually bless God's name and accept his will as not only just and right but also as good and salutary for us. We are to willingly accept what he sends us, so that on the one hand we are sad, but on the other hand we do not fail to bless God deliberately and of our own accord and not because of external constraint.

When at last we calm down after having lost control of our emotions, we can greatly sweeten our sadness by remembering that nothing can hinder us from going to God. That is what we must keep in mind.

FOR MEDITATION: Calvin has been called a theologian of moderation, always balancing the concerns of this life in the light of eternity to come. Here he exemplifies this talent in the matter of sorrowing over loved ones. An excellent example of this can be found in Abraham, who grieved deeply over the loss of his dear Sarah, yet pressed on with the Lord's work and agenda (Gen. 23:1–4; 24:1–4). When you have lost loved ones, or have faced some great personal trial, did you moderate your sorrow by contemplating the great joys that await you in the fast-approaching eternity of glory?

Asking for Guidance

And it came to pass after this, that David enquired of the Lord, *saying, Shall I go up into any of the cities of Judah? And the* Lord *said unto him, Go up. And David said, Whither shall I go up? And he said, Unto Hebron.* 2 Samuel 2:1
SUGGESTED FURTHER READING: Luke 11:9–13

When the text says God told David that he should go to the country of Judaea, it teaches that we have only ourselves to blame if we do not accept good advice. For Scripture says we are to knock on the door and it will be opened to us, we are to seek and we shall find, we are to ask and it will be given to us (Matt. 7:7). David had this promise engraved on his heart, but it had not yet been stated in its fullness as we have it today. Instead, he sought God's will by the ceremonial means of the priestly ephod.

Today we have far more than that. Our Lord Jesus Christ came to earth to fulfill his promise to his disciples that he would no longer call them his servants but his friends (John 15:15). That means he has come so close to us that we, like good pupils, can learn all we need to know.

When we clothe ourselves in humility, God will certainly respond to our need. Are we lacking in wisdom? James says the "Father of lights" (James 1:17) is ready and able to help us in our weakness and needs. Thus, let us go to him. Above all, when we need wisdom, let us realize that God reserves the right to give it, and we should not be so foolish as to attribute wisdom to ourselves. Instead, let us worship him for such an excellent gift.

We should be persuaded that if we ask God to give us the Spirit of understanding, we can be assured that he will respond if we are ready to subject ourselves to his Word. We will find him ready and inclined to grant our requests, and we will never be frustrated for having waited to make our requests to him.

FOR MEDITATION: God has not changed since the time of David. David asked and he received what he asked for; we too can ask and know that we will receive what we ask for. The New Testament clearly states this. Believing this is a great test of our faith because it is difficult. Be encouraged by David's example.

Using God's Gifts to Us

And David perceived that the LORD had established him king over Israel, and that he had exalted his kingdom for his people Israel's sake.
2 Samuel 5:12
SUGGESTED FURTHER READING: Esther 4

David knew to what end God had exalted his reign: it was because of his people, Israel. David could easily have thought that God was making him prosper to maintain him as ruler over the kingdom. But to know the intention of God and to what end he does something takes far more prudence. David perceived that God was exalting him because of his people Israel. So David knew the reason why he was reigning. It was not for his personal profit but for the common salvation of all.

This is well worth noting, for we must always remember that it is not enough for us to recognize the blessings of God. We must also always *use* those properly. How? When God has brought us back from some illness, when he has saved us from some danger, we must realize that he does this so we might thank him and honor his name. Moreover, let us realize that we must apply everything we are granted to his service.

In sum, let us learn that, whenever God shows mercy to his people or to an individual member of the body, it is so that we will call on him and recognize him as the author of every good, then give ourselves to his service and dedicate all that we have to it.

On the other hand, when I see that God has set me apart for some service, I must realize that it is not because of me that he has prolonged my life but because he wants to use me in the service of his church. This is the prudence we should manifest whenever God favors us. Let us realize that these blessings are not to be useless but always think: God has preserved me so many times. I must, therefore, show that I am aware of this.

FOR MEDITATION: God has determined roles for each of us to fill within his plan. He has given us specific gifts and blessings to suit us for the task we must do. We should study God's Word and the way Christ is leading us and consult with other believers to determine how to best use the gifts he has given us for his service.

Glorifying God's Strange Ways

And when David enquired of the LORD, he said, Thou shalt not go up;
but fetch a compass behind them, and come upon them over against the
mulberry trees. 2 Samuel 5:23
SUGGESTED FURTHER READING: Judges 7

There was a reason why God commanded David to go behind his
enemies and not to attack them directly. For our faith must be proved in
various ways, and if David had always conquered his enemies in one
way, he would not have been so keenly aware of the help of God.

There was another benefit in David's recognizing that God could
smite his enemies both from the back and from the front. He could
punish them one way now, and another way later, thereby cleverly
surprising them. When one means fails us, God has more than a million
more in his hand to offer us. That is what David recognized.

Likewise, let us carefully recognize that when God uses different
methods that we do not understand with our own minds, we must
humble ourselves and adore his wisdom. When he is hidden from us and
we cannot see the reason why he acts as he does, we must turn everything
over to him and accept as good everything that he declares to be his will.
This is how the foolishness of God overcomes the wisdom of the world
(1 Cor. 1:25).

When we cannot understand why God does something, we show
arrogance in our nature when we presume to be his judges and boldly
condemn him. Men have tried all sorts of trickery to find ways to
contradict God, but they only remain confounded. Well, then, that is the
point: God takes care of his people in such strange ways that we cannot
understand why he uses various approaches. But when God's way seems
foolish to us, let us learn to receive with deep sobriety and reverence
what we know has proceeded from him.

FOR MEDITATION: God often chooses to accomplish his will in ways we
did not expect and may not like. In such situations, however, we see that
it is God who is accomplishing his will, not us. He does not need to
follow our plans or obey our council; we must follow his. In this way he
keeps us humble and dependent on him. Is there an area of your life
where you are struggling with this truth today?

Bringing the Ark Home

And they brought it out of the house of Abinadab which was at Gibeah, accompanying the ark of God: and Ahio went before the ark. 2 Samuel 6:4
SUGGESTED FURTHER READING: John 4:1–42

David decided to remove the ark from the house of Abinadab and take it to another place. He wanted the ark to be lodged in the center of the country rather than in the remote location where it had been left by the Israelites when the Philistines were forced to return it.

When the ark was in a corner, it could scarcely be honored as it deserved, and the people had an excuse for not coming to the solemn feasts to worship God. David brought the ark back to Israel so it would be in a place where people could more easily come, and everyone could more readily do their duty.

People seek all kinds of excuses to draw away from God, as we too frequently see. When things are not easy, we think we can wash our hands of the matter. We pretend that we would like to do something but lack the opportunity. David knew this and wanted to remove every obstacle to worship so that those who were already too careless could not say that the ark of God was in an unreachable place.

We note the same kind of laziness in ourselves, along with the lack of inclination to worship God when there is no convenient means of worship. If we use such excuses, we will never profit from worship as we should. Why does the church choose the hours that are the most appropriate, a definite place to assemble, and a bell to ring, with all these matters carefully arranged? It is because we humans have practically no desire to give ourselves to God unless we are first drawn to do so.

On the one hand, let us note how feeble we are when we ought to be stirring ourselves to honor God. On the other hand, let us use every available means to break through the coldness and laziness to which we are so strongly inclined so we may worship God wherever he is.

FOR MEDITATION: We are highly skilled in finding excuses to avoid our Christian duties. How many excuses do we have when it comes to evangelism or attending a prayer meeting? David removed obstacles for the people so that they would have no excuse for avoiding their obligations. We should be diligent in removing the obstacles in our own lives so that we cannot use them as excuses for disobedience.

Singing Together

And David and all the house of Israel played before the Lord on all manner of instruments made of fir wood, even on harps, and on psalteries, and on timbrels, and on cornets, and on cymbals. 2 Samuel 6:5
SUGGESTED FURTHER READING: Psalm 87

David and the Israelites sang a hymn to God with instruments and music. David assembled a multitude of people so that everyone might worship God with one accord. He knew that God had not made himself known only to David but to the entire family of Abraham. David thus provided the way to mutual accord so that everyone, small and great, might together demonstrate their desire to serve God.

Here we see the true use of hymns. We are to encourage one another in celebrating and magnifying the name of God in our hymns (Eph. 5:19–20). It would be enough for each person to pray to God in his heart and to give him thanks. This is true worship of God, for he says, as it were, "Call upon me in the day of trouble and then praise me when you know that I have answered" (Ps. 50:15).

But even though people may privately invoke God, we also have the privilege of assembling in public to testify of our faith and to encourage others by our example. When we pray to God in the church and sing psalms, we do that not to show ourselves off but to declare that we seek nothing but that God may be glorified among us.

Assembling in his name should also serve as a thorn to prick us because of our laziness. We are to encourage one another continually (Heb. 3:13); people are not to sing hymns of praise to God for only a temporary period of time but until the end of the world. We are surrounded with flesh and blood; we need means such as this to lift our spirit up to God. Thus the obligation to sing hymns of praise is given to us as well as to people in David's time.

FOR MEDITATION: It is God who calls us to corporate worship. This call is not to be taken lightly or treated as optional; extra personal devotions do not make up for a lack of corporate worship. We should cultivate love for this worship and the glory God receives from it.

God's Inscrutable Ways

And when they came to Nachon's threshingfloor, Uzzah put forth his hand to the ark of God, and took hold of it; for the oxen shook it. And the anger of the LORD was kindled against Uzzah; and God smote him there for his error; and there he died by the ark of God. 2 Samuel 6:6–7

SUGGESTED FURTHER READING: Jonah 4

We have the very strange story here of a man who burns with good and holy devotion. He attempts to honor God but then is punished like a criminal. This certainly offends our feelings, even though we know the main cause of offending God is our wicked will. On the other hand, when our desire is to glorify him and we have no ill will in us, it seems that God should not hold that against us, especially when we do not willfully get out of line or go beyond the rule that he gives us.

Well, here is Uzzah, walking in front of the ark of God. He sees that the ark is in danger of falling because the oxen are shaking it. He puts his hands on the ark to hold it up. But then God kills him for touching the ark. Was being zealous to protect the ark of God so that it would not be shamed a crime worthy of punishment? If not, why was Uzzah punished? How should we understand God's actions here?

Let us take closer heed to ourselves. Many people who do not dare to openly blaspheme God privately murmur when the judgments of God do not agree with their understanding and fantasies. Let us note that Scripture often warns us that the judgments of God are a profound abyss. This should make us so utterly astonished that we fear God and his judgments and find good in all that he does, even when we are confused about it.

Let us have the sober attitude to be totally persuaded that nothing proceeds from God that is not just and irreprehensible. If many of his works do not agree with our appetites or our reason, let us remain his captive, realizing that it is quite necessary that God and his ways surpass all our senses.

FOR MEDITATION: "Why?" is a question haunting many of us. Surely it must have haunted those who gathered around Uzzah's body. In many cases, we will never obtain an answer to our "whys" in this life. We must simply submit ourselves to God's good will, even when life's circumstances go beyond our understanding.

Rightly Fearing God

And David was afraid of the LORD *that day, and said, How shall the ark of the* LORD *come to me?* 2 Samuel 6:9
SUGGESTED FURTHER READING: Psalm 25

In fearing God, we must maintain perspective in knowing where this fear should lead us. Well, where should it lead us?

We will never answer this unless we first see a specific illustration of it. Many who truly fear God are unnecessarily agitated with despair when they hear certain sentences from Scripture, such as: "God is a consuming fire" (Deut. 4:24; Heb. 12:29), and he consumes all before him (Joel 2:3). Or they hear such statements as: The day of the Lord is terrible, and, "Who can dwell with a devouring fire?" (Isa. 33:14). These verses can make them draw back from the service of God, saying, "Alas, what will happen to a poor creature like me? Since God is so severe and strict, how shall I approach him?"

For this reason, Paul advises us not to be overwhelmed by our disappointments (2 Cor. 2:7). When we only think about our sins, that may serve to abase and confound us, but let us also remember how to find in the goodness of God the remedy to sweeten our grief. Let us not let unbelief plunge us into the depths of an abyss.

When we come to God, let us fear, let us be stunned by his majesty, and let us above all realize that we are full of nothing but rottenness and infection. However, let us also not fail to taste the goodness of God, indeed, to drink in the infinite number of good benefits that we receive from him.

So, let us realize that, however innumerable our needs may be, God will always continue to be generous toward us and answer our requests. This is the kind of fear we ought to have of God.

FOR MEDITATION: We are to tremble before the majesty of God, but we must also remember that he is full of grace and mercy. If we are in Christ, we have the assurance that we are forever safe from the consuming fire of God's majesty. Knowing that we are safe from total destruction, our fear of God should be childlike rather than slavish. How should you be fearing him today?

Praying for Family Blessing

Then David returned to bless his household. 2 Samuel 6:20
SUGGESTED FURTHER READING: Psalm 127

This verse tells us that David returned to "bless" or "save" his house. He came to ask God to prosper his family, or, as we say today, to "save" his family. The word *save* here refers to God having us and our lives in his hands, and to safekeeping those for whom we pray. Therefore, since David has already publicly declared that all the good and prosperity of the people depend on the pure grace of God, he now offers the same prayer privately for his family, namely, that God would watch over them and be their protector.

This point here is well worth noting. It is certainly true that fathers of families and heads of houses ought to carefully do their duty in governing those who are placed under their authority. But the main thing parents should do is to take refuge in God. Those who have children should recognize that they will never reach their goal and their pain can produce no good fruit unless God takes the whole matter in hand and controls it.

Those who have servants and handmaids must also recognize that if God does not preside over their house, everything will go badly, and there will be much confusion. Even when a man only has his wife in his household, he must know that when his household is not blessed by God, there will be nothing but poverty.

It is true that David expressed this dependence by means of a public ceremony. But there is no doubt that the Holy Spirit praised David here for clearly recognizing that in all things he sought refuge in God.

FOR MEDITATION: Psalm 127:1 says, "Except the LORD build the house, they labour in vain that build it." Every day and in every way, we and our families need God's blessing. This dependency on God should motivate us to storm his mercy seat for divine benediction at the very beginning of our day! Robert Murray M'Cheyne said, "I would see the face of God before the face of man each day."

Besides morning prayer and devotions, what other means can we use to foster a greater consciousness of our dependency upon God's daily blessing?

Waiting for God's Direction

And it came to pass, when the king sat in his house, and the LORD *had given him rest round about from his enemies; that the king said unto Nathan the prophet, See now, I dwell in an house of cedar, but the ark of God dwelleth within curtains.* 2 Samuel 7:1–2

SUGGESTED FURTHER READING: Psalm 27

David's basic motive to build a temple for God was good and holy. But he was too hasty in failing to wait for God to order him to do this. David thus took upon himself more than was appropriate for him.

We note here that God gently guides his people by definite degrees. He does not immediately employ all of his treasures, but just what seems good to him at the time. We should pay careful attention to this because we are greedy and want God to immediately give us everything that comes into our imagination.

In brief, we cannot tolerate God keeping us in a low condition. That comes in part from our arrogance, for we often would like to do more than is right or legitimate for us. We are full of covetous follies, yet we want God to fulfill us and gratify us in everything, everywhere. We want that with such intense desire that we do not cease being angry and vexed when it pleases God to keep us in a lowly state. Even if we do not openly cry out, yet we privately have much chagrin in our hearts.

Seeing that it is so difficult for us by nature to be content, let us even more remember and practice the doctrine to be governed as God knows best. If, at first, God does not elevate us above the clouds but makes us crawl upon the earth, keeping us in weakness and generally teaching us to be humble and small, let us learn to walk patiently and bow our necks to receive the yoke that he puts on us. Let us learn to exert ourselves in all the afflictions to which the church is subject and to allow God to do his work, which will turn to our good, since he knows what is best for us.

FOR MEDITATION: Once again, Calvin directs us to be active for the Lord's cause, even as he recognizes that God's sovereignty directs all things. Thus, we should be content to remain in a humble posture and in humble circumstances before the Lord, recognizing that God often has unknown reasons for denying us the freedom to do on his behalf that which we feel inclined to do. Sometimes we must discover that letting God be God is more than half of all true religion, as Luther once said. Are you, by God's grace, exercising this kind of submission and moderation before the Lord?

Keeping your Promise

And David said, Is there yet any that is left of the house of Saul, that I may show him kindness for Jonathan's sake? 2 Samuel 9:1
SUGGESTED FURTHER READING: Matthew 5:33–37

When we have made a promise in the name of God and have called upon him, let that promise restrain and govern us in the future.

For example, when a man marries, let him think, "When we promised faith and loyalty to one another, was this not done before God in his name?" Remembering that vow helps a husband to carry out his duty to live chastely with his wife and foster peace and harmony in his household. The wife, also, in remembering that she is joined with her husband in the name of God and that marriage is a sacred thing, will carry out her duty.

Likewise, fathers clearly promise to nurture their children because they have made the solemn promise in baptism to instruct those children in the fear of God. A magistrate who takes the oath of duty to carry out his office will carefully think of this in remembering that he made this promise before God. People by and by will take delight in keeping this magistrate's laws, and everything else will fall into place. Also, when people make contracts with one another, their agreements will be faithfully observed when they can say, "We have in this called on the name of God."

So, then, what shall we think when we see people using the courts to rescind all their promises, so that nothing prevents their reversing their contracts, and they spend their time working out ways to be relieved of their promises? They bring forward excuses such as: "I have been defrauded in a certain situation that would cause me too much loss."

In the end, equity and fairness will not be maintained unless people remind themselves, "God was witness when I promised a certain thing. Therefore, I must not seek to be absolved before men. The main thing is that I look to God, bring myself before his judgment seat, and examine my conscience so I may keep the obligation to which I once committed myself."

FOR MEDITATION: We have all made promises that we later regretted. We need to remember two things. First, we should not make promises lightly. Second, we should keep those promises that we have made, even if fulfilling them no longer seems advantageous to us. Remember, God is present at every promise we make.

Doing Good Anyway

And David said unto him, Fear not: for I will surely show thee kindness for Jonathan thy father's sake, and will restore thee all the land of Saul thy father; and thou shalt eat bread at my table continually. 2 Samuel 9:7
SUGGESTED FURTHER READING: Matthew 10

When David wanted to show kindness to the house of Saul, he showed immense strength of character. For in showing kindness to his enemy, he overcame and put underfoot painful thoughts that could have caused him to take vengeance and act unkindly.

The devil presents us with objects of fear and doubt in such matters, saying, "If you do that, it may please God, but it will cause you trouble." When, therefore, we think of such things, let us see that by following God's commands we will be protected. We will be upheld when tortuous paths are ahead of us.

For example, magistrates, whose responsibility is to rebuke everything evil, often cover it up. Why? Because they do not want to be hated. That is not only the case in one place, but everywhere. Ministers of the Word of God should open their mouths to rebuke the faults that they see, but they cover things up and pretend not to see evil. They do that because they fear being disdained by some, and they do not want to lose that friendship.

More often, we refrain from doing good when we see that few are taking the straight path, and most only half carry out their duty. We are cold when it comes to carrying out our duty because we are afraid of what it may cost us.

We must resist these fears by letting faith be our guard. We must believe that, when we follow the path that God proposes for us, he will make all our enterprises prosper and make things turn out well. He will certainly find the means to deliver us whenever we are oppressed or tossed about with many doubts.

FOR MEDITATION: Doing what is our duty to God and our neighbor may result in trials and tribulations. God never promised that faithfulness would bring us a life of ease. It will bring joy and blessing, to be sure, but that will often be our experience in the midst of great trials. This should not deter us, however, from fulfilling our duties; we are a great witness to those around us when they see us persevering despite the trouble that lies ahead.

Running from Guilt

But Uriah slept at the door of the king's house with all the servants of his lord, and went not down to his house. 2 Samuel 11:9

SUGGESTED FURTHER READING: Isaiah 57:15–21

David was frustrated when Uriah did not want to sleep with his wife, so he racked his brain, seeking time and ways to still bring that about. Previously David had sent Uriah "as a present to his house" (2 Sam. 11:8). Now David called Uriah to his table (2 Sam. 11:13).

By his own actions, David would prove himself guilty, though he was trying to do the opposite. In this we see how God removes every vestige of prudence and discretion from those who operate with a bad conscience. No one had yet accused David of wrongdoing, but even when his sin was unknown, he felt under pressure to cover it up. He began running in strange directions, first seeking one way out of his sin, then another.

When we despise the judgment of God and try to conserve our good reputation before others, God gives us our just reward by drawing us in the very opposite direction from where we want to go. He thus brings us by force to judgment. Let us carefully note, therefore, that a bad conscience will always be accompanied by torment, anxiety, and anguish.

If we wish to have true peace, let us have a good conscience and do right. Furthermore, let us not hope to have peace when we flee the presence of God, especially when we attempt to abolish his justice. Now the wicked, at times, are certainly dead to the disturbing pain of guilt, but this kind of peace is not lasting. The reason is that, instead of presenting themselves before God, they go farther from him.

To have sure and permanent peace, let us be careful to present ourselves before God and deeply examine our conscience. When we feel guilty, let us groan and sigh over our sins, then ask pardon of him who is ready to give us mercy when we come to him in sincerity of heart.

FOR MEDITATION: The peace David was frantically trying to find was false. It only made him run farther from God and dragged him down into greater sin. Do you find yourself in the same frenzy? Do you try everything to escape the just reward of your sin? Turn *to* God, rather than *from* him, and find the peace that passes all understanding in the gospel of Jesus Christ.

Treasuring Grace and Peace

Grace be to you and peace from God the Father, and from our Lord Jesus Christ. Galatians 1:3
SUGGESTED FURTHER READING: 2 John

Notice that, in all his epistles, Paul constantly reminds us of the grace of God and the love he bears toward all believers. He says, *Grace be to you and peace.* This word *peace* includes all worldly prosperity. By it Paul is asking God to provide those things that he considers for our good. He will shower his riches upon us and reveal his bounty so that we might praise him for his goodness.

However, the wealth of this world will be harmful for us unless we have found favor with the Lord. Hence, Paul speaks here in an orderly way, always placing God's grace and free pardon before an increase in worldly prosperity. Though we may ask God to bless us with those things he thinks we need, we must not forget the most important blessing is to be members of his church and assured of God's love in our hearts.

The light of God's countenance should suffice us. Although God permits us to ask for good things from his hand, we must keep a tight rein on our desires. God may afflict us with many sorrows, and at such times we need to value his grace above anything else. We should then be content, even if everything else was taken away. If we live in comfort, surrounded by all kinds of pleasures and delights, we will still be miserable if we do not have the peace of conscience that comes from knowing that God loves and accepts us.

We should not desire earthly goods more than the love of God. For what if God, who loves us, wishes to test our patience by making us suffer in this world and subjects us to many trials? Even then, we must prize his love above all else and patiently bear all trials, though it seems as if everything is against us.

FOR MEDITATION: How quick we are to assume that if we were greatly blessed with earthly goods, we would be happy. The broken lives of many of the rich and famous should be enough to convince us otherwise. Earthly blessings must be combined with the grace of God in our hearts if they are to bring us true joy. What is your attitude toward earthly wealth?

Separated for Service

But when it pleased God, who separated me from my mother's womb, and called me by his grace, to reveal his Son in me, that I might preach him among the heathen; immediately I conferred not with flesh and blood. Galatians 1:15–16

SUGGESTED FURTHER READING: Jeremiah 1

Faith is purely a gift from God, so people may not praise themselves for having come to the light of the gospel, in which they have found happiness and salvation. Instead, they ought to glorify God, for they are indebted to him for choosing and calling them to salvation.

It is the same with every calling that God has given us. We choose people on the basis of their ability to do work. One is fitted to lead a nation, another to be a preacher of the Word of God, and someone else to other work. We discern the gifts God has given to each person, and we are right to do so. Yet one who is chosen, no matter what skills he has to fulfill his office, must still acknowledge that God had set him apart beforehand for that work.

If this is so, let us not think that a person with a more advanced and skillful mind has himself to thank for it. After all, why are we not all slow-witted, like many of the creatures we see around us that have no powers of reasoning? Surely, all we are is from God, who chose us before we were born and ordained what we would be like.

The person with a more gifted mind than others should acknowledge that God has created him this way. Whatever we do, God leads and governs from above; therefore, everything must be attributed to him. Paul says that God revealed his Son to him and called him to preach Christ. Paul did that because God had already set him apart from others. Indeed, God chose Paul, knowing very well to what use he would put him.

FOR MEDITATION: We must acknowledge that our various talents are gifts from God, not merited by us; but we must also acknowledge that they were given to us because God has some purpose for those gifts. He set us apart for this work even before we were born. Thus, we are not free to use our gifts anyway we want. Rather, we must cultivate them and use them for the service to which God calls us. Are you striving to use your gifts in God's service?

Uniting under One Head

Then after three years I went up to Jerusalem to see Peter, and abode with him fifteen days. Galatians 1:18
SUGGESTED FURTHER READING: 2 Corinthians 15:20–58

Paul came to Jerusalem to declare his unity with the other apostles and to testify in front of the whole church. We learn from this that he desired to serve God and to unselfishly exalt the Word of God above all creatures. We also learn that he was very human and very humble.

We ought to be of the same mind as Paul, seeking to submit to one another as members of one body, with Jesus Christ as our head. We should not separate or be parted over the slightest thing nor think we are in a category apart from the rest. Instead, let us seek to communicate one with another so that each of us may guide our neighbor.

May we all work toward the same end, encouraging one another so that people may see the warm fellowship that is among us. It is true that we cannot be at peace with everybody. That is why Paul says in another passage that we should seek to live at peace with all men as far as it is possible for us to do so (Rom. 12:18). By this, he implies that we will be at war with many people. The devil has many demons, and there are many people who oppose the Word of God.

However, when someone wishes to submit to the Lord Jesus Christ, we must welcome this person and go before him in the way. We should identify with him and not consider ourselves more important than him, thinking, "What? If I associate with him, it will seem as if I am lowering myself to his level." Let us instead simply desire that Jesus Christ should be our head and we members of his body, worshiping him and calling upon him with one voice in unity of faith.

FOR MEDITATION: The church has only one head, and we should not be too quick to judge whether others are under it. Nor should we dissociate ourselves from anyone under that head who does not fit our particular tastes, or set ourselves apart as if we are on a different level than him. The church is a body and must be united. That so many people from so many different backgrounds and with so many different characters can be united in Christ is a powerful witness to our world.

Affirming God's Gifts to Others

But they had heard only, That he which persecuted us in times past now preacheth the faith which once he destroyed. And they glorified God in me. Galatians 1:23–24

SUGGESTED FURTHER READING: Philippians 2:19–30

In envying someone whom God has honored and in seeking to deny the gifts and graces that we see in this person, we not only do wrong to mortal creatures but also to God, the author of those very gifts.

I may meet someone who can build up the church, and God may have gifted him with such graces that the church could profit from his labor. But, fearing that he may advance too far and that I might have to fade too much into the background, I seek to conceal and weaken what God has done in him by my slander and other devious methods. It is as if I willfully seek to hide all the gifts of God and cause them to be despised.

Where does this come from, if not from that cursed ambition that I have already described? If we stir ourselves up this way, there will always be strife and grumbling. In short, this will lead to the kind of disunity that offends God. For whom are we wronging? I wrong my neighbor by undervaluing him this way, yet I also blaspheme against God. How is this? It is because God wants to be known through all his gifts.

If we see some of the evidences of the Holy Spirit's workings in a man, and if we trample them underfoot, or spit at them, or loathe them, is this not an attempt, as far as it lies in us, to undermine the majesty of God? While we may not admit this to be so, this does not alter the truth. We ought to give heed to what is said here regarding the believers who glorified God in the person of Paul when they saw that God was working in him. This warns us to give God the glory that belongs to him when he grants his gifts to us and others.

FOR MEDITATION: How beautiful it is when a very gifted person embraces and cultivates the gifts he finds in another, not caring if his own are overshadowed. And what an ugly and shameful thing it is if the opposite occurs because of pride and ungodly ambition. How do you perceive others with gifts greater than your own: as a threat to your own honor, or do you see the potential glory these people might give to God with their gifts?

Holding Fast to our Liberty

And that because of false brethren unawares brought in, who came in privily to spy out our liberty which we have in Christ Jesus, that they might bring us into bondage: to whom we gave place by subjection, no, not for an hour; that the truth of the gospel might continue with you.
Galatians 2:4–5
SUGGESTED FURTHER READING: Galatians 4:9–20

When Roman Catholics ask us to abstain from eating meat on Fridays and Saturdays, on fast days, and other days they think it is forbidden, we are traitors to the gospel if we agree to this. We would rather die a hundred times over than submit to such rules.

Why is this? We must have respect for the liberty that was bought for us by the Lord Jesus Christ. May what God permits in his Word be condemned because men have so resolved according to their own whim and fancy? Surely we can see this diminishes God's authority by taking what belongs to him and what is rightfully his by giving it to mortal creatures.

Further, such duties imposed upon poor souls serve to rob the Lord Jesus Christ of his honor. If he has obtained liberty for us to set us free from the ceremonies of the law, this is a greater reason for us to cast aside and abolish all that has been invented by man. Let us, therefore, understand that in all these secondary matters we must be motivated by the desire to edify. Thus, even if it is lawful for us to act or to abstain from an action, love ought to constrain us in all our dealings with others.

This involves the willingness to be self-controlled and to refrain from exercising our freedom for the sake of the edification of our neighbor. At the same time, we must not disobey God's truth or mix it with error to the confusion of others, who are unsure about how our lives here on earth are to be guided or what laws they ought to follow, even if our motive is to maintain peace and unity. Rather, we must hold fast the liberty which Paul speaks of here to the best of our ability.

FOR MEDITATION: How can we hold fast to our liberty in Christ and yet not offend our weaker brother (see Rom. 14)? How can we discern between adhering to some man-made traditions that are fitting and beneficial and rejecting other man-made traditions that bring us into bondage?

Speaking Freely to our Neighbor

But when I saw that they walked not uprightly according to the truth of the gospel, I said unto Peter before them all, If thou, being a Jew, livest after the manner of Gentiles, and not as do the Jews, why compellest thou the Gentiles to live as do the Jews? Galatians 2:14
SUGGESTED FURTHER READING: Proverbs 27:1–10

We know how important it is to feel at peace with the world. We are like this because we think we will have no friends unless we tolerate our neighbors.

Well, indeed, there is a kind of forbearance that is commendable. It involves being gentle when we rebuke those who have fallen, always seeking to draw them back in a friendly way. We must not be too harsh, for if we constantly are ready to reprove others, we only exasperate them. Too many people are continually on the prowl for something they can attack; their holiness amounts to nothing more than mocking one person or chiding another. In short, they are the world's greatest critics.

We must keep ourselves from such attitudes and not always be waiting to reprove others. However, the kind of flattery which surrounds us today is also a sin that we ought to shun as we would a deadly plague. So let us learn that to love our neighbor, we must speak freely to him, as Paul does here, especially when God's truth is at stake. We must not fear anyone, for the zeal of God must rise up within us and overwhelm us. Even if that means we acquire a bad reputation and become the object of all kinds of calumny and slander, nevertheless, we must enter into combat.

We must follow the example set for us here by Paul. What he did with his companion Peter ought to serve as a law and a rule for us. We must prove that we want people to listen to God and not to exchange his truth for a lie. Also, we must teach that no one should obscure his truth or add leaven to it. The truth must remain in its purity and simplicity.

FOR MEDITATION: It seems that we are often falling into one of two extremes: constant criticism or flattery. We should pray for the grace to know when to praise, when to criticize, and when to remain silent. Is your tendency toward excessive criticisms or compliments? Know this tendency and be careful not to slip into one extreme or another.

Fighting for the Truth

But when I saw that they walked not uprightly according to the truth of the gospel, I said unto Peter before them all, If thou, being a Jew, livest after the manner of Gentiles, and not as do the Jews, why compellest thou the Gentiles to live as do the Jews? Galatians 2:14
SUGGESTED FURTHER READING: 1 Timothy 6

When a sin deepens and spreads because of silent acquiescence, we must deal with it. If we only respond after the illness has become deep-rooted, we will be too late.

When those who corrupt God's truth by adding their own inventions are drawing others to themselves and attracting a large following, it is time to arm ourselves for the fight. If we have shown ourselves cold and indifferent to the problem and then finally decide to act, God will not bless us with his grace. Let us be warned, therefore, that when evil increases and becomes contagious, or when one person corrupts another, we must vehemently oppose them. This not only applies to errors that corrupt pure gospel truth, but to all corruption and vice.

However, when it comes to heresies and wicked perversions of the truth that distort everything, we should react as if we have been punched in the stomach, for in what does the life and well-being of the church consist if not in the pure Word of God? If someone poisoned the meat that we needed for food, would we tolerate it? No, it would make us strike out!

The same reasoning applies to the gospel. We must always raise our hands to defend the purity of its doctrine, and we must not allow it to be corrupted in any way whatever. If we tolerate corruption, or make it a laughing matter, then subsequently try to deal with it, we will be surprised to find that God has shut the door on us and that Satan has won. That is a just reward for our cowardice and coldness for failing to be prepared to heal the sicknesses which corrupt and infect the body of the church the moment we saw them arise within her.

FOR MEDITATION: Sometimes it is difficult to discern whether pointing out and confronting an aberrant teaching will root it out or simply compound the problem. If the heart of the gospel is threatened, however, silence is not much different from approval. The gospel must be preserved, even if it means unpleasant confrontation.

Believing without Extras

Knowing that a man is not justified by the works of the law, but by the faith of Jesus Christ, even we have believed in Jesus Christ, that we might be justified by the faith of Christ, and not by the works of the law: for by the works of the law shall no flesh be justified. Galatians 2:16

SUGGESTED FURTHER READING: Romans 4

Since God has loved us and has showered his grace upon us, we are obliged to do our part by forgetting about self and devoting ourselves completely to him. In other words, the two main factors in our religion are, first, to recognize that God is to be served and glorified; and second, to understand how we can present ourselves to him and be accepted and acknowledged as his children, owning him as our Father. Then we can have full assurance of the salvation of our souls.

These words of humble confession define the sacrifice that God requires of us. I speak of humility, not simply the right facial expression but rather being affected in such a way that we willingly accept God's condemnation and cast away all trust in our works.

In addition, we learn from this text that when God commanded the ceremonial law, he did not intend for us to cling to such external things. He wanted the children of Israel to exercise patience, acknowledge their poverty and misery, and rid themselves of all the corruptions of the flesh. Indeed, his purpose was to lead them to the Lord Jesus Christ so they would put their trust in him and lean on him completely for salvation.

Those who sought to keep the ceremonial law as if it were absolutely vital and a sin not to do so were establishing a pattern of worship that was against God's will and contrary to his intention. Those who did so were therefore false teachers, distorting the real significance of the law. In addition, they were instructing people to exalt themselves and to boast of their own works. That does not bring glory to God, for if we attribute to ourselves even a little merit, we are robbing and spoiling God of what rightfully belongs to him.

FOR MEDITATION: Few Christians have denied the necessity of faith in Christ, but many have consciously or unconsciously added more requirements for salvation. This tendency lives in the heart of every man, and we should learn from church history to inspect our own hearts carefully to make sure that we are exclusively trusting in Christ. Are you harboring any other grounds for your salvation?

Offering our Works in Christ

For I through the law am dead to the law, that I might live unto God.
Galatians 2:19
SUGGESTED FURTHER READING: Ephesians 2:8–22

We can serve God freely and boldly, even though our consciences accuse us and we know we are full of sin.

How is this possible? Well, we are not grounded upon our own merits but purely upon the mercy of God. Because of this, we know that God accepts our works, even though much is wrong with them. God thus says by the mouth of the prophet that he will receive the service we render as a father accepts the works of his child (Mal. 1:6).

Picture a child who is seeking to obey his father. When the father asks the child to do something, he will accept what the child does, even though the child may not understand what he is doing. The child may even break something in the process, yet the father will not fret about the broken object when he sees his child's affection and willingness to obey.

But if a man hires a servant, he expects that servant to perfectly perform his task because he is going to receive wages and therefore cannot afford to ruin what has been committed to his hands. If the task is not done well, the master will not be content with it.

In speaking of the days of gospel grace, our Lord says that he will accept our service just as a father accepts the obedience of his child, even if what is done is of no value. He shows himself bountiful and kind to us by accepting what we do as if it were fully pleasing to him, even though there is no inherent merit or worth in our works. Thus, we can have the freedom and the courage to serve God, knowing that God will bless all that we do for him because whatever is wrong with our offerings is washed away in the blood of the Lord Jesus Christ.

FOR MEDITATION: The heart of the Christian gospel is the understanding of how good works function in the Christian life. They do not merit or preserve eternal life. Rather, they are the feeble offerings of a grateful soul saved by grace. They are pleasing to our dear heavenly Father only because they are cleansed in Christ's blood and thus fit for the Father's service. Praise God for this great mercy and privilege.

Trusting God as Father and Savior

Even as Abraham believed God, and it was accounted to him for righteousness. Galatians 3:6
SUGGESTED FURTHER READING: Ephesians 1:11–23

It is helpful here to understand how Abraham believed in God. If Abraham had simply believed there was a God in heaven, that could not have justified him, for the pagans believed as much. If Abraham had simply believed that God was the judge of all the earth, that would not have sufficed, either. But God said to Abraham, "Abram, I am thy shield, and thy exceeding great reward," and "I will be a God unto thee, and to thy seed after thee." He also said all nations would be blessed in Abraham (Gen. 15:1; 17:7).

God spoke with Abraham, testifying that he counted him a member of his family and one of his own children. He also said that he would be Abraham's God. When Abraham accepted this promise, he was justified. How is this? Well, when God presented Abraham with his bounty and grace, Abraham believed and accepted God's word. In this his salvation was completely secure.

Now we have a much clearer idea of what it means to be justified by faith. It does not mean we possess a vague notion that God exists, but rather that we know him as our Father and our Savior, since he reveals himself thus in his Word. Through Jesus Christ, we are united and joined to God.

Although we are wretched creatures, full of wickedness, God will still accept us as his own and find us pleasing in his sight. This is only possible because our Lord Jesus Christ mediates between God and man. Having such a promise, we must entirely rest upon it and not doubt that God will be favorable to us to the end. When we call upon him, we may find all our refuge in him, leaving the world behind us and pressing on in the hope of eternal life.

FOR MEDITATION: Saving faith is trust in Christ. It is falling helplessly into his arms and resting there, confident that he will take care of us. Though Christ had not yet appeared, Abraham had this same trust. He did not simply believe that God had promised something; he trusted in the promise. Do you trust Christ?

Becoming a Curse to Bless Us

Christ hath redeemed us from the curse of the law, being made a curse for us: for it is written, Cursed is every one that hangeth on a tree.
Galatians 3:13
SUGGESTED FURTHER READING: Philippians 2:5–11

Two facts must be carefully held together; that God has said whoever hangs upon a tree is cursed, and that it was his will for his own Son to suffer thus. It may seem harsh and strange at first sight that the Lord of Glory, who has all sovereign authority and before whom all the angels of heaven tremble and prostrate themselves, should be subject to such a curse.

But we must remember that Paul said gospel teaching is foolishness to the human race, who regard themselves as wise (1 Cor. 1:18, 23). Indeed, in this way God humbles us for our folly. For there is enough wise and good instruction (if we care to heed it) in the heaven and earth around us, yet we are blind and shut our eyes to God's wisdom displayed in nature. This is why he has opened up a new way to draw us to himself through something that we deem foolish! So we must not judge by our human reasoning what we read here concerning the curse to which the Son of God was subject.

Instead, we should delight in such mystery and give glory to God that he loved our souls so much that he redeemed them at such inestimable cost to himself. Indeed, may we all glorify God, for our Lord Jesus Christ refused to consider it robbery (as Paul expresses it) to reveal himself thus in his infinite glory (Phil. 2:6). He willingly emptied himself, not only taking upon himself a human nature and becoming a man, but also submitting to a most shameful death in the sight of both God and man.

How precious we must have been to him for experiencing such extreme suffering for our redemption! If we could taste something of what this implies, we would forever magnify his unspeakable grace which surpasses all human understanding.

FOR MEDITATION: The great cost of redemption should never cease to bring us to our knees. That Christ was willing to bear the sins of the world and to die such a shameful and accursed death for sinners like us is shocking and glorious and humbling. We did not deserve such sacrifice, yet God did it out of sheer love and grace. What a glorious truth to meditate on throughout today!

Accepted into the Family of God

That the blessing of Abraham might come on the Gentiles through Jesus Christ; that we might receive the promise of the Spirit through faith. Galatians 3:14

SUGGESTED FURTHER READING: Ruth 4

By faith we receive the promise of the Spirit and become united to the Lord Jesus Christ. We also become part of the spiritual seed of Abraham. Though we do not physically descend from his family, it is enough that we are united together with him by faith.

Indeed, we have been regenerated by incorruptible seed, as Peter says, by the Word of God (1 Peter 1:23). Having been transformed, we understand that God accepts us as part of the body of his only Son. Though of Gentile descent, we can still be joined to his church, since faith is all that is required.

Here, all pride in human virtues and merits must cease, and people must recognize that they shall be utterly confounded unless they seek God in the way that he has appointed. Let Jesus Christ be sufficient, since our salvation depends entirely upon him. We will lack nothing if we have an interest in him. This is the point to which Paul frequently returns in this book. Furthermore, he wants us to hold fast to God's truth, knowing that it does not allow any additions. Were we to add to it, we would corrupt, pervert, and falsify the covenant upon which our salvation depends.

Having embraced our Lord Jesus Christ, we must fully remain dependent on him, because this one man has sufficient grace for us all. In him, we can boldly call upon God, knowing that though we descend from the accursed race of Adam, we nevertheless receive blessing in Jesus Christ, and God now accepts us as his children and freely adopts us. He wants this message to be heard throughout the world since there is now an open door and free access by which we may draw near to him.

FOR MEDITATION: Calvin presents us here with a wonderful confirmation of how the Reformers emphasized *solus Christus* ("Christ alone") for salvation. Does your mind and heart resonate with the Christ-centeredness of his approach? What a blessing and what a relief it is for poor sinners like us to find all our salvation in Jesus Christ! Thank God today for his "unspeakable gift" (2 Cor. 9:15), our Emmanuel.

What It Means to Believe

For ye are all the children of God by faith in Christ Jesus. Galatians 3:26
SUGGESTED FURTHER READING: Matthew 15:21–28

Jesus Christ is the head of the church, and for his sake God owns and accepts us as his children. Believing this means much more than people generally imagine.

Those who are not familiar with Holy Scripture may find it strange that we can receive blessing simply by believing. They may think faith is not enough of a virtue to earn us such a reward. However, believing in Jesus Christ is not equivalent to believing a story that we were told or that we have read; it means truly receiving him as presented to us by God the Father. We must embrace the Lord Jesus Christ as the one who has paid for our sin to reconcile us to God. We must entirely trust in him for salvation, assured that he has provided all that we need to gain our eternal inheritance.

If we are certain of these things, it will not surprise us that we become children of God simply by believing. Yet we must also remember that faith has no merit in itself; it is not a question of weighing our faith in the balance to assess its value as a virtue. No, we become children of God through free adoption.

If you are looking for the cause of this, I tell you the true source of salvation is in the mercy of God alone in choosing to take pity upon us. This is achieved by means of faith, as we have said before. When all our pride and vain presumption has been taken away and we recognize that we are lost by nature, then we take refuge in the Lord Jesus Christ. This is what Paul is teaching us here.

FOR MEDITATION: Here Calvin brings together three mottos of the Reformation: faith alone, grace alone, and Christ alone. For Christ's sake, faith and grace are best of friends, not competitors. Gracious faith, then, embraces Christ the way a ring embraces its diamond, as Luther put it. Faith gets all its value from its object, Jesus Christ. Even if your faith is as weak as a single strand of a spider's web, if that strand is attached to the rock, Christ Jesus, your salvation is absolutely secure. If you are a believer, meditate humbly on your security in Christ today.

Finding Blessing in Rebuke

Brethren, I beseech you, be as I am; for I am as ye are: ye have not injured me at all. Galatians 4:12

SUGGESTED FURTHER READING: Psalm 141

When we are reproved for our faults, we are not to raise barriers against that by falsely imagining that the person hates us and is therefore out to criticize us as part of an attack of Satan.

Though we are by nature inclined to analyze whether or not we are being vilified and criticized out of hatred, our first thought must not be that the person is against us because of any personal reason. The devil stirs up such thoughts within us. If we have fallen and someone rebukes us, the message has surely been sent to us by God, regardless of who conveys it to us. For God does not want us to perish but seeks to bring us back to the right path, even if the messenger is motivated by less than righteous intentions. Even if a person only seeks to criticize to avenge himself, God can use that to help us so that we do not perish.

Satan, on the other hand, will not allow us to accept this medicine, for he puts in our heads the idea that the other person, when reproaching us for our faults, is motivated by something other than holy zeal. He convinces us that the person is on the attack and is ready to kick us in the teeth because he is driven by some hidden ill-feeling toward us. Satan puts these imaginary ideas into our minds whenever we are bothered over something to make us so angry that we reject what we have been told and consequently rebel against God himself.

Let us, therefore, remember this lesson when we are next challenged because of our sin. Then we will realize that the messenger has been sent to judge us on behalf of God so that we may not have to face him as our judge in this matter.

FOR MEDITATION: The greatest problem we face when receiving rebuke is pride. Unable to conceive of the possibility that we might be wrong, we immediately think of how the other person must be wrong. But if we are genuinely in error, others have been sent by God to bring us back into line. It would be a terrible thing if our pride were to keep us from receiving God's rebuke.

Listening to our Accusers

Brethren, I beseech you, be as I am; for I am as ye are: ye have not injured me at all. Galatians 4:12
SUGGESTED FURTHER READING: Galatians 2

When someone reproves me for my sin, Paul says it is because God has ordained this and has sent the person to me in his stead. The person does this so I will not have to stand before the majesty of God to give an account of myself for this sin. For if I do, I will be condemned a hundred thousand times more severely. Thus, when God sends us human judges, it is because he has taken pity on us. He hopes that we will be ashamed of ourselves and return to the right path.

If God is gracious enough to take pity on us in this way, we ought to take advantage of his grace rather than become embittered against him and full of imaginary thoughts that we are hated, persecuted, envied, or victimized by any kind of evil treatment that we can conceive. Let us banish all such thoughts and accept warnings and reproaches, if they are indeed true. In short, the best thing we can do when we are accused is to consider whether or not our own consciences have been giving us the same message.

Next, we must conclude that we have been rightfully challenged. How strange that those who become enraged when they are criticized and who rant and bare their teeth would find plenty of reasons to condemn themselves if they truly searched their own hearts. But they prefer to act like madmen when face to face with God, despising his warnings rather than judging themselves and being humble before him.

Therefore, this is what we must do: when rebuked, we must listen to our accusers.

FOR MEDITATION: What a positive view Calvin presents to us of criticism! Though our critics seldom present their case against us without at least some exaggeration, few criticisms don't hold at least a grain of truth. Who is being critical of you at the present time? Isn't he or she in some way helping you to see some aspect of your distorted emphases, blind spots, areas of neglect, attitudes and actions contradictory to stated commitments, and perhaps even outright failings of faith and practice? Try being less defensive, and ask yourself: Even if my critic doesn't intend my betterment through his criticism, how can I grow from this criticism?

Accepting our Guilt

Ye know how through infirmity of the flesh I preached the gospel unto you at the first. Galatians 4:13

SUGGESTED FURTHER READING: 2 Corinthians 10

Above all else, we must know ourselves as we really are. How can we do this? By examining what is written and engraved upon our consciences. If we are not aware of any wrongdoing, let us be on our guard, for none of us are competent when it comes to judging ourselves.

God has given us some ability to judge our own actions, but it is safer to accept condemnation, even of a fault that we are unaware of, than to resist it without thorough consideration of the extent of our guilt. Many people simply shut their eyes or blindfold themselves so they do not have to admit their baseness. When they are told to repent of a sin, they bolt at the first opportunity.

If they are so depraved, there is no hope for them; they will not be convinced of their sin even if they are told of it a hundred times over. They wipe their mouths as a gesture of self-justification. Though they are acting like little children, they do not much care because they revel in what they do since they are so hardened in sin and corruption.

Let us beware of ever becoming so stubborn; for it is our responsibility to judge our own shortcomings in truth and without hypocrisy. We need a spirit of humility to be submissive and to overcome all our pride. Then nothing will prevent us from freely confessing our failings to God. This is what we are to remember from this passage.

FOR MEDITATION: Humility is the mother of submission and acceptance of guilt. Humble people are not easily offended but often admit they are far worse than their critic makes them out to be. The critic only sees their outward appearance, but they themselves know something of the wretchedness of their own wicked heart. Let us remember two things: first, no matter how we are criticized, we are never criticized as much as our sin merits, even if we are innocent of the accusation leveled against us; second, if we have Christ, who, being innocent, suffered infinitely more for our sake than we shall ever suffer for his sake, we have more than enough to cope with any trial (1 Cor. 10:13; 2 Cor. 4:7–12). Drink deeply of the love of Christ, find your delight in the triune God, and you will conquer pessimism and be able to love your critic (Ps. 37:4).

Forming Christ in Us

My little children, of whom I travail in birth again until Christ be formed in you. Galatians 4:19
SUGGESTED FURTHER READING: Colossians 1:9–20

When Paul speaks of Christ being formed in us, he is warning us that it is not enough to have a sketchy knowledge of our Savior; we must have a real-life experience of him. We need to have a vision of his power, his grace, and all his benefits impressed upon our hearts to the extent that his image in us can never be erased.

Earlier in the epistle, Paul says that whenever the gospel is preached in true power, as it should be, it is as though Jesus Christ is crucified in our midst (Gal. 3:1). He is not only vividly depicted but is presented before us upon the cross, with his blood flowing from him, offering the ultimate sacrifice to God the Father to blot out all our sins and transgressions. Since God has been so gracious to us, our response should be never to allow the message to pass us by unheeded.

Many people seem to blossom after hearing only three words of the gospel, as it were. They believe that is sufficient, yet in reality their understanding of Scripture is very shallow. We ought not to be surprised if they fall into temptation, however small, and become forever lost. All they thought they believed is of no avail in such circumstances, for God is punishing them for their lack of true commitment.

Therefore, now that God has graciously permitted us to know his Son, we should have this vivid picture impressed upon our hearts whenever we hear a sermon. We need to remind ourselves and refresh our memories of this so that the devil, who seeks to cloud our minds and to overcome our faith, will not have the victory.

True believers will have such a clear picture of Christ engraved deeply upon their hearts that they can say that Jesus Christ is truly formed in them.

FOR MEDITATION: Jesus' accomplishment of redemption was graphic. It was substantial and visual. Christ should likewise be vivid inside us. We should not be content with blurry concepts and ideas but with a clearly defined and experientially known Son of God. Do you have Christ formed in you?

Loving your Neighbor

For all the law is fulfilled in one word, even in this; Thou shalt love thy neighbour as thyself. Galatians 5:14

SUGGESTED FURTHER READING: Matthew 5:43–48

If we give way to selfish interests, it is a sure sign that we do not know what it means to bear the yoke of God, for we are simply following our natural instincts.

Indeed, as we shall shortly see, people are wholly inclined to evil and therefore give rein to their appetites, waging war upon God. Their whole life is spent in rebellion against God. This proves that the devil controls our affections, indeed, so much that God cannot make use of us until he has overcome everything that pertains to our nature.

The person who loves his neighbor demonstrates that he is not looking after his own interests and is not selfish. Loving our neighbor is a sure and certain mark that we are seeking to obey God and to regulate our lives according to his Word. The Lord Jesus begins with this when summarizing his own teaching by saying that we must first learn to deny ourselves. For if we followed our natural course, we would undoubtedly walk in the opposite direction to the path set out by God. Thus Paul has good reason to say in this passage that the law is fulfilled by this one thing: that we love our neighbor.

We must realize that when God uses the word *neighbour*, he does not only include our relatives and friends, from whom we hope to gain some profit or advantage, or who deserve some kind of reward from us. He wants us to be aware of the kinship that he has placed between all of us. We are all made in the image of God and bear his stamp, so we share a common nature. That means we ought to maintain a sense of unity and brotherhood among all of us.

FOR MEDITATION: Loving our neighbors as ourselves takes incredible selflessness. It is not so difficult to be pleasant or civil toward another person, but to actually love him or her requires much more. This kind of love thus serves as a great test of the genuineness of our desire to fulfill the law. How are you loving your neighbors?

Giving up Anger

But if ye bite and devour one another, take heed that ye be not consumed one of another. Galatians 5:15

SUGGESTED FURTHER READING: Proverbs 14:16–27

This warning of Paul's is not superfluous, for in it he wishes to shame those who become so enraged that they refuse, even from the very first, to be subdued or restrained by reason. When a man is thus fiery-natured and throws caution to the winds, we need to give him an appropriate reproof that will make him ashamed and draw him back to obedience unto God.

Paul therefore seeks to help us so that we might overcome our passions little by little, for they are far too powerful. Then, the next time we feel prompted to hate someone or to take vengeance upon him, we will first think, "What will happen in the end? If we fight like cats and dogs, we will only consume one another!'"

Have we really taken note of this? Indeed, we could go further and say that, even when hatred would be the most useful thing in the world to us and would mean that we could have greater victory over our enemies when we have come to the end of all our projects and schemes, yes, even when we could only profit by giving vent to our anger, yet we would provoke the wrath of God if we did not submit to him so far as to love the unlovable.

This being the case, let us submit to each other in all humility. If this is difficult for us, let us more earnestly work at it until God has mastery of us and until we have denied ourselves. For we must leave behind everything that pertains to our nature and preserve the sacred union that God has placed among us by making us one body.

FOR MEDITATION: Proud creatures that we are, most of us find it very difficult to love our enemies. How can we love those who criticize us? Here are six helps:

- Consider how Christ treated those who hated him.
- Become better acquainted with your enemies; you cannot love those you don't know. Seek to understand them.
- Assure them that you want to learn from them and that you want iron to sharpen iron—and mean what you say.
- Ask the Spirit for grace to be willing to forgive any injury done to you.
- Pray *with* your critic when you are with him and pray *for* him in private. It is difficult to stay bitter against a person for whom you pray.
- Follow 1 Peter 2:1 in putting away anything that inhibits love.

Walking in the Spirit

This I say then, Walk in the Spirit, and ye shall not fulfil the lust of the flesh. Galatians 5:16

SUGGESTED FURTHER READING: Romans 6

Paul tells us here that we are to walk in the Spirit. If we do this, "we will not fulfil the lust of the flesh." By this he issues a warning to all who revel in their sins and allow themselves freedom to do evil under the pretext that they cannot resist it. He stirs them up here and shows them that they have no excuse for sin; that though completely disposed toward evil, they nevertheless ought to search for the remedy.

What is the remedy? It is true that we will not find the answer in ourselves, but God is sufficient for this. He will give us grace to fight against our carnal appetites and evil desires. He will make his Holy Spirit reign in us and have the victory. God has no intention of disappointing us when he makes such a promise. Flee to him, therefore, like a sick person running to a doctor.

Paul anticipates the excuses yet to be made as well as those to which people are already accustomed. They say, "Look at us—we are carnal. Love is an angelic quality; therefore, how can we be expected to exhibit this if we are wholly disposed to evil and overtaken by sin? If we were not under the dominion of sin, we could be expected to be united under God, but we are too weak for that!"

This is what many people say, and they expect to be absolved as a consequence. However, Paul, as it were, says, "It is true that we are full of evil, and yet men choose to remain in this state; they are serving the devil and their minds are increasingly darkened. Nevertheless, we are to seek a remedy. God calls us to himself through the gospel and offers us his Holy Spirit. Therefore, we must condemn evil and hate it. Then God will work in us and overcome all our fleshly desires."

FOR MEDITATION: Without the Holy Spirit's power, we are unable to conquer our natural sinful inclinations. But believers have the Holy Spirit and thus are without excuse if they do not walk in that Spirit and refuse to fulfill the lusts of the flesh. We are no longer slaves to sin! Rejoice and be encouraged to press on in your daily fight against sin.

The Remedy against Sin

For the flesh lusteth against the Spirit, and the Spirit against the flesh: and these are contrary the one to the other: so that ye cannot do the things that ye would. Galatians 5:17
SUGGESTED FURTHER READING: Romans 7

Though we fervently pray and strive to tame our evil desires, we will always have weaknesses in whatever we do. I am not speaking about hypocrites here but the true children of God. Even those who increase in holiness can only approach God by limping. They do not do as they would want to, as Paul goes on to say.

Yet believers, once they have become aware of their wickedness, sincerely and without pretense seek the remedy in God. They feel the need for him to help them overcome their evil desires. Hence, Paul says, "ye shall not fulfil the lust of the flesh" (Gal. 5:16). This does not mean that for the rest of our lives we will never again be tempted by Satan to do evil. For, indeed, our flesh still has many goads urging us to do wrong. All kinds of sin will tempt us, but we can still resist those through the grace of God.

Paul, in exhorting believers not to allow themselves to lose control, speaks of "the flesh having no dominion over them." He does not say that evil desires and sinful lusts will no longer dwell within us. We will only be rid of sin when it pleases God to take us to himself. Until the day that we leave this world, we will always have spots and stains within us, and we will always be bent down with the burden of our sins and weaknesses. This is to humble us and to show us that our life is a constant battle against sin.

Though sin dwells within us, it must not have dominion, for the Spirit of God must conquer it. This can only happen if we flee to God with fervent zeal, praying that he will remedy the evil that we cannot change and that he would grant us more gifts of his Spirit so that we might overcome everything that has weighed us down.

FOR MEDITATION: Do not lose heart if your struggles with sin continue until the day you die. You should not be pleased with the status quo or make a truce with sin; we must fight it tooth and nail! But do not doubt your salvation because you cannot perfect yourself. Instead, hope in God and his unfailing promise to help you battle sin.

Producing Fruits of the Spirit

But the fruit of the Spirit is love, joy, peace, longsuffering, gentleness, goodness, faith. Galatians 5:22

SUGGESTED FURTHER READING: Matthew 13:1–9, 18–23

Love is the summary of the law; thus, Paul places it first in listing the fruits of the Spirit. However, he does not wish us to neglect calling upon God, to abandon the trust that we ought to have in his promises, or to forget any service that is described in the first table of the law.

Paul despises none of that and therefore does not wish us to reject it, but he is concerned that we testify before men whether or not we truly desire to obey God. We have already said that such testimony is clearly seen if we love our neighbors and are not devoted to self-advantage. Collectively, we should be trying to foster a healthy and peaceful unity, using the faculties and the means that God has given us to serve those to whom his Word declares that we have a responsibility. That is why Paul puts the word *love* first. He does not mean that we should love our neighbors so much that we leave God out of the picture, but rather that we declare our true dedication and devotion to God by the friendship that we have with one another.

Of course, this cannot happen unless we have placed all our trust in God and taken refuge in prayers and petitions. Indeed, since that is known as virtue in the fruits of the Spirit, we will not be equipped to approach God by faith nor will we have the will to pray to be armed against all temptations unless the Holy Spirit is at work within us.

By nature, we have no ability to understand the gospel, nor are we agile enough to rise up to God and personally communicate with him in prayers and supplications. We need the Holy Spirit to enable us by enlightening us by his grace and encouraging our hearts to call upon God. That is what we need to remember.

FOR MEDITATION: If we have the Holy Spirit within us, we will be so united with Christ and in love with God that we will yearn to do nothing but manifest the fruits of the Spirit. Those fruits will flow out of our relationship with the triune God. We cannot expect to find any of those fruits in our lives if we are not in this living relationship. By the Spirit's grace, are you manifesting these fruits?

Living in True Joy

But the fruit of the Spirit is love, joy, peace, longsuffering, gentleness, goodness, faith. Galatians 5:22

SUGGESTED FURTHER READING: Nehemiah 8:9–18

Paul here adds *joy* to love in naming the fruits of the Spirit. He not only means that we will be at peace with God and have cheerful hearts because God has mercifully received us and declared his kindness to us. He also implies another kind of joy here, which is that we ought not to grieve or upset one another or to alienate ourselves from our neighbors by disdaining them.

We are to be easy-going and friendly, even finding pleasure in being able to help and assist those who require our aid. In Romans 14:17, Paul says the kingdom of God is joy in the Holy Ghost. However, here he uses this word in a different sense. He says we can rejoice in God when we testify that we have found acceptance in the name of the Lord Jesus Christ. Without this, we would be transfixed and numbed with fear. For this reason, we would always be troubled in spirit.

Those who have contempt for God may seem happy enough in their pride, but they do not have true peace or joy. Inwardly, they are burning, for God pricks their consciences with remorse so they are always sorrowful and agitated. Even when they want to rejoice, their minds become increasingly darkened. They have no more feeling because their ability to discern between good and evil is dead.

When people stray from God in this way, their joy is cursed, and they forget who they are. But, as I have already said, Paul speaks here of the joy we have when we rightly relate to our neighbors in love.

FOR MEDITATION: True joy is in short supply these days. When Christians let their true joy shine—not shallow silliness, but deep happiness—people around them notice. A Christian without joy is a contradiction in terms. Do not be afraid to let your Christian joy shine in this dark world.

Being Faithful to One Another

But the fruit of the Spirit is love, joy, peace, longsuffering, gentleness, goodness, faith. Galatians 5:22

SUGGESTED FURTHER READING: 1 Peter 2:11–25

The word *faith* here means faithfulness and integrity. The faith that relates to God is the certainty that we will see the fulfillment of his promises. Scripture says we are justified by faith (Rom. 5:1), meaning that God begins the process of mortifying everything in us that pertains to our sinful nature. We need to be grounded upon the mercy of God alone, as revealed to us in the Lord Jesus Christ.

How do we possess this gift of faith? By believing the promises of God and accepting them in obedience; also by entirely leaning upon God once we have confessed that we are lost and condemned. Thus, the faith that relates to God is the assurance of his goodness and love, making it possible for us to approach him with confidence because we know that he will hear us.

Paul says those who have such faith steadfastly trust in God and therefore possess the liberty and boldness to come to him in repentance.

But in this passage, Paul speaks of another kind of faith. It is the faithfulness we show to one another when we walk in integrity. With this kind of faith, we do not attempt to cheat anyone out of malice or craft. We are not two-faced. There should be no deception in us whereby we seek to influence the simple-minded, but we should treat others as we ourselves would like to be treated. That is the faith that Paul refers to here as a fruit of the Spirit.

FOR MEDITATION: When Christians maintain integrity in the face of criticism and persecution, the world sits up and pays attention. The integrity of a clear conscience is priceless. Rendering good for evil is always far better than rendering evil for evil. Ask for grace to maintain integrity by refusing to descend to the level of your persecutors. Pray for strength to fight God's battles, not your own, and you will discover that he will fight yours.

Led by the Spirit

But the fruit of the Spirit is love, joy, peace, longsuffering, gentleness, goodness, faith, meekness, temperance: against such there is no law.
Galatians 5:22–23
SUGGESTED FURTHER READING: 1 Corinthians 2:10–16

Paul now adds *gentleness* and *goodness* to the fruits of the Spirit. Without these fruits, it is impossible for us to unite together; there would be no harmony among us whatever. For if each of us was determined to be horrible and unkind to one another, we would do better as wild beasts. We must show that we want to communicate with those whom God has placed around us. In short, we must maintain love by the gentleness, goodness, and meekness that Paul refers to here.

He also mentions *temperance*, which means that we must abstain from plundering one another's goods and that we must live sober lives and keep ourselves from intemperance and excess.

To summarize, the virtues that Paul mentions here are for Christians. It is as if he were saying, "If we are led by the Spirit of our Lord Jesus Christ, it will be evident and visible in our lives. We will be kept from wandering like those who lead dissolute lives; we will be loving and kind to everyone and will not harbor iniquity, deception, or extortion within us. We will be content with what we have and will seek only to serve one another."

We have seen, therefore, that all good proceeds from the Spirit of God.

But we also see here that our Lord Jesus is the fountain from which we must draw water; if we are in him and belong to him as members of his body, he will demonstrate in our lives that it was not in vain for him to have received and acknowledged us as his own.

FOR MEDITATION: How dependent we are on the Holy Spirit to work real and abiding virtues and graces in us! Ask God for more of the leading of his Spirit. Find honest friends who will alert you to any word or action you indulge in that runs counter to the fruit of the Spirit.

Rebuking with Gentleness

Brethren, if a man be overtaken in a fault, ye which are spiritual, restore such an one in the spirit of meekness; considering thyself, lest thou also be tempted. Galatians 6:1

SUGGESTED FURTHER READING: Colossians 3:1–17

We must aim to bring back to the right path those who have turned away from it. If we have no kindness or humanity within us, we may plunge someone deep into despair the minute we see him committing a sin. This is why Paul says the children of God must show kindness and gentleness so those who have fallen through weakness can be helped up, knowing that we seek their salvation.

There are two extremes here. The first is that we often close our eyes if one of our friends offends God and creates a scandal; we let it slip by because we do not want to stir up ill will by reproaching them. This is how friendships work today; each person permits all kinds of evil.

No one wants to have their sore skin scratched; therefore, people will not listen to warning unless God first touches them and gives them an obedient spirit that makes them teachable. Such people would say with David that they would prefer to be scolded harshly, indeed, even with austerity, rather than to be surrounded by a crowd of flatterers who would lull them to sleep in their sins (Ps. 141:5).

However, generally speaking, people want to be spared this shame. They prefer that we not utter a word against them, let alone assail their ears with a list of their vices and transgressions. People are happy with this silence, yet in it God is forgotten. As the prophet Isaiah says, no man was found in any of the streets who upheld the truth (Isa. 59:14–16). There is confusion and worse injustice than ever before, yet we let it continue unchecked.

FOR MEDITATION: Our best friends are those who tell us the most truth about ourselves in a loving and caring way. Are we serving our friends in this manner as well?

If we do not remember from where we have come and the grace God has shown to us, we will rebuke our brothers and sisters in a harsh and unloving manner. But if we remember God's grace, we will restore those who have fallen in meekness, knowing that only God's grace keeps us from the same fault.

Reproving without Harshness

Brethren, if a man be overtaken in a fault, ye which are spiritual, restore such an one in the spirit of meekness; considering thyself, lest thou also be tempted. Galatians 6:1

SUGGESTED FURTHER READING: Proverbs 4

The opposite sin in rebuking one who has fallen is excessive harshness.

Hypocrites often use this kind of rebuke, for when they see a speck in their neighbor's eye, they cry out in alarm, yet they have a large beam in their own eye that they do nothing about, as our Lord Jesus says (Matt. 7:4). Since many people enlarge their consciences to swallow an entire camel yet strain at a gnat when it comes to the faults of others, we must guard against being too harsh or too severe when we reprove others. It seems to some that they are only correctly doing their duty if they loudly sound the trumpet when another person falls.

How many cautionary words today spring from righteous concern? If a person sees his neighbor doing evil, he should, if he has an opening and an opportunity, show him his fault, yet we see nothing of this! For if each one spies on his friends and listens as he keeps watch to see if he can find anything to reprove, then he will be severe in the extreme.

However, those who are severely dealt with in this way certainly cannot complain. After all, why else has evil become so prevalent in today's society? Indeed, few people are admonished in private anymore to bring them back to God; rather, the sins that were hidden are slanderously published abroad.

Why? We cannot bear to hear the truth about ourselves. We want to cleave to our sins, as if no one has any authority or jurisdiction over us. True community cannot exist among us without such mutual correction, in which we all willingly submit to one another.

FOR MEDITATION: Paul's advice explained here by Calvin is sorely needed in our families, churches, and work environments today. Loving correction of an offending brother that follows Matthew 18:15–17 is seldom followed today. Most people operate in one of two extremes: either they think that this is the work of a minister or a church and they neglect their own responsibility as a member of Christ's corporate family, or they overreact in harshness and neglect to approach their bother in love and humility. Are you lovingly and tenderly correcting your brothers and sisters in the faith when they fall into some sin?

Sowing Seeds in Well-Doing

And let us not be weary in well doing: for in due season we shall reap, if we faint not. As we have therefore opportunity, let us do good unto all men, especially unto them who are of the household of faith. Galatians 6:9–10

SUGGESTED FURTHER READING: James 1:26–2:13

Here we learn we must use all that God has bestowed to serve him and his own, even all people in general. As God distributes different abilities and gifts to each of us, we are obliged to use them for those who need us and whom we can help. We must, therefore, make up our minds not to be idle or fruitless and consider the means that God has given us so that each one of us can use those gifts as an offering to him.

To further encourage us, Paul tells us that by doing this we are sowing seeds. God will not allow us to be disappointed when we have sought to do what he has commanded. It may seem to us that we waste our efforts when we do not seek our own profit and give ourselves over to self-advantage, yet the opposite is true. For even though a person who helps his neighbor loses whatever he has given, he is laying up treasure like the one who sows seed upon the soil to reap a crop in due season.

On the other hand, all is lost when we are too anxious to become wealthy in this life and only care about our own advancement, for in that we will reap corruption. Indeed, this entire world is passing away and its shadow is fading, yet this is the only treasure that those who study to enrich themselves in this world can possess. Just as our lives are transitory and fleeting, so are the goods we have collected, for everything will rot away to nothing.

But if we rid ourselves of earthly cares and consider God's kingdom, even though it seems that in well-doing we are becoming impoverished and depleted, nevertheless, this treasure will never perish. It will be well guarded by the hand of God until the last day.

FOR MEDITATION: Doing good to others may not be the best way to gain earthly goods, but it does provide a harvest of its own. It can often be wearying and draining, but the harvest will come. Let us take this as an encouragement, then, to not give up on treating others well when the rewards seem few.

Rightly Motivated to Serve Others

And let us not be weary in well doing: for in due season we shall reap, if we faint not. As we have therefore opportunity, let us do good unto all men, especially unto them who are of the household of faith. Galatians 6:9–10

SUGGESTED FURTHER READING: Matthew 22:33–40

Paul says we must seek to do good to all, even to those who are not worthy and are even our mortal enemies!

It is true that this is hard work and contrary to our natural instincts, but it is how God proves and tries us. For if we were to do good only to those who deserved it or to those who could repay us, we would not be showing that we are motivated to serve God at all, for it is possible that we would have an eye only toward our own profit. As our Lord Jesus says, the pagans do as much, and so do the worse people in the world (Matt. 5:46).

Why? They reason, "I need to be looked after; therefore, I must acquire some friends."

If, therefore, we seek to distinguish those who are worthy of our good deeds and have the means to return our favors, this is not proper proof or a sure test of our desire to do what has been commanded by God. But if we close our eyes to people's ingratitude and feel led to pity people solely because of their poverty and misery, then we serve God.

If we operate like this, it is certain that we will seek to do good to all, for we cannot destroy the unbreakable bond by which God has joined and united us to others. Even the most distant strangers in the world are our neighbors, though they are neither our relatives, cousins, nor members of our household. We are all of one flesh, and we bear a mark that ought to induce us to do all that we possibly can for one another.

FOR MEDITATION: How easy is it to press on when our efforts to show kindness are met with nothing but ingratitude? If gratitude and reward are our motivations for doing good, we will do good to very few people. If, however, our motivations are based on unconditional love for humanity, we will press on, no matter what the response, displaying the love of Christ as we go.

Doing Good in the Household of Faith

As we have therefore opportunity, let us do good unto all men, especially unto them who are of the household of faith. Galatians 6:10
SUGGESTED FURTHER READING: Luke 10:25–42

Paul tells us that believers and those who profess to follow the same gospel form a household; in other words, they are of the same house. Indeed, the church is called the house of God, and he dwells among us (1 Tim. 3:15).

When Scripture speak thus, it does not mean that we need to be in a material building to be joined together; for even when we are in our own homes, we are still members of the same household. We are in that household because God has truly gathered us to himself. Thus, when Scripture says that the children of God are of the same household, it is to show that we have fellowship with each other.

Although earthly brothers and sisters separate and go different ways, we always remain in this union established by God among us. When we hear these things, are we not worse than stupid if we are not moved to use what God has given us to help our neighbors as well as fellow believers?

We now see Paul's intention here; since God has given us the responsibility of doing good to all people because they are made of the same flesh, let us not be hindered by malice of any kind from striving to carry out our general duty toward those whom God sets before us to test our humanity. But since he has gathered believers into his flock and united us in his name, and since we call upon him with one voice as our Father, we must show love to one another in the family.

If we want God to acknowledge us as his children, we must value the adoption by which he has chosen us. To do this, let us sincerely declare by our lives that we long to demonstrate that we regard those whom God has called into his household and church as our brothers and sisters.

FOR MEDITATION: Are you taking every opportunity to reach out to your neighbors—especially your believing neighbors—with kind words, loving actions, and all kinds of good? Can your neighbors see and feel that you are a giving Christian?

Living the Word

Ye see how large a letter I have written unto you with mine own hand.
Galatians 6:11
SUGGESTED FURTHER READING: 1 Peter 1:13–25

When our Lord Jesus Christ was sent to the world in the fullness of time, he declared everything that was needful for our salvation. Even today, he still raises up people as instruments of his Spirit to proclaim his will, to bring others the message of salvation, and to bear witness to that which otherwise would be hidden from us.

In light of these things, may we all be of one mind, and, whether we read in private or are taught in public, let us become stronger in the Word that God has been pleased to communicate to us. We need to remember that so we might have much greater love for his holy Word and give ourselves wholly to it. May we receive Scripture with more reverence, as, indeed, it is most worthy to be received.

Now let us fall before the majesty of our great God and Father, acknowledging him as our judge, who buries our sins in his infinite mercy. Let us pray that it might please him to accept us in mercy in the name of our Lord Jesus Christ.

May he also give us grace to walk in such a fashion that we truly confirm that we are his children and that he has not called us in vain. May this grace so benefit our hearts that we grow in it and become increasingly enabled to serve and adore him throughout our lives in true obedience to his holy Word. May he show this grace, not only to us, but also to all people and nations on earth.

FOR MEDITATION: Too often we do not realize the specialness of the Word of God. I recently read a study of boat owners in Florida and in Michigan. The former could use their boats twelve months a year; the latter, about four months. The study concluded, rather surprisingly, that Michigan boat owners used their boats more than their peers in Florida. Michigan boat owners take advantage of nearly every nice summer day, while Floridians postpone, thinking there is always another day to sail.

Don't treat the Word of God this way. Ask for grace to live more fully out of God's Word next year. Search the Scriptures, know the Scriptures, love the Scriptures, and live the Scriptures. You will never be sorry.

Scripture Index (daily reading)

Scripture index (suggested further reading)

Scripture index (suggested further reading)

Scripture index (suggested further reading)

Scripture index (quoted in text)

About Day One:

Day One's threefold commitment:

- To be faithful to the Bible, God's inerrant, infallible Word;
- To be relevant to our modern generation;
- To be excellent in our publication standards.

I continue to be thankful for the publications of Day One. They are biblical; they have sound theology; and they are relative to the issues at hand. The material is condensed and manageable while, at the same time, being complete—a challenging balance to find. We are happy in our ministry to make use of these excellent publications.

JOHN MACARTHUR, PASTOR-TEACHER, GRACE COMMUNITY CHURCH, CALIFORNIA

It is a great encouragement to see Day One making such excellent progress. Their publications are always biblical, accessible and attractively produced, with no compromise on quality. Long may their progress continue and increase!

JOHN BLANCHARD, AUTHOR, EVANGELIST AND APOLOGIST

Visit our website for more information and to request a free catalogue of our books.

www.dayone.co.uk

About Reformation Heritage Books:

Our Mission:

To glorify God and strengthen His church through the publication and distribution of Puritan and Reformed literature around the world at discount prices.

Reformation Heritage Books is a non-profit organization that was founded in 1994 with the sole purpose of disseminating Puritan and Reformed literature around the world. Since our beginning in 1994 we have published 125 titles. In 2008, RHB acquired Soli Deo Gloria and we have begun to reprint numerous Puritan titles. Our bookstore also distributes approximately 3,000 Puritan and Reformed titles from a variety of publishers at discount prices. We also provide numerous books free of charge to seminaries and pastors in Africa as enabled.

For a complete listing of all available titles visit our web site at **www.heritagebooks.org** or request a catalog by calling **616–977–0599**.